96304

331.15

EUROPEAN MANAGEMENT GUIDES

IRISH MANAGEMENT
LIBRARY
INSTITUTE

Industrial relations

IMI *information service*
Sandyford, Dublin 16
Telephone 2078513 Fax 295 9479
email library@imi.ie
Internet http://www.imi.ie

4 JAN 1999

0 6 MAR 2000

3 APR 2000

10 AUG 2001

28 NOV 2001

D1422302

European Management Guides

The European Management Guides, written and researched by the International Department of Incomes Data Services, provide a reliable and up-to-date overview of employment law and practice in Europe. They now include Austria, Sweden and Switzerland as well as the eleven major member states of the European Union. There will be three volumes:

Contracts and Terms and Conditions of Employment
Industrial Relations and Collective Bargaining
Recruitment, Training and Development.

The Institute of Personnel and Development is the leading publisher of books and reports for personnel and training professionals and students and for all those concerned with the effective management and development of people at work. For full details of all our titles please telephone the Publishing Department on 0181 263 3387.

EUROPEAN MANAGEMENT GUIDES
General editor: Pete Burgess

Industrial relations and collective bargaining

Incomes Data Services

Institute of Personnel and Development

© Institute of Personnel and Development 1996

Published 1996

All rights reserved. No part of this publication
may be reproduced, stored in an information storage
and retrieval system, or transmitted in any form
or by any means, electronic, mechanical, photocopying,
recording or otherwise, without written permission
of the Institute of Personnel and Development,
IPD House, Camp Road, Wimbledon, London SW19 4UX.

Phototypeset by The Comp-Room, Aylesbury
and printed in Great Britain by
Short Run Press, Exeter

British Library Cataloguing in Publication Data
A catalogue record for this book is available
from the British Library

ISBN 0 85292 612 X

The views expressed in this book are the
contributors' own, and may not necessarily
reflect those of the IPD.

INSTITUTE OF PERSONNEL
AND DEVELOPMENT

IPD House, Camp Road, London SW19 4UX
Tel: 0181 971 9000   Fax: 0181 263 3333
Registered office as above. Registered Charity No. 1038333
A company limited by guarantee. Registered in England No. 2931892

Contents

General Introduction

European Management Guides

The internationalisation of businesses within the European Union (EU), the creation of new corporate entities as a result of mergers and acquisitions across national boundaries, and the complexities of meshing cultures and practices – often accompanied by painful rationalisation – are set to continue unabated in the 1990s. The management of the human resource dimension to these processes will continue to pose fresh challenges to personnel practitioners, especially those confronted with international personnel issues for the first time.

The programme to realise a Single European Market by 1993 triggered a new raft of European-level legislative proposals intended to complement the commercial and economic aspects of European integration with a 'social dimension'. Although influential, and occasionally decisive, in a number of areas of employment regulation, EU legislation has left the diverse institutional structures of the member states largely untouched. Substantial differences in cultures, institutions, law and practice will persist for the foreseeable future, tempered more by broader economic exigencies than by legislative intervention from the European Commission. Indeed, the philosophy behind the 1993 Treaty on the European Union (the Maastricht Treaty) and the European Commission's more recent approach to employment policy is that greater scope should be left to negotiation and local implementation rather than monolithic prescription from Brussels.

Understanding and working with national diversity will therefore continue to be vital for personnel or line managers entrusted with European responsibilities. Although professional advice is indispensable when approaching a European venture or major personnel decision, access to basic and structured information can help in shaping the agenda for decisions – as well as saving precious time and money. The European Management Guides series aims to meet this need for accessible and comprehensive information on employment in the major economies of Western Europe. The second edition of the series, researched and written by Incomes Data Services Ltd (IDS) and published by the Institute of Personnel and Development (IPD), consists of three volumes covering:

- contracts and terms and conditions of employment
- industrial relations and collective bargaining
- recruitment, training and development.

European Management Guides are based on research carried out by the International Department of IDS using original national sources: this embraces the business press, specialist publications (including those from employer associations, trade unions, and personnel management organisations), legislation, collective agreements, and material on policy and practice supplied by companies and consultants, including extensive and regular face-to-face interviews with specialists and practitioners. The main sources, including published secondary material, are listed at the end of each country chapter.

Each volume presents information on a country-by-country basis, structured to allow easy comparative reference. Appendices detail local organisations which can provide further help and information. However, European Management Guides are not intended as a substitute for expert advice tailored to an individual situation and provided in the context of a professional relationship. Every effort has been made to ensure that the information contained in them is accurate and relevant. The publishers and authors offer them to readers on the understanding that neither organisation seeks to take the place of a lawyer or a consultant.

Incomes Data Services

Incomes Data Services has monitored employment developments in Europe since 1974. IDS's International Service publishes:

- *IDS Employment Europe*, a monthly subscription journal on pay and employment law and practice in member states of the European Union. Each issue includes news on pay, collective bargaining and legal developments in EU member states, a Country Profile drawing together trends and developments in the economy, pay, employment law, labour costs and executive remuneration for an individual country, together with regular supplements on European Union-level legislation and issues, with features, and regular statistics on pay trends and prices.
- *IDS International Documents* comprise two series of in-depth reference sources on an individual country basis covering i) Pay and Conditions, ii) Recruitment and Dismissal. Updated regularly, each series provides both context and detail in these crucial areas of personnel management.

For more details contact: IDS Subscriptions, 193 St John Street, London EC1V 4LS (tel. 0171-250 3434, fax 0171-608 0949).

Acknowledgements

European Management Guides are researched and written by the staff and contributors of the International Department of Incomes Data Services Ltd, London. Individual country chapters were prepared by Angela Bowring, Pete Burgess, Fintan Hourihan, Sally Marullo, Tony Morgan, David Shonfield, Steve Steadman, George Tsogas, Caroline Welch, Marion Weißkirchen and Josef Wöss. The series editor is Pete Burgess. The authors would like to thank the many individuals and companies who helped in the research for their time and co-operation; the staff of the publishing department of the Institute of Personnel and Development for their patient and scrupulous editorial input; and the national committees of the IPD for their support and advice.

Introduction

Industrial relations and collective bargaining

Industrial Relations and Collective Bargaining is the second volume of the new three-volume edition of IDS/IPD European Management Guides. It sets out to provide detailed information and context for 14 European Union (EU) member states on the following subjects:

- national systems of industrial relations
- trade unions and employers' associations, and the involvement of the state
- national institutions for consultation
- statutory and agreed systems of employee representation and employee participation
- collective bargaining rules, structures, and trends
- industrial action and conflict resolution.

This book aims to provide an overview of the institutions and structures of industrial relations, and in particular to outline any statutory or agreed obligations on employers in the fields of employee participation, information disclosure, and consultation. It also indicates where coverage through binding collective agreements may impose terms and conditions on employers either through membership of an employers' association or where the 'extension' of collective agreements by the authorities may also embrace non-signatory companies.

However, we do not set out to characterise the national features of the organisation of personnel management as such or the cultural aspects of workplace industrial relations. These issues, set in some cases in a broader examination of national industrial and commercial cultures, are explored in, for example, the Price Waterhouse/Cranfield Study, and in works by Hofstede, Lane, Trompenaars and Hampden-Turner (see 'Further reading' at the end of this Introduction).

National patterns of industrial relations

Industrial relations and bargaining arrangements in the 14 countries covered in this volume present a highly diverse picture. The table on pages xx–xxi illustrates some of the main dimensions of difference, including: level of trade union density, coverage of the labour force by collective agreements, the main levels of bargaining, and the degree of co-ordination and state involvement in bargaining.

Levels of trade union membership differ enormously, from the 80–90 per cent seen in Nordic countries, the 65 per cent in Belgium (often aided in all cases by the involvement of unions in disbursing social benefits), a middle core of 30–35 per cent in the UK, Germany, and Italy, to low-membership countries such as France and Spain (below 15 per cent). Virtually all the countries looked at here have experienced a decline in trade union membership and density since the early 1980s, though at widely varying speeds. The UK and the Netherlands were deeply affected during the 1980s, but since the late 1980s trade union membership in the Netherlands has stabilised; in fact it may have increased slightly. In Germany and Italy trade unions managed to sustain their memberships through the 1980s. However, membership fell seriously in Germany as a result of the 1992/93 recession, which hit manufacturing. Trade union density has fallen massively in France and Spain since the 1970s, although some commentators have suggested that the fall in Spain may not be so precipitate as has often been thought, and that some recovery may have taken place since the mid-1980s.

The incidence of industrial disputes (measured in terms of working days lost per 1,000 employees – see the table on page xxii) varies markedly between countries, although statistics on industrial action are notoriously difficult to compare internationally. Virtually all EU member states have experienced a steady downward movement in industrial disputes since the early 1980s, although it is hazardous to generalise about the causes of this; they remain hotly debated and a simple, transnationally applicable model is difficult to construct. Moreover, the meaning and impact of strikes in any given national context can be properly judged only by looking at national institutional arrangements, sectoral differences, the state of the economic cycle, and the broader political culture. For example, the organisation of workplace industrial relations in Germany – with the constraints on works councils preventing them from initiating lawful industrial action, and industry bargaining tending to keep conflict over pay outside the establishment – means that there are both opportunities for resolving disputes and limits on starting them at company level. On the other hand, industrial action – when it occurs – can take the form of highly organised and disciplined set-piece struggles over basic issues, with the outcome transmitted to a wide range of firms through the mechanism of industry agreements, often following one pattern-setting settlement. In France, however, where unions lack the capacity to organise such broad conflicts (especially outside the public sector) and where the right to strike is an individual right, industrial action is more sporadic, with a greater propensity to direct action and organisation outside the orbit of trade union institutions; the immediate impact may be dramatic, but the capacity to turn the outcomes into durable settlements is more doubtful (for a fuller discussion see Edwards and Hyman in 'Further reading').

Compared with the UK, collective bargaining and mechanisms for employee representation in Contintental Europe tend to be highly formalised and are often subject to statutory regulation.

- Collective agreements are always legally enforceable, not only when embodied in the individual contract of employment but also through the establishment of a contractual relationship between the signatory parties. For trade

Collective bargaining systems in Western Europe

Country	Trade union density %	Coverage by collective agreement (and extension to non-signatories) %	Main level of bargaining *Trends*	Co-ordination of bargaining *Role of state*
Austria	45	95+ Extension possible	Industry level, with occasional multi-industry national-level agreements. Scope for workplace negotiation with elected works councils on non-pay issues.	Tripartite consultation on price and incomes with co-ordination on bargaining through highly centralised national employer and employee organisations.
Belgium	55	90 Extension possible	Industry level, with company bargaining growing in importance. National multi-industry agreements set framework for sectoral bargaining on non-pay issues. Also scope for 'negotiated legislation' where national agreements made mandatory by royal decree eg on minimum wages collective dismissal, and equal pay.	National tripartite and bipartite institutions for consultation on economic and social issues. State has played active role on pay issues with statutory incomes policies.
Denmark	80–85	90 No formal extension procedures	Industry-level has replaced multi-industry bargaining, with one agreement covering much of manufacturing. However, industry agreements often effectively implemented through additional workplace-level bargaining, especially on pay.	Some tripartite consultation, with institutionally established national bipartite consultation on IR issues.
France	10	c. 85 Extension possible	Industry-level agreements provide framework, with some national multi-industry agreements. Formal bargaining rights at workplace have led to some decentralisation, but company bargaining seen as weak in practice.	Centralised system provides for minima, with limited co-ordination at sectoral level. State traditionally active in employment regulation.
Germany	37	85–90 Extension possible	Industry by region, complemented by arrangements agreed at workplace with works councils. Formal company bargaining covers c. 6 per cent of workforce. Growing formal decentralisation to workplace level on working time, and informally on other issues.	Tight co-ordination within sectors – moderate co-ordination via national employer/union institutions but fairly narrow range of settlements. No formal tripartism but much informal consultation, boosted by round-table talks initiated by Chancellor Kohl.
Greece	30 (in private sector)	Virtually all employees Extension possible	National multi-industry agreement sets minimum wage and framework for industry, company and – in some cases – occupational bargaining.	In the past, high degree of state intervention in private-sector bargaining but state now withdrawing, with more scope for bipartite resolution.

		Mechanisms for setting pay minima in poorly organised industries		
Ireland	47	n.a.	Company level, within the framework of nationally negotiated pay accords since 1987.	Pay settlements since 1987 have been subject to a series of national tripartite pay accords. Although non-statutory, compliance is high.
Italy	38	90+ Extension via court rulings on status of sectoral agreements	Industry level. Company-level bargaining intended to reward performance under new arrangements.	State does not intervene in bargaining but brokered new negotiating arrangements: tripartite economic consultation.
Netherlands	25	70 Extension possible	Industry level still predominates; company-level bargaining covers 8 per cent of workforce with influence of workplace regulation of terms and conditions growing since 1980s.	State has reserve powers to intervene on pay bargaining – and has used influence to achieve pay pauses. Extensive tripartite consultation on non-pay issues.
Portugal	25–30	80 Extension possible	Industry level, although agreements often minimal and tied to statutory provisions. Very weak formal company bargaining.	Tripartite consultation on prices and incomes 1984–92, with possibility of renewal.
Spain	10–15%	70 Extension possible but rare	Industry bargaining at provincial level predominates setting framework for company agreements; company bargaining in engineering. The incidence of company bargaining has declined slightly since the early 1980s.	Tripartite consultation on non-pay issues; no national pay accords since 1986.
Sweden	80	80 No extension	Industry level, with extensive scope for company-level implementation, especially where national agreement provides for 'kitty' bargaining.	No formal tripartite consultation. Incomes policies imposed in the past, most recently in 1991/92. Previously a high degree of co-ordination by each side, but weakening with decline of centralised bargaining.
Switzerland	27	53 Extension possible	Industry level, but agreements often leave major issues to be implemented at company level. In engineering, for example, pay is set wholly by the employer at company level. Growing trend towards industry-level agreements on paybill increases with scope for employer discretion on distribution.	No formal co-ordination at national level, but employer associations co-ordinate at sectoral level.
UK	32	45–50 No extension mechanisms	Company level. Industry-level bargaining much reduced since early 1980s but still important in some sectors (eg construction). Decentralisation of pay-setting often to business-unit level within centralised corporate financial framework.	Little co-ordination of company bargaining, but some lead settlements (eg Ford) still influential. Some industry associations may attempt to regulate pay. No state intervention in private sector and no tripartite consultation.

Sources: IDS, *Employment Europe*, October 1995; OECD, *Employment Outlook*, July 1994; national sources and authors' estimates.

Labour disputes in selected EU member states: 1984–93
(working days lost per 1,000 employees)

Country	1984–88*	1989–93*
France	60	30
Germany (West)	50	20
Italy	360	(250)
Netherlands	10	20
Spain	740	430
Sweden	100	70
UK	400	70

Source: *Employment Gazette*, December 1994.

* Annual averages for years within period for which data is available, weighted for employment.
( ) indicates the figure is based on incomplete data.

unions, this usually implies a binding agreement not to take industrial action or pursue claims during the lifetime of an agreement. The power to conclude collective agreements is seen as part of the legal hierarchy: collective agreements are a type of negotiated law, and have the force of law. In a number of countries matters typically regulated by statute law in the UK may be regulated by national, universally applicable collective agreements, sometimes given a stamp of legality to ensure universal application. This approach has also informed the shaping of social dialogue between EU-level employer organisations and trade unions in the Treaty on the European Union (see below).

- In many countries collective agreements concluded at national or industry level may be applied to non-signatory companies through 'extension' procedures (see the table on pages xx–xxi for incidence): this means that the coverage of the workforce by collectively agreed terms is much greater than would immediately appear warranted by the level of trade union membership. Some national employer associations, for example in Germany or Switzerland, are extremely sceptical about the worth of such provisions, and differences of view between employers' associations in Germany have boiled over into a row about the use of such mechanisms to implement legislation intended to shield the construction industry from low-wage competition.

- Furthermore, high levels of coverage of the labour force by collective agreements in themselves give no indication either of the 'intensity of regulation' (ie the number of issues covered) or the 'authenticity' of regulation (ie the degree to which agreements represent a genuine compromise between reasonably equal negotiating parties and the degree which they have a genuine and autonomous impact on the pay and conditions of individual employees). In the case of France, for example, it has been argued that the growth in the coverage of the workforce by collective agreement since the early 1980s simply reflects statutorily created opportunities and requirements, and does not correspond to a real change in the effectiveness of trade unions on the ground.

- Negotiated pay increases have the force of law – and have to be implemented by employers. In practice, most companies (especially large ones) exceed agreed industry minimum pay rates; this typically emerges at 10–20 per cent, but in some circumstances can be higher still. This 'two-tier' structure creates particular problems in the field of the management of remuneration – but also scope for absorbing shocks and giving an element of management discretion over the pay package.
- The signatory parties themselves are often assigned their roles or attain the competence to bargain by statute law, as amplified by case law. For example:

  - Trade unions may have to meet criteria of representativeness, such as a certain number of members or seats won in workplace-elections (as happens in Spain).
  - Trade unions may have to establish their genuine independence of the employer or their capacity to back up negotiation with industrial action if necessary (as happens in Germany).
  - Under laws on employee representation in several countries such as the Netherlands, Germany, and France bodies such as works councils, elected by the whole workforce, do not usually enjoy full bargaining rights; these are reserved for trade unions ('dual structure').

However, compared with the UK, Continental European countries have much less statutory regulation of trade union internal organisation and the right to take industrial action.

- Levels of bargaining and the legal precedence of different types of collective agreement (the so-called 'hierarchy of agreements') may also be prescribed by law. Typically this gives legal precedence to national or industry-level agreements; workplace agreements or individual contracts of employment may not worsen the terms of national- or industry-level agreement.
- Withdrawal from an employers association, de-recognition of a trade union, or a collective agreement may not necessarily free an employer immediately from agreed provisions. Collective agreements may continue to have effect until replaced with a new agreement of equivalent legal status, for example. A good illustration is the situation in Germany; this may inhibit and modify any trend towards company-level bargaining.
- Moreover, the implantation of statutory forms of employee representation at workplace level, which managements must recognise by law, still leaves an agency in place with some rights to strike collective accords.

Existing national systems of employee representation in the EU–15

Country	Name of body By law/agreement	Composition	Method of electing employee reps	Role of body
Austria	Betriebsrat Statute	Employees	Whole workforce (separate colleges for blue- and white-collar)	• information • consultation • monitoring
Belgium	Conseil d'entreprise Statute and national C/As	Joint	Whole workforce on TU lists (separate colleges for blue- and white-collar)	• information • consultation • co-determination*
Denmark	Samarbejdsudvalg National C/A	Joint	Whole workforce	• information • consultation • co-determination
Finland	Form not specified Statute	Joint	Unions and workforce	• information • consultation • co-determination
France	Comité d'entreprise Statute	Joint	Whole workforce on TU lists (separate colleges for employees, middle management, and executives)	• information • consultation • co-determination
Germany	Betriebsrat Statute	Employees	Whole workforce (separate colleges for blue- and white-collar)	• information • consultation • co-determination
Greece	Works Councils Statute	Employees	Whole workforce	• information • consultation • co-determination where no C/A or TU in workplace
Ireland	Voluntary agreement	Joint	Usually whole workforce	Variable
Italy	(1) Rappresentanza sindacale unitaria National C/A (2) Consiglio dei delegati Statute and C/A	(1) Employees (2) Employees	(1) Whole workforce (2) Work groups	(1) • consultation • information • bargaining (2) • information • monitoring • co-determination
Luxembourg	Délégation du personnel Statute	Joint	Whole workforce on TU lists	• information • consultation • co-determination • bargaining
Netherlands	Ondernemingsraad Statute	Employees	Whole workforce on TU lists	• information • consultation • co-determination
Portugal	Commissão de trabalhadores Statute	Employees	Whole workforce	• information • consultation • some informal bargaining
Spain	Comité de empresa Statute	Employees	Whole workforce: can be on TU lists	• information • consultation • bargaining
Sweden	Form not specified Statute + national C/A	Joint	Unions	• information • consultation • co-determination by agreement
United Kingdom	Voluntary agreement	Joint	Usually whole workforce	Variable

Source: *IDS*

* Subjects for, and powers of, co-determination vary widely between countries

Employee representation

With the exception of the UK and the Irish Republic, every EU member state has either statutory provisions on employee representation or structures established via collective agreement with widespread application; however, the precise arrangements are highly diverse, and their roles and organisation depend crucially on the pattern of collective bargaining, and also on the strength and structure of trade unions at various levels (see the table on page xxiv). Each national system is also the product of national histories and cultures, many of which have embraced traumatic convulsions directly bearing on industrial relations. Structures of employee participation, for example, have rarely been drawn up as rational models but have typically been the product of, and response to, periods of dramatic political and industrial strife: works councils in Germany were born out of the 1918 revolution, the first initiatives in France emerged during the 1930s Popular Front, and workplace industrial relations in Italy were crucially shaped by the 'Hot Autumn' of 1969 and its accompanying social turbulence. The transformation from dictatorship to democracy in Greece, Spain, and Portugal is also sufficiently recent for many of the current actors to have been directly affected by the suppression of trade unionism, corporatist arrangements for business representation, or the acute conflicts that marked the transition.

Although there is an obligation on employers to bargain with a trade union in only a small number of countries, employers' duties are more tightly circumscribed – at least in theory – in the area of employee representation. In France and the Netherlands, for example, it is the employer's statutory duty to set up a works council, provided the establishment meets the relevant criteria of workforce size. Where employees elect works councils or other workplace bodies under law or collective agreement, representatives customarily enjoy legal protection and a range of enforceable rights. Such rights are probably strongest in Germany and the Netherlands, as set out in the relevant country chapters in this book. Although lacking such formal trade union rights as the right to take industrial action or to conclude collective agreements proper, these forms of workplace representation have often effectively underpinned trade unions lacking membership on the ground. At the same time they also offer an opportunity to weaken trade union loyalties, especially under industry-level bargaining, by tying workplace representatives more closely to corporate imperatives and allowing flourishing companies to pay wage supplements in boom periods; wage drift built up in such periods also offers a buffer over which the employer has greater control, and which can be cut – often unilaterally or via workplace negotiations outside formal collective bargaining – in downturns.

The reality of workplace representation often fails to correspond to the stringent requirements of the law, especially outside large and medium-sized firms, where employee representation throughout Europe tends to be strong – irrespective of the formal system. In France, for example, only a minority of firms complies with the law, and even then the quality of information supplied to employee representatives may be far below that required. Even in Germany, the paragaon of employee representation, a substantial minority of employees is not represented by works councils, either through apathy or employer hostility. In small companies works councils often exercise their role in a rather nominal fashion. In the case of the UK, the 1990 Workplace Industrial Relations Survey found that around a quarter of private-sector establishments with more than 25 employees has some form of joint consultative committee at workplace level; where trade unions were recognised, this figure rose to 41 per cent – not wholly out of line with the incidence in France or Germany, although lacking legally or contractually enforceable rights. Levels of informal participation and influence on managerial decision-making in the UK are also widely held to be higher than more formalised systems, and may afford employees greater power at the workplace and on job-control issues than a panoply of formal but underused statutory rights.

None the less, enforceable rights to information about corporate developments and, in Germany and the Netherlands, the right of employee representatives to resort to the courts to prevent or at least to delay managerial decisions in areas regarded as within management's prerogative in the UK can prove at best a novelty and at worst a shock to managers with a British or American background. However, both these systems continue to be characterised by a high level of consensus between unions and management on many industrial fundamentals, and are part of wider structures in which employee representatives at plant level do not play a direct and formal part in negotiations over pay increases, for example, which removes a good deal of the raw material for conflict from the immediate workplace.

Challenges and national adaptation

All systems in Europe are being confronted with the need to respond to very similar problems and challenges, as well as to a common external environment. This includes:

- greater international competiton within the EU as a result of the Single Market and also with low-cost producers in East Asia and Eastern Europe. Changed supplier–purchaser relationships are also intensifying competition for component suppliers in manufacturing, with pressure to improve on price and quality as well as a greater choice of international suppliers for end-users.
- a more stringent financial and macro-economic framework for collective bargaining as a result of efforts to pursue the convergence criteria for Economic and Monetary Union set by the 1993 Treaty on the European Union (the Maastricht Treaty). The most immediate impact is on the public sector, already under pressure because of sweeping changes in service provision as a result of privatisation, competitive tendering, and increasingly demanding consumers.

- new approaches to personnel management, such as total quality management (TQM), teamworking, and attempts to introduce performance and results-based pay to wider groups of employees. These approaches have a tendency to make the immediate workplace the site at which the regulation of terms, conditions, and working practices is best achieved, often challenging the existing relationship between levels of bargaining and the role of established institutions for employee representation.

Widely differing national systems have managed to produce responses to external challenges through their specific institutional frameworks. For example, the pressure on real pay as a result of the 1991–93 recession yielded national competitiveness programmes, incomes policies and/or pay freezes in Belgium and the Netherlands; industry-level concessions bargaining on pay in Germany; and individual company-level responses in the UK. On balance, the more centralised systems – once goaded into action – tended to produce a swifter and more generalised response, but arguably, as a corollary, also a less differentiated one in terms of the fortunes of individual companies.

In broad terms there are as yet few signs of a generalised and discernible convergence of overall structures; national institutional and legal differences are likely to persist for the foreseeable future. However, this judgement does need to be qualified in a number of respects. Although different national systems may respond in varying ways to the broad exigencies of cost and price competition, a number of forces at corporate level may be weakening existing institutional arrangements and nourishing a trend towards a devolution of the regulation of employment from industry to company or workplace level. For example, internationalisation of firms is weakening the identification of managers with a particular national model and impelling companies to develop transnational approaches, weakening both national ties and undermining national systems of industry bargaining (see Marginson and Sisson in 'Further reading'). This trend amongst large firms may be further encouraged by the establishment of pan-European mechanisms for information and consultation of employees (see below). New approaches to personnel management – TQM, 'Lean Production', and the development of forms of performance-based pay dependent on company criteria – are also likely to foster greater workplace regulation.

Where structures exist – workplace trade unions, works councils – this process may mean a rebalancing of institutions to new tasks, and could upset established equilibria in these industrial relations systems. Where local structures are either non-existent or weak it could mean that important areas of employment regulation are driven outside the ambit of collective bargaining or joint determination altogether.

Commentators in some national systems have also pointed to the fact that industry-level bargaining is not only being eroded from below but is also subject to a loss of function from above as statutory regulation, and possibly national-level agreed provisions, is losing ground to legislation and (if only embryonically) to accords struck at EU level between the European social partners: the European Trades Union Confederation (ETUC), UNICE (representing the private employers), and CEEP (representing public employers).

The 'European dimension' in industrial relations

Enhanced role for European social partners

Since the mid-1980s, and more especially as a result of the Social Protocol with its Agreement on Social Policy, annexed to the Treaty on the European Union (TEU), the role of European-level social dialogue and that of the social partners has assumed greater importance in shaping the future of social and employment policy within the EU.

The Single European Act 1987

The main aim of the 1987 Single European Act (SEA) was to introduce institutional changes in order to establish a basis for the single European market, and to facilitate and accelerate decision-making on measures necessary to achieve it through the introduction of qualified majority voting in the Council of Ministers. Under the SEA employment matters still required adoption by unanimity, unless related to health and safety issues or to the completion of the internal market, such as free movement of labour.

However, Article 118b of the Act – an offshoot of the Val Duchesse deliberations between the social partners (see below) – opened the possibility for European-level social dialogue 'if the two sides consider it desirable', leading to relations based on agreement. This had no immediate impact in terms of leading to any free-standing agreements, but was later developed by the Agreement on Social Policy under the Maastricht Treaty (see below).

The Social Charter

The 'social dimension' of the single market began to be developed following the signature of the Community Charter of the Fundamental Social Rights of Workers in 1989, the so-called Social Charter. This was a statement of principles subscribed to by 11 of the then 12 member states (excluding the UK) which, it was agreed, should shape future Community social policy. The 1989 Social Charter Action Programme, outlining proposals for legislation and other measures, gave substance to these objectives.

Many of the more controversial Directives under this Programme (controversial, at least, from the UK government's viewpoint), such as the re-organisation of working time and the protection of pregnant women and young people, have been adopted by qualified majority voting as health and safety measures.

Val Duchesse and intersectoral social dialogue

The 1985 Single Market White Paper omitted the social dimension. But in presenting the European Commission's programme to Parliament in January 1985, incoming President Jacques Delors declared that the creation of an internal market should be accompanied by the organisation of a European social area. He identified social dialogue between employers' and workers' organisations at European level as a key element in this process.

Flagging intersectoral social dialogue was revived by the President in 1985 in the form of discussions at Val Duchesse between representatives of all national organisations affiliated to employers' organisations UNICE and CEEP, and trade unions affiliated to ETUC. The parties confirmed their endorsement of the single-market objective, and also committed themselves to develop closer understanding on a range of matters of mutual interest through the establishment of a number of working parties.

The upshot was a series of joint, nonbinding opinions on aspects of labour relations, including the introduction of new technology, access to further training, and adaptability of the labour market. The motivation for engaging in talks, however, was quite different for the respective parties. The unions viewed the dialogue as preliminary to a process of eventual European collective bargaining, whereas employers regarded it as entirely separate from negotiations. This difference of views meant that opinions did not lead to spontaneous agreements, an option under Article 118b of the Single European Act (although possibly a notional one given the absence of a European-level bargaining framework); nor was there any commitment to implement them at national level through the appropriate channels. Discussions did however demonstrate the capacity of the social partners to present a joint supranational viewpoint on often highly complex issues.

The most concrete achievement of this phase of the intersectoral dialogue was a text agreed by the European-level social partners in 1991 outlining their proposals to amend articles 118(4), 118a and 118b on their role in the new institutional setting. This text later became the Agreement on Social Policy, part of the Social Protocol, endorsed by 11 of the 12 member states (see below).

New tasks aimed at strengthening the social dialogue lie ahead and have been given particular significance by efforts to revive employment prospects in Europe in the shape of a set of coherent EU policies. Some objectives are contained in the medium-term Social Action Programme for 1995–97; others arise in the context of the 1996 Inter-Governmental Conference (IGC), which will revise the 1993 TEU. For example, the Standing Committee for Employment, set up in 1970 and the only EU-level forum where representatives from EU institutions and the social partners (not just members of UNICE or ETUC) sit, is likely to see its role enlarged. It is on course to become the main institutional channel for consultation on the EU's employment strategy.

The European Commission will be reviewing the operation of the social dialogue, specifically in connection with the functioning of Articles 3 and 4 of the

Agreement on Social Policy. There is pressure that this should become part and parcel of any new treaty. In addition, it will complete a review of sectoral social dialogue committees with the idea of forging stronger links with the intersectoral dialogue process. In some sectors, social dialogue has developed fruitfully, but in others employers have been reluctant to enter into any sort of institutional relationship – a stance adopted by UNICE.

There are also plans to revise the Community Charter of Fundamental Social Rights of Workers in the light of developments since 1989, which will involve consultation with a range of organisations beyond those normally associated with the social dialogue.

The Maastricht Treaty

The Maastricht Treaty, intended to establish the European Union, introduced a number of major changes in the scope for regulating social and employment policy at Community level. Article 118 urges closer co-operation, for example, between the social partners on employment, labour law and working conditions, vocational training, social security, workplace safety, and the right of association and collective bargaining. The strictures imposed by the voting methods laid down by the 1957 Treaty of Rome and the 1987 Single European Act (subsequently incorporated into the TEU) resulted in a lack of progress on some key issues, primarily as a result of the exercise of the UK government's veto on a number of measures advanced by the European Commission after 1989 which required unanimity.

During negotiations in 1991 leading up to the TEU, attempts were made to amend Articles 117–122 (the 'social' clauses of the Treaty of Rome as amended by the Single European Act) in order to facilitate and broaden the scope of decision-making on employment matters, and to allow for greater qualified majority voting on employment-related matters. The UK government's refusal to co-operate compelled the other (then) 11 member states to find an alternative solution.

The Social Protocol

The outcome was the Social Protocol, which constitutes an accord between all member states. This states that all member states – except the UK – may, under the accompanying Agreement on Social Policy (commonly known in the UK as the Social Chapter), take action in the social and employment field to further the overarching aim of providing an effective social dimension to the Single European Market set out in the 1989 Social Charter and concretised in its associated Action Programme.

In practice, the Social Chapter allows progress to be made on issues that are unlikely to command unanimous or even qualified majority support of all 15 EU member states, as required by the precedures contained in the main treaty. Social policy is therefore now subject to autonomous and complementary legal frameworks. Specifically, the Social Chapter states that measures may be adopted by qualifed majority voting on:

- improvements in the working environment to protect health and safety
- working conditions
- information and consultation of workers
- equality between men and women with regared to labour market opportunities and treatment at work
- the integration of people excluded from the workforce.

Measures which still require unanimity (but now only of the EU–14) include:

- social security and social protection of workers
- employee protection in the event of termination
- representation and collective defence of workers and employers, including co-determination (but excluding pay, rights of association, and the right to strike and to impose lock-outs).

The Social Protocol came into force with other parts of the Treaty on the European Union on 1 November 1993. This Agreement is now observed by the original 11 signatories plus the three new member states of Austria, Finland, and Sweden. It is regarded by the European Commission, and indeed most member states, as a transitional arrangement. They are keen to see the Agreement incorporated into the main treaty when it is revised following the Intergovernmental Conference (IGC) in 1996; however, the UK government remains implacably opposed to this. The consultation elements in the Agreement on Social Policy in no way displace procedures outlined in other TEU provisions for consulting with other bodies.

The aims of the Agreement on Social Policy

The agreement on Social Policy has three main aims:

- to extend the scope of the Community's power to regulate on social matters beyond that provided for in Articles 117–122 of the TEU (which constitutes the Treaty of Rome together with the changes introduced by the 1987 Single European Act)
- to enhance the role of management and labour through greater consultation on proposed European legislation on social and employment matters
- to offer management and labour the option of regulating issues through European-level agreements as an alternative to legislation, in addition to the rather notional possibility foreseen under Article 118b of the TEU.

The preference within EU institutions remains for measures that bind all member states in order to avert the dangers of a two-track Europe and 'social dumping'. However, a number of factors will be taken into account when determining how proposals for possible regulation should be handled. These are the nature of the proposal; the attitude of the social partners; the need to ensure that social issues progress at the same rate as other policies; the need to ensure that all EU workers can benefit from any proposed measures; and the prospects for progress via either route.

Two-stage consultations

The Agreement gives the European-level social partners the right to be formally involved in two stages of consultation, each intended to remedy previous criticism that policies were formed by the European Commission without sufficient consultation, and that the scope for enhancing local implementation in accordance with the idea of 'subsidiarity' was inadequate. In the first stage, at the behest of the Commission under Article 3 of the Agreement on Social Policy, the social partners can give their views on the possible direction of EU policy on a specific issue prior to the presentation of a formal proposal (for which six weeks is allowed). In a second stage, there is an option under which the social partners can comment on the content of a substantive proposal with a suggested legal base (for which a further six weeks is allowed). Any such proposal can then become the subject of either EU-level legislation or an agreement between management and labour at European level.

Legislation or agreement?

Once a substantive proposal for legislation arises, the social partners may:

- give an opinion, outlining points of agreement or disagreement in a draft text
- give a recommendation outlining a joint position
- express a wish to conclude an agreement on the matter, for which they have nine months (extendable by mutual agreement).

If legislation is the preferred option, then the proposal will pass through the modified legal procedure outlined in the Agreement on Social Policy. If the social partners opt to negotiate on an issue, they may:

- request a Council Decision to endorse the agreement in its entirety, thus making it binding on the EU–14
- opt to implement it according to the national procedures and practices
- continue to negotiate beyond the nine-month deadline
- indicate a failure to agree.

Alongside this procedure, any Directive adopted under the Agreement on Social Policy may also be implemented in the form of an agreement, if management and labour jointly request it; this could apply, for example, under national systems where social and employment policy is typically embodied in national, universally binding collective agreements.

Two examples of Social Protocol route

Two matters have so far been fully progressed through the Agreement on Social Policy, with different outcomes. The social partners tried but were unable to reach agreement on European Works Councils, and therefore the matter became subject to legislation (very much along the lines of previous failed draft Directives). An agreement was, however, achieved on parental leave, and the social partners have requested this to be adopted by Council Decision and then implemented by the member states.

European Works Councils

After 20 years of failed attempts at adopting a Directive on European Works Councils (which required a unanimous vote on the Council of Ministers prior to the TEU) the matter was finally introduced into the Agreement on Social Policy procedures. The outcome was a Directive adopted on 22 September 1994 to be transposed into national legislation by 22 September 1996 (Council Directive 95/45/EC). The Directive excludes the UK. However, it is binding on Norway, Iceland, and Liechtenstein through the European Economic Agreement (EEA).

The Directive on European Works Councils has aroused much interest and debate about its long-term implications, not only because of its pioneer status under the new post-Maastricht machinery, but primarily because it is probably the most direct encroachment by 'Brussels' upon company decision-making in the employee relations field, as well as upon existing practices in national industrial relations systems. As such, it has become an important element in the debate about whether, and how, a distinct supranational form of 'European industrial relations' might develop.

The Directive's starting-point is the necessity to inform and consult employees 'if economic activities are to develop in a harmonious fashion'. Although most member states have either statutory or agreed national consultation systems for information and consultation, the Directive addresses the transnational dimension of international business. It covers undertakings, or groups of undertaking, irrespective of ownership (or location of head office), with at least 1,000 employees located within the EEA–17 states subject to the Directive (including at least 150 employees in each of at least two member states). The measure will include certain firms with headquarters in the UK, North America, and Japan that meet these criteria. In such cases, companies must designate a 'representative agent' within a member state of the EEA–17 to fulfil the role of 'central management'.

Although UK staff do not have to be included in the headcount, or have a formal right to be included in the consultation exercise set up for other staff, experience has so far shown that companies covered by the Directive – with headquarters both in the UK and in other member states – have included their UK staff.

The Directive gives a choice of how its provisions are to be implemented. Under Article 13 of the Directive, inserted at the insistence of the employers, a body providing for information and consultation may be established by an agreement between employers and employees. Provided such a body covers the particular employer's entire workforce, the agreement can stand after the September 1996 deadline, by which time the Directive is to be transposed into national law. Many companies immediately set about concluding such agreements, attracted by the fact that they could do so on their own agenda and free from the direct, detailed prescription of the Directive. By autumn 1995 well over 60 multinational enterprises had indeed done so – although not all had complied with the basic requirement that staff in all countries must be covered by arrangements. Moreover, this remains a small proportion of the c. 1,000–1,500 companies estimated to fall under the Directive.

If no action is taken by September 1996, then the provisions of the Directive on the form of consultation apply. In the first instance, this entails negotiation between management and a 'special negotiating body' established subject to the provisions of the Directive. Negotiations can be initiated either by management or by a minimum of 100 employees (or their representatives) from at least two member states. Should these negotiations fail, or be unjustifiably delayed, then the detailed provisions for a European Works Council (EWC) laid down in the Directive's Annex will apply. This Annex, the 'Subsidiary Requirements', sets out matters such as the size and composition of the EWC, the frequency of meetings, and specifications on the manner in which information should be disclosed. Given that these requirements would become operative automatically within three years of the Directive's coming into force in member states, in the absence of another agreement or a total lack of interest on the part of employees, the 'subsidiary requirements' are likely to emerge as the yardstick by which employee representatives will approach earlier negotiations.

Many employers are concerned about the technical problems of transposing and implementing the Directive. An expert working-group has been set up within the European Commission to deal with such matters as common implementation dates, mutual recognition of voluntary agreements, and definitions of such concepts as 'controlling undertaking'. In addition, the European employers' organisation, UNICE, has also set up an advice point for companies.

Parental leave: first EU-level agreement

Parental leave looks set to be the first issue to emerge from the Agreement on Social Policy in the form of a European-level agreement to be turned into a binding provision via a Council decision, as opposed to the directly legislative approach resorted to for EWCs. A first draft Directive was presented in 1983 and re-presented in revamped form in 1993, needing a unanimous vote of the Council of Ministers for adoption.

Owing to the UK government's opposition to an EU–15 Directive, in February 1995 the Commission launched consultations with the social partners under the terms of the Agreement on Social Policy on a somewhat broader remit: reconciling professional and family life. The social partners decided that they had no objection to regulation, but preferred this to be by means of an agreement. A draft accord was signed in December 1995, with the intention of its being submitted for Council Decision.

The basic entitlement is for an individual right to three months' parental leave (in prinicpal non-transferable) on grounds of the birth or adoption of a child up to a maximum of 8 years. Workers must be protected against unfair dismissal for applying for, or taking, leave and be entitled to re-instatement to their job. No payments are guaranteed during the leave period. In addition, the agreement gives a right to time off for *force-majeur* for urgent family reasons. The provisons are subject to no company threshold size-limits, but member states can make special arrangements for small firms or to allow postponement on specified grounds.

A common mind was reached quickly, probably because most member states already have in place provisions broadly similar to those of the agreement. However, both unions and employers regard the outcome as satisfactory and an improvement on the draft Directive text.

Other measures in the Social Protocol pipeline

In September 1995 the European Commission launched the first stage of consultations under the Social Protocol on the question of non-standard employment contracts (part-time, fixed-term and temporary work). A text entitled *Flexibility in Working Time and Security for Workers* invites the social partners' views on the need for EU-level regulation, its forms, and how it should be implemented. The background to this is the failure to agree proposals contained in the 1989 Social Charter Action Programme. Consultations are also taking place on the issue of reversing the burden of proof onto employers in sex discrimination cases, although this may be best dealt with by legislation, given the technical nature of the subject matter. Any substantial development would involve the withdrawal of pending proposals.

In November 1995 further consultations were launched on forms of employee information and consultation in national undertakings. This move, spurred on by the European Works Council Directive, is intended to achieve some progress in unblocking four outstanding employee consultation proposals (but whether by using the EU–14 or EU–15 procedures is unclear). These are contained in draft Directives that accompany Statutes for, respectively, a European Company, a European Association, a European Co-operative, and a European Mutual

Society. The draft Fifth Directive, on company law, also contains employee involvement proposals.

Other Directives with transnational implications

Several Directives have been, or are in the process of being, amended to take better account of the transnational dimension. The 1975 Collective Dismissals Directive (75/129/EEC) requiring consultation with employees before collective redundancies take place was amended in 1992 (92/56/EEC) to ensure that the obligation to consult remains even if the decision is taken outside the member state concerned. It also gives greater priority to putting in place measures that could mitigate the effects of a collective dismissal. (These are well developed, in law, in a number of EU member states.)

The Transfer of Undertaking Directive (77/187/EEC) [Acquired Rights], which safeguards employees' rights when a business is transferred, is currently being revised. It is envisaged that a new Directive will result. A number of key issues need to be clarified in the light of changing business operations and decisions from the European Court of Justice (ECJ).

Further reading

BIRD, DEREK. 'International comparisons of labour disputes in 1993', *Employment Gazette*, December 1994, 433ff.

BREWSTER, CHRIS and HEGEWISCH, ARIANE (eds). *Policy and Practice of European Human Resource Management*, findings of the 1992 Price Waterhouse/Cranfield survey, London, Routledge, 1994. Results of the 1995 survey will be published during 1996

EDWARDS, P. K. and HYMAN, RICHARD. 'Strikes and industrial conflict: peace in Europe', in Richard Hyman and Anthony Ferner (eds), *New Frontiers in European Industrial Relations*. Oxford, Blackwell, 1994

ETUI. *Collective Bargaining in Western Europe 1994–1995*, Brussels, European Trade Union Insititute, 1995

ETUI. *Transfer*, 'Modernisation of trade unions in Europe', Vol. 1, No. 1 (January 1995). Quarterly journal of the European Trade Union Institute

HAMPDEN-TURNER, CHARLES and TROMPENAAR, FONS. *The Seven Cultures of Capitalism*. London, Piatkus, 1994

HOFSTEDE, GERD. *Culture's Consequences*. London, Sage, 1980

IDS. 'European Works Councils: millstone or milestone?'. *IDS Employment Europe*, Issue 401, May 1995

LANE, CHRISTEL. *Management and Labour in Europe*. Aldershot, Edward Elgar, 1989

MARGINSON, PAUL and SISSON, KEITH. 'The stucture of transnational capital in Europe, the emerging Euro-company and its implications for industrial relations', in Richard Hyman and Anthony Ferner (eds). *New Frontiers in*

European Industrial Relations. Oxford, Blackwell, 1994

MILLWARD, NEIL ET AL., *Workplace Industrial Relations in Transition.* Aldershot, Dartmouth, 1992

TRAXLER, FRANZ. 'Collective bargaining levels and coverage', in *OECD Employment Outlook.* Paris, OECD, 1994

TROMPENAAR, FONS. *Riding the Waves of Culture.* London, Economist Books, 1993

1

Austria

Industrial relations in Austria are characterised by highly developed corporatist arrangements which have endured and exhibited a high level of stability throughout the post-war period. Both employers and employees are represented through a number of centrally organised institutions with wide-ranging powers. Unusually, these not only consist of the customary voluntary associations – employers' federations and trade unions – but also representative bodies based on compulsory membership for both sides established under public law.

The most important associations are, for employees, the Austrian Trade Union Confederation (Österreichischer Gewerkschaftsbund, ÖGB) and the chambers of labour (*Kammer für Arbeiter und Angestellte*). For the employers, there are also two main national organisations: the chambers of business (*Wirtschaftskammer*) and the Confederation of Austrian Industry (Vereinigung Österreichischer Industrieller). Chambers of agriculture also constitute an important interest group.

The key institutions for the practical regulation of employment matters are the ÖGB and the chambers of business. Both organisations are institutionally dominant over the parties at individual establishment level. For example, no binding agreement on pay may be concluded at company level without the express authorisation of a collective agreement (*Kollektivvertrag*) concluded between the main representative bodies.

Moreover the main representative associations enjoy a significance which goes far beyond the immediate context of employee relations. Within the broader framework of social and economic partnership in Austria they play a major role – in conjunction with the government – in shaping economic and social policy as a whole.

Although the Austrian system continues to display considerable stability, there have been some indications in recent years that the political influence of the central organisations has weakened somewhat compared with the 1960s and 1970s. This is primarily attributable to the changed external context now confronting traditional domestic arrangements – but is also rooted in the loss of influence of the nationalised industries, in changes in the structure of the Austrian economy, shifts in broader social values, and shortcomings within the organisations themselves. The most marked change in the external context is the narrowing down of the scope for the pursuit of independent policies by a small country such as Austria in the face of the rapid globalisation of the economy, characterised by the liberalisation of goods' and capital markets. Arrangements negotiated on a consensual basis between the social partners in response to primarily domestic

1

forces, which had long characterised politics in Austria, are now increasingly required to respond to external exigencies. In part, these developments have been promoted by the social partners: both sides supported the entry of Austria into the European Union on 1 January 1995.

The decline in the influence of the social partners is also evident in voter disenchantment with the political parties with which they have been traditionally associated. Despite this, the main central associations continue to dominate the sphere of employee relations: there have been no massive changes in recent years, either organisationally or in terms of the content of employment regulation. This high level of stability is principally attributable to the fact that the existing system has served well in the past, and has been seen as instrumental in Austria's, in general, positive post-war economic development.

Many commentators have emphasised the particular contribution of Austria's mechanisms for pay-setting to the long-term and stable growth of the economy. Wage settlements are negotiated at central level, are oriented to the medium and long term, and always take into account the macro-economic environment – that is, the international economic environment, productivity growth, and inflation.

The main players

National structures for employee representation

Employee representation at national level is characterised by two peculiarities. First, there is only one trade union, the Österreichischer Gewerkschaftsbund, which organises employees irrespective of occupation and political affiliation. The main political groupings in Austria are represented *within* the ÖGB via a number of political tendencies with close affiliations to the established political parties (see below). Second, in contrast to the ÖGB, which is a 'voluntary' employee organisation, there is also a statutory forum for employee representation, the chambers of labour, with compulsory membership (see below).

Historical development of the trade union movement   The establishment of free associations was legalised in 1867 with the creation of the Basic Law (*Staatsgrundgesetz*), or constitution. Following this, in 1870 freedom of trade union association was granted through the ending of the criminalisation of combinations to enforce working conditions. However, the practical achievement of trade union rights still required several decades and numerous conflicts before bans on freedom of assembly and on the prosecution of picketing were lifted.

The first all-Austrian trades union congress, organised by social democrat trade unionists, was convened in 1893. Towards the end of the nineteenth century Christian and national trade unions also gained in influence.

The steady growth of trade union strength and influence in the late nineteenth and early twentieth centuries, illustrated in the conclusion of numerous collective agreements, was brought to an abrupt halt by the outbreak of the First World War. Between 1914 and 1916 the trade unions lost 60 per cent of their members. After the war, organised workers gained in power and, together with the Social Democratic Party, were able to achieve wide-ranging reforms in both structures of representation and working conditions. This period saw, for example, the introduction of the eight-hour day and unemployment insurance. In 1919 legislation introducing and regulating works councils was introduced (Works Council Act, *Betriebsrätegesetz*), and in 1920 it was followed by the law establishing the chambers of labour, with extensive statutory rights to consultation on social policy. In all, therefore, this period saw the crystallisation of three forms of institutional representation for employees: the trade unions, establishment-based works councils, and the chambers of labour. Far from weakening the position of trade unions, these additional bodies have been viewed as a source of considerable support for trade union activity.

The year 1920 also saw the passage of legislation on conciliation and collective agreements, which together with the Works Councils Act represented a precursor of the 1973 Labour Constitution Act (*Arbeitsverfassungsgesetz*).

The period between the wars was characterised by major conflicts between the different political camps and political trade unions, especially between the social democratic and the Christian trade unions. Under the authoritarian regime which took power in 1933 independent trade union activity was severely restricted and both the social democratic trade unions and the Social Democratic Party were banned. With the incorporation of Austria into National Socialist Germany in 1938 all trade union activity was forbidden.

One consequence was that the formerly hostile representatives of the Christian and social democratic trade unions found themselves fellow prisoners in the National Socialists' concentration camps – an experience which almost certainly played a major role in the subsequent resolve of the main actors to settle their differences in a non-conflictual way.

One further factor which contributed to *rapprochement* between the various political tendencies within the trade union movement, and their respective political camps, was the occupation of Austria by the allied powers, which continued until 1955. The joint aim of achieving national political independence overrode many other conflicts of interest.

The Austrian Trade Union Confederation (Österreichischer Gewerkschaftsbund, ÖGB) The ÖGB was established as a central confederation in 1945 as the result of co-operation between a number of political tendencies. As virtually all trade union members belong to the ÖGB, the organisation in practice exercises a monopoly of employee representation (on the special position of the chambers of labour see below). The ÖGB exists as a registered association, with its internal arrangements and field of activity set by its own rulebook. There is no specific trade union legislation in Austria.

The ÖGB consists of 14 individual trade unions; however, these have no legal personality, and in formal terms have no power to act on their own behalf. The dominance of the ÖGB within the overall structure is illustrated by the fact that the supreme authority on financial and personnel questions lies with the ÖGB and not with the constituent trade unions. Although employees who become trade union members join one of the individual trade unions, their formal membership is with the ÖGB.

The individual trade unions nevertheless exercise substantial practical independence in the sphere of collective bargaining, where they are responsible for negotiating with employer representatives. Once agreement has been reached, however, it is the ÖGB which formally signs the resultant collective agreements.

The 14 individual trade unions within the ÖGB are basically structured on industrial lines. All employees in a particular branch are members of the same trade union, irrespective of occupation. There is one major exception to this rule: virtually all white-collar workers in the private sector are organised in a specific trade union, the Gewerkschaft der Privatangestellten, mirroring some of the differences in treatment of blue- and white-collar employees established in labour law (see 'Austria' in *Contracts and Terms and Conditions of Employment* in this series) .

In addition to the trade union for white-collar workers there are eight private-sector blue-collar trade unions, four trade unions for the public sector and the trade union for the arts, the media and the independent professions. In 1994 there were 1.6 million trade union members, including pensioners, out of the total of 3 million dependent employees. This yields a union density of currently employed union members of some 45 per cent. The largest ÖGB affiliates were the trade union for private white-collar workers (330,000 members), the public services union (230,000), the engineering, mining and energy union (220,000) and the construction and woodworkers' union (190,000). Membership has remained remarkably stable over 40 years – and has actually increased from the 1.4 million members recorded in 1956 – although the level of union density has gradually declined over the years with workforce growth.

The executive and policy-making bodies within the ÖGB are staffed according to a formula negotiated between the various political tendencies represented within the ÖGB. There is no membership balloting for senior positions. However, indirect influence is exercised through elections to works councils, on lists nominated by the tendencies, which serve as an important benchmark for the relative strength of the tendencies within the ÖGB. By far the biggest tendency is the social democratic one, aligned with the Social Democratic Party (SPÖ). Only in one affiliated union, that for the public services, does any other tendency – the Christian one – exercise a dominant influence.

Neither the ÖGB nor its constituent unions are directly represented at establishment or enterprise level. Rather, the work of trade union representation at workplace level is done by works councils (*Betriebsräte* – see below). It is made possible through the intimate links between works councils and the ÖGB, embodied in the fact that more than 80 per cent of works council members belong to the ÖGB. Conversely, the ÖGB's main decision-making bodies are made up primarily of members of works councils. In consequence, works council members have a direct and decisive influence on trade union collective bargaining strategies.

Although the ÖGB is engaged in a wide range of representative and policy-shaping activities, its core task is that of seeking to exert influence over the terms and conditions of employment of its members. This aim is pursued via political lobbying on employment-related legislation, by collective bargaining with employers and their representatives, and not least through direct assistance to individual trade union members in the form of legal advice and representation.

The chambers of labour (*Kammern für Arbeiter und Angestellte*) The chambers of labour are institutions established by statute 'to represent and promote the social, economic, professional and cultural interest of workers'. They were founded in 1920 at the instigation of the trade unions, and were intended as a counterweight to the chambers of trade, which were established after the 1848 revolution.

Each of Austria's nine constituent federal states (*Länder*) has its own chamber of labour, with the Vienna chamber acting as the overall federal chamber for the whole country. Under the law regulating the chambers (*Arbeiterkammergesetz*), all employees but those who work in central or local government must be members of the relevant chambers (including the unemployed who retain their membership). The approximately 2.5 million members elect a parliament (*Kammerparlament*) every five years which determines the policy and strategy of the organisation. Membership contributions of 0.5 per cent of gross earnings are deducted direct from pay each month.

The chambers' activity encompasses evaluating draft legislation, participating in social administration (with delegates to a number of institutions, such as the employment service), research and policy development, and legal advice and representation for members.

The existence of the well financed chambers of labour plays a major role in evening out the balance of power between employer associations and employee representation, and as such is a key component in the operation of social partnership in its specifically Austrian form.

In recent years the Austrian system as a whole, and the chambers of labour in particular, have become the target of criticism from some areas of the daily press and the opposition parties. The chambers themselves were very concerned when participation in the most recent elections in the autumn of 1994 fell dramatically to only 31 per cent of those eligible to vote.

Relations between the ÖGB and the chambers of labour Close co-operation is maintained between the chambers of labour and the ÖGB. In fact the activities of the chambers of labour should be seen as complementing and supplementing the ÖGB's work – although the ÖGB is clearly the more powerful partner and has greater freedom of manoeuvre should a conflict of interest with employers arise. The chambers of labour are bound by the requirements of the law, which, in theory, could be changed by parliamentary decision at any time.

Co-operation between the ÖGB and the chambers of labour is ensured through the fact that the dominant political tendency within the ÖGB, the social democrats, also holds a majority of seats on the chambers of labour. There are non-social democrat majorities in only two of the chamber parliaments at *Land* level – Tirol and Vorarlberg, whose chambers are dominated by Christian trade unionists.

Employer organisations

As with the institutions for employee representation, there are a number of features of collective employer representation which are unique to Austria. Notably, every undertaking operating in the spheres of industry, trade, the handicrafts, finance, transport or tourism must be a member of the appropriate chamber of business (*Wirtschaftskammer*), established under statute. As a consequence of the comprehensive form of organisation offered by the chambers of business, which are broken down into a number of sub-bodies specific to each area of economic activity, there are few employer associations based on voluntary membership.

The first employer chambers were established shortly after the revolutionary upheavals of 1848, initially as chambers of commerce (*Handelskammer*). In their early period there was controversy over the separation, called for by those in handicrafts, between trade and handicraft chambers. The tasks of the chambers of commerce during the period of the monarchy consisted primarily in obtaining a voice for employers at governmental level. Among other things, they had the right to send representatives to the imperial Diet and the *Land* parliaments.

After the First World War the chambers of commerce were formed into three departments covering commerce, handicrafts and industry. This subdivision largely eliminated the risk of separate chambers being set up for handicrafts and industry.

In the immediate wake of the Second World War the organisation, scope and remit of the chambers changed markedly and they subsequently became the most important employer organisation in Austria. Crucially for the field of employee relations, the chambers were given responsibility both for representing the interests of their members and for maintaining industrial peace.

The strengthening of the chambers as a result of this extension of their activities has left little scope for voluntary employers' associations concerned with employment terms. In contrast to the employees' side, where the ÖGB is responsible, collective bargaining for employers is carried out by the chambers of business.

The chambers of business In contrast to the institutional arrangements for employees, where the ÖGB operates in a conventional sense as a freely constituted trade union, on the employer side the dominant vertical influence lies with the statutory form of interest representation. As with the chambers of labour, there is a chamber of business in each of the nine constituent federal states, the *Länder*. In addition there is an independent organisation at federal level, the Austrian Federal Chamber of Business (Bundeswirtschaftskammer Österreichs – see 'Organisations' below).

The internal structure of the individual chambers is highly complex. The organisational foundations consist of a large number of trade groups within the federal organisation (known as *Fachverbände*) and corresponding groups at *Land* level (known as *Fachgruppen*). These bodies, which have extensive powers, usually embrace an entire sector of industry. At federal level some 130 individual branches have their own trade groups.

The trade groups are organised into six sections both at federal and at *Land* level, namely handicraft, industry, commerce, finance/credit/insurance, transport, and tourism. As far as employee relations are concerned, of paramount importance to the activities of the chambers is the fact that the individual trade groups are authorised to conclude collective agreements.

Virtually all independent traders and proprietors must be members of the appropriate chamber, with the exception of individuals engaged in the liberal professions and farmers, who have separate organisations. Membership is automatically acquired with the granting of the right to engage in independent economic activity, and ceases if permission is withdrawn. Membership is compulsory both of the trade groups at *Land* level and also of the Federal Chamber and its specialist associations.

For individual employers the most important consequence of membership of a particular trade group is coverage by any industry agreement it has concluded.

In addition to their activities in the sphere of employee relations the chambers of business also perform a variety of other tasks, ranging from evaluating draft legislation to maintaining an extensive network of foreign trade offices.

The marked internal subdivision of the overall system of chambers of business combined with the extensive scope for independent activity by the individual organisations means that many employers see their own trade group as an autonomous institution for representing their interests. This is one factor, for example, which has inhibited the growth of employer associations established on a voluntary basis.

The Confederation of Austrian Industry   Politically the most important organisation representing employers outside the statutory framework is the Confederation of Austrian Industry (Vereinigung Österreichischer Industrieller, VÖI). This organisation was established in 1946 as a successor to the Central Federation of Industry. In contrast to the chambers of business, the VÖI is not structured by industry but organised on a regional basis. Around 70 per cent of industrial establishments are members of the confederation. The VÖI is seen as representative more of large-scale and export-oriented industry than of the chambers. Moreover, it does not conclude collective agreements.

National consultation

The horrendous experience of occupation and war, together with the aspirations of all political parties to secure political independence, served to dampen rivalries between the Christian conservative and social democratic currents which had marked the inter-war years. At government level the *rapprochement* between the two political camps was expressed in the coalition between the two major parties – the Social Democratic Party (SPÖ) and the conservative Austrian People's Party (ÖVP) – which lasted from 1945 until 1966.

Political co-operation at the national level was reflected in the field of industrial relations by a model of conflict resolution primarily through the forging of a consensus via negotiation.

The central institution for social partnership at the national level is the Joint Commission on Wages and Prices (Paritätische Kommission für Lohn- und Preisfragen) established by the government, although not on a statutory basis, in 1957 at the instigation of the ÖGB. The original aim in setting up the commission was to contain wage–price spirals. Subsequently its role expanded to embrace economic and social policy as a whole. The commission is composed of the Federal Chancellor and Ministers responsible for economic matters together with two representatives each from the ÖGB, the chambers of labour, the chambers of business and the chambers of agriculture. Unanimity is required for decisions: members of the government do not vote.

In the course of time the commission has expanded to embrace a number of subcommittees: at present, these consist of a subcommittee on pay, a subcommittee on prices, one on international questions and an advisory council on economic and social matters. The advisory council consists of experts in the various fields, and its major responsibility is producing studies on economic and social policy issues.

According to the commission's procedural rules, member organisations must seek the commission's authority to negotiate before bargaining can begin: in practice, this is now virtually a formality.

Co-operation between senior members of the government and leading representatives of employer and employee bodies has had a marked impact on the political atmosphere in post-war Austria, one clear illustration of which is the relative absence of industrial conflict.

The commission continues to operate on the basis of nonbinding accords which can be revoked by any of the participating organisations. The fact that the commission has none the less survived for 40 years illustrates the extent to which all parties involved are still committed to resolving their differences via discussion and negotiation, not only with each other but with the active involvement of the state.

Employee representation at establishment and enterprise level

As in Germany, there is statutory employee representation at all levels of the private sector; the individual establishment, the enterprise, and the group. These systems of representation embrace all employees, irrespective of whether they are union members.

How works councils are to be constituted and to function, the rights and duties of employee representatives, and their legal status, are regulated by the Labour Constitution Act (*Arbeitsverfassungsgesetz*).

Works councils

Works councils (pl. *Betriebsräte*) may be established in any establishment with at least five permanent employees, provided the workforce wishes it. Works councils may not be established at any level below that of an establishment, for example in individual departments. Works councils have the 'task of safeguarding and promoting the economic, social, health and cultural interests of employees in the establishment'.

The number of works council members depends on the size of the workforce in the establishment. In establishments with no more than nine employees the works council consists of one member; for workforces of 10-19 employees, two members; between 20 and 50 employees, three members; between 51 and 100 employees, four members. For every additional 100 employees the number of works council members is increased by one person. If the establishment has a workforce of more than 1,000 employees there is a further works council member for each 400 additional employees.

If there are at least five blue-collar workers and five white-collar workers, separate representative bodies may be established for each of the two groups, although they may be merged into a joint works council, given workforce approval. Works councils are elected for a period of four years.

All employees are entitled to vote in elections to works councils upon reaching the age of 18. Citizenship is irrelevant. However, candidates for works council office must be Austrian citizens or citizens of EU member states. Moreover, anyone who wishes to be elected to the works council must have also worked at least six months in the establishment or with the company.

Where a works council consists of at least four members, executive board members and full-time officials of trade unions may also be elected; however, at least three-quarters of a works council must consist of employees of the establishment. Voting is by secret ballot, equal and direct. Postal voting is allowed.

Co-determination rights Works councils have a number of broad rights to information, consultation and participation. The Labour Constitution Act distinguishes:

- general powers (such as monitoring compliance with statutory protective regulations; the right to information on all matters affecting employees; the right to intervene either with the employer or, if necessary, with outside bodies, on all matters affecting employees, and to put forward proposals for improvements; the right to be consulted regularly by the employer on all issues, with provision for inviting external participants from representative bodies on major questions affecting the workplace)
- participation rights on social matters, including participation in the management of company welfare and training facilities
- participation rights in personnel matters (for example, participation in decisions on the transfer of employees)
- participation rights in economic matters (for example, to consultation about changes in the operation of the establishment).

On some matters the works council has the statutory right to conclude binding works agreements with the employers. These are detailed below (see 'Works agreements'), as is the right of representation on the supervisory board of companies.

To cover the cost of operating the works council and maintaining welfare facilities, a works council contribution of up to 0.5 per cent of gross pay may be levied on employees with workforce approval. Receipts from the contributions are paid into an independently established works council fund managed by the works council. The conduct and use of the fund are audited at least once a year by the local Chamber of Labour.

Central works councils If a company consists of several centrally administered establishments a 'central works council' (*Zentralbetriebsrat*) may be established at company level at the initiative of the individual establishment works councils.

Central works councils consist of, and are elected by, the members of establishment works councils. Each works council member has as many votes as the number of employees whom they represent. In undertakings with up to 1,000 employees a central works council consists of four members. For each additional 500 employees a further central works council member has to be elected. Where the workforce exceeds 5,000 a further central works council member is elected for each additional 1,000 employees. The period of office on the central works councils is four years.

A number of powers are automatically transferred to it once a central works council has been established. Of these the most important is the right to participation in decisions on economic matters. In addition, individual works councils are free to delegate such other powers as they wish to the central works council. On issues which fall within the scope of their powers central works councils may conclude binding agreements with company managements.

Group-level representation   Under an amendment of the Labour Constitution Act introduced in 1986, employee representation within the works council system was allowed at group (*Konzern*) level initially simply through a 'working party' of central councils. In 1993 the 'working party's' powers were extended and formalised to create a body now known as the 'group representation' (*Konzernvertretung*). Group-level representation can be established with the agreement of two-thirds of the central works councils in a group of companies, provided they represent more than 50 per cent of the group's whole workforce.

The group-level representation consists of a council of two delegates from each central works council in the case of companies employing fewer than 500 employees. For each additional 500 employees the number of members delegated by each central works councils is increased by one.

Powers may be delegated by central works councils or, where none is elected, by individual establishment-level works councils. The tenure of office of representatives at this level lasts four years. Group-level representatives enjoy comparable powers to central works councils: for example, they have the right to a voice in decisions on important changes in the running of the business where they affect more than one company in a group, and a right to information and consultation on all matters which affect the interests of the group's whole workforce.

Group-level representatives may also conclude binding works agreements provided specific authorisation is given by lower-level works councils.

Employee co-determination on supervisory boards

The main element in employee involvement in the conduct of the employer's business is via employee representation on the supervisory boards (pl. *Aufsichtsräte*) of companies. Supervisory boards may be established in public limited liability companies, private limited liability companies and co-operatives, and their main task is to exercise control over the firm's executive board, which deals with day-to-day management. In a public limited company the supervisory board also has responsibility for appointing – and recalling – members of management boards. ('Recalling' means here that the board has the right to remove members from office by a vote.) One-third of the seats on the supervisory board are reserved for employees.

The delegation of employee representatives to supervisory boards takes place through the works councils. Only works council members may be nominated, and then only those entitled to vote in works council elections in the company (excluding external trade union delegates).

As a rule employee representatives are delegated for an indefinite period which ends when their period of office as a works council member ends, or as a result of recall by works councils. Employees on the board have the same legal status as shareholder members. There are a small number of exceptions to this rule. For example, employee representatives have restricted rights over the election and recall of members of the management board.

European works councils

The adoption of the EU directive on European works councils triggered a good deal of activity in Austria, beginning with intensive training of their memberships by trade unions, chambers of labour and business organisations. In all, some 30 groupings with headquarters in Austria are expected to be affected by the directive. In addition, around 300 companies located in Austria are subsidiaries of foreign concerns which will be required to establish European works councils.

Other forms of employee representation

In addition to the works councils structure the following institutions represent employee interests:

- disability representation. Disability representatives are to be appointed in establishments in which there at least five disabled employees who may elect a disability representative. This person has the job of protecting the interests of workers with a disability in conjunction with works councils.
- youth representatives. A youth representative should be appointed in workplaces where there are at least five employees under the age of 18. These employees may elect a youth representative body to represent their interests. This operates in conjunction with the works councils.

Although not institutions of employee representation in the strict sense, other bodies which are of importance in employee relations include: safety representatives, safety committees, the technical safety service, and occupational physicians. In the appointment of such individuals works councils have a right of co-determination.

Collective bargaining

Binding collective employment norms are set at two distinct levels: on the one hand through the representative institutions of employers and employees, and on the other directly between individual employers and workforces via works councils.

Collective agreements

Collective agreements (pl. *Kollektivverträge*) between employer associations and trade unions are negotiated primarily at branch level. General collective agreements, with a multi-industry impact, are a rarity. One important agreement of that nature was the one introducing a general cut in working hours in the late 1960s. Similarly, few company-level collective agreements are concluded between the employers' organisations and trade unions, although it may happen on occasion. There is a specific legal instrument for regulating terms and conditions at establishment level, the works agreement (*Betriebsvereinbarung*), dealt with below.

Which organisations are entitled to conclude collective agreements, whom the agreements apply to, their legal effect and the legal consequences of terminating a collective agreement are all regulated by statute law under the Labour Constitution Act.

Collective agreements are recognised in law as an autonomous regulatory instrument over substantive employment terms and hence have quasi-legal standing. The Labour Constitution Act states: 'The provisions of collective agreements, inasmuch as they do not govern the legal relation between the signatory parties, are directly binding within their occupational, spatial and personal sphere.'

The terms of a collective agreement cannot be altered to the disadvantage of the employee either by works agreement or by the individual contract of employment.

Competence to bargain   The Labour Constitution Act distinguishes between organisations which are competent to conclude collective agreements by law and those which may be allowed such competence upon application. In law the capacity to conclude binding collective agreements is assigned to the statutory bodies representing employees and employers – on the employees' side the chambers of labour, on the employers' the chambers of business – and their various subordinate bodies, as well as the chambers of the liberal professions.

However, the competence to conclude collective agreements possessed by the statutory representative bodies does not apply where voluntary interest associations conclude collective agreements; 'If a voluntary occupational association is granted the power to conclude collective agreements, and then concludes an agreement, the relevant statutory body for interest representation shall surrender its capacity to conclude collective agreements for the duration of the agreement and for the scope of the collective agreement concluded by the occupational association' (Labour Constitution Act, article 6). That is, the law gives precedence to voluntary forms of interest representation over statutory bodies in the conclusion of collective agreements.

In order to acquire the capacity, representative institutions established on a voluntary basis must apply to a department of the Federal Ministry of Labour known as the Bundeseinigungsamt. Recognition for collective bargaining purposes will be granted provided certain statutory conditions are met: these include the requirements that

- the constitution of the applicant body should permit it to regulate conditions of employment
- the association should cover a reasonably large occupational and geographical area

- the association is of reasonable economic significance in terms of number of members and the scope of its activities
- it is independent of the other party to the contract.

On the employees' side this competence has been granted only to the ÖGB and a small number of professional associations such as the association of pharmacists and the dental technicians. On the employers' side, the capacity to conclude collective agreements has been devolved to a larger number of associations. Voluntary employer associations authorised to conclude collective agreements exist principally in the field of financial services, together with the association of pharmacists, the association of newspaper publishers and the association of electricity generating companies. Individual employers are granted the capacity to enter into collective agreements only in exceptional circumstances.

In practice, on the employers' side 95 per cent of collective agreements are concluded by the appropriate specialist trade group of the chambers of business, and only 5 per cent by voluntary employer associations.

On the employees' side, all collective agreements are concluded by the ÖGB. However, the ÖGB is only formally the contracting party. In practice, negotiations are conducted by its affiliated trade unions. The organisational structure of the ÖGB also means that separate negotiations are carried out for blue-collar and white-collar employees, culminating in separate collective agreements.

A collective agreement covers all employment relations with an employer who is subject to it. An employee's specific occupation at an establishment is relevant only in as much as there are separate agreements for blue-collar and white-collar workers. Thus, for example, the collective agreement for the engineering industry applies to the canteen staff of an engineering works as much as to the engineering workers themselves.

Under the Works Constitution Act the substantive terms of a collective agreement apply equally to employees who work in an undertaking subject to the collective agreement but are not members of the relevant trade union (*Außenseiterwirkung*).

On occasion examples occur of regional collective agreements, but in most instances agreements apply to the whole country.

Extension of collective agreements   Under certain circumstances the federal Ministry of Labour, via the Bundeseinigungsamt, may extend a collective agreement to cover employers who are not members of a signatory organisation (in a process known as *Satzung eines Kollektivvertrages*) or issue its own minimum pay scales (*Mindestlohntarif*).

An extension can be granted only upon the written application of one of the two parties to a collective agreement. The prerequisite of extension is that the employment relationship which is to be subject to the extended agreement is essentially the same as that covered by the existing arrangements and that the collective agreement already has overwhelming importance in the industry concerned.

Minimum pay scales can also be set for employees in sectors where there is no collective agreement to extend for lack of an employers' association with the power to sign an agreement. This applies, for example, to people working as domestic helps in private households.

The practical importance of extension has declined considerably over the past few decades, especially in the immediate post-war years, as collective agreements became more comprehensive.

According to a recent OECD study some 98 per cent of all non-public-sector employees are covered by a collective agreement or minimum wage scale. Although this estimate may seem on the high side, it does illustrate the central role which collective agreements play in employee relations. This high degree of collective regulation is attributable to two main factors: first, the preference on both sides for negotiated solutions to problems of employment regulation and income distribution – a product both of historical experience and the strength of organised labour; second, the institutional and legal context, in particular compulsory company membership of employer associations with the power to sign agreements, and statutory extensions of agreements to non-union members. Furthermore, in those few sectors of the economy in which collective agreements are signed by employers' organisations based on voluntary membership, the regulations are usually extended to non-signatory employers in the relevant trade or industry upon application by the relevant trade union.

The course of collective bargaining   There is no obligation to bargain. The Labour Constitution Act merely sets out rules for registering and publishing collective agreements. It is entirely up to the negotiating parties to determine the form and course of the bargaining.

Economic forecasts and analyses are prepared both by experts from the various interest groups and by independent institutions. Customarily, negotiations centre on the rate of productivity growth and inflation. The trade unions have also sought to pursue a 'solidaristic' negotiating strategy, aimed at limiting differentials. In contrast, the employers have tried to maximise flexibility.

The main pay round takes place in the autumn, with the pace being set by the agreement for the engineering industry. However, there is no formal linkage between that sector and other settlements.

The content of collective agreements   The primary substance of collective agreements is the regulation of pay. This is due in part to the fact that Austria has no statutory minimum wage, combined with the fact that at workplace level the parties have no power to enter into binding provisions on pay (see below). In consequence, pay-setting on a collective basis is left almost entirely to trade unions and employers' organisations.

There are a number of forms of agreed pay regulation. The most prevalent is the setting of a structure of minimum pay rates by grade. Most white-collar agreements also contain seniority increments, with progression to a higher rate every two years. Pay rates are normally adjusted by the annual pay round. Companies may pay more than the industry minimum on an individual basis or via plant-level supplements. On average, company-level supplements mean that individual contractual pay (*Ist-Löhne*) exceeds industry minima (*KV-Löhne*) by some 20–5 per cent.

However, one factor of some importance in pay-setting, which contrasts with many other countries with a two-tier structure, is that Austrian employment law provides for the collective regulation not only of agreed minimum pay rates but also of contractual pay. Such provisions are found only in sectors where trade union organisation is strong. None the less, it does limit the scope for employers to offset mandatory increases in industry minima against their own higher in-house rates.

In addition to setting minimum pay, agreements also regulate bonus payments, primarily holiday bonuses and Christmas bonuses. Both these additional salary payments (thirteenth- and fourteenth-month payments) are now customary throughout the economy.

In recent years, employer associations have increasingly called for agreed pay increases to take the form of a fixed element and a flexible component in an attempt to extend the scope for plant-level discretion over pay. However, the pay agreement in the engineering industry in 1993, which allowed scope for plant-by-plant variations, has remained an exception.

For their part, the trade unions have not succeeded in minimising inter-sectoral differentials, which have continued to grow and which are high by international standards.

The second main focus of collective regulation is working time and in particular weekly working hours. As with pay, while the trade unions have been primarily concerned to achieve a cut in working hours, employers have pressed for greater flexibility.

In contrast to pay, where the trade unions have generally been able to resist employer calls for flexibility, the past few years have seen a number of steps towards greater flexibility on hours of work, mostly implemented at plant level through hours-averaging arrangements, seasonal variations and flexible shift work.

At the same time trade unions have succeeded in winning shorter working hours. Since the mid-1980s, beginning with engineering and printing, many industries have concluded agreements reducing actual working hours below the statutory 40 hour week, although often in combination with flexibility options. In leading sectors the actual agreed working week is now 38.5 hours.

More recently the debate on working time has been linked with questions of further training and work humanisation. For example, the ÖGB has proposed further cuts in working time, with the hours released to be used for further training. Arrangements on training have already been agreed in some industries. White-collar workers in industry, for example, can now take one to two weeks' unpaid leave in order to prepare for professional examinations.

Compared with weekly working hours, agreed arrangements have little impact on annual leave. Provisions which go beyond the statutory minimum holiday of five weeks' per year are a rarity.

Periods of notice are an important component of collective agreements for blue-collar workers, as, in contrast to white-collar workers, they do not enjoy statutory protection. In some blue-collar agreements trade unions have succeeded in recent years in harmonising notice periods with the statutory minimum for white-collar workers (between six weeks and five months, depending on length of service).

Most collective agreements also include provision for days off on personal and family grounds.

Works agreements

At company level the employer (proprietor) and the works council may agree on a different form of collective provision, the 'works agreement' (*Betriebsverein-barung*). Works agreements can apply to several establishments within a firm, and in certain instances to an entire group of companies.

According to the Labour Constitution Act, 'Works agreements are written agreements concluded by the owner of the establishment on the one hand and the works council on the other on issues the regulation of which has been assigned by law or collective agreement to works agreements.' Works agreements have the same quasi-legal status as collective agreements: 'the provisions of works agreements, in as much as they do not regulate the contractual relationships between contractual parties, are directly binding within their sphere of application'. Arrangements which are governed by works agreement may not be changed to the disadvantage of employees either unilaterally by the employer or through the individual contract of employment.

Any change in a works agreement concluded between the employer and the works council is directly applicable to individual employees, who are not required to give their assent in order to make the change effective. This means that not only works councils but many employers prefer to negotiate and conclude works agreements, rather than proceed via individual agreement, on a variety of issues.

There is no statutory right for the parties at establishment level to regulate pay, unless authorised by an industry collective agreement. Such authorisations are extremely rare. Should a provision on pay be adopted at establishment or enterprise level without the authorisation of a collective agreement it will not enjoy the status of a works agreement but instead will become part of the individual contract of employment, which as a rule can be changed only with the consent of the individual employee.

The Labour Constitution Act lists those measures which do not necessarily require the conclusion of a works agreement and where, even if the works council or the employer wishes to conclude one, there is no right of recourse to a conciliation panel.

The following types of works agreement can be distinguished:

- obligatory works agreements
- enforceable works agreements
- voluntary works agreements.

An obligatory works agreement regulates matters on which the employer may take no action without the agreement of the works council. They include the introduction of a company rulebook with disciplinary provisions, employee questionnaires, measures which serve to control the movement of employees, and the introduction of performance-related payment systems (including payment by results).

The Works Constitution Act also lists a number of issues on which the agreement of the works council should be sought; however, if no agreement can be reached then the employer may obtain a ruling from an external conciliation panel instead (and conversely a works council could also do the same if the employer refused to agree to a works council proposal). Any such decision is binding on both sides and has the legal effect of a works agreement. Enforceable works agreements may be concluded on the following main issues: general provisions on company handbooks, daily working hours and breaks, the manner of wage payment, the establishment of social compensation plans to mitigate hardship in the event of major changes in the operation of the establishment, and the employment of temporary workers.

Voluntary works agreements, with no right of resort to a conciliation panel, may be freely entered into on a range of matters. These include: profit-sharing systems, anniversary bonuses, the allocation of company-owned housing, occupational pension schemes, and employee safety.

Industrial action

Industrial action is rare in Austria. The application of pressure by trade unions is normally confined to organising works meetings and the threat of a strike. The reasons for this low level of industrial unrest lie primarily in the culture of social partnership and in the positive experiences which both sides have had with negotiated solutions – and in the ability of central organisations to exert control over their members.

The law on industrial action is characterised by a marked lack of formal regulation. Although there is no legislative and express recognition of the right to take industrial action, neither is there any ban on organising strikes or on participation in them. Unemployment benefit is not payable if unemployment is the direct result of a shutdown caused by a strike. Furthermore, companies may not recruit the unemployed to work in plants which are affected by a strike or lockout.

In 1993 6,869 employees took part in strike action with an overall loss of 13,000 working days.

Organisations

Labour Ministry (Bundesministerium für Arbeit und Sozialordnung)
Stubenring 1
1010 Vienna
Tel. + 43 1 711 00
Fax + 43 1 711 00

Federal Chamber of Labour
(Bundeskammer für Arbeiter und Angestellte)
Prinz-Eugen-Straße 20–22
1041 Vienna
Tel. + 43 1 50165
Fax + 43 1 501 65 2230

Austrian Trade Union Confederation
(Österreichischer Gewerkschaftsbund, ÖGB)
Hohenstaufengasse 10
1010 Vienna
Tel. + 43 1 534 44
Fax + 43 1 533 5293

Austrian Chamber of Business
(Wirtschaftskammer Österreich)
Wiedner Hauptstraße 63
Postfach 180
1045 Vienna
Tel. + 43 1 50105
Fax + 43 1 50206

Confederation of Austrian Industry
(Vereinigung Österreichischer Industrieller)
Schwarzenbergplatz 4
1031 Vienna
Tel. + 43 1 711 35
Fax + 43 1 711 35 25 07

Austrian Centre for Productivity and Efficiency (personnel management association) (Österreichisches Produktivitäts- und Wirtschaftlichkeitszentrum)
1014 Vienna
Rockhgasse 6
Tel. + 43 1 533 8636
Fax + 43 1 533 863618

Main sources

Arbeit und Wirtschaft, various issues; 'Bundeskammer für Arbeiter und Angestellte/ÖGB'

CERNY, JOSEF. *Arbeitsverfassungsrecht*. Vols. I-III, Vienna, 1992, 1994, 1995

DORALT, WERNER (ed.). *Kodex des österreichischen Arbeitsrechts*. Linde, Vienna, 1990

GUGER, ALOIS. 'Corporatism: success or failure? Austrian experiences' in Pekkarinen *et al.*, *Social Corporatism. A superior economic system?* Oxford, 1992

KORINEK, KARL. 'Interessenvertretungen im Wandel' in Gerlich and Neisser (eds), *Europa als Herausforderung*. Vienna, 1994

SCHWARZ, WALTER, and LÖSCHNIGG, GÜNTHER. *Arbeitsrecht*. Verlag des österreichischen Gewerkschaftsbundes, Vienna, 1995

TRAXLER, FRANZ. 'Österreich' in Bispinck and Lecher (eds), *Tarifpolitik und Tarifsysteme in Europa*. Bund Verlag, Cologne, 1993

TRAXLER and SCHMITTER, 'Arbeitsbeziehungen und europäische Integration' in Mesch (ed.), *Sozialpartnerschaft und Arbeitsbeziehungen in Europa*. Vienna, 1995

2

Belgium

Industrial relations in Belgium are highly systematised, still largely centralised and very formally structured, with a strict hierarchy of agreements. A series of joint bodies established at all levels regulate the labour environment, contributing to the web of institutions for the airing and resolution of differences both within and between the main interest groups, political formations, and linguistic and religious communities. Although the structure helps shape exchange and consensus between the social partners, the state has also been active in intervening where voluntary agreements have proved elusive, as exemplified in the current incomes policy.

The linguistic dimension plays a crucial role in the structuring of social and political relations: Belgium has been a federal state since 1993. Regional parliaments exist for Flemish-speaking Flanders in the north and French-speaking Wallonia in the south, with limited powers to sign international agreements. The two communities plus the bilingual region of Brussels have responsibility for foreign trade, public works, the infrastructure, the economy, job creation and training. (We use French terms here; an English, Flemish and French glossary is provided in Volume One of this series, p. 74.)

Although as yet the federal structure has had a limited direct impact on the industrial relations system itself, it nevertheless constitutes an important factor in the industrial relations climate and the weight attached to specific issues in the different regions. Employment legislation is still enacted at national level, although some services such as training and job placement are administered regionally.

Government intervention in industrial relations has become more frequent over the past decade, a trend which is expected by most commentators to continue. Nevertheless the nature of the bargaining system is such that the social partners are often left to reach their own agreements and arrangements within the clearly defined legislative system. There are numerous bodies in which the social partners meet, formally or informally, to exchange views, with much overlapping in membership of various organisations from company level upwards. An important element of the industrial relations system is the high level of trade union membership, embracing some 65 per cent of the workforce. Trade unions have a long-established role in official bodies and as a bargaining partner. They are deemed to be very representative and place much emphasis on training their members and officials. They have a well-developed presence at all levels of bargaining: national, sectoral and company.

The system of collective bargaining may appear rigid and bureaucratic, especially in terms of procedures, but it offers considerable flexibility on substantive issues, such as working time, within a protective system of labour legislation.

It is important to note the statutory differentiation between blue-collar staff and white-collar staff, with their separate representation, negotiations, agreements and (some) terms and conditions of employment. There have been moves to integrate terms and conditions, but these have been greeted with little enthusiasm by either blue- or white-collar staff and representatives.

The main players

Freedom of association

Freedom of association is guaranteed by law. Individuals have the right to join or not to join a trade union, and closed shops, as such, do not exist. Trade unions have no status in law and exist as *de facto* organisations. However, they are recognised for certain purposes and the law does make stipulations about their representativeness. The unions are unwilling to have legal status imposed on them, since they believe it would restrict their freedom of action. They cannot be sued for damages, nor as an organisation can a union be served with an injunction.

In order to be considered nationally representative and entitled to sit on the National Labour Council (see below), a trade union confederation must have a membership of at least 50,000 across several industries. It is not required to register and may set its own rules. A union affiliated to any of the three nationally representative confederations is entitled to sign collective agreements.

Trade unions

The trade union situation is marked by a high degree of pluralism. Most organised workers belong to a union affiliated to one of the three nationally representative trade union confederations. These represent three distinct political/confessional strands, although neither of the two major centres has any formal link with a political party. Confederations co-ordinate the strategy and work of their constituent union federations. All are organised along both industry and geographical lines, with a distinct organisation according to the three main regions of the country.

- The Confederation of Christian Trade Unions of Belgium (Confédération des Syndicats Chrétiens de Belgique, CSC/ACV), which represents the Christian strand in the trade union movement, was formed as a confederation in 1912. It has its origins in an anti-socialist trade union alliance and places particular emphasis on family values and reconciliation between work and family responsibilities. In 1991 the CSC had some 1.4 million members. It is particularly strong in Flanders, with 68 per cent of its membership there.
- The General Federation of Belgian Workers (Fédération Générale du Travail

de Belgique, FGTB/ABVV) is socialist-oriented and started as a trade union grouping within the organisation which eventually became the Socialist Party. Although now formally separate, the FGTB co-operates closely with the Socialist Party. It adopted its present form in 1945. It has 1.1 million members, spread evenly over the two main regions of the country (43 per cent of the membership each in Flanders and Wallonia, and 14 per cent in Brussels). Both the CSC and the FGTB are structured along industry and regional lines.

• The smallest trade union confederation is the General Confederation of Liberal Trade Unions of Belgium (Centrale Générale des Syndicats Libéraux de Belgique, CGSLB/ACLVB). It has a liberal outlook and was established in 1930. It was recognised as a representative union in 1946 and has some 210,000 members.

The two main trade union confederations (the CSC and FGTB) have considerable power and influence. The government frequently consults them on social and economic matters (see above). They are involved in collective bargaining at all levels, and as they have strongly disciplined structures they are capable of implementing some of their industrial strategies with greater effect than their counterparts in many other countries.

The National Confederation of Managerial Staff (Confédération Nationale des Cadres, CNC/NCK) has been recognised by the government as representative of managerial staff for the purposes of forming a separate college for works council elections since 1986 (see below). However, it is not recognised in other respects and has not been granted a seat on the National Labour Council, despite repeated applications. This is partly because the other major union confederations also claim to represent managers as part of the total workforce, despite not having separate affiliates for management staff. The CNC claims to represent just over 10,000 managers.

The FGTB and CSC are both organised along industry lines for manual workers in the private sector, with separate federations crossing industry boundaries for white-collar staff. The CGSLB has no industry federations. There are also a small number of autonomous trade unions, usually for the self-employed as well as for the army and police. In addition, there is one autonomous union for train drivers.

Union membership is high, with a density of 65–70 per cent of the workforce – somewhat less if retired and unemployed members are excluded. Unionisation rates approach 90 per cent in the public sector and 60 per cent in the private sector. Around 80 per cent of blue-collar and 55 per cent of white-collar workers are unionised, although the level varies across different sectors. Union dues are most frequently collected by standing order, more rarely through collection at the workplace or by check-off. Unions hold strike funds, and, owing to their role in consultation and bargaining, trade union training is an important issue, regulated frequently by sectoral collective agreements.

The high level of membership is explained, in part at least, by the fact that there are still direct financial advantages to be gained from being a member of a trade union. The most obvious is the payment of the union bonus (*prime syndicale*). This was negotiated by the unions in the 1960s as a form of compensation to unionised employees for the payment of their trade union membership fees. It is a bonus paid indirectly by the employer, usually via the sectoral social hardship funds which are jointly administered and offer additional benefits over and above those provided by national legislation in the event of unemployment, long-term sickness or short-time working. The *prime syndicale* is agreed at sectoral level and may be paid out only to employed trade unionists (for example, in construction or textiles) or distributed also to trade union members in a given sector who are retired or unemployed (for up to one year). The amount varies from sector to sector but is approximately BFr 2,500 to BFr 3,500 per union member (£55–£77) a year.

Employers' organisations

There is no obligation on employers to join a federation to promote their interests. Like trade unions, employers' organisations have tended not to opt for constitution as a legal entity, although some affiliates of the largest federation have done so.

The Federation of Belgian Enterprises (Fédération des Entreprises de Belgique, FEB/VBO) is the main employers' confederation, representing members in both manufacturing and services in the private sector. Constituted in its present form in 1973, it is estimated to account for organisations employing approximately a million workers. The presidency of the FEB is held for three years, and alternates between Flemish- and French-speaking business leaders. It co-operates with three regional employers' organisations: the Vlaams Economisch Verbond (VEV) in Flanders, the Union Wallone des Entreprises (UWE) in Wallonia and the Union des Entreprises de Bruxelles (UEB) in Brussels. However, these organisations do not formally bargain collectively. It is the FEB which negotiates national agreements with the main union confederations.

For small businesses there are also separate organisations which are regionally based.

Consultation at national level

The National Labour Council is the main national body for bipartite consultation and negotiation. It is often dubbed the 'social' parliament of Belgium, and has a central role in industrial relations. It was established in 1952 and comprises 24 members, half from the main employers' organisations and half from the trade union confederations deemed to be nationally representative. The chair is an independent expert appointed by the Crown. To qualify for a seat on the council, unions must demonstrate a membership of at least 50,000. The following organisations currently sit on the council: for the employers' side, the Federation of Belgian Enterprises, one organisation representing small and medium-sized enterprises, and a representative of the agricultural organisations; on the employees' side, the three trade union confederations, the CSC, FGTB and CGSLB, which are considered nationally representative. There are also two associate members from the 'non-commercial' sector (one from the employers and one from the employees): they have been appointed for two years, after which there will be a review of their status and they may be admitted fully to the council.

The council's original role was consultative, and this continues through advice to Ministers or to Parliament (in the form of recommendations, or *avis*) on social matters where regulation is proposed or needs clarification. Advice may be offered either at the request of the politicians or on the council's own initiative. The council can also examine an issue at the request of either the union or the employers' side.

The council may make recommendations on jurisdictional disputes between the individual joint sectoral committees (*commissions paritaires*) responsible for bargaining at national or sectoral level (see below) – for example, where their coverage overlaps. In addition the council may recommend the creation of joint committees where new activities have become established – for example, for non-profit-making organisations.

Some individual acts of parliament specifically give the council the right to advise on matters within the scope of the law. For example, the 1978 contracts of employment legislation gives the council the right to advise on days off for family occasions (*petits chômages*).

The act of December 1968 on collective bargaining and joint committees empowered the council to conclude binding nationwide collective agreements (*conventions collectives du travail*, CCT). These normally cover the whole of the private sector but sometimes apply only to individual branches of activity (see below). In the first instance such agreements are binding only on organisations affiliated to the signatory bodies, that is, the employers' organisations and trade union confederations represented on the council. However, such agreements can be extended by royal decree at the request of (one of) the signatory parties, to become generally legally binding. More generally the council gives advice on issues that may later take the form of legislation or other regulation. For example, an opinion on the subject of outplacement was embodied in a national collective agreement in February 1992 and later ratified by royal decree, rendering it applicable throughout the whole economy.

The council may also conclude collective agreements on behalf of joint committees which do not function fully – these have gradually been reduced in number and there remains now only the 'non-commercial' sector – or for those few sectors where no bargaining machinery has been established.

The council operates on a consensual basis, with members acting under mandate from their organisations but referring back where appropriate. The council aims at joint regulation of employment matters without government intervention. However, if progress on a given issue is slow, the government may announce or introduce draft legislation to speed matters up. Some 80 per cent of the council's recommendations are unanimous; it has issued over 1,100 to date. The council is assisted by a secretariat. Most matters are dealt with in committees of members of the council plus experts from employer and union side. These committees prepare draft recommendations (*projets d'avis*) which are then debated in full council, and voted upon. Full council meetings are held once a month, and may be assisted by experts from the various committees and by outside specialists.

The Central Economic Council

Although the National Labour Council has no formal links with its sister organisation in the economic field, the Conseil Centrale de l'Economie (CEC), the two co-operate frequently. The Economic Council comprises 50 members, 22 from each side of industry, six experts and an independent chair. It has a similar advisory role on economic matters. Under the 1989 law on industrial competitiveness it is charged with producing twice-yearly reports on the country's competitive position *vis-à-vis* its seven principal competitors. The social partners give their view on these reports, and if the position is unfavourable, according to a set of predefined indicators, the government can resort to special powers to intervene in the economy, including modification of the pay indexation system. These powers were evoked at the end of 1993 under the government's Global Plan (*Plan global pour l'emploi, la compétitivité et la sécurité sociale*) in direct response to the declining competitive position of the economy highlighted in the 1993 reports from the CEC (see below).

There are a number of other forums in which the two sides of industry can meet, formally through the hierarchical bargaining mechanism, but also in the joint administration of several funds and bodies. For example, there are a number of sectoral funds (*fonds de sécurité d'existence*) which provide supplementary payments in parallel with the national social security system (see below).

Incomes policies and government intervention

The state played an active and interventionist role in the shaping of pay throughout the 1980s and 1990s in response to concern about national competitiveness and persistently high unemployment. This intervention has taken the form of altering the operation of the system of pay indexation and of imposing limits on pay growth or freezes (sometimes absolute, sometimes merely for sums on top of cost-of-living adjustments).

In the early 1990s a job creation and vocational training levy of 0.5 per cent was introduced which was allocated to a national fund unless companies could show they were devoting an equivalent amount to the same purpose themselves.

Broader action on competitiveness culminated in November 1993 with the Global Plan on Employment, Competitiveness and Social Security – heir to several previous recovery programmes – which was an attempt to restore the declining position of the Belgian economy. This three-year plan, introduced when talks between the social partners broke down, tackled a range of issues, including revision of the indexation mechanism and the implementation of a wage moderation package. It applies to the period 1994–96 and stipulates that no pay increases other than those awarded prior to 15 November 1993 or via the operation of the indexation mechanism can be awarded for the period 1 January 1994 to 31 December 1996. This affects all elements of remuneration, including benefits, bonuses, individually awarded special payments and payments in kind. Penalties are imposed for breaching the terms of the plan. A few exceptions are allowed: increases agreed for 1994 but spread over 1994–96; age, length of service or promotion increases; partial compensation for hours reductions agreed under working time redistribution plans (see below). In addition the wage indexation mechanism was revised, effectively delaying most indexation payments by at least six months in 1994.

Consultation at industry level

Consultation at national and sectoral level is mainly carried out within the sectoral joint committees (*commissions paritaires*). These exist for almost all sectors of the economy and, like the National Labour Council, have both a bargaining and a consultative function. The committees, set up by royal decree, reflect the make-up of the National Labour Council: they have an equal number of representatives from employers' organisations and trade unions, with an independent chair appointed by the government. Their scope is defined according to their status (branch, regional and occupational groups – blue- or white-collar workers). There are some 130 committees and sub-committees covering 90 per cent of the private sector. Employers can find out which joint committee governs their business from the Ministry of Labour. The main responsibility of the committees is the conclusion of sectoral collective agreements (see below). However, they also act as an important forum of debate for the social partners.

Although there is no formal set-up for consultation and the conclusion of collective agreements at regional level, other than in the chemical and engineering sectors, where it is limited and conducted through the national joint committees, there are a number of regional bodies in which the social partners meet. Flanders and Wallonia have their own economic councils: the Sociaal Economische Raad voor Vlaanderen (SERV) and the Conseil social économique pour la région wallonne (CESRW). These act as important arenas for debate and for gathering information which invariably, if informally, feeds back into the national industrial relations framework.

Regional employers' organisations also exist – the VEV and UWB – which again are not formally linked with the FEB, although they co-operate on a number of issues such as representation to the European-level private-sector employers' association UNICE (see Introduction). One of the lingering problems in this complex of national, sectoral and federal bodies is that many regional structures do not want to be seen as lower in the hierarchy than their national counterparts, while established national bodies resist moves towards increased regional powers over labour relations.

In any case, all laws are determined at national level, while the regional level tends to cover such issues as training and job creation measures.

Workplace employee representation

Works councils

The establishment and functioning of works councils (*conseils d'entreprise*) is governed primarily by an act of 20 September 1948 (*Loi portant sur l'organisation de l'économie*). A number of agreements concluded within the National Labour Council, notably collective agreement No. 9, also elaborate upon certain aspects of works councils, such as the financial information which must be disclosed to them. In addition, certain matters may be regulated by agreement within a joint committee – although this is extremely rare – and by the councils' own regulations.

Composition   Under the law works councils must be set up on the initiative of the employer in all establishments employing on average at least 100 workers. All workers employed under a contract of employment or an apprenticeship, even temporaries, with at least three months' service are taken into account when calculating the size of the establishment's workforce. Employees working less than full time count as the equivalent of half an employee.

Works councils are joint bodies chaired by the employer. Apart from the head of the company, the employer side comprises employer nominees, who may not outnumber the employee side. Employee-side members are elected by secret ballot in the private sector every four years over a period declared by decree for the whole country; the latest elections were held between 8 and 20 May 1995. There is separate representation for blue- and white-collar staff and for young workers, provided there are at least 25 of them. Managers (*cadres*) may also be represented provided 15 at least are employed by the firm – see below.

Election of works councils   The electoral processes for both works councils and health and safety committees are similar though distinct and they are conducted at the same time. The procedure is complex and only the main points are set out below. (A number of comprehensive guides are available.)

In 1995 over a million employees were eligible to vote for members of the employee side of works councils, which generally represent both unionised and non-unionised employees. The criteria for calculating the size of an establishment's workforce (see above) are also used to define entitlement to vote. Senior management can neither nominate candidates nor participate in the elections of employee representatives. There are separate electoral colleges for blue-collar workers and white-collar employees. If there are at least 25 employees under the age of 25, then separate seats are reserved for them. In works council elections, managers qualify for separate representation through their own electoral college only if they number at least 15 members.

The electoral process must be carried out in the appropriate language, according to the region in which the establishment is situated – broadly, Flemish in Flanders, French in Wallonia, either language in Brussels, depending on local criteria, and German in some of the eastern provinces.

Trade unions affiliated to confederations which are deemed representative on a national basis, in practice the CSC, FGTB and CGSLB, have a monopoly of presenting lists of candidates, and the outcome of the election is seen as a test of the popularity of the various organisations. To qualify as candidates, people must be employed by the firm, aged between 18 and retirement age (16–25 for youth candidates), have six months' service and belong to the occupational group for which they are standing. There would be nothing to prevent a non-unionist appearing on a union list, but it rarely happens. The number of employee seats ranges from six (in firms with 101 employees) to eight in firms with up to 1,000 employees, and to 22 for firms with 8,000 employees or more. There are either one or two management seats where there are between 15 and 99 managers. The allocation of seats between blue- and white-collar employees depends on their numbers at the workplace; the same principle applies to the number of seats reserved for young workers. There are precise rules governing the replacement of a member by a reserve.

The result must be published within two days of the election, together with details of the management side of the council. In the 1995 elections the vote was generally evenly split between the two major unions, the CSC and FGTB, with some variations reflected in the separate regions.

In effect the domination of works councils by trade union members enables close co-operation between the works council and the official trade union delegation (see below), which has sole collective bargaining rights. Trade unions frequently provide extensive training for works council staff, more often than not in tandem with training for trade union delegations; for example, the metalworking and engineering affiliate of the FGTB provides six weeks' training over a four-year period for both trade union delegation and works council members.

Information rights   The works council must be given information on a wide range of economic, financial and social matters. At the first meeting of a new council it must be supplied with basic data on the company's legal status, its financial structure, its investment plans, the volume and value of production and productivity rates, and wage and labour costs. The standing orders must also be approved.

Each year the works council must consider a written report on the company's financial position, the profit and loss account, and the auditor's report. The works council takes part in the selection of an auditor, who may attend meetings and must assist if called upon to do so by a majority of the members. Every three months information must be provided on orders, sales, costs, prices and employment. The works council must also be advised of any company plans which could have an impact on the workforce, for example the introduction of new technology or a proposed take-over.

These information rights are broadly respected. Trade unions have their own experts to assist in the interpretation of data, and auditors have a much more independent role than previously. Unions put considerable effort into training their representatives to carry out these functions.

Council members are bound by confidentiality and may be specifically requested to withhold particularly sensitive information from the rest of the workforce. It is also possible for employers to obtain the authorisation of the labour authorities to withhold information of a highly confidential or prejudicial nature.

Consultation rights   Works councils have a general right to be consulted and to give advice on any measure affecting working conditions or work organisation and on personnel practices in general. Reports on the employment situation must be submitted to works councils on both a quarterly and an annual basis, with consultation taking place on proposed measures such as criteria for recruitment and dismissal, arrangements for the induction of new recruits, consultation over collective training or retraining, and the scheduling of flexible hours or working time changes.

Decision-making rights   The works council may also take decisions in certain areas. There are differences of opinion over whether these have to be unanimous to be valid; a works council's own standing orders will often clarify the position, and there is also case law. The areas include

- internal works rules
- methods of paying salaries
- criteria for hiring temporary staff
- setting the dates of annual holidays and alternative days off when a public holiday falls on a Sunday
- managing the enterprise's social funds.

Where there is no works council, some of its functions may be assumed by the health and safety committee under certain circumstances. Similarly the trade union delegation may assume functions of works councils or health and safety committees in companies below the legal threshold at which such bodies become a requirement.

Because the role of works councils is quite wide and encompasses matters such as the organisation of production, initiatives such as quality circles have not become a normal part of the industrial relations scene, although they do exist and give rise to trade union apprehension. The most widespread initiatives in this field have been in the metalworking sector.

Meetings   The works council meetings take place on company premises, usually within normal working hours. Meetings must take place at least monthly, or at the request either of the chair (the head of the company or deputy) or at least half the works council's members.

The law provides that employee representatives should be given sufficient time off within normal working hours to fulfil their duties. This is often further defined by industry agreement. Time off is paid at normal rates. Members also have a right to circulate freely within the enterprise. Works council and health and safety committee members are protected against dismissal, except for genuine redundancy or serious misconduct. In either case the proposed termination must meet a set of stringent criteria and be accepted by a joint committee or labour tribunal.

Health and safety committees

The establishment and functioning of health and safety committees (*comités de sécurité, d'hygiène et d'embellissement des lieux de travail*, CSH) are governed by the law of 10 June 1952 (*Loi concernant la santé et la sécurité des travailleurs*), articles 54 and 837-9 of the 1947 General Regulations for the Protection of Work (*Règlement général pour la protection du travail*, RGTP) and national collective agreement No. 6 on facilities for works councils and health and safety committee members.

All establishments employing an average of 50 workers, in the private as well as in the public sector, must set up a health and safety committee comprising an equal number of employer and employee representatives.

The employee side is elected on the same basis as works council members, except that there is no separate managerial representation; however, the separate representation of white-collar, blue-collar and youth employee groups remains the same. The size of the employee side ranges from four members in establishments with fewer than 100 workers to 22 in those with a workforce of 8,000 or more.

The employer side must include the head of the company, who chairs the committee. The works medical officer has an independent consultative non-voting role, whilst the head of the firm's health and safety service does have a vote although acting in an independent capacity.

The committee's functions are defined by the RGPT and involve being informed and consulted on all matters relating to health and safety in the workplace. Great emphasis is placed on the prevention of risks and on the active promotion of health and safety. The committee is deemed competent to take decisions, make recommendations and obtain information in all these areas. The head of the firm's health and safety services may not be appointed or dismissed without the approval of the committee. The committee can also demand the dismissal of the works medical officer if it is dissatisfied with the way his or her duties are being discharged. The CSH can also intervene to call work to a halt if it deems there is a serious and immediate risk to health or safety.

Meetings must be held at least monthly, or at the request of the chair or at the request of a third of the committee's members. Members may be assisted by outside experts. The head of the firm must submit to the committee for approval a draft annual plan to promote health and safety. Employees who have lodged a complaint against the employer also have the right to express their point of view. Under certain circumstances the labour inspectorate can call a meeting and chair it.

Trade union delegations

Trade union delegations, the other arm of employee workplace representation, are dealt with under 'Collective bargaining' below, as their role lies primarily in that area.

European works council directive

With Belgium's highly developed national system of employee representation and a large number of small- to medium-sized companies, it is still unclear how the EU directive on European Works Councils will affect industrial relations. The majority of companies likely to be affected will be subsidiaries of foreign multinationals. Nevertheless few companies are expected to implement any measures until the directive has been enacted into national law. This in itself is also under debate, as a collective agreement within the National Labour Council may be the preferred route to implementation, rather than statute law.

Collective bargaining

The 1968 act on collective bargaining and joint sectoral committees (*Loi sur les conventions collectives de travail et les commissions paritaires*) recognises and defines collective agreements, which are legally enforceable, and specifies the various levels at which such agreements can be concluded.

According to the Act a collective agreement is 'an agreement concluded between one or more employees' organisations and one or more employers, determining individual or collective employment relations between employers and employees within a company or branch of activity, and laying down the rights and obligations of the contractual parties'. Such an agreement may either be concluded within a joint body (that is, the National Labour Council, joint committees or sub-committees) or outside it, at company level.

An agreement must be in writing and in both French and Flemish, except where it covers a geographical area in which only one language is spoken. Representatives signing agreements are presumed competent to do so on behalf of their respective organisations; when concluding company agreements, union representatives must be mandated by their union to do so, although almost always it is a district official who will sign. Agreements must be concluded for either a definite or an indefinite period. Notice to terminate must also be given in writing. The agreement must specify

- the signatory parties
- in appropriate cases the number of the joint sectoral committee
- the agreement's coverage (sector, area, occupational group, company) and duration
- the implementation date (if it is different from the date of signature).

An agreement concluded within a joint body must normally be signed by all parties. Only very rarely will an agreement which one trade union or employers' organisation has refused to sign be concluded. In such cases (of which there has been only one in 20 years) it is binding only on those employers affiliated to the signatory party, but must be applied to all workers within those organisations regardless of whether they belong to the trade union that has signed or not.

All agreements must be registered with the Ministry of Labour, from which anyone may obtain a copy on payment of a fixed sum. Although the statutory registration requirement excludes company agreements, many are still registered in order to establish that specific expenditure requirements have been met, such as training fund allocations. In addition, if there is a dispute over the terms of a collective agreement (at any level), provided it is registered, either party can appeal to a tribunal for adjudication. If a company collective agreement is to be registered the signature of the district trade union official is required. Notification of collective agreements is published in the official gazette, the *Moniteur Belge*.

At the request of the appropriate joint body, or a party represented on it, a collective agreement can be extended by royal decree to become generally binding in its entirety on all employers within the defined area. An employer may wish to adopt the terms of an agreement, for example where it covers the sector but has not been extended. Such a request would normally be conceded, provided the signatory parties have no objection; reasons for a refusal must be given. Details of these association arrangements are also published in the official gazette.

Levels of bargaining

The 1968 legislation sets out a hierarchy of legal sources and obligations governing employment relations, as follows:

- law
- collective agreements which have been extended by royal decree. In descending order of priority these are those that have been signed within: (a) the National Labour Council, (b) joint sectoral committees, (c) joint sectoral sub-committees
- collective agreements concluded at any of these three levels which have not been extended but are still legally binding on signatory parties (ie they have been registered)
- other collective agreements, ie those concluded at company or plant level
- individual contracts of employment
- works rules (*règlement de travail*).

An agreement or individual contract may not include provisions that contravene those agreed at a higher level and its terms must be no less favourable where the company falls within the scope of their application. Most collective agreements are cumulative, that is, they will not only build on the agreement at a higher level but will usually only add to or amend existing agreements. This explains why a number of sectoral or company agreements may have apparently few provisions in any one year. Collective agreements are binding on members of signatory parties and on any organisations affiliated to them, from the date of signature, from the date of adherence to the agreement or from another date specified in the agreement itself. Parties can go to court to enforce the normative clauses of a collective agreement, that is, those referring to pay, hours and other conditions of employment.

Collective bargaining may take place at four different levels:

- national, multi-industry (*interprofessionel*) within the National Labour Council
- industry-wide (within the joint committees)
- regional or group of companies
- company.

National multi-industry framework agreements

Periodically, in practice every two years, the main employers' organisation and the three trade union confederations negotiate a national, multi-industry framework agreement (*accord interprofessionel*, AIP) on various issues which sets the guidelines for bargainers at industry and company level. The latest agreement, covering 1995 and 1996, focuses on job creation, work redistribution and early retirement.

These agreements are not collective agreements as such and are negotiated outside the framework of the National Labour Council. They are not legally binding but set guidelines for industry negotiations within the joint sectoral committees. Specific terms may also require regulation by statute – such as social security reductions proposed in the 1995/96 agreement – or through the conclusion of a binding collective agreement within the National Labour Council such as the early retirement provisions agreed in 1995 (see below). In effect the AIPs agreed between the social partners carry a good deal of weight, and both the government and the National Labour Council generally go along with whatever proposals they may contain. However, this is not always done without controversy; for example, the reduction of social charges proposed in the 1995/96 agreement gave rise to much wrangling in parliament before it was finally passed. Although the government is not officially involved in negotiations over the AIPs, it monitors them closely, and the government is not keen on any suggestion that it may be toeing a line drawn by the social partners. On the other hand, measures and guidelines which are agreed voluntarily between employers and unions are more likely to be adhered to when implemented at industry and company level.

The 1995/96 multi-industry framework agreement, which was concluded within the limits on pay imposed by the Global Plan, largely extended the 1993/94 agreement and the terms were fairly general. The social partners were keen to demonstrate their unity after difficult talks in 1993.

National collective agreements

Within the National Labour Council the main employers' organisation and the unions have concluded over 50 national collective agreements (*Convention collective du travail*, CCT), the vast majority of them legally binding on the signatory parties and their affiliated members. However, most of these agreements are also rendered mandatory across the whole economy by royal decree. They cover such issues as the national minimum wage, collective dismissal, equal pay, part-time work, shift working, the status of trade union delegations, the introduction of new technology, and temporary work. The majority contain minimum conditions below which no employee should be allowed to fall: for example, the setting of a national guaranteed minimum monthly income. Others lay down the principle which must be followed or the framework within which a particular system must be operated – such as early retirement, which is possible from the age of 55 under certain conditions – but require details to be established in a sectoral collective agreement.

Agreements can be identified by breaking down the various codes attached to their official designations. For example, CCT No. 42 (*Convention collective de travail sur l'introduction de nouveaux régimes de travail dans les entreprises 02 06 1987, AR 18 06 1987, MB 26 06 1987*) refers to collective agreement No. 42 on the introduction of new working time schedules in companies, concluded on 2 June 1987, extended by royal decree on 18 June and published in the official gazette, the *Moniteur Belge*, on 26 June.

Industry agreements within joint committees

Sectoral joint committees (*commissions paritaires*) were set up after the First World War, initially in the iron and steel, mining and engineering industries.

They are responsible for conducting collective bargaining at nationwide industry level. It is at this level that the vast majority of bargaining takes place and most terms and conditions are set. The 1968 legislation on collective agreements and joint committees provides for the formation of a joint committee for every sector of activity in the private sector, outlining the procedure for instituting joint committees and sub-committees and the scope of their activities by branch, regional and occupational group. All committees are numbered; those in the 100–199 range relate to blue-collar committees, those between 200 and 299 are for white-collar employees, and any integrated committee is numbered between 300 and 399. Around 100 joint committees and 70 sub-committees exist, covering 90 per cent of the private sector.

New employers can ascertain from the Ministry of Labour which joint committee covers their business. The labour inspectorate normally verifies within the first year whether the employer has applied to the correct joint committee. Complications may arise when a company's activities straddle more than one sector, and the overriding criterion is the company's main or principal activity. The size of each joint committee is defined by statute and comprises a chair, a vice-chair and an equal number of employer and employee representatives, plus one or more secretaries. The committee's term of office lasts four years. Meetings must be attended by at least half the members and decisions must be taken unanimously.

The main role of the joint committees may be summarised as follows:

- the conclusion of collective agreements between all the organisations represented on the committee in order to regulate pay and working conditions
- the prevention and settlement of disputes between employers and employees
- advising the government, the National Labour Council and local trades councils on the issues falling within their scope
- the management of sectoral hardship funds (*fonds de sécurité d'existence*).

Industry agreements are particularly important, since they cover an enormous range of issues but centrally, and most commonly, pay and working hours. Typically such an agreement will set minimum rates or pay scales for different grades of workers and premiums for shift work, night work and other bonuses. Industry agreements may also regulate matters such as the employer's contribution to travel costs, or the rates payable by employers into a sectoral hardship fund which provides workers in the sector with benefits additional to those received from the state social security system. Some have established sub-committees to advise on these issues. Some committees, particularly in sectors where small to medium-sized companies predominate, set minima very close to real pay rates in companies. Others have industry minima far below company rates, such as banking and insurance, where large companies predominate. However, even in these cases companies will base their pay scales on the industry scales.

Regional bargaining

This type of collective agreement is rare but is found in the engineering and chemical industries, where some terms for workers – for example, in the Liège region – may be different from those for workers in the Charleroi area. Such agreements are also negotiated through joint committees. With the increasing federalisation of Belgium there have been calls by the regional powers for the regionalisation of collective agreements, but the idea has been resisted by the social partners (see above). Companies are also generally reluctant to encourage regionalisation of bargaining, as they can be caught in the crossfire: already some regional funds or subsidies (for example, Flemish employment subsidies) mean, in effect, discrimination between groups of workers in the same national company doing the same job but in different regions.

Company-level bargaining

Some companies have no agreement of their own but simply apply the terms set by the relevant industry agreement. Others may have an agreement covering only limited terms, while in some sectors, particularly those in which the industry agreement sets only minimum terms, may have more complete coverage of terms and conditions: this applies, for example, in the chemical industry, where the industry agreement sets only a minimum pay rate.

The importance of company bargaining has grown in recent years. In 1980 341 company agreements were concluded, compared with 442 at industry level; by 1992 the figure had risen to 2,027 out of a total of 2,314 agreements signed at all levels.

Employer associations may also exert pressure on companies not to diverge from the association's position on bargaining by offering terms too far above sectoral minima, because this can open the door to comparability claims by trade unions.

Trade union delegations

Company agreements are negotiated with trade union delegations (*délégations syndicales*) within the company. Such delegations are established under the provisions of a national collective agreement (No. 5) and consist solely of trade union representatives. The status and rights of trade union delegations are also regulated by industry and, occasionally, company agreements. Since the delegation is regulated by a binding agreement at national level, recognition of the trade union does not normally constitute an issue for an individual employer.

A delegation may be established in any firm if one or more unions affiliated to nationally representative centres request it. A joint sectoral agreement often lays down the rules governing the establishment of a delegation, including the threshold number of workers necessary to qualify, the requisite union density, the number of delegates, the manner of appointment and delegates' time-off rights.

Delegates may be appointed by their union members or may be elected; in the latter case, elections may be timed to coincide with elections to works councils and health and safety committees. In many cases the threshold for setting up a union delegation is lower than those required for works councils and health and safety committees. For example, the metalworking agreement sets it at 20 blue-collar workers (for a blue-collar trade union delegation), and in the metal trade sector requires the unions to prove (usually by petition) that at least 25 per cent of the workforce want a delegation and stipulates the number of delegates as follows:

- 15–30 workers: two delegates
- 31–50 workers: three delegates
- 51–150 workers: four delegates plus four reserves
- 151–200 workers: five delegates plus five reserves.

For every 50 workers beyond 200 another delegate is elected. Trade union delegates must be aged 18 or over, and must have six months' service with the company; those eligible to vote are trade union members aged at least 16 with three months' service in the company. This means that often trade union delegations are the only employee representative body in small companies. They can therefore take on some of the functions both of a works council and of a health and safety committee. Most delegations hold their mandate for four years, after which it can be renewed.

The workplace trade union delegation is the recognised channel through which workers make their demands and negotiate with the employer – collectively and individually. Delegations are recognised as competent to sign agreements provided they have a mandate from the trade union of which they are members, although normally a district union official will be the signatory. Trade union delegations also have a duty to the individual worker and can lodge claims on his or her behalf.

The principal object of a trade union delegation is the defence of workers' interests through

- regular bargaining, leading to the conclusion of collective agreements within the company
- monitoring the implementation of labour legislation generally in the company (statute law, collective agreements, works rules and individual contracts), including whether trade union rights are being respected
- undertaking some of the functions of a works council or a health and safety committee if none exists
- the resolution of collective and individual grievances.

Trade union delegations can also call in full-time trade union officials, as can the employer.

In consequence trade union delegations have extensive rights to information, particularly concerning changes in working conditions. Delegates are able to communicate with the workforce through meetings, which may be held during working hours, or by notice boards and in premises put at their disposal by the employer. Delegates enjoy some protection against dismissal for the period of their mandate (four years, renewable). However, the criteria are not as stringent as in the case of works council and health and safety committee members. There can be some conflict between the different trade union delegations where such exist (blue-collar and white-collar) but in general they tend to co-operate, as they do with the works council and the health and safety committee – indeed, in many companies there is considerable overlap of members on each of these bodies, particularly as works council candidates are normally put forward on union lists. Most employers are none the less keen to maintain a clear distinction between the role played by the works council and that of the trade union delegation, even where the bodies essentially consist of exactly the same individuals!

Works rules

Works rules (*règlement de travail*) are required by statute to be set up in consultation with the works council (or trade union delegation, where no works council exists) in all private-sector firms. The rules cover matters such as workplace discipline and grievance procedures, including the range of warnings, suspensions and fines that may be used as part of the disciplinary procedure. The proceeds of any such fines must be used for the good of the employees as a whole, and details of the uses to which they may be put are agreed in the works rules themselves.

Employees not covered by bargaining

Blue-collar workers outside the scope of an industry collective agreement are invariably covered by some national minima such as the minimum wage, laid down by collective agreement within the National Labour Council and made generally binding by royal decree. Most white-collar employees not specifically covered by an industry agreement are covered by the joint committee 218, a catch-all committee for white-collar employees. This committee has established a four-category job classification system, minimum pay scales and average weekly working time, among other terms. It applies to some 270,000 employees across the whole economy.

Middle-ranking white-collar and technical employees are covered by a few industry agreements, for example in banking and insurance. Executives not specifically covered by white-collar industry agreements are none the less covered by their non-monetary terms. For this group, pay is largely the province of management decision or individual negotiation. The wage moderation measures implemented via the Global Plan apply equally to management and executives. However, extra pay or bonuses may be generated through existing merit or profit-related schemes which will largely benefit managerial staff.

The pay round and current trends

As described above, the collective bargaining system is highly developed and still largely centralised at industry level. An important starter for the main bargaining round is the biennial multi-sectoral national framework agreement (AIP), which sets the tone and provides the guidelines for industry and company bargaining. These two-year agreements are usually signed in late autumn; the latest one covers 1995–96. Although the framework agreement does not usually detail specific pay issues, it none the less sets the overall parameters, leaving the industry joint committees to fill in the details. It often covers issues affecting labour costs such as training or child care funds, incentives for recruitment or holiday entitlement.

The other main influence on pay bargaining is the twice-yearly competitiveness report which charts the country's overall economic position in relation to its seven main competitors. Economic forecasts are published regularly by the Bank of Belgium and the Bureau du Plan, and also influence pay-setting. Most pay bargaining occurs at the beginning of the year, with unions presenting claims from December onwards. The leading settlements tend to be the larger industry agreements such as metalworking and engineering, chemicals or banking.

Wage increase freeze, 1994–96

In November 1993 the government published its Global Plan to restore the country's economic position after the failure of talks between the social partners to conclude a wage moderation package. The Global Plan's wage restraint measures were implemented by royal decree in December 1993, and the remainder of the package was implemented by legislation in March 1994. The main element of the package is wage restraint for the period 1994–96, which involves revision of the automatic wage indexation mechanism and a freeze on all other pay increases (see above). This means that agreements signed for 1994 onwards do not include pay: the focus has instead been on job creation through early retirement schemes, work redistribution plans and hours reductions.

The 1995/96 national multi-industry framework agreement provided for some of these changes, such as enabling industry collective agreements to instate early retirement from age 55 as a temporary measure (until March 1996). However, measures must be detailed at industry and, where necessary, company level for individual workers to be able to claim the right.

Agreed provisions

Industry minima   Binding minima are set for the majority of workers by the relevant industry collective agreements negotiated within the joint committees.

Rates are normally a function of qualification and, for white-collar employees, seniority. The law requires all industry minima to be brought up to at least the national minimum wage.

Blue-collar pay is usually reckoned on an hourly basis and pay progression is commonly based on age. White-collar pay is calculated on a monthly basis and salary scales are usually related to age, experience and, more rarely, length of service. The number of age-related increments laid down varies widely. Annual salary for white-collar staff can be broadly calculated by multiplying one month's pay by 13.85 to include holiday and end-of-year bonus payments (see below).

In most cases the industry agreement will set minimum levels, which may or may not be improved upon at company level. For example, one large bank has pay scales of nine job categories with increments based on age. The first four categories and pay levels are taken directly from the industry agreement, while the top five levels are based on the top three levels in the industry agreement but improve upon them by approximately 15–20 per cent. As well as age increments, these five levels also incorporate merit pay assessed by individual managers at an annual review.

In times of extreme economic hardship companies can apply for exemption from certain payment conditions laid down in collective agreements; however, this is extremely rare.

Pay indexation Despite the wage increase freeze implemented under the Global Plan, Belgian workers' pay is still being raised more or less in line with inflation through the automatic wage indexation mechanism. The system is set up by national collective agreement, not by law, but is the fastest-working and most comprehensive indexation system in Europe. The Global Plan included a revision of the price index used to calculate increases in indexed pay, the new index being dubbed the 'health index' (*index santé*), as it excludes such items as tobacco, petrol and alcohol. The introduction of the new index was intended to slow down the pace of indexed pay increases, and it effectively delayed them by up to seven months in 1994.

In principle most pay is indexed in line with national consumer prices, as measured by the *index santé*. In practice most joint industry committees have devised their own systems through binding agreements. The mechanisms tend to be complex and diverse. However, agreements typically make provision for say a 2 per cent increase in pay when the consumer price index rises by 2 per cent (or a lower threshold), though some systems specify automatic review dates.

Bonuses The two most common bonus payments are holiday pay and thirteenth-month payments.

Full-time employees are entitled by law to four weeks' annual paid leave after one year's service, with additional leave granted by agreement. The employer must pay employees for the whole period of leave at the normal rate (*simple pécule*) plus a double rate (*double pécule*) for most of the leave, according to a somewhat complicated formula which differentiates between white- and blue-collar workers. However, in essence three weeks and two days must be paid at double the normal rate. In addition the national framework agreement for 1993/94, extended to 1995/96, provided for all workers to receive an additional sum equivalent to double pay for the third day of the fourth week. Total holiday bonus therefore now consists of double pay for three weeks and three days, and normal pay for the remainder.

The practice of paying a thirteenth-month bonus is also widespread. Although in most cases it is provided for in industry agreements, arrangements can also be made at company level, in individual contracts or via internal works rules. Often it is awarded as an end-of-year bonus (*prime de fin d'année*) and paid with December's salary. White-collar staff usually receive a straight extra month's pay. Industry agreements covering blue-collar workers employ formulae such as a percentage of gross annual pay or a multiple of basic hourly rates. Some qualifying conditions may apply, such as length of service, all subject to negotiation.

Executives are also usually awarded a bonus, which may be considerably enhanced as a form of merit pay and may be equivalent to a fourteenth-, fifteenth- or even sixteenth-month bonus.

Other bonuses and supplements laid down by collective agreement include: overtime, shift- and night-work supplements; performance-related or merit pay; long-service awards; dangerous or dirty work; travel allowances; union bonus (*prime syndicale*) and luncheon vouchers.

Financial participation   Belgium has a large number of small to medium-sized companies, many of which are family owned. In consequence, financial participation schemes are not widespread. The legal and tax regimes applying to different types of scheme are relatively unfavourable and the social security obligations are somewhat unclear. Employers are broadly in favour of developing schemes and have been pressing for a legal and tax framework. The trade unions are less well disposed towards them and maintain that financial participation would magnify wage inequalities and income insecurity. However, the debate is continuing as more schemes are introduced in practice.

Share option schemes, which must be set out in a written agreement, can be granted, by statute, to employees with one year's service for the eventual purchase of shares at a fixed price. There are also convertible loan schemes. A specific legal framework was created in 1991 for the issue of shares to employees at less than market price. Companies that have declared a dividend to shareholders for two of the previous four years may reserve all or part of the increase in capital to their employees, provided it does not exceed 20 per cent of capital over five years. Companies may determine the basis of employee participation in consultation with the works council. Other forms of share ownership include the purchase of shares for distribution to employees, the creation of shares for distribution, and company savings plans, but these are rarer.

Working time arrangements   Although hours of work are extensively regulated by legislation, reforms of the law during the 1980s introduced substantial derogations allowing a large measure of flexibility for operations, provided that official authorisation and the agreement of employee representatives is obtained.

The law states that hours of work may not exceed eight per day or 40 per week, based on a six-day week. In practice working hours are governed by collective agreement, with an average agreed working week in 1995 of 38 hours.

Some exceptions to the statutory limits are provided for in law: daily hours, for example, may be increased to nine where a five-day week is standard and 10 if the workplace is a long way from the place of residence. Shift workers can work up to 11 hours a day and 50 per week, as long as a weekly average of 40 is maintained over a three-month reference period. Other departures from this rule, such as flexible hours arrangements, require prior authorisation and typically must be provided for in a collective agreement, either at industry or at company level.

Under the 1985 Economic Recovery Law arrangements on annual hours may be introduced by collective agreement. The agreement must set out the weekly average to be worked (calculated over a 12 month period) and a maximum that can be worked, which may not exceed the statutory limit of nine hours per day or 45 per week. The maximum departure from the weekly average is five hours in any direction. This would allow an industry with an average 38 hour week to vary its hours from 33 to 43 per week, provided the average is achieved within the stated reference period of up to one year. In some industries additional days off are granted in order to maintain the average: for example, the construction industry agreement allocates six fixed days.

Further options for flexibility were created under a 1987 law on new working time arrangements. The act allows private-sector companies to draw up hours schedules within collective agreements with the approval of the relevant joint committee. Agreements may include Sunday working and work on public holidays; night work; a 12 hour day and the removal of the 40 hour week limit, provided an average 40 hours are worked over 12 months; and an extension of evening work for women and young people.

The Global Plan encouraged the reorganisation of hours of work to create new jobs (such as part-time work, overtime limits, career breaks, flexitime) and in return employers may claim reductions in social security contributions relating to new staff taken on (see below).

Holidays   Full-time employees have a statutory right to four weeks' paid annual leave per year (24 days based on a six-day week). In a few industries collective agreements award additional leave for long service, while others give young employees extra time off. However, agreements which award extra holiday for age are rare.

There are 10 public holidays and it is standard practice to award an additional day's leave when there is one normal working day between a weekend and a public holiday – often called a bridging day (*pont*). In addition, 11 July and 27

September are regional holidays in Flanders and Wallonia respectively, with most sectoral agreements providing for a day's paid leave in the relevant region.

Time off   In addition to annual leave and public holidays, employees may be entitled by law to a certain amount of time off for personal reasons (*absences légitimes/petits chômages*). Such time may be paid, and the list is fairly comprehensive including the marriage of an employee (two days) or of a close relative (one day), a death in the family, political duties, etc. Collective agreements may improve on the statutory minimum, and most sectors now have their own agreement on the subject: for example, every worker has a statutory right to two days' leave when getting married, but most workers are awarded three days by collective agreement. Unpaid leave for urgent and unforeseen reasons (*congé pour raisons impérieuses*), including a child's illness, hospitalisation, etc., may also be expanded in collective agreements.

Other agreed provisions   With pay not covered (under Global Plan wage restraint) the emphasis in the 1994 and 1995 bargaining rounds was on job creation through part-time employment, hours reductions, early retirement and work redistribution.

The government tried to encourage job creation through company-level work redistribution schemes. These were plans drawn up by management and works councils or trade union delegations to change working patterns so as to facilitate the recruitment of staff; the employer was entitled to reduced social security charges relating to each new recruit. However, few companies produced such plans and in 1994 only 3,000 extra jobs were created in that way.

Industrial conflict

Industrial conflict is regulated and formalised by peace obligation clauses in collective agreements. Since these concern the procedural aspects of the agreement, they are not legally enforceable *per se* but constitute an implied obligation on the parties. A social harmony clause specifies that no collective or individual claims may be introduced in respect of issues covered by the agreement during its life span: neither party may seek to enhance, expand or enlarge the provisions made in a collective agreement. Most agreements specify a period of notice of termination unless they are temporary agreements signed for a specific length of time, eg one year only. The harmony obligation is usually respected, and the number of strikes is small; between 1989 and 1993 Belgium lost on average 36 days per year per thousand employees to strikes. This compares with an average 586 per year per thousand employees in Greece; 70 in the UK and three in Japan over the same period.

An obligation to implement the contract in accordance with its terms is also an implied term, which means that signatories have to persuade their affiliates to abide by all its provisions.

The right to strike

There is no specific statutory right to strike. However, international law and conventions, including the European Social Charter, offer some legal basis. In addition the right to strike has been recognised by case law. A 1981 Supreme Court ruling on 1948 legislation providing for the maintenance of essential services (see below) has long been regarded as recognising a right of employees to strike in that the court decreed that participation in strike action does not constitute an unlawful act. Case law also holds that picketing is not unlawful; nor are wildcat strikes necessarily unlawful. The lack of a legislative framework is evidenced in the absence of regulation over forms of industrial action, including notice to strike or picketing, although industry collective agreements do often stipulate a notice period. Sympathy strikes are rare. However, there are some restrictions on the right to strike in certain key sectors of the economy – for example, the ports – on the grounds that strike action would harm the national interest by restricting essential services. In most sectors the joint committees have specified which services are deemed essential, and employees called upon to maintain those services during strike action cannot refuse. In the gas and electricity sectors, essential services are regulated by government.

The individual contract of employment is suspended, not terminated, by strike action: once work resumes continuity of employment is guaranteed. Theoretically an employer could dismiss strikers, except those who enjoy special protection (eg employee representatives, pregnant women, etc.). However, the employee would still be entitled to due notice, or payment in lieu.

Because trade unions have no legal personality, and have been sufficiently powerful to resist all past attempts to have it conferred on them, they cannot be sued, nor can an employer take out an injunction against them to prevent or stop strike action, even if the action may entail breaching a peace clause in a collective agreement. However, since the early 1990s there have been a number of cases in which employers, seeking court action against strikes, have successfully applied for fines to be levied upon individual employees.

Since the late 1980s there has been a tendency for court intervention in the area of industrial action to increase. More and more employers are resorting to the courts to stop strikes on the basis of the right to work. They can submit an *eenzijdse verzoekschrift*, a written request to the courts to give out a ruling without requiring a hearing. However, some courts are reluctant to be used as 'strike police', and insist on calling a full hearing before making a decision. Injunctions may also be granted on the grounds that a strike could do irretrievable harm to an enterprise – an argument successfully used by Volkswagen in 1994, leading to the court sanctioning fines of up to BFr 100,000 on individual pickets preventing other employees from entering the car plant.

Lockouts are not in themselves unlawful, unless intended to attack trade union organisations as such, but in any case they are rare.

Each trade union is bound by its own rules in calling a strike. Normally an internal ballot is conducted in which a majority of two-thirds must support the action. Unions exercise strict internal discipline; wildcat strikes are infrequent. Those that do occur are often sparked off by non-unionists. Collective agreements usually include a period of notice, often seven days, of strike action, as well as conciliation procedures.

Industrial disputes are typically short, unregulated, and aimed at disruption rather than protracted conflict. Employee reluctance to engage in protracted disputes is also prompted by the loss of a number of bonuses.

Conciliation and arbitration

Each joint sectoral committee has a conciliation committee (*bureau de conciliation*), usually presided over by the sectoral committee chair. The conciliation committee is responsible for the interpretation of an agreement and can intervene at the request of the employer or the trade unions. Conciliation meetings normally take place at the Ministry of Labour, but are sometimes convened elsewhere. It is up to the conciliation committee to decide on the procedure, in terms of whether a joint or separate meeting of the parties should take place. The latter course of action is adopted when the initial standpoints are far apart. The conciliation procedure is used to positive effect.

Organisations

National Labour Council (Conseil nationale du travail, CNT/Nationale arbeidsraad, NAR)
Avenue de la Joyeuse Entrée 17–21
1040 Brussels
Tel. + 32 2 233 8811
Fax + 32 2 233 8859

Ministry of Employment (Ministère de l'emploi et du travail/Ministerie van tewerkstelling en arbeid)
Rue Belliard 51–3
1040 Brussels
Tel. + 32 2 233 4111

Belgian Trade Union Confederation (Fédération générale du travail de Belgique, FGTB/Algemeen belgisch vakverbond, ABVV)
Rue Haute 42
1000 Brussels
Tel. + 32 2 506 8211
Fax + 32 2 513 4721

Christian Trade Union Confederation (Confédération de syndicats chrétiens de Belgique, CSC/Algemeen christelijk vakverbond, ACV)
Rue de la Loi 121
1040 Brussels
Tel. + 32 2 237 3111
Fax + 32 2 237 3300

Belgium Employers' Confederation (Fédération des entreprises de Belgique, FEB/Vereniging van belgische ondernemers, VBO)
Rue Ravenstein 4
1000 Brussels
Tel. + 32 2 515 0811
Fax + 32 2 515 0913

Main sources

Commentaire Social de Poche, Samsom, 1994/95.

Guide de Législation Sociale, Confédération des Syndicats Chrétiens.

Collective Agreements for the following industries: chemicals, engineering, foodstuffs, retail, transport; also various national collective agreements supplied by the Conseil National du Travail.

Legislation: 1968 Law on collective agreements (*Loi sur les conventions collectives de travail et les commissions paritaires*); 1971 Law on Employment (*Loi sur le travail*); 1978 Law on contracts of employment (*Loi relative aux contrats de travail*).

VILROKY, JAQUES, and VAN LEEMPUT, JIM. 'Belgium: a new stability in industrial relations' in A. Ferner and R. Hyman (eds), *Industrial Relations in the New Europe*, Blackwell, Oxford, 1992

3

Denmark

Four elements are generally considered to be characteristic of the Danish approach to industrial relations:

- a comprehensively organised labour market, with strong organisations for both workers and employers
- a high degree of commitment to collective bargaining, with agreements covering virtually the entire labour market, but with scope for flexible implementation, especially on pay issues, at company level; at industry level the process of bargaining remains centralised – a fact emphasised by the role of the public conciliator
- a consensus-based relationship between the opposing organisations, and a relatively low level of industrial strife
- regulation of the vast bulk of terms and conditions of employment, together with employee representation, by collective bargaining rather than legislation.

Industrial relations are extensively based on collective agreements. These do not just cover substantive terms and conditions of employment. National agreements concluded between the central employers' association and the trade union confederation also regulate the fundamental procedures for the conduct of industrial relations, such as resolving disputes. Union membership is high, and procedures for employee participation are based largely on institutions agreed with and operated through the trade unions. Despite the priority accorded to collective bargaining, the government has on occasion been prepared to intervene directly on a variety of issues, including forced conciliation to end strike action. Resort to mediation is also common, and – controversially – has been virtually the norm throughout the 1980s and 1990s in many negotiations.

The 1980s saw a major shift from a system of centralised bargaining between a cohesive union confederation (the LO) and a central employers' organisation (the DA) to a more decentralised system, with the focus on developing industry-level bargaining and considerable scope for either bargaining or managerial discretion at company level. This transformation has created strains for the existing central union and employer organisations, both of which are being compelled to examine and adjust their role in the overall system. The move to decentralisation took place during the long period of centre–right coalition government from 1982 to 1993, in which many of the traditional links between trade unions and government were weakened. This has allowed room for greater employer discretion and has enhanced the power of some groups of skilled workers, who felt that the previous centralised model limited their ability to negotiate higher differentials.

Decentralisation of pay bargaining to industry level has been paralleled by a growth in the importance of minimum-pay systems, in which industry agreements merely specify the lowest rate for new starters, leaving grading and progression to company bargaining – a step which has given added impetus to the widening of pay differentials.

Despite Denmark's vigorous voluntarist industrial relations traditions – issues governed by statute in most other EU countries are dealt with through central collective agreements – until the mid-1980s the government frequently intervened in the bargaining process to impose a settlement by law when the parties could not agree, and still has the power to do so.

The main players

Trade unions

Trade union structure   By comparison with trade unions in many other EU countries, those in Denmark weathered the storms of the 1980s well: although their influence over national policy has been weakened somewhat by several years of liberal–conservative government, they succeeded in retaining their memberships, and the coverage of the workforce by collective agreements has remained virtually unchanged. No deregulation of industrial relations has taken place, and the trade unions themselves have been instrumental in reshaping their organisations. Indeed, the fact that many conditions of employment are regulated by agreement rather than statute would render intervention by the state problematic.

Three union confederations, the LO, the FTF and the AC, organise a total of some 2.1 million employees, approximately 80–5 per cent of the workforce.

LO (Landsorganisation), which is closely aligned with the Social Democratic Party, is the largest, representing over 1.4 million employees in 23 individual unions. Around one-third of the LO's members are in private companies affiliated to the employers' confederation, the DA. The organising principles of the constituent unions vary. The most significant constituents are

- the National Union of Commercial and Clerical Workers (HK), with approximately 320,000 members in both the public and the private sectors
- the National Union of General Workers (SiD), with approximately 313,000 members in industry, transport and agriculture
- the National Union of Engineering Workers, with 140,000 employees
- the National Union of Women Workers, with 100,000 employees.

The FTF union, which represents some 350,000 white-collar employees and civil servants, is not affiliated to the LO and was established in 1952 as a politically neutral trade union.

The AC, the Confederation of Professional Associations, was established via a merger of several professional organisations in 1972 and has some 140,000 members.

Although initially regarded as a competitor of the LO, the FTF has been recognised by the Social Democratic Party, and since 1972 has had an agreement with the LO on mutual recognition and to prevent inter-union competition. All three union groupings customarily present common demands to employers.

Unlike central union confederations in other EU countries, the LO is competent to bargain, a right delegated to it by the constituent unions, reflecting the primacy of central organisations in the 'Nordic model'. In practice the LO no longer bargains directly on pay, a fact which testifies to the erosion of some of the central axioms of the model. However, the central agreements between the LO and the DA on the basic framework of industrial relations, covering issues such as the basic principles of bargaining, industrial co-operation, conflict resolution and unfair dismissal, set the context in which bargaining takes place. Despite the shift to industry-level bargaining, these LO–DA agreements – allowing scope for resort to the central organisations for help should negotiations stall – still play a fundamental role as a backdrop to bargaining.

Since the late 1980s the LO has been attempting to rationalise its representation by establishing sectoral 'cartels' into which the individual unions – many of which straddle industrial boundaries – would transfer part of their membership for bargaining purposes. The original proposal was for three cartels in the private sector, covering construction, manufacturing, commerce and services, with a further two in the public sector. The ultimate aim of many of the advocates of the change is the creation of industrial unions, with the implication that existing general and occupational unions should eventually be disbanded and their members allocated to the new structure. However, movement in that direction has been halted by opposition within the General Workers' Union (SiD), which would stand to lose out under such an industry-based arrangement. As a result, the original LO proposal has stalled, although the establishment of cartels through direct links between trade unions, including parts of the SiD not opposed to the change, is continuing.

Despite several years of discussion on this issue the only functioning cartel remains CO-Industri (which grew out of the long-standing bargaining group CO-Metal). CO-Industri brings together in one bargaining unit the skilled engineering workers' union, the women's union, the semi-skilled union and the commercial workers' union (see below). It covers all employees within the orbit of the parallel employer's organisation Dansk Industri (see below). The creation of the CO-Industri cartel in 1992 represented an attempt by unions in CO-Metal to sidestep the process of cartel formation which had stalled under the direct guidance of the LO.

The generally high levels of union membership reflect not only the culture of Danish industrial relations, with its emphasis on collective agreements, but also the involvement of the trade unions in the administration and payment of unemployment benefit. This applies particularly, some commentators feel, in the area of white-collar trade union membership, where bargaining plays a less important role in pay determination.

The right to organise   Complementary to the constitutionally guaranteed right to form associations for any legal purpose, section 1 of the General Agreement between the DA and the LO provides that the two organisations 'undertake not to hinder employers and workers, either directly or indirectly, in organising themselves within the organisational framework of the central organisations . . . an act by one party against another party on grounds of organisational affiliation rather than industrial issues shall be regarded as an act against the national organisation itself'. Employers may not, for example, discriminate against unionised employees by refusing to employ them.

The closed shop is valid in the private sector. Although the DA prohibits affiliated companies from entering into closed shop agreements without special permission, employers not in the DA – who account for one-third of the LO's membership – often do so. As a consequence of the British Rail judgement at the European Court of Human Rights in 1981, the Danish Parliament passed legislation providing for protection in the event of dismissal either for being or for not being a member of a trade union. Accordingly, an employer may dismiss an employee for not being a trade union member only where the employee knew that union membership was a condition of employment.

Employers' organisations

The largest and most significant private-sector employer organisation is the DA (Dansk Arbejdsgiverforening), with a membership of some 30,000 companies organised into 31 industrial groupings. Individual companies join the industrial groupings rather than the DA itself, although there are some exceptions in the case of conglomerates whose activities are difficult to classify. In the past the DA concluded central agreements with the LO, which – although covering only 500,000 workers – set the trend for the rest of the economy. As pay-setting has moved increasingly to industry level, the main tasks of the DA and LO have been to maintain procedural agreements, co-ordinate the activities of their affiliates, and clarify national issues such as pensions. The DA, in particular, has the power to refuse to endorse branch-level agreements, and it has been used in the most recent pay round to force employers to re-negotiate.

The largest groupings in the DA are the Danish Industries Employers' Association (Dansk Industri), the Trade, Transport and Services Employers' Association (AHTS), the Retail and Office Sectors Employers' Association (BKA) and the Construction Industry Employers' Association (BA).

Apart from the DA, there are two other major employers' associations in the private sector: the Financial Sector Employers' Association and SALA, the Confederation of Danish Agricultural Enterprises, both of which conclude their own agreements with LO affiliates.

National-level consultation and co-operation

Denmark has a tripartite national Economic Council (Det Økonomiske Råd), established in 1962, which reports to the government on economic issues. Trade unions are represented by the LO and FTF (see below), which regard the council as a valuable forum for discussing national economic developments. Trade unions also participate in the Council of Nordic Trade Unions (NFS). The NFS advises and lobbies the Nordic Council of Ministers and the Nordic Council.

During the 1980s there were tripartite negotiations and consultation on a number of issues, although relations between the trade unions and the Conservative-led coalition government were at times severely strained. In 1984, for example, union confederation LO pulled out of tripartite discussions on whether and how to implement cuts in working hours after accusing the government of taking the employers' side: a report produced by the Ministry of Labour on the issue at the request of the trade unions identified a number of criteria which had to be met before shorter hours could be introduced, such as no impact on wage costs and greater flexibility, which the employers claimed could not be met. The government eventually intervened to end strikes over the LO claim for shorter hours in March 1985.

In the mid- to late 1980s tripartite discussions took place about models for profit-sharing, although no specific proposals emerged, the implications of an ILO ruling which had found against the government's suspension of pay indexation, and, in 1987, measures to contain wage costs through a major reduction in employers' overall social insurance contributions which were cut to approximately 5 per cent of employees' pay. In 1988 discussions centred on trade union demands for supplementary occupational pensions (*Arbejdsmarkedspensioner*), which have subsequently been progressively introduced via collective bargaining. More recently attention has been directed at the structural problems of the labour market.

Central bipartite consultation and bargaining on the fundamental principles and structures of industrial relations takes place between the LO and DA, and is embodied in two core agreements. The General Agreement (Hovedaftalen) regulates each party's rights of organisation and association, recognition of managerial prerogatives, the status of collective agreements (see below), unfair dismissal, and enabling provisions – to be fleshed out by industry agreements – on shop stewards. The Co-operation Agreement (*Samarbejdsaftalen*), the main provisions of which are set out in the section on employee representation below, establishes a framework for industrial co-operation, information and consultation on a wide range of issues.

Collective bargaining on pay and conditions of employment in the private sector is the responsibility of individual sectoral or occupational trade unions and industry employers' organisations, based on framework agreements on procedures, and in the past on basic terms, arrived at centrally between the DA and the LO.

Under the Co-operation Agreement, which regulates the setting up of co-operation committees (see below), the DA and the LO have established a jointly financed Co-operation Board charged with promoting co-operation between managements and employees, assisting in setting up co-operation committees, and settling any disputes which may arise out of the operation of co-operation committees: the procedures here are dealt with in the following section.

Workplace employee representation

There are three forms of employee representation at workplace level: via shop stewards, through 'co-operation committees', with the two structures closely related, and through health and safety committees. Only health and safety committees are regulated by statute law. However, as noted above, the underlying collective agreements which provide for shop steward and co-operation committee rights are central and therefore binding throughout the private sector, subject to size criteria. There is no statutory form of employee representation comparable with the works councils found elsewhere in the European Union.

The role of the shop steward (*tillidsrepræsentant*)

There is a long tradition of workplace representation via trade union shop stewards, with agreed provisions on their election, status and role. Such provisions through national framework agreements, fleshed out by industry agreements, now cover most of the private sector. There is no statutory provision in this area. Section 8 of the General Agreement (see also below) – which sets out the general agreed principles for the conduct of industrial relations – provides that industry agreements should make provision for shop stewards to be elected and recognised, unless the nature of the activity renders this impossible. Industry agreements prescribe detailed regulations on the election of shop stewards, and on their specific rights and duties. On average there is one shop steward for every 50 employees, the precise arrangements depending on the structure of the individual enterprise.

The minimum requirements for candidacy as a shop steward typically include

- *union membership*, because the shop steward serves as the local/workplace representative of a trade union
- *length of service*. Normally a year's seniority is required, reflecting the requirement that the shop steward should have a sound knowledge of the undertaking
- *recognition as a 'capable worker'*. Candidates for election as a shop steward must be acknowledged as a 'capable worker' (*anerkendt dygtig medarbejder*), although this may be interpreted broadly. The reason lies in the special protection against dismissal enjoyed by shop stewards, giving the employer a

legitimate interest in having only capable employees in such a secure position. The onus is on an employer who contests the election of a shop steward to show that the candidate does not meet this requirement.

In larger companies with many stewards, the stewards may establish a joint union delegation. Agreements also provide for the establishment of trade union 'clubs' in larger organisations, which can embrace members of several trade unions, who elect a common shop steward. Under industry agreements, employers may be required to provide facilities for 'club' meetings.

Collective agreements often require that, as the representative of the workforce *vis-à-vis* the employer, as well as the workplace representative of the trade union, a shop steward, once elected, must be approved in office by the relevant union, and the employer informed.

Shop stewards serve as a direct link between employees and management on issues relating to workplace terms and conditions, and as such figure as the central channel through which employee grievances are articulated, although collective agreements generally state that relations between the parties should be co-operative rather than confrontational. For example, the agreement covering clerical employees states that: 'shop stewards are required to behave with diligence towards their colleagues, their organisation [i.e. the trade union] and the employer, to seek to resolve conflicts and to maintain industrial co-operation at the workplace'.

Collective agreements also establish grievance procedures, specifying the stage at which individual problems may be referred to stewards, and at what point a grievance can be taken to the relevant trade union.

Shop stewards customarily enjoy time-off rights to carry out their activities, although specific amounts of time are not usually set out.

As a rule, collective agreements contain special provisions protecting shop stewards against dismissal. In general, a shop steward can be dismissed only where the employer has 'compelling grounds', such as serious misconduct.

Co-operation committees (*samarbejdsudvalg*)

'Co-operation committees' have existed in the private sector since the immediate post-war period and function under a central collective agreement negotiated between the DA and the LO: the most recent agreement dates from 1986. Such committees exist in around 1,700 companies in the private sector. Co-operation committees are envisaged as a means of furthering employee participation and industrial co-operation, with the objective of promoting 'competitiveness and employee job satisfaction'. The preamble of the Co-operation Agreement stresses the importance of 'motivating management systems' and 'active participation by employees and their elected union representatives', with particular emphasis on the need for management, co-operation and communication systems to 'induce as many employees as possible to participate in arranging and organising their daily work'.

Co-operation committees may be set up in enterprises with 35 or more employees, and may be proposed either by the employer or by a majority of the employees. The Co-operation Agreement recommends 'informative meetings' between management and employees 'at frequent intervals' should neither side wish to establish a formal co-operation committee. A committee consists on the one hand of managers and senior personnel ineligible for trade union membership, and, on the other, all the remaining employees of the enterprise. The size of the committee varies according to the size of the company, with six representatives for each side, up to a maximum of six for each side in companies with more than 500 employees. Election of employee representatives to the committee, which takes place every two years, is by direct vote of the whole workforce.

Elected shop stewards are *ex officio* members of the co-operation committee. Should the number of stewards exceed the number of places available on the committee, election is solely from among the stewards. Committee members, like shop stewards, enjoy dismissal protection in the form of an extended period of notice of six weeks in addition to their contractual notice.

The co-operation committee is chaired by a senior manager, with the employees nominating the deputy chair. Meetings must be held six times a year, unless an individual local agreement provides otherwise.

Co-operation committees have the following rights and responsibilities (Co-operation Agreement, 1986, section 3):

- establishing principles for the local working environment and human relations, as well as the principles of the personnel policy pursued by the enterprise towards the employees represented in the staff group of the co-operation committee
- establishing principles for training and retraining employees who are to work with new technology
- establishing principles for the in-house compilation, storage and use of personal data
- exchanging viewpoints and considering proposals for guidelines on the planning of production and work, and the implementation of major changes in the enterprise
- assessing the technical, financial, staffing, educational and environmental consequences of the introduction of new technology, including computer-aided technology and systems which entail the introduction of such technology or changes on an extended scale
- informing employees about proposals for incentive systems of payment, including details of their basic structure, effect and application. Also informing employees about the possibility of setting up funds for educational and social security purposes.

Under the 1986 agreement any employees displaced through the introduction of new technology have a right to up to four weeks' time off to attend retraining and reorientation courses, with the employer covering loss of pay and course fees for any employee with at least one year's service.

Employers are required to inform the committee, 'in plain language' and in good time, of the firm's financial position and future prospects, the employment outlook, and any major changes contemplated, including the application of new technology. Information disclosed must not harm the employer's interests, and the committee may be bound to secrecy on some issues. The committee, in turn, is required to develop appropriate means of communicating information to the workforce.

Co-operation committees are not empowered to deal with issues which are in the province of collective bargaining proper – that is, industry or company pay matters.

Disputes arising out of the operation of co-operation committees, if irresolvable at company level, may be taken to the Co-operation Board set up under the national agreement. If discussion at that level is unable to settle the dispute, an arbitrator may be appointed – if necessary, by the president of the Labour Court.

Health and safety representatives and committees

Under the 1985 Health and Safety at Work Act, originally passed in 1975, employees in companies with a workforce of at least 10 people must elect a safety representative who, together with a supervisor, constitutes a safety group for the enterprise. In companies with at least 20 employees a safety committee (*sikkerhedsudvalg*) must be set up to ensure that working conditions are in accordance with the relevant regulations. Inspectors from the Health and Safety Executive (Arbejdstilsynet) must make regular contact with safety representatives and members of the committee. Safety representatives – as well as other employees – are free to discuss issues relating to health and safety at the workplace with the Executive.

Safety representatives have a right to time off and, like shop stewards, are protected against certain types of dismissal.

Employee representation at board level

Provision for board-level representation was introduced by the 1974 Companies Act, amended in 1980. All limited liability companies and companies limited by guarantee are required to establish a two-tier board structure, with a supervisory board and a management board. While the management board is concerned with day-to-day operations, the supervisory board – which must consist of at least three members – is responsible for overall policy, and must be consulted on important decisions. Secondary legislation specifies the regulations on employee representation at board level.

In companies which have employed at least 35 workers over the previous three years, employees have a legal right to vote on whether to elect employee representatives. Any employee who is of age and has at least one year's service is

eligible. Employees may elect at least two and up to half the number of shareholder representatives elected by the shareholders' meeting. Employee representatives have the same rights and duties as other board members, are elected for
four years, and have the same dismissal protection entitlement as shop stewards.
The supervisory board must ensure that employees are given information on the
circumstances of the company, including its finances, employment and production plans.

Implementation of the EU works council directive

Given the Danish tradition of relying upon collective bargaining rather than legislation to regulate employment matters, it is perhaps unsurprising that this
seems to be the route which is likely to be followed in implementing the EU
directive on European Works Councils.

There is a recent precedent for this approach. The industrial agreement concluded by the DA and CO-Industri in the 1995 bargaining round contains provisions implementing three EU directives – those on working time, the protection
of young people at work and the amended directive on collective dismissal. This
effectively means any infringement of these directives may be pursued through
the Industrial Court as breaches of a collective agreement (see below).

At the moment it seems that the most likely result will be sectoral agreements
implementing the requirements of the directive. The Ministry of Labour will then
examine the agreements and see whether complementary legislation is needed to
'top up' provisions on the question.

Collective bargaining

Collective bargaining in Denmark presents both a complex and changing picture.
The past 15 years have seen a substantial shift away from centralised bargaining
between the national trade union confederation, the LO (Landsorganisation i
Danmark), and the employers' confederation, the DA (Dansk Arbejdsgiverforening),
towards industry-level bargaining, with greater emphasis on supplementary or
implementing agreements at company level. However, the process has been
uneven and has entailed major upheavals in the trade union structure and restructuring among employers.

Although industry bargaining has now supplanted central agreements on pay,
the picture is still complicated by the existence of some occupational and general
unions whose members span industry boundaries. Of these the most important is
the white-collar union, the HK (see below), which until the latest bargaining
round negotiated a national agreement for its members with an affiliate of the
national central employers' organisation, the DA. However, in 1995 members of
the HK in the relevant sector were for the first time included in the Dansk
Industri/CO-Industri industrial agreement.

There are also unions for some special crafts (electricians, plumbers) whose pay rates are also set nationally. Where that is the case a company must ensure that its own grading and pay scales mean that employees covered by national agreements are paid at least these rates. In the event of doubt, the most favourable agreement covering an employee prevails.

The coverage of the workforce by collective agreements is high, matching the high levels of trade union organisation. However, this does not mean that pay structures at company level or annual increases for all employees are tightly pre-scribed by central collective agreements. Many agreements set only minimum rates for the unskilled, with rates for other categories set either by local agree-ment (typically for blue-collar workers) or management decision and individual negotiation (in the case of many white-collar employees).

Extension procedures

There are no procedures through which a collective agreement can be declared binding on non-signatory parties. However, many companies choose to sign an 'adherence agreement' (*tiltrædelsoverenkomst*) with a trade union under which they accept the terms of an agreement already concluded between a union and an employers' association. It is estimated that around one-third of all Danish employers accede to collective agreements by this procedure rather than through direct membership of a signatory organisation. Such an agreement would cover the range of agreed terms and conditions, including pay.

Levels of bargaining

The extent to which bargaining over pay and other terms is conducted centrally by the LO or predominantly by the individual unions has varied over the past decade or so, but with an overall strong movement to decentralisation. Decentralisation to industry bargaining began in the early 1980s, was interrupted by a government-imposed settlement in 1985/86 following a failure of central negotiations, and returned from 1987.

The movement towards industry bargaining, with greater encouragement of company negotiations, has reduced the role of the LO and DA and enhanced the importance of industry-level employers' associations. The need to parallel this heightened profile with appropriate union structures has been one force driving the formation of union industry cartels, to which the individual occupational unions can affiliate a certain number of members. However, as noted above, there have been problems in implementing the approach and the pace has been set by the only functioning cartel, CO-Industri.

To some extent the negotiating role of the LO and the DA has been supplanted by CO-Industri and its counterpart, the employers' association Dansk Industri. However, there have been problems of co-ordination between employer group-ings. The DA also has to agree formally to what its industry affiliates have negotiated. (At the moment Dansk Industri is numerically the most important force on the DA's General Council.)

The shift in the locus of bargaining is also being reinforced by the replacement of so-called 'standard pay' systems, which specify the actual rate to be paid across a range of positions, to a 'minimum wage' system, in which the collective agreement merely specifies the lowest rate for an unskilled worker. All additional payments are then negotiated, or unilaterally awarded, at company level, with actual pay on average around 35 per cent more than the minimum (see below). In the recent past around half of all workers were covered by 'minimum' pay agreements and half by 'standard' pay agreements. The 1991–93 agreement in the metalworking industry, in which the women's and semi-skilled unions moved from a 'standard' to a 'minimum' system, has decisively changed the balance, and around two-thirds of blue-collar workers are now estimated to be covered by minimum pay agreements. This shift towards minimum pay systems, with greater local bargaining, is part of, and parallels, a move to widen differentials between the skilled and the unskilled, and to tie increases more firmly to local ability to pay.

Pay in the public sector is overwhelmingly 'standard', with actual rates set out in the relevant collective agreements.

In the engineering industry local bargaining over pay structures and pay increases for blue-collar workers building on the single industry minimum rate is carried out by shop stewards whose rights are set out in the General Agreement concluded between the LO and the DA, with more detailed regulations in the industry agreement. Following the conclusion of the industry agreement in engineering, usually in March, local negotiations may be carried on by shop stewards. According to the agreement, an individual employee's wages are set by agreement between the employer and the employee without the involvement of unions: however, this may be overruled if a party feels that 'abuse' is taking place, allowing scope for collective negotiation and local agreements.

Under the agreement, negotiations on wages can take place only once a year. Local agreements require at least two months' notice should either party wish to cancel them. However, longer periods of notice at local level can be agreed, allowing a local agreement to be concluded that matches the industry agreement.

There is no right to strike at local level: under the General Agreement between the LO and the DA any proposal for industrial action must be submitted to the executive committee of the relevant organisation.

Agreed increases at industry level may be offset against actual pay at company level, either through the implementation of a merit system or through a company pay pause/freeze, provided that company pay still exceeds the binding agreed minimum. There have been isolated examples of this taking place.

Pay agreements

Industrial relations are characterised by the fact that many issues customarily regulated by statute elsewhere are organised between employers and employee organisations through collective agreements: this applies to basic matters such as the rights to organise, to take industrial action, settlement procedures in the event of a dispute, and industrial co-operation. One consequence is a relative paucity of legislation on collective agreements, most matters of practical relevance being specified in the General Agreement between the LO and the DA. This agreement, and any others concluded centrally, is binding on all member organisations. Within these very general rules the conclusion of collective agreements is fairly informal, and in theory a collective agreement could be verbal.

Collective agreements are normally concluded every other year, with most private-sector agreements expiring on 1 March. In general, once this agreed period has expired, an agreement can be terminated by either of the parties upon three months' notice. Collective agreements bind signatory organisations, and the terms must be applied by signatory employers to all employees, whether unionised or not. Should an employer pay a non-unionised worker less than the agreed wage, the union concerned may take the employer to the Industrial Court and obtain payment of a fine to itself for at least the difference between the two payments.

Agreements involving the DA and LO are subject to the 'peace obligation' (*fredspligt*) contained in the General Agreement, which outlaws industrial action during the lifetime of an agreement, save for exceptional circumstances set out in the *Standard Rules for Handling Labour Disputes* first agreed in 1908. The rules include situations where there is risk 'to life, welfare or honour'. This means in effect that industrial action (by employers or employees) is usually legal only when an agreement has expired – such action is most common in conjunction with the renegotiation of agreements. However, there are other circumstances in which action may be legal – for instance, against unorganised employers, or if a dispute concerns a new type of work not yet covered by an agreement.

All collective agreements must be ratified by union members in a secret ballot before they can be signed and put into effect by the negotiating parties. In practice balloting often follows the intervention of the public conciliator, who has come to play a major role in finalising the pay round – generating considerable controversy (see 'Mediation' below).

Agreements apply to the signatory employers' organisation (or company) and the relevant trade union (or trade unions in the event of the agreement being negotiated by a cartel). Because of the possibility of conflicting or parallel agreements (with occupational, general and industrial unions all represented), an employers' organisation, and/or a company, may engage in single-table bargaining with all unions though formally concluding separate agreements – respecting any national/industry agreements – for different employee categories. In the event of conflicting collective agreements for an individual employee or group of employees, the most favourable provision must apply.

Agreements between member organisations of the LO and the DA remain in force after they have expired, or if the agreement has been duly denounced by one of the parties, until a new agreement has been concluded or procedures for initiating a lawful industrial dispute have been begun. Moreover a union, employers' organisation or company leaving one of the central organisations cannot avoid obligations arising out of the General Agreement. (This would not necessarily apply if the employer entering into a collective agreement was not a member of the DA but negotiated its own agreement with a trade union.)

One single agreement usually covers a variety of topics, not simply pay. The Industrial Agreement, for example, includes the rights of shop stewards and industrial co-operation, working hours and holidays, wages, employment and dismissal, holiday pay and arbitration rules. On pay itself, the agreement specifies minimum rates for adult and young workers, basic rules on local negotiations, procedures for calculating time rates, procedures for negotiating piece rates and rules for wage systems based on work study.

The pay round

The tripartite national Economic Council, established in 1962, reports to the government on economic issues and publishes an annual economic forecast. During the 1980s there were tripartite negotiations and consultation on a number of issues, although relations between the trade unions and the Conservative-led coalition were severely strained at times. However, there is no central tripartite accord on pay as such.

Pay bargaining is normally conducted every two years, with most private-sector agreements expiring on 1 March. The leading settlement is typically that in the engineering industry, from 1993 negotiated between the union cartel CO-Industri and its counterpart, Dansk Industri. Where agreements set only a minimum rate there is usually a further round of bargaining at company level between managements and workplace employee representatives where the increase in the industry minimum is applied to company rates, with the possibility of additional locally negotiated increases. Where there is no local negotiation, member companies of signatory organisations can simply develop their pay structures unilaterally – provided they observe the agreed minima.

Both the DA and the LO seek to co-ordinate negotiations through specific bargaining committees which meet regularly. In the case of the DA, the organisation issues a recommendation to its members, which is made known to the LO, on what it regards as reasonable increases in minimum rates. The DA's position is bolstered to some extent by the fact that its General Council must consent to any agreements negotiated by affiliated organisations. This was illustrated in the 1995 bargaining round, when the DA rejected three deals struck by its member organisations on the grounds that they were too expensive.

In the case of pay reviews for salaried employees, which may or may not be built on a structure of agreed pay, employers can ascertain market trends through salary clubs: the Danish Institute of Personnel Management currently runs about 30 such clubs.

Recent trends

The 1993 biennial pay round led to most deals giving rises of around 3 per cent over two years, in line with projected inflation. Another 2 per cent was added to labour costs by new sick-pay terms and increases in labour market pension contributions. For the first time many blue-collar agreements introduced full pay for the first 14 days of sickness – something to which white-collar employees are entitled by law.

'Labour market pensions' – supplementary occupational pension schemes for blue-collar workers – were introduced in some agreements in the 1991 round. The 1993 round saw schemes set up for most of the remaining sectors. For existing schemes, contribution rates generally rose to 2.1 per cent, with employers paying 1.4 per cent of the wage bill and employees 0.7 per cent of earnings.

In manufacturing industry the previous seven individual branch collective agreements were incorporated into a single industry-wide agreement.

There were difficult negotiations in some sectors, notably in the meat industry, where a three-week strike preceded the conclusion of a settlement. The main bone of contention was employers' right to set flexible working time unilaterally, a right which was surrendered in the subsequent deal.

The supposedly decentralised nature of the collective bargaining system was called into question when the DA expelled the haulage employers' federation for signing a deal which the DA judged too expensive.

Agreements signed in the 1995 round imply an overall increase in wage costs of around 4.2 per cent in 1995 and of 4.0 per cent in 1996. With wage costs in competitor countries estimated by the LO at 4.0 per cent in 1995 and 4.3 per cent in 1996, international competitiveness over the next two years is expected to remain broadly unchanged.

The increases agreed amount to a rise of 6.1 per cent over the two-year period, with inflation of 4.4 per cent forecast over the period, allowing real pay to rise.

Agreements signed in many sectors extend the period of sickness on full pay to three weeks, although the industrial agreement now specifies four weeks (from 1 March 1996). Those sectors which did not negotiate such a right in the 1993 round now generally have two weeks. A ceiling of DKr 95 per hour – sometimes marginally higher – is usually specified.

Some agreements (covering just over half of employees in the DA–LO area) contain a new clause entitling those on maternity or paternity leave (but excluding the parental leave scheme) to have their social security payments topped up to 100 per cent of previous earnings by their employer (from 1 March 1997). Again there is an hourly maximum of DKr 95. The LO's ambition of a central fund for this was not, however, realised.

Further increases in contributions were agreed – 1.25 per cent for employers and 0.6 per cent for workers, bringing total contributions to 3.9 per cent, 2.6 per cent by employers and 1.3 per cent by employees. Increased contributions to the ATP supplementary pension scheme were also generally agreed.

Some agreements, most notably the industrial agreement, will now last, unusually, for three years, compared with two years in other sectors. This means that key collective agreements in the DA–LO area now expire in different years for the first time since 1916, which will complicate future bargaining.

One of LO's bargaining demands for 1995 had been the establishment of 'training funds', financed by an employer contribution of 1 per cent of the wage bill, to top up state benefits to full wages during training. Although it was unsuccessful, around 75 per cent of agreements in the DA–LO area now have some kind of commitment from employers to pay full wages during relevant training – periods range from one week per year to an unspecified period. Some also set an hourly ceiling – usually DKr 90–5.

There has been some very cautious movement towards acceptance of the idea of employing some categories of worker on less than collectively-agreed minima. Although some 40 per cent of agreements in the DA–LO area have some kind of 'social chapter', as these formulas are known in Danish, many go no further than setting up working parties to examine the possibilities. Such 'chapters' usually refer to older workers and those with a reduced working capacity, although the long-term unemployed are sometimes included.

Although there has been no attempt to reduce working time, there has been some relaxation of the rules on, for example, the placement of normal daily working hours, the introduction of four-day weeks and weekend work and an extension of the averaging periods for variable weekly working time. However, in the vast majority of cases any variations from the norm must be agreed by the partners at local level.

Attempts have been made to preserve the values of the 'Danish model' in an EU context by including in some agreements clauses that apply the directives on working time and the protection of young people at work. However, in the case of the working time directive, for example, it is thought that as yet only 50 per cent of the labour market is covered by such clauses, less than the EU's requirement of 80 per cent. It may now be that the government will have to legislate on such matters, undermining the traditional emphasis on collectively agreed solutions.

The DA's rejection of three draft agreements reached by member organisations again highlighted the danger of viewing the collective bargaining system as thoroughly decentralised. The part played by the DA's largest member – the industrial employers' association, Dansk Industri – in the rejection (mainly because it felt the agreements granted rises which would set too generous a precedent for the negotiations then still in progress in its own sector) led some to question whether the DA still had an independent role to play.

Employees outside the scope of collective bargaining

White-collar workers

Although many white-collar workers are unionised, collective agreements will often set only minimum pay levels, with scope for employers to set effective salaries and award increases by unilateral decision or negotiation with the employee. Moreover, many white-collar workers are not covered by any agreement at all. In contrast to blue-collar employees, whose rights are mostly provided for by collective agreement, white-collar employees are covered by a specific statute, the Salaried Employees Act (*Funktionærloven*). Under this law employees have right to negotiate individually, and be represented either by a trade union official or by a lawyer. Collective discussions – rather than negotiations – may also take place involving local union representatives, followed by individual increases.

In industries where there is still a standard pay agreement, increases and salary levels will be specified in the settlement.

White-collar workers may also find themselves part of a bonus scheme negotiated by the appropriate blue-collar union for all the employees of a company. In that case, bonus or merit payments and the system of appraising employees will be determined collectively, although any general increases will be decided individually.

Pay for senior specialists and managers in the private sector will invariably be individually negotiated. There is a national collective framework agreement – the General Regulations (*Almindelige Bestemmelser*) – between the DA and a cartel of organisations representing supervisors, middle managers and technical specialists. The agreement sets out a broad range of provisions on the status of managers during industrial disputes, on severance payments and on training. On pay the agreement emphasises that salaries should be determined by individual negotiation, though with an appropriate and sustained differential *vis-à-vis* other grades. Pay should be reviewed annually.

Agreed provisions

Pay   There are no statutes governing general pay determination, nor any provisions on a minimum wage or on pay indexation. These matters are left entirely to individual bargaining or, as in the case of around 90 per cent of the workforce, to collective bargaining. As the law makes no provision for collective agreements to be extended to non-unionised workers, pay-setting for such employees is theoretically a matter entirely for the employer and the employee concerned. In practice, however, the terms of the relevant industry agreement – including pay levels – are usually applied.

Pay agreements generally use two systems: standard wages (*normalløn*), where a range of pay rates is set by collective agreement for different grades or occupations, and minimum pay (*minimalløn*), where industry-level minima (or a single minimum rate for adult employees) can be supplemented by local-level bargaining, resulting in real pay levels which are usually much higher than the minima. The number of employees covered by standard wages is shrinking steadily, and is around 17 per cent at present.

In both types of agreement it is common to find provisions which allow the introduction, subject to local agreement, of various types of incentive-based wage systems such as piecework or productivity agreements.

Overtime pay is also generally set by industry-level collective agreement. Agreements will usually include limits on overtime, and periods of notice and provision for time off in lieu. Payments for shift work and work in specialised areas, as well as other supplements relevant to the industry, are also the subject of collective bargaining.

Working time   Working time is also left largely to collective bargaining; statutory regulation of working time is limited to provisions in the Work Environment Act specifying the daily and weekly rest periods to which employees are entitled.

The present centrally collectively agreed working week is 37 hours. Agreements typically include detailed provisions on how these hours are to be distributed and allow some degree of local flexibility.

Industrial action

Official and unofficial action

In principle, employers as well as employees have a right to resort to industrial action, subject to the constraints imposed by agreements, such as the peace obligations noted above, and partly also by law. The General Agreement concluded between the DA and the LO also provides that no stoppage of work may take place 'unless approved by at least three-quarters of the votes cast by a competent assembly under the rules of the relevant organisation and due notice has been given to the other party'. The executive committees of the DA and LO must be informed of any intention to stop work at least 14 days before the proposed stoppage, and the other party must be given seven days' notice.

The Labour Court may fine anyone engaged in unofficial strike action, or in any other action which breaches the General Agreement. Following a case which came before the court in 1989, the standard fines in force were raised to DKr 32 per hour (£3.68) for skilled workers and DKr 27 per hour (£3.11) for unskilled workers, at which levels they remain today. If industrial action continues after the Labour Court has ordered it to be stopped, these rates may be raised by a further DKr 20 (£2.30) per hour. Action may not be proceeded with if the central organisations meet to resolve the problem and those engaged in the action resume work immediately. Unions can be fined if they fail to use all reasonable means to prevent an unlawful stoppage.

Conciliation machinery

The Standard Rules commit the parties to seek to resolve disputes by mediation or, if necessary, by arbitration. If one of the parties requests it, mediation must take place within a maximum of five working days. Should mediation fail, the matter is initially handed back to the negotiating parties for further talks.

If the dispute concerns the interpretation of an existing agreement ('dispute of rights'), the matter may be submitted to a court of arbitration if one of the parties so requests. If a party refuses on the grounds that the dispute is one of interests – for example, over the terms of a new agreement – the matter can be referred to the Industrial Court, which includes representatives of both sides of industry. Before appearing before the court the parties must hold a further meeting – in the presence of the central organisations – to attempt to resolve, or at least clarify, their differences. If that fails, the Industrial Court can issue a binding ruling, and also has the power to fine unofficial strikers.

Disputes over interests during negotiations can be referred to the state Conciliation Board established by the Ministry of Labour. Preliminary notice of industrial action (strike or lockout) can be given if no agreement has been reached after negotiations involving the Conciliation Board. The conciliator has the power to postpone industrial action twice, each time for 14 days.

The role of the public conciliator in the bargaining round is to assist employers and unions in reaching agreement when talks break down.

In theory there is absolutely no need for the conciliator to become involved in bargaining – that is, if all parties reach a satisfactory conclusion within a reasonable time frame. In such a situation all that needs to be done is for the agreement to be put to the ballot among the members of the organisations involved, according to their internal voting rules.

In practice, this state of affairs hardly ever arises. The last time it occurred was in 1981. What tends to happen is that, while some sectors will reach agreement with little difficulty, there are usually areas where talks break down. In such a situation the conciliator has wide-ranging powers, including the right to intervene in negotiations on his or her own initiative, even if deadlock has not been reached, and to postpone any planned industrial action for two periods of two weeks.

When agreement has been reached, the conciliator has the right to submit a 'concatenated proposal' for approval by ballot – that is, all the numerous agreements with all their different provisions are linked together. This means that all trade unions and employers must vote to accept or reject the package of agreements as a whole. In effect it means peace for everyone or industrial conflict for everyone. Concatenation may take place only in areas covered by central employer and union bodies, such as the DA and LO. If these agree that a certain sector should not be included for voting purposes, their wish must be respected. It seldom happens, but meat industry workers obtained such a dispensation in 1993.

The most controversial aspect of this process concerns the rules laid down in law for voting on such a concatenated proposal. The rules state that, for a proposal to be rejected, a simple majority will suffice, but it must represent at least

35 per cent all of those entitled to vote. The turnout for these ballots is tradition-ally low, and has recently been below 35 per cent (33.1 per cent in 1995). This means that it is practically impossible to reject a proposal, even with a 100 per cent 'no' vote. The pooling of votes raises another problem. It is possible (and happens) that members of a small union may vote to reject the agreement reached for its sector, but since voting covers a proposal covering several sectors an overall 'yes' vote means that they are forced to accept it.

There is growing discontent with this state of affairs. The LO has called for reform of the voting rules after the last three bargaining rounds. Even the DA, which has been opposed to reform, expressed cautious support after the 1995 round. It seems likely that any change will involve a lowering of the 35 per cent threshold.

The ease and frequency with which the public conciliation service may – and does – intervene in a supposedly decentralised free collective bargaining system has led one study to suggest that a better description of the Danish system would be 'centralised decentralisation'.

Organisations

Danish Confederation of Trade Unions
(Landsorganisationen i Danmark, LO)
Rosenørns Allé 12
DK-1634 Copenhagen V
Tel. + 45 31 35 35 41
Fax + 45 35 37 37 41

Danish Employers' Federation (Dansk
Arbejdsgiverforening, DA)
Vester Voldgade 113
DK-1790 Copenhagen V
Tel. + 45 33 93 40 00
Fax + 45 33 12 29 76

Ministry of Labour (Arbejdsministeriet)
Laksegade 19
DK-1063 Copenhagen K
Tel. + 45 33 92 59 00
Fax + 45 33 12 13 78

Danish Institute of Personnel Management
(IP)
Hauser Plads 20
1127 Copenhagen
Tel. + 45 33 13 15 70
Fax + 45 33 32 51 56

CO-Industri (industrial unions' bargaining
cartel)
Vester Søgade 12, 2
DK-1790 Copenhagen V
Tel. + 45 33 15 12 66
Fax + 45 33 15 12 66

Dansk Industri (industrial employers'
federation)
H.C. Andersens Boulevard 18
DK-1553 Copenhagen V
Tel. + 45 33 77 33 77
Fax + 45 33 77 37 00

Main sources

ARBEJDERNES OPLYSNINGSFORBUND, Erik Stubtoft (ed.), *Arbejdsmarkedets Håndbog 1994*. Copenhagen. Arbejdernes Oplysningsforbund, 1994

DANSK ARBEJDSGIVERFORENING. *Personalejurahåndbogen*, Copenhagen, Dansk Arbejdsgiverforening, 1990

DANSK ARBEJDSGIVERFORENING. *Direktøren, ansættelses- og arbejdsvilkår.* Copenhagen, Dansk Arbejdsgiverforening, 1990

DUE, JESPER, *et al. The Survival of the Danish Model.* Copenhagen, DJØF Publishing, 1994

NIELSEN, RUTH. *Lærebog i arbejdsret.* Copenhagen, Jurist- og Økonomiforbundets Forlag, 1990

DA/LO. *Hovedaftalen* (General Agreement). Copenhagen, 1993

DA/LO. *Fællesordning for arbejde i holddrift* (Shift-work Agreement). Copenhagen, 1993

DA/LO. *Mægling i arbejdsstridigheder* (Dispute Resolution Agreement). Copenhagen, 1991

DANSK INDUSTRI/CO-INDUSTRI. *Industriens overenskomst* (Industry Agreement) Copenhagen, 1993

LAND- OG SKOVBRUGETS ARBEJDSGIVERE/SID. *Overenskomst for jordbrug.* Copenhagen, 1993

DA/BKA/HK. *Landsoverenskomst* (National White-collar Workers Agreement). Copenhagen, 1993

4

France

Industrial relations in France present a complex and mixed picture of statutory mechanisms for employee representation and extensive coverage of the workforce by industry-level collective agreements combined with low union membership, weakly developed bargaining at plant level and a continuing – if diminished – view of the workplace as a site of employer–employee confrontation rather than co-operation.

The main players

Trade union density is among the lowest in Europe and has fallen markedly since the late 1970s. None the less, trade union representatives remain the main force behind statutory workplace participation, with the consequence that such mechanisms often fail to function at all in sectors with low union membership. The law provides principally for information and consultation rights at establishment level, with effective decision-making confined to the organisation of cultural activities.

The 1980s saw the growth of employer-led structures of employee involvement, paralleling and often supplanting statutory structures because of the greater resources devoted by employers to making them function, and their perceived greater relevance to employees' working life compared with the 'rights of expression' conferred by the law. From being traditionally underdeveloped, workplace collective bargaining has been fostered by legislation passed in 1982 (the 'Auroux laws'). This gives every nationally represented trade union the right to form a trade union section (*section syndicale*) in any company, provided that the union is represented significantly among its employees. The law further requires firms with over 50 employees and at least one union delegation to negotiate annually with workforce representatives on pay, working time and work organisation. However, there is no obligation to come to agreement.

The political orientation of trade unionism – albeit stronger in the past – has been viewed as contributing to low union density, currently around 10 per cent of the workforce as a whole, and as low as 6 per cent in the private sector. This in turn helps explain why collective bargaining has remained weak at workplace level, despite supportive legislation. Apart from the statutory national minimum wage (SMIC), the single most immediate determinant of wages in French industry remains not collective bargaining but unilateral management decisions.

These features of industrial relations have reinforced the focus on the state, which in turn – notably under the Mitterrand presidency after 1981 – has sought to use the law to widen collective bargaining and encourage employee representation. In the past, unions have had only limited scope to improve pay and conditions across the board without the support of a sympathetic government. And improvements achieved elsewhere by collective bargaining – such as cuts in working hours – have tended to await legal regulation in France. Change has been spasmodic rather than smooth. The weakness of organised unionism also underlies the occasional outbursts of unofficial industrial action, the formation of *ad hoc* groupings, and difficulty in resolving disputes. An approach rooted in consensus and negotiation has also been regarded as difficult to implant in the broader industrial culture of France, where companies tend to be hierarchical and less value is attached to achieving agreed technical goals.

Some commentators have argued that, despite the marked weaknesses of trade unionism, the 1980s saw progress towards a 'normalisation' of industrial relations and convergence with other European countries – notably through the spread of company-level bargaining, the acceptance of union presence at the workplace, and the consonance between the aims of some progressive, usually large, employers and modernising unions in the private sector (see Goetschy and Rozenblatt in 'Further reading'). However, major differences, especially in workplace industrial relations and industrial culture, remain between France and her neighbours.

Trade unions

Trade unions in France are general unions, with divisions – not absolutely rigid or consistent ones – along political and religious lines. There are five major, and essentially competing, trade union confederations in the private sector, each with a larger or smaller number of affiliated unions organised by industry or sector. Each also has a white-collar affiliate. In the 1970s there were efforts to reconcile differences between the communist – CGT – and more social democratic – CFDT – confederations during the period of Communist Party and Socialist Party co-operation. However, the break-up of the Union of the Left in 1977 ended this phase, and relations remained difficult throughout the 1980s. However, in February 1995 all five accepted an invitation from the national employers' confederation, the CNPF to engage in a series of national round-table discussions on major current employment issues (see below). Relations between the confederations are markedly more co-operative at workplace level than at branch or national level, as illustrated by the different initial positions of the CFDT on the one hand and the Force ouvrière (FO) on the other in the late 1995 strike over welfare reforms and public-sector employment.

Union confederations and their industrial affiliates play a role in collective bargaining at industry level (see below) but their strength at workplace level is patchy, and this has been crucial in reducing their overall influence as effective collective bargaining has increasingly been decentralised to company and plant level.

Estimates of the membership of the trade union confederations should be treated with caution, as there is no wholly reliable way of measuring their size. The confederations produce figures with considerable delay. However, in a move towards greater openness, in June 1995 the head of the CGT union (see below) admitted that his confederation's membership was, in fact, only 630,000, compared with the 780,000 publicly claimed as recently as mid-1994.

Although nominal union membership is low, and accounts for less than 10 per cent of the workforce, unions enjoy indirect and latent workforce support through elections to works committees and industrial tribunals. Union candidates, all told, account for some 90 per cent of the votes cast for employee representatives on industrial tribunals (*conseils de prud'hommes*) and 70 per cent of the votes cast for employee representatives on works committees – a decline in support for union nominations from the 80 per cent or so of the early 1980s. The largest single bloc of union votes in recent elections, some 25 per cent, went to the CGT, with the CFDT winning the second largest bloc. Non-aligned candidates receive about a quarter of the votes cast. Trade unions also enjoy the advantage of having preferential rights to nominate candidates as staff representatives at workplace level. (Works committee results in the 1993 elections are set out in Table 1.)

Confédération française démocratique du travail (CFDT)   The CFDT, which claimed 650,000 members in May 1995, is the largest union confederation of the five recognised by the government at national level. It was established in 1964 via a split from the Christian CFTC (see below), with the CFDT breaking its link with the Catholic tradition and adopting an explicitly socialist orientation after 1968. The union grew rapidly in the 1960s and 1970s, embodying many of the aspirations of the radicalised workers' movement to self-management but retaining a radical Christian tradition. Membership fell off in the 1970s, and the union adopted a more conventional trade union agenda after 1978. It is especially active in engineering, chemicals, the nationalised sector and certain white-collar sectors such as banking and teaching. It retains close links with the Socialist Party. In contrast to its principal 'rival', the CGT, the CFDT has a more even balance of members at all employee grades, including middle managers and specialists. It is one of the few unions, if not the only one, to have actually increased its membership, at least on the basis of its own figures. However, some confirmation can be seen in the results for works committees (see Table 1), where the CFDT has managed to cling on to its share of the vote since the mid-1980s. According to the union, this is mainly thanks to an intensive recruitment campaign started in the 1980s, taking into account the changing nature of unionism and putting more emphasis on participation and involving members, offering them special services, such as, for example, legal advice and strike pay (a modest daily sum). The CFDT has been taking an increasingly reformist rather than confrontational stance and did not officially support the all-out resistance in 1995 to change in the public sector.

Confédération général du travail (CGT)   The CGT claimed 630,000 members in June 1995, publicly correcting the figure of 780,000 it had claimed a year before. It is associated with the Communist Party of France (PCF), has tradition-ally maintained a militant stance in industrial affairs and continues to be rooted primarily in manufacturing industry, with heavy representation among skilled manual workers in general engineering, chemicals, mining, steel and the docks. Until *c*. 1980 it was the largest single trade union confederation. The CGT often refuses to sign collective agreements at national level, where until recently it has maintained its traditional political stance, but is willing to sign agreements at company level – quite frequently with the CFDT – and seeks representation on works committees and European works councils. However, goaded by the rela-tive success of the CFDT, and in response to the manifest crisis in trade union-ism, the confederation has been seeking to reposition itself by, for example, withdrawing from the World Federation of Trade Unions (and hence clearing the way for membership of the ETUC), participating in social dialogue at national level, and attending the CFDT's congress.

CGT–Force ouvrière (CGT-FO)   The FO was formed in 1948, when a minority group within the CGT rejected Marxism and established a separate organisation, in part at the instigation of the SIFO (the Section française de l'Internationale ouvrière), the predecessor of the social democratic PSI (Partie socialiste française). The FO regards free collective bargaining, rather than political activ-ity, as the principal method of advancing workers' interests and retains a broadly socialist orientation. It had 400,000 members in 1995, and is particularly strong in the public sector, commerce and finance; its role in administering the welfare state also caused it to oppose social policy changes, and it formed a bloc with the CGT in the public-sector strikes.

Confédération française des travailleurs chrétiens (CFTC)   The CFTC is the Christian trade union confederation. It had an estimated 120,000 members in 1995, mainly in health, teaching and engineering. It was established by the Christian minority in the 'old' CFTC when the CFDT was established in 1964.

Confédération générale des cadres (CGC)   The CGC is a union for *cadres* (engi-neers, executives, supervisors and technicians) and had an estimated 100,000 mem-bers in 1995. Its membership is strongest in engineering and chemicals.

Union density   Traditionally union density has never been high in France, and it has been steadily declining since the late 1970s – with traditionally well unionised sectors hard hit by a wave of corporate and economic restructuring. Only around 10 per cent of the overall workforce is estimated to be unionised, falling to 6 per cent in the private sector. Union representation and activity are virtually non-existent in small undertakings with fewer than 50 employees.

There are many reasons for the low level of union membership, rooted in the political and industrial orientation of the main unions, with emphasis on the creation of an activist *cadre* rather than a mass membership – with major personal and career implications for those who join. The large number of small firms, and a tradition of employer hostility to unions, have also contributed to the lack of recognition of unions as players in workplace industrial relations. The protection of employee rights by a written labour code, with its corollary of legislation rather than negotiation on substantive issues, reflects and compensates for weak union organisation. At the same time, it does little to highlight the need for independent collective representation.

Many employees, around half the workforce, are employed in small companies where there is no union representation and where the culture militates against individual membership. Furthermore, under the system of extending collective agreements across sectors, everybody benefits from an agreement, whether or not they belong to a trade union. The changing structure of the workforce has also resulted in lower union membership; in the 1980s the workforce became more skilled and educated, and the proportion of women in it rose. Traditional areas of unionisation such as heavy industry and shipbuilding shrank, to be replaced by an enlarged tertiary sector.

Rights of association   The freedom to join a trade union (*la liberté syndicale*) is a constitutional right and is also provided for in the Labour Code (article L411-5): 'All employees, regardless of sex, age and nationality, are free to join the trade union of their choice.' Membership of a trade union may not influence any recruitment or dismissal decision on the part of an employer, and questions about union membership must not be included on application forms. Employees also have the right not to join a union: there is therefore no legal basis for the closed shop. Under the law of 28 October 1982 trade unions are 'organisations with a particular legal status, grouping individuals in the same or a similar profession, having the sole object of defending the rights and material and moral interests of their members'. Trade unions are free to organise and meet as they wish. Unions may also set their own rules, but when they are set up they must lodge a copy of their articles with the local authority (the *mairie*).

Trade union representation   Trade unions are recognised in negotiation at national, industry and company level. At *national* level, trade union representatives sit on the National Collective Bargaining Board and the Social and Economic Council (see below); at industry level, at least one trade union must sign a collective agreement before it can be regarded as valid – and under some circumstances trade unions that have not signed have the power to veto the extension of the agreement to cover a whole sector.

Trade union representation in the workplace became formally entrenched following the events of May 1968 (the Grenelle agreement), and was initially used primarily to wrest from employers conditions better than those provided for in industry agreements, especially, and effectively, in large firms. Current arrangements are substantially determined by legislation dating from 1982, passed under the first Mitterrand presidency.

The 1982 legislation, the Auroux laws, set out to bolster the position of the trade unions at *company level* and to encourage company-based collective bargaining. Under the law, every nationally represented trade union, such as the CGT, CFDT, CGT-FO, CFTC, CGC or any other union, has the right to set up a trade union section (*section syndicale*) in a company, regardless of the company's size, if it can prove that it is adequately represented within the company. The law stipulates that trade union sections should 'ensure the representation of the material and moral interests of employees'. Trade union sections are normally set up at company rather than plant level, unless it can be shown that the plant is of a separate character from the company as a whole. Trade union sections may appoint a representative to the company works committee, but this is not obligatory.

Trade union delegates (*délégués syndicaux*) may be appointed only in companies with 50 or more employees, unless otherwise stipulated by collective agreement. Trade union delegates are appointed by the relevant trade union and not by the section within the company. The number of delegates appointed varies from one to five, according to the size of the workforce. There is no fixed mandate, and delegates must be over 18 years of age, have one year's seniority within the company and not be related to the employer. The presence of a trade union delegate in a company obliges the employer to bargain with him annually on pay, working time, training and the right of expression. However, the obligation is only to negotiate and not necessarily to reach agreement.

By law, trade union delegates should represent the standpoint of their union and its workplace members to the employer, but in practice they can intervene on all matters relating to the material or moral well-being of the employees, unionised or not.

Trade union delegates are entitled to time off for the purpose of carrying on union activities ranging from 10 to 20 hours a month, according to the size of the company. They also enjoy protection against dismissal during their term of office and for 12 months following the end of their mandate. Candidates for appointment as trade union delegates are protected against dismissal for six months following their candidacy.

Employers' organisations

The main national employers' organisation is the CNPF (*Conseil national du patronat français*), also known simply as the Patronat, which represents around 75 per cent of employers. The CNPF has a mandate to negotiate with trade unions on all matters concerning companies at multi-industry and national level. The CNPF does not bargain direct, except on national framework agreements, but does issue an annual statement on pay. This used to include a specific recommended increase but since 1986 has consisted of broader guidelines. National framework agreements concluded in recent years have covered technological change, flexible working time, working conditions, equality of opportunity in the workplace, and training.

Two employers' organisations represent small and medium-size companies: the CGPME (Confédération générale des petites et moyennes entreprises), which has been representing those with up to 500 employees since it broke away from the CNPF in 1948; and the SNPMI (Syndicat national du patronat moderne et indépendant). Employer associations at sectoral level are involved in the negotiation of minimum pay and conditions, and may issue pay recommendations for company-level bargaining. The SNPMI split from the CGPME in June 1977, and since then has pursued an independent strategy. Unlike all the other organisations listed above, it is not represented on the National Collective Bargaining Board (see below).

There is also a sectoral employers' organisation for each industry which is covered by a sectoral collective agreement. The two largest and most prominent are, in chemicals, the Union des industries chimiques (UIC) and in engineering the Union des industries métallurgiques et minières (UIMM). Bargaining on terms and conditions is carried out both nationally and regionally; in most industries, negotiations on pay are conducted by the regional sections of industry employer organisations and union confederations.

Consultation at national level

There is no institutionalised form of national tripartite negotiation. However, there is a tripartite forum, the National Collective Bargaining Board, which consists of representatives of the central employers' organisation, the trade union confederations and the government: its main task is to monitor legislation related to collective agreements and to decide on increases in SMIC, the minimum wage. Bipartite consultation does not take place through an institutional forum as such. Nevertheless, the main employers' organisation, the CNPF, and the main union confederations have met regularly at national level in recent years, and a new initiative on 'social dialogue' was set in train in February 1995.

National negotiations have generally resulted in a multi-industry agreement (*accord interprofessionel*) which is not itself legally binding but which serves as a framework within which enforceable collective and company agreements can be drawn up. These national agreements have also served as a forum for airing topics on which new legislation is planned, and agreements may precede a new law.

The Economic and Social Council (*Conseil économique et social*) is a research and advisory body which publishes reports on economic and social policy. Its members include employee organisations, business representatives, the professions and individuals engaged in social activities such as housing associations.

In February 1995 the newly elected leader of the CNPF employers' federation, Jean Gandois – widely seen as representing the interests of larger firms –

expressed a desire to 'revive the social dialogue' and convened a round-table meeting with the five major trade unions. It was agreed to focus debate on such pressing issues as unemployment, following the EU Essen summit, social protection and working time, and to tackle the integration of the young unemployed into the labour market. Subsequently negotiations between the CNPF and the trade unions were initiated, and working groups were set up on a variety of issues – in particular the question of encouraging job creation by lowering employer social charges on low-paying jobs. Union and employers' federation commentators alike have viewed these negotiations partly as a response to a recent increase in industrial unrest (see below) and partly as evidence that the two sides are eager to demonstrate their independence and autonomy *vis-à-vis* the state. The round-table talks are unprecedented in that all unions agreed to attend, possibly presaging a change in the pattern of industrial relations. However, it remains to be seen whether the habit of looking to the state to resolve industrial problems will be stifled entirely. Following the public-sector strikes in November/December 1995 there were further initiatives for a 'social summit' on employment issues; however, the Patronat declared itself unwilling to allow such a forum for bargaining on pay or cuts in working hours.

Workplace/enterprise employee representation

Employee representation (*représentation du personnel*) is determined largely by statutory provision requiring representative bodies to be directly elected by the whole workforce at establishment or company level. Trade union representation in the workplace is also provided for by law. Hence there is a dual system of employee representation – through statutory bodies, outlined below, and through trade unions. However, the proliferation of bodies with rights rooted in statute law, with occasionally overlapping functions and personnel, may create complex and often opaque relations at workplace level, assuming that the mandatory requirement to establish representation has been complied with at all. The extent to which elected bodies and trade union sections in the workplace complement each other varies considerably, and in practice depends crucially on the ability of trade unions (and of the individual confederations) at workplace level to make use of the full range of rights offered by the law. The proliferation of bodies can also overstretch employees who put themselves forward as candidates, and may explain some of the reluctance of individuals to stand for posts – one factor cited behind the low compliance with the law.

Statutory elected workplace representative bodies do not negotiate or conclude collective agreements: that is solely the prerogative of trade unions, including their workplace delegations. The type and size of representative organisation required depends on the size of the undertaking:

- In undertakings with 11 or more staff, representatives (*délégués du personnel*) must be elected.

- Undertakings with 50 or more employees are required also to establish works committees (*comités d'entreprise*).
- In smaller enterprises, with 50–199 employees, a change in the law introduced in 1993 allows both bodies to be combined into a unitary employee representative body (*délégation unique du personnel*).

Staff representatives or works committees may also be established in smaller companies than those specified by law under a collective agreement.

Staff representatives (*délégués du personnel*)

Under legislation dating from 1936, during the period of Popular Front government, there is a statutory requirement for staff representatives to be elected in public and private undertakings, under the current law provided they have at least 11 employees. (The legislation was initially promoted by the employers with the aim of weakening trade union representation.) Companies with fewer than 11 employees may do so by collective or house agreement. The responsibility of ensuring that the law is complied with rests upon the employer. The number of representatives to be elected depends on the size of the workforce, ranging from one representative and one deputy in companies of 11–25 employees to 10 representatives and 10 deputies in companies of 1,000 employees, with a further one representative and one deputy for every 250 employees further.

All employees are eligible to be elected as staff representatives provided they are not related to the employer, are above 18 years of age, speak French and have at least one year's service with the company. Staff representatives are elected on a two-year renewable mandate; since December 1993, following the 'five-year law' (*loi quinquennale*), the election of staff and works committee representatives is now to take place simultaneously every two years. Where the size of the workforce requires more than one representative, separate representatives are elected for blue- and white-collar workers, on the one hand, and for technicians and supervisory staff on the other. Election is by secret ballot on lists of candidates proposed in the first instance by the trade unions represented at the workplace. Should the number of votes cast be fewer than half the total number of eligible votes, a second round must be held within 15 days. Independent candidates are entitled to stand in the second round: however, the majority of staff representatives are trade union nominees.

The 1982 legislation also provides for the election of inter-company staff representatives in cases where several undertakings with fewer than 11 employees operate on a single site, provided there are at least 50 employees in all on the site and the undertakings are likely to experience common difficulties connected with the working environment. Such may be the case on a building site, a business park or a shopping centre. The local labour inspector may enforce the regulation if he deems it appropriate or if trade union sections request it.

The rights and duties of staff representatives Staff representatives are empowered to represent employees' interests to the employer, individually or collectively, on matters concerning the Labour Code, social protection, health and safety and any matters covered in a company or relevant industry collective agreement. In practice they function as the main agency representing the day-to-day concerns of employees to management. They may also raise individual or collective pay grievances but do not bargain on pay as such: wage negotiations are a matter for the employer and trade union representatives. Employees have the right to go direct to the employer with a grievance if they so wish.

Staff representatives must be consulted by the employer on matters relating to length of holidays and holiday planning, health and safety matters, redundancy, and any reassignment of employees to new duties following an industrial accident. Staff representatives also communicate with other employee representative bodies, where such exist. If no works committee exists in a company – that is, if the company employs fewer than 50 people, or no works committee has been set up for lack of candidates – staff representatives must be informed by the employer about such matters as the general economic and financial situation of the company, the introduction of new technology, changes in working conditions, and training.

Status of staff representatives Staff representatives have the right to 15 hours' a month paid time off in companies with at least 50 employees and to 10 hours in companies with fewer than 50 employees, in addition to time spent at meetings. The number of hours may be increased in exceptional circumstances. If there is no works committee, it is increased to 20 hours a month. Staff representatives have the right to meet the employer at least once a month and can request additional meetings, which the employer cannot refuse. If there is a works committee, as well as staff representatives, the employer must arrange separate meetings. Wilfully hindering the election or functioning of employee representation constitutes a criminal offence (*délit d'entrave*), punishable by fine and, in theory, a prison sentence of up to two months.

Staff representatives enjoy statutory protection against dismissal, except for gross misconduct (*faute grave*), during the whole of their term of office. Candidates for election also enjoy protection against dismissal for six months from the publication of the list of candidates. Former representatives are protected for six months following the expiry of their term.

Compliance with the law is patchy, especially in smaller enterprises, and may have deteriorated since the mid-1980s. According to a 1992 study carried out by the Institut supérieur du travail, only about 60–70 per cent of establishments in which employee representation is mandatory have actually set up the appropriate bodies. Evidence from a Labour Ministry survey, published in 1990, also found a fall-off in compliance with the law between the mid- and late 1980s. According to the survey, 52 per cent of companies which should have had representatives had none in 1985, the figure rising to 57 per cent by 1988.

Low rates of staff representation appear to be typical in small and medium-size companies (11–49 employees); larger companies show a much higher rate of compliance with the law. For example, 78 per cent of companies with 100–499 employees and 98 per cent of larger companies had staff representatives.

In the Ministry's view this may have been due in some measure to the general decline of trade union membership – partly owing to structural changes in the economy which have reduced the number of large well unionised plants – lowering the pool and motivation of potential candidates. The growing influence of 'new' industrial relations practices, in which direct contract between employees and managers has supplanted or overshadowed representative structures, is also felt to have played an important role in the 1980s.

It is also acknowledged that employers, especially in small and medium-sized enterprises, remain hostile to trade unions (often a mutually conditioned phenomenon rooted in the political character of the unions) and simply ignore the law.

Works committees (*comités d'entreprise*)

Under legislation passed in 1945, with amendments in 1975, 1982 and 1993, the election of works committees is a requirement in companies employing 50 or more staff and voluntary in smaller companies by collective agreement. Works committees can be elected at three different levels – the group (*groupe*), the undertaking (*entreprise*) or the establishment (*établissement*) – provided the company is large enough to employ more than 50 people at all three levels. In practice, however, as a Ministry of Labour survey conducted in the late 1980s discovered, some 25 per cent of companies employing 50–99 staff had no works committees in place. According to the Ministry survey, the reason was mainly a lack of candidates. It also found that works committees in small and medium-size companies do not carry out all their statutory functions, some concentrating wholly on the administration of cultural activities. Only 30 per cent of companies surveyed were keeping works committees fully informed, in line with the law, and 25 per cent of all committees received no information at all from the employer. Consultation took place regularly in only 10–15 per cent of committees.

Works committees are bipartite bodies and consist of the employer or the employer's representative, who chairs the committee, elected employee delegates and trade union representatives if there are any. Any nationally recognised trade union is entitled to elect a member to sit on the works committee as an observer. A maximum of four members of the works committee are also elected to sit on the administrative or supervisory board of the company, in order to represent employees' views. However, these representatives have no voting rights.

The number of elected members on a works committee varies according to the number of employees in the company, from three in companies with 50–74 employees to 15 in companies with over 10,000 employees. The number may be modified by collective agreement. Each member has an elected deputy. Council members are elected for a period of two years which is renewable. Eligibility is the same as for staff representatives. Table 1 sets out the results of the 1993 elections, indicating the support for the nominees of the main trade union confederations and independents, with a comparison of results from earlier years.

Table 1 *Works committee election results, 1981–93 (by percentage of votes)*

Confederation	1981	1985	1989	1993
CGT	32.0	25.9	23.0	19.6
CFDT	22.3	20.8	20.3	20.8
CFTC	2.9	4.7	4.4	4.9
CGT-FO	9.9	13.0	11.6	11.5
CFE-CGC	6.1	6.5	5.9	6.5
Other unions	4.1	5.1	5.6	6.3
Non-union	22.2	23.8	29.1	30.3

Source Liaisons Sociales, *Bref Social*, 9 March 1995

Works committees are funded by the employer, by a minimum annual amount equal to 0.2 per cent of the gross wage bill. Larger companies may devote a larger proportion of the payroll to financing works committees – in one study, as much as 5.5 per cent of the pay bill was encountered (see Lecher and Wendeling-Schröder, 1995). This money finances council members' travelling expenses, all relevant and necessary documentation and administration costs. The funds devoted to 'social and cultural activities' can be substantial (see below).

The rights of works committee members   Works committee members are entitled by law to 20 hours' a month paid time off in order to carry out committee duties. (Extra time off may be awarded under exceptional circumstances.) Under the law of 28 October 1982, on initial election works committees are entitled to attend an economic training course (*formation économique*) lasting up to a maximum of five days at a recognised institution. As with staff representatives, works committee members enjoy protection against dismissal during their period of office and for a period of six months thereafter. Candidates for election to the works committee are protected against dismissal for a period of three months following the announcement of the list of candidates.

Depending on the size of the undertaking, sub-committees must be created to deal with specific topics. For example, a vocational training committee (*commission de la formation professionelle*) must be set up in companies employing 200 or more staff, a housing committee (*commission d'information et d'aide au logement*) in companies employing 300 or more staff, and an economic committee (*commission économique*) in companies employing 1,000 or more staff.

The functions and powers of works committees   Works committees exist as an organ of collective representation for employees – but not of negotiation – on issues relating to pay, working conditions, training, and changes in working practices or working time. Compared, for example, with German works councils, their powers and status are limited. In the main, their rights are confined to consultation with and information from the employer. However, there are a limited number of matters on which the employer *must* obtain the agreement of the works committee. These are

- the hiring or dismissal of a company medical officer
- the conclusion of a profit-sharing agreement
- the institution of a four-day week or the reorganisation of individual working time
- the formation of a health and safety committee.

The greatest area of autonomy is in the field of company social and cultural activities, where works committees manage their own budget and may become involved in substantial projects, in some cases jointly managed and funded with works committees from other companies. Favoured areas of expenditure include holiday provision (including vacation homes) for employees: one observer has dubbed works committees 'the biggest travel agency in France'. This aspect has been seen as fostering an essentially consumerist attitude to works committees on the part of employees, rather than seeing them as representing broader employee interests in the workplace.

Works committees cannot directly affect management decision-making through full rights to co-determination, although it is possible that they may influence policy decisions in areas such as training, and in cases of redundancies (see below).

Works committees must be *consulted* by the employer before action can be taken on a number of issues, including changes in the structure of the workforce, working time, working conditions, training, mergers and acquisitions, the introduction of new technology, changes in maximum overtime, the implementation of short-time working, dismissals and redundancies.

Works committees must be *informed* by the employer on matters such as the economic situation of the company, minimum and actual rates of pay, the structure of the workforce – including the number of part-timers, disabled employees and those on temporary contracts – annual overtime provisions, improvements in production methods and sabbatical or other leave.

Works committees are also *responsible* for organising company social and cultural activities and managing the budget for that purpose, the budget being based on expenses incurred in the three previous years.

Meetings between the works committee and the employer are held once a month, or twice a month if the majority of works committee members prefer. Under the 1994 Five Year Employment Plan the number of meetings of the works committee in companies with under 150 staff is reduced from once a month to once every other month, although a second meeting can be held if the majority of members demand it. Employers who refuse to meet the works committee risk being found to have wilfully hindered the functioning of employee representation and may be subject to penalties.

In the event of *collective redundancy* the works committee has a legal right to detailed prior information on a proposal, and a right to one or two special meetings with the employer. The time which may elapse between these meetings was extended by the collective dismissal legislation of 2 August 1989. Works committees have the right to call in an expert of their choice to help assess the information supplied by the company. Works committees may also give their views on a company's social compensation (redundancy) plan: any company employing 50 or more staff must draw up such a plan, specifying measures to be taken to reduce the impact of economic dismissals. Under the 1989 legislation, works committees must be informed each year not only of employment movements over the past 12 months but also of forecasts for the coming year, steps to be taken to prevent redundancies, and training contracts available, particularly for older and vulnerable workers.

Under the 1994 Five Year Employment Plan information procedures have been simplified in companies with up to 300 staff. Information previously supplied by the company to workplace representatives, either in writing or verbally throughout the year, may now be replaced by a single annual written report. Topics to be covered by the report include

- the financial situation of the company and forecasts for the coming year
- workforce numbers
- types of contract
- part-time working
- atypical working
- the situation of male and female workers in the company.

Employers, or their representatives, now have the right, if they so choose, to be accompanied by two colleagues at works committee meetings.

Unitary employee representation (*délégation unique du personnel*)

The 1994 Five Year Employment Plan takes some account of the frequent criticism that employee representation arrangements are over-complex, especially in small and medium-sized enterprises. Under the plan, in companies or establishments of 50–199 staff, employers may now merge the functions of staff representatives (*délégués du personnel*, mandatory in companies of 11 or more employees) and the works committee (*comité d'entreprise*, mandatory in companies of 50 or more employees) into a unitary body (*délégation unique du personnel*). In that case the number of staff representatives would be increased, according to the size of the company, from three in companies with 50–74 staff to eight in companies with 175–199 staff. These representatives are each allowed 20 hours paid time off a month to carry out their duties. This provision is optional and is at the discretion of the employer.

According to official estimates the new arrangements could affect a substantial number of enterprises – up to 60 per cent of those required by law to have a works committee. The first elections under the proposals were held in 1994, when some 1,200 companies chose to adopt this approach. The results, set out in Table 2, give some indication of trade union support in smaller enterprises. Compared with the results for industrial tribunals and works committees (see Table 1), trade unions are much more weakly represented in small firms, with non-union candidates holding the majority of places in firms with fewer than 99 employees. (The fact that some workplaces are indicated as having 200+ employees is attributable to part-timers, temporary workers and workers on fixed-term contracts who are included in the overall head count but with a value of less than 1.)

Table 2 *Election results for unitary employee representation (as percentage of total votes)*

Workforce	CGT	CFDT	CFTC	CGT-FO	CGC	Other union	Non-union
Under 50	11.4	6.1	2.2	4.4	0.5	7.6	67.7
50–99	12.5	10.2	2.2	4.4	1.4	3.7	65.5
100–49	10.9	18.6	5.7	8.4	2.4	5.2	48.8
150–99	10.4	15.0	4.6	10.3	3.2	6.6	49.8
200+	13.4	8.4	0.0	0.0	0.0	0.0	78.3
Total	11.6	13.2	3.6	6.4	1.9	4.7	58.5

Source DARES, *Premières informations*, 21 April 1995

Employee 'rights of expression'

The law of 4 August 1982 (one of the Auroux laws, so named after the then Labour Minister), amended on 3 January 1986, recognises a general right on the part of all employees in the public and private sectors to express their views (*droit d'expression*) concerning the content, conditions and organisation of work. Individual employees may go straight to members of management with an opinion or problem, without having to go through the usual employee representation channels. However, these rights are essentially collective, and the legislation deliberately allows a great deal of scope for interpretation by employers' and employees' organisations. It stipulates that agreements on employees' rights of expression should be concluded between employers and representative trade unions if the company employs 50 or more staff and has a trade union delegate, or if it has fewer than 50 staff but has a trade union delegate by collective agreement.

Any such agreement should contain information concerning measures to be taken to ensure freedom of expression within the company and should set out the level, frequency and duration of self-expression meetings. All meetings and consultation should take place in the workplace and during paid working hours. Where no agreement has been concluded the employer must consult staff representatives at least once a year on the general subject of the right of expression. If an agreement does exist, employers should appraise the operation of the provisions with the trade unions once every three years.

A Ministry of Labour report published in the mid-1980s showed that such agreements covered employees in 45 per cent of eligible companies, with the majority of agreements providing for meetings in the context of a particular unit, such as a department. In 1989 446 agreements on the right of expression were signed, compared with 194 in 1988.

However, some studies question the success of such agreements and self-expression groups. An ILO study (see Delamotte, 1988) indicated that such groups may founder if not given a specific and relevant brief. The study found that quality circles, which expanded in the mid-1980s, tended to be more favoured by employees and management alike as they set out to tackle specific problems, with the outcome often directly affecting the individual's job, and were well supported by managements. Union representatives often remained unconvinced about expression groups, and this allowed such groups to be used more readily as a means of management communication than for true dialogue.

Health and safety committees (*comités d'hygiène, de securité et des conditions de travail*)

Under legislation passed in December 1982 health and safety committees must be set up in companies employing 50 or more staff. The committees must consist of the employer, or the employer's representative, and an employee delegation, the size of which will depend on the size of the company and which may range from three in companies with up to 199 employees to nine in companies with 1,500 or more employees. A proportion of the employee delegation must consist of supervisors (*agents de maîtrise*) or managers (*cadres*). All employees are eligible to sit on the health and safety committee; the term of office is two years, renewable.

Health and safety committees are enjoined to protect the health and safety of all employees at the place of work, to oversee and improve working conditions and to ensure that legal provisions are complied with. The committee has a right to consultation and information but has no funds of its own and cannot make decisions directly binding on the undertaking. Committees must be consulted before any decision is made regarding significant changes in health and safety at work, changes in work stations, changes in methods of production, or any other matters affecting the health and safety of employees. Committees are entitled to appoint an expert to examine any situation it deems to pose a serious risk. Committees are also empowered to carry out their own regular inspections of the workplace. In the event of disagreement between the employer and the committee the matter may be taken to the high court (*tribunal de grande instance*).

Employers must present the committee with a written report, at least once a year, on the general health and safety situation of the company, and on current measures, or steps that have been taken during the previous year, to improve health and safety in the workplace. The committee will then give its response to the report and can propose priorities in the order of tasks to be undertaken. Members of health and safety committees must treat the information disclosed to them by the employer with discretion and must respect the confidentiality of information regarding production processes.

Health and safety committee members in companies with 300 or more employees are entitled to attend an initial training course lasting up to five days. Members are also entitled to time off of two to 20 hours a month, depending on the size of the company. Members are entitled to the same protection against dismissal as members of works committees.

Employee participation at board level

There is no statutory provision for employee representation at board level. However, under the decree of 21 October 1986 companies may provide for a number of employee representatives to sit on the board of management (*conseil d'administration*) which should not exceed four (or five in a quoted company) or a number equal to a third of the number of board members. The maximum period of office is six years, renewable.

Since 1994, where the employees of a company own more than 5 per cent of the capital – acquired through the distribution of shares under capital participation schemes – there is provision in the law for an extraordinary shareholders' meeting to be held to change the articles of association to allow up to two employees to join the board.

Implementation of the EU works council directive

Employers' organisations were very active during 1993/94 in EU-level negotiations on the works council directive. With the directive in force, the central employers' organisation has largely handed the matter over to individual companies to decide how they will take the issue on board. Some degree of co-ordination is taking place at branch federation level only.

National legislation, due to be implemented by September 1996, seems likely to offer a mechanism resembling group councils (*comités de groupe*). Action on legislation is expected to be taken in spring 1996.

In France some 250 companies are expected to be affected by the directive and at the time of writing some 18 have already made moves to establish voluntary agreements under the directive prior to national implementation in September 1996. Large undertakings, such as Bull or Saint-Gobain, in the public sector, were pioneers in establishing European consultative bodies in the mid-1980s. However, there remain a substantial number of companies which are choosing not to pre-empt the imposition of the directive but which prefer to wait and observe the experiences of other undertakings.

Collective bargaining

Collective bargaining, promoted in the pre-war period by legislation dating from the Popular Front government of 1936, did not really begin to take root until the law of 11 February 1950 established the present system. French employers have traditionally been very unwilling to give up their unilateral control over wages, and collective bargaining – principally at industry level – began to gain ground only in the 1960s. Although an estimated 75 per cent of private-sector employees are covered by collective agreement, industry-level agreements set only a minimum provision, which most employers exceed.

A number of amendments have been made to the framework law on collective agreements since 1950. There are two in particular, both intended to strengthen the process of collective bargaining, especially at workplace level. The law of 13 July 1971, introduced in the wake of the 1968 upsurge in industrial militancy, recognised in principle the right of workers to negotiate over the entire range of their conditions, assimilated plant and company-level negotiations, and widened the scope of agreements which could be 'extended' (that is, made binding on non-signatory employers). The law of 14 November 1982 – the third Auroux law – set out to strengthen collective bargaining, principally at company and plant level, where there is now a legal duty to negotiate (though not to reach agreement) annually on wages, working time and work organisation if there is at least one trade union delegation present.

This has considerably changed the style of bargaining, which had typically used to take place only as the sequel to a dispute. The parties now look to inflation predictions rather than simply seeking to catch up with previous inflation, and explicit consideration is given to issues of competitiveness, at industry as well as company level. At the same time there has been drastic decentralisation of bargaining to individual workplaces, where union influence tends to be weak, with a corresponding lowering of the status and importance of industry-level agreements, over which unions traditionally had greater influence.

A collective agreement at industry level normally determines *minimum* wage rates and basic conditions, usually within an industry at regional level, and – unless 'extended' by the Ministry of Labour (see below) – it binds only those companies whose representatives have signed (though it is applied to all employees in such companies, whether or not they are members of a signatory union). Actual pay rates (*salaires effectifs*) are decided at company level and by law must not be lower than the minima agreed at sectoral level. These rates comprise all elements of pay, including individual increases.

Figures from the Ministry of Labour show that, after increases in the late 1980s, the number of company agreements declined slightly during the recession years of 1992 and 1993. An estimated fifth of employees are covered by a company or workplace agreement (supplementing and industry agreement), compared with some 75–85 per cent covered by industry agreements. Nevertheless, overall company bargaining has increased markedly since the early 1980s.

The emphasis on company bargaining, in terms of the number of agreements and their weight in setting terms and conditions, is partly the result of a conscious effort by employers to shift the locus of pay determination, detach pay increases from inflation and link them more closely to profitability and individual performance, leading – during periods of economic expansion – to a widening gap between industry minima and actual salaries paid at company level: it is now of the order of 20–30 per cent. In fact by 1990 some 80 per cent of sectoral agreements contained minimum rates below the level of the national minimum wage, SMIC – a situation remedied fairly rapidly following intervention by the Prime Minister, Michel Rocard. Should an agreement include a rate below SMIC, employees automatically receive the statutory minimum.

Government intervention in pay bargaining

Since the mid-1970s successive governments have sought to influence private-sector pay determination. For the most part their efforts have normally been confined to the direct or indirect manipulation of SMIC, exhortations to voluntary restraint (backed up by the *franc fort* policy of a strong currency and high interest rates to dampen inflation and inflationary expectations) and the use of the public sector – including nationalised trading concerns – as an exemplar.

Other forms of intervention, such as wage-fixing, are forbidden under the law on collective agreements dated 11 February 1950. However, following an unsuccessful appeal to the social partners to keep wage rises down in November 1981, Jacques Delors, then Finance Minister, imposed a statutory pay and price freeze in June 1982 as part of the government's austerity programme (and shortly after the second successive devaluation of the franc within the ERM). The policy ran from 11 June until 31 December 1982.

Levels of bargaining

A collective agreement is defined under the Labour Code as an agreement relating to conditions of work and social guarantees concluded between employers and representative trade unions. The code adds that such agreements may be concluded at four levels: national, regional, local and company or workplace level. The law offers no definition of 'regional' or 'local', leaving it to the negotiating parties to establish territorial limits.

A *convention collective* is a collective agreement dealing with the totality of terms and conditions; an *accord collectif* deals with a single issue, such as pay or hours.

Collective agreements are most common at industry level and usually improve upon the statutory position in matters such as holiday entitlement, time off and severance payments.

National level   National multi-industry (*interprofessionel*) agreements are occasionally negotiated between the CNPF and the union confederations. The most recent national agreements cover

- technological change, signed in September 1988 by the CNPF, and the unions CFDT, CGC and CFTC
- flexible working time, signed on 21 March 1989 by the CNPF and CGPME and the unions CFE-CGC and CFDT
- working conditions, signed on 20 October 1989 by the CNPF and the unions CFTC, CFE-CGC, CGT-FO and CFDT
- sex discrimination, signed on 23 November 1989 by the CNPF and the unions CFDT, FO and CGC
- apprenticeships, signed on 8 January 1992
- training, signed on 5 July 1994.

There are no national multi-industry agreements on pay.

Industry level   The prime vehicle for setting agreed minimum rates in France is the industry-level agreement: it is estimated that some 85 per cent of employees are covered by around 400 such agreements. Some agreements set pay for all employees, including up to middle management, whereas others may have separate arrangements for managers.

The Auroux law of 14 November 1982 lays down that employers' associations and unions which have signed such industry-level agreements must meet at least once a year to negotiate on pay, and at least once every five years to determine whether the job grading structure (*grille de classification*) used in agreements needs revision. However, there is no obligation to make any alterations, and some grading systems still date from the 1970s. Wage negotiations must also include an examination of the economic and employment situation of the sector, and employers must supply the unions with relevant information at least 15 days before negotiations begin.

The CNPF employers' organisation usually issues an annual pay recommendation. In keeping with practice over the last few years, recommendations for 1995 did not include specific figures. This reflects the growing emphasis on the performance of the company and the individual (especially managerial staff) in determining pay. In its 1995 statement the CNPF argued that employment considerations should figure in negotiations but that it would be mistaken to argue that pay growth should be suppressed in every situation for the theoretical possibility of creating more jobs.

Regional/*département*/district   The law does not define these levels but leaves the negotiating partners to agree the meaning in each case. A common form of agreement is one which covers a sector or industry at regional, departmental or local level by adapting a national agreement to the lower level.

Company and workplace level   Whereas industry-level bargaining sets a floor for pay levels, actual rates of pay (*salaires effectifs*) are determined, either by negotiation or by unilateral management decision, at company level. Rates may not be lower than the sectorally agreed minima set out in the collective agreement covering the company, and are typically 10–30 per cent above sectorally agreed minima, depending on the company's size, its ownership, the skills profile of the workforce, and the sector it is in. Levels of pay are also affected by skill shortages in particular sectors or specialisms.

Collective bargaining at company and plant level remains fairly weak, despite the marked shift in pay setting to that level. Indeed, many employers claim that engaging in company-level negotiations has little effect on their eventual decision regarding pay increases. The law of 14 November 1982 puts employers under an annual obligation to negotiate on pay, working time and work organisation in companies where there is at least one union delegation – if not to come to a negotiated conclusion. Should an employer fail to open negotiations for more than 12 months, a union can now demand them, in which case talks must begin within two weeks. There is no obligation to increase actual pay in line with minimum pay, allowing for increases in agreed minima to be offset against actual rates.

Company agreements tend to be concentrated among large firms. Around 70 per cent of employees covered by company agreements work in undertakings with 1,000 or more employees.

Duration and validity of agreements   At both industry and company level, pay agreements are normally signed for one year. Increases are commonly staged in two or three separate rises throughout the year. The sectoral agreement in the chemical industry is an exception, as it provided for staged increases over a period of three years from 1992. Most agreements, at industry or company level, include reopener clauses. Agreements tend not to contain an automatic mechanism for pay increases, as indexation is prohibited by law in France.

In order to be valid, an agreement need be signed only by one nationally representative union along with the individual employer or an employers' organisation. However, under the 1982 legislation a union may revoke certain clauses of an agreement within one week of signing it provided the union obtained at least 50 per cent of the total potential number of eligible votes in the most recent elections to the company's works committee.

Employees are covered by collective agreements in a variety of different ways. In some industries, integrated pay scales cover all employees from unskilled blue-collar to middle manager; in others, separate agreements apply to blue-collar workers, white-collar staff, supervisory staff, engineers and managers. For example, the agreement in the chemical industry covers managers up to middle management level, while the national agreement in general engineering has a separate agreement for technical specialists and managers. Senior managers, however, fall outside the scope of collective agreements and their pay is determined by individual contract.

Although many collective agreements appear to be single-status, there are in fact a number of invisible divides which render movement between categories difficult. This was recognised by the engineering sector when, in response to a shortage of engineers, an extra grade was added to the top of the technical and supervisory scale. The aim was to facilitate the move up to engineer/manager (*ingénieur-cadre*), with training introduced for the purpose.

The public sector

Pay in the public sector is negotiated annually between the government and civil service and other public-sector unions. Negotiations usually take place at the end of the year or early the following year. They are shaped by government inflation predictions, a recommendation issued by the Prime Minister (*lettre de cadrage*), and are also linked with budget expenditure and fiscal policy for the year. Reopener clauses are common and usually provide for further negotiations in September in the event of official economic forecasts proving inaccurate; government forecasts are often optimistic. Pressure to meet economic convergence criteria to allow France to qualify to be part of the proposed single currency led to a major clash over public-sector pay and conditions in autumn 1995, triggering the biggest industrial unrest since May 1968.

The pay round

The prelude to the annual pay bargaining round starts in the autumn with employer recommendations and official forecasts. The CNPF national employers' organisation issues a pay recommendation each year. Until 1986 it took the form of definite figure. Since then the CNPF has issued more general guidelines in order to allow sectors and companies greater scope to award pay increases according to their individual situation and the situation of the economy and the business climate generally. Some of the larger employers' organisations, such as the UIMM, also issue recommendations around this time. As with the CNPF, and for the same reasons, their recommended blue- and white-collar minimum rate increases, which are negotiated regionally, have not specified a figure since 1986. In practice this means that small companies feel freer to set rates in line with their own needs and ability to pay, whereas previously they adhered closely to the UIMM recommendation. Larger companies, such as Peugeot, usually set their own rates anyway, sometimes before the recommendation is officially issued.

Pay recommendations, and expectations, are influenced by a number of economic forecasts issued by a variety of independent economic forecasting organisations in addition to that of the government. The most important are the OFCE

(Observatoire français du commerce extérieur), the BIPE (Bureau d'informations et de prévisions économiques) and the national statistical office, INSEE (Institut national de la statistique et des études économiques). These institutions issue forecasts twice a year and tend in general to be less optimistic about the economic prospects than the government.

Although there is no legal stipulation as to when pay negotiations should take place, most settlements, whether at company or industry level, are concluded between November and March. Negotiations tend not to have a fixed anniversary date because the statutory requirement to negotiate does not stipulate talks precisely every 12 months. Pay agreements do not include a fixed expiry date and so frequently overrun, although unions have the right to request the reopening of talks twelve months after the conclusion of the agreement.

No one industry or company settlement has emerged as the lead settlement and there is a marked, and increasing, emphasis on each industry or company setting rates according to its individual situation. This has been particularly the case since the CNPF and UIMM stopped making a precise pay recommendation and it is what was intended by that move. However, settlements in the larger companies in major industrial sectors, such as Renault, usually at the end of the year, are seen as important. Smaller companies tend to look at what the larger companies are awarding but large company settlements generally have no direct influence on the rest of the sector except where companies are in direct competition for staff.

Recent private-sector bargaining

During 1993 and 1994 there was a continuation of the trend towards bargaining on non-pay issues, accentuated by the recession. Negotiated reductions in working hours, with government support to maintain incomes, in an effort to conserve and create jobs, marked a novel trend during the 1992/93 recession: the CFDT was particularly active in this area. Although not of great quantitative significance set against the unemployment total, such arrangements had a local impact, as well as helping the unions to maintain a positive profile during a difficult phase.

The economic recovery saw some revival in pay militancy, with instances of industrial action in some larger enterprises and in the public sector in spring 1995. However, pay growth barely remained above inflation in 1994/95, and some industry-level deals at less than the going rate of inflation were imposed unilaterally during the 1994 pay round. At company level, increases were just above inflation in the 1995 round as companies emerged from recession into recovery.

Since 1990 there has been further movement away from branch negotiations to negotiations at company level. This trend arose with economic recovery in 1990 and then deepened with the onset of recession in 1992, but has continued into the recovery.

One strategy advocated within the union movement to resolve the problem of the weakness of company-level bargaining would be to enlarge the range and the mandate of the people who are entitled to negotiate, for example by making it possible for an employee to get a mandate to negotiate from a signatory union. Another option, advocated by the employers but resisted by the trade unions, would be to amend the law and make negotiations directly accessible without the need for a union delegation. The Ministry, however, is reluctant to agree to this as it could put independent bargaining at risk and shift the balance of power further towards employers.

Although the rapid move towards the individualisation of pay in the 1980s was not without problems, especially the complexity of managing reward and the possibility of weakening teamwork, many employers – including the CNPF – remain attracted and committed to greater flexibility, particularly in times of economic uncertainty.

In the past, major cuts in working hours – notably the introduction of a 39 hour week – were achieved via legislation. However, moves to the 35 hour week in Germany and elsewhere, combined with persistently high unemployment, have raised the possibility of further working time cuts as a matter for collective bargaining: at its 1995 congress the CFDT indicated that this issue could figure in future negotiations. However, employers' organisations oppose a uniform reduction and prefer to allow individual employers more flexibility on the issue.

Part of the on-going debate is the contentious question of negotiated trade-offs of pay increases in return for job creation. These played a major symbolic role in negotiations during 1993, especially for the CFDT, but their overall economic significance is difficult to quantify.

Non-wage labour costs have also figured in discussions on employment creation, especially in view of the high level of employers' social insurance contributions in France – over 40 per cent. However, the scope for negotiated alterations remains limited, as the vast bulk of employer payments go to state-administered funds.

Even though the on-going round-table negotiations seem to reflect a degree of consensus on issues such as the need to reduce unemployment and youth unemployment in particular, it is widely accepted that employers are in a stronger position to influence which route will be taken. To quote one union observer, 'In reality the state decides and the social partners manage.'

Proposals for reform of bargaining include

- reviewing existing branch definitions. The grouping of undertakings with similar activities into branches is becoming increasingly difficult, given the existence of large conglomerates and rapid changes in products.
- the CFDT union demand for measures to privilege branch negotiations in order to put a brake on decentralisation to company level. The union also favours broadening the right to oppose agreements. The idea is unlikely to be popular with employers, as the current system gives them more control in choosing which union to conclude agreements with.

Validity and duration of agreements

An agreement – at whatever level – becomes binding once it has been signed by one or more unions recognised by the government as representative (currently the CGT, CFDT, FO, CFTC and CGC) and by an employers' organisation or an individual employer. The signature of even one minority union may therefore validate an agreement. The CGT is noted for its traditional reluctance to sign industry-level collective agreements.

The law of 14 November 1982 stipulates that, under restricted circumstances, a union may veto certain clauses of a company – or plant-level – agreement, provided that it obtained at least 50 per cent of the total potential eligible number of votes (not of votes actually cast) in the most recent elections to the company's works committee and that it does so within a week of the agreement being signed. These conditions were tightened up further by amendments introduced in late 1992 which set time limits on challenging proposed changes of eight days at company level and 15 days at industry level. In practice, however, unions are rarely able to meet the conditions required to challenge an agreement.

Procedures and notice periods for revoking an agreement are laid down in the agreements themselves, but where an agreement is revoked by only one of several signatories it remains valid for the other parties. On the other hand, where all employer signatories or all union signatories wish to revoke it, new negotiations must be held within three months.

Should an employer leave an employers' association, the employer will continue to be bound by any provisions agreed by the association during the period of the employer's membership.

Most collective agreements cover a 12 month period and are automatically renewed, unless notice is given to terminate. The vast majority of bargaining at industry and company level takes place between December and March each year.

'Extension' of collective agreements

Under powers granted by statute dating from 1936 the Ministry of Labour may, by decree (*arrêté*), 'extend' the provisions of a collective agreement to non-signatory companies. Either industry-wide agreements or multi-industry agreements at national/regional level may be extended in this way. Company agreements may not be extended. Such extension may take one of two forms:

- The agreement may be extended to all companies – whether signatory or not within the same sector and geographical area (*procédure d'extension*).
- The agreement may be extended to all companies in the same sector but in another geographical area (in cases where attempts to sign an agreement have persistently failed) or to other job classifications where it is considered necessary (*procédure d'élargissement*).

The Ministry of Labour requires a number of conditions to be met before an agreement may be extended. A multi-industry or industry agreement, for example, must provide for recognition of employee and union rights, recognition of vocational qualifications for the purposes of job classification, and conciliation procedures in the event of industrial disputes.

In all cases, extension can be decreed only after consultation with the National Collective Bargaining Board. Any organisation which has not signed the agreement in question may veto its extension.

Industrial conflict: conciliation, mediation and arbitration

All private-sector employees and most public-sector employees, except those in the police, prison or security services, have a constitutionally guaranteed right to strike, understood principally as an individual, rather than collective, right. Apart from these provisions, industrial action is not generally subject to statutory regulation, and case law plays a major role in determining whether actions are lawful.

Lawful and unlawful action

A strike is defined as entailing a total stoppage of work. Strikes are lawful only if conducted in pursuit of industrial demands (*fondée sur des revendications professionnelles*). Employees are required to put their demands to the employer before taking action but they are not obliged to wait for a response or give notice, except in the public services. There is no requirement to hold a ballot before embarking on a strike. According to a ruling of the Supreme Court (the Cour de cassation), handed down in July 1995, collective agreements may not seek to constrain the individual employee's right to strike – for example, by imposing mandatory periods of advance notice.

Strikes undertaken from political motives are not legal unless directed against the government's social and economic policy; most sympathy strikes (*grèves de solidarité*) are also illegal unless they are in support of demands deemed to be of direct relevance to the striking employees, either by virtue of membership of the same organisation or in pursuit of broader objectives. Sympathy action over a sectoral collective agreement would generally be legal. Rolling strikes (*grèves tournantes*) are forbidden in the public sector but have been recognised by the courts as generally legal in the private sector unless the motive is deemed to be to disrupt production seriously or to endanger the existence of the company.

Go-slows, or 'irritation strikes' (*grèves perlées*) are not considered as strikes under the definition of a total stoppage of work, and the courts have viewed them as a failure to meet the employee's obligations. Unannounced and repeated short stoppages (*débrayages inopinés et répétés*) are deemed legal as long as the motive is not to harm or disrupt the company. Sit-ins (*grèves avec occupation des locaux de travail*) are generally deemed illegal unless the action does not hinder the running of the company. Wildcat strikes (*grèves sauvages*) are deemed legal in that they are total stoppages of work and employees are under no legal duty to give notice of strike action or go through formal union procedures: employees in the private sector do not have to give notice before taking indus- trial action, nor are they obliged by law to wait for the outcome of conciliation or organise a ballot.

Public-sector employees must give five days' notice before taking industrial action. In certain industries, such as television, broadcasting and air traffic con- trol, a skeleton service must be maintained.

The incidence and pattern of strikes

French unions do not usually grant strike pay and disputes tend to consist of short stoppages: one result is that France loses comparatively few working days to industrial conflicts. In 1993 a total of 533,100 days were lost to strikes, according to the Ministry of Labour. This represents an increase of 8.7 per cent on 1992 and marks the end of a downward trend in days lost to industrial action recorded since 1988. According to comparative figures produced by the UK Department of Employment, France lost an average of 30 days per thousand employees per year to industrial action in the period 1989–93, compared with 70 in the United Kingdom, 20 in Germany, and some 250 in Italy.

Strikes are predominantly organised – or resorted to spontaneously – at plant or company level. Despite the extensive coverage of the workforce by regionally based industry agreements, organised strikes affecting a whole region are almost unknown.

In line with the individual nature of the right to strike, strikes are seen as a rapid and immediate response to stalled negotiations, often taking place without formal trade union support or a ballot. Although this makes private-sector indus- trial action a spontaneous and short-lived phenomenon, the lack of union answer- ability has, on occasion, made it difficult to persuade small groups of determined employees to abandon strike action, despite a general lack of support from the rest of a firm's workforce. The strong role of the state in economic and social organisation has also generated the potential for politically directed industrial action, seen most dramatically in May 1968 but most recently in the strikes of late 1995, triggered by government efforts to reduce social spending and some established conditions of public-sector employees. Trade unions also continue to be most effective at national level and in the public sector.

Lockouts

Lockouts are generally held by case law to be illegal, and an employer might be liable to pay employees for any period during which they were locked out. Lockouts are not permitted as a response to a lawful strike. However, they have been ruled legal under certain circumstances, such as where a strike has caused a total breakdown in the functioning of the company (a case of 25 February 1988) or threatened the safety of staff or other persons and property (a case of 7 November 1990), or as a response to other forms of industrial action which do not enjoy legal protection.

Consequences of industrial action

Under statute law the act of going on strike does not constitute a breach of contract and since 1985 employees have had the right to be reinstated if they are found to have been unfairly dismissed for striking. Employers are under no obligation to pay employees for the period during which they are out on strike. However, they must carry on paying those not on strike even if their work is disrupted by the strikers. Employers may be relieved of this obligation if it is deemed impossible to offer employees work, for example if machines are not running or if the employer has applied for an injunction to remove pickets or workers engaged in a sit-in.

Employees who have damaged stock, assaulted supervisors or threatened other employees during the course of a strike are liable to summary dismissal for flagrant misconduct. Strikers participating in illegal strikes may also be liable to summary dismissal for flagrant misconduct.

If the majority of the workforce vote to return to work, a minority may continue to strike as long as they put new demands to the employer, assuming that the employer has met the original demands.

Conflict resolution

In law there are three complementary procedures for settling disputes: conciliation, mediation and arbitration.

Many collective agreements set out conciliation procedures which must be adhered to before strike action can be taken. If no such provision exists, parties to a dispute may go before a regional or national conciliation committee (*commission régionale/nationale de conciliation*). This procedure is voluntary, but if conciliation procedures are initiated both parties are obliged to appear in person. Conciliation will lead to either agreement or failure, in which case the matter can be taken either to mediation or straight to arbitration.

Should conciliation fail, the dispute may go to statutory mediation. This may occur at the parties' own initiative or if either the chair of the conciliation committee or the Minister of Labour requests it. Having brought the parties together in an attempt at conciliation, the mediator has one month in which to submit his/her own proposals, which, if accepted, become the terms of a new agreement. The recommendation is not binding and the parties are entitled to reject it within one week, giving their reasons for doing so. Should this happen, the mediator must inform the Ministry of Labour within 48 hours: the Ministry then registers a failure to agree and publishes all the relevant documents on the case within three months.

Arbitration mechanisms may be provided for in a collective agreement but, if not, a matter which has not been resolved at either conciliation or mediation level may be taken to arbitration if both parties wish. The arbitrator, who is chosen jointly by the parties in dispute, may rule both on the interpretation of the law or the collective agreements still in force and on pay and conditions where these are not subject to the law or collective agreement. The arbitrator must give reasons for the award, which may be contested by the parties only in the high arbitration court (*cour supérieure d'arbitrage*) and then only for alleged infractions of the arbitrator's powers or the relevant laws.

Organisations

The Ministry of Labour (Ministère du travail, de l'emploi et de la formation professionnelle)
127 rue de Grenelle
75700 Paris
Tel. + 33 1 40 56 60 00
Fax + 33 1 40 56 67 24

Agence nationale pour l'emploi (state employment agency)
13 rue Galilei
93198 Noisy-le-Grand
Tel. + 33 1 49 31 74 00
Fax + 33 1 43 05 67 96

Confédération générale du travail (CGT)
263 rue de Paris
93515 Montreuil
Tel. + 33 1 48 51 80 00

CGT–Force ouvrière (CGT-FO)
198 avenue du Maine
75014 Paris
Tel. + 33 1 45 39 22 03

Confédération française démocratique du travail (CFDT)
4 boulevard de la Villette
75955 Paris Cédex 19
Tel. + 33 1 42 03 80 00

Confédération française des travailleurs chrétiens (CFTC)
13 rue des Ecluses-Saint Martin
75010 Paris
Tel. + 33 1 42 05 79 66

Confédération générale des cadres (CGC)
30 rue de Gramont
75002 Paris
Tel. + 33 1 42 61 81 76

Conseil national du patronat français (CNPF)
31 rue Pierre 1er de Serbie
75016 Paris
Tel. + 33 1 40 69 44 44
Fax + 33 1 47 23 47 32

Union des industries métallurgiques et minières (UIMM)
56 avenue de Wagram
75854 Paris Cédex 17
Tel. + 33 1 40 54 21 34
Fax + 33 1 47 66 22 74

INSEE (National Institute of Statistics)
18 boulevard Adolphe Pinard
75675 Paris Cédex 14
Tel. + 33 1 4540 12 12

Main sources

AMADIEU, JEAN-FRANÇOIS. 'Labour–management cooperation and work organisation change: deficits in the French industrial relations system', in OECD, *New Directions in Work Organisation*. Paris, 1992

Code de Travail. Fifty-fifth edition. Paris, Editions Dalloz, 1993

DELAMOTTE, YVES. 'Workers' participation and personnel policies in France'. *International Labour Review.* Vol. 127, No. 2, 1988, 221–41

Direction de l'Animation de la Recherche, des Etudes et des Statistiques, *Premières Informations,* various issues

GOETSCHY, JANINE and ROZENBLATT, PATRICK. 'France: the industrial relations system at a turning point', in Anthony Ferner and Richard Hyman (eds.), *Industrial Relations in the New Europe.* Oxford, Blackwell, 1992

LANE, CHRISTEL. 'Industrial order and the transformation of industrial relations: Britain, France and Germany compared', in Richard Hyman and Anthony Ferner, *New Frontiers in Industrial Relations.* Oxford, Blackwell, 1994

LANE, CHRISTEL. *Management and Labour in Europe.* Aldershot, Edward Elgar, 1989

LECHER, WOLFGANG, and WENDELING-SCHRÖDER, ULRIKE. *Betriebliche Interessen-vertretungsstrukturen in Frankreich und in der Bundesrepublik Deutschland.* Düsseldorf, 1995

Liaisons Sociales, *Bref Social,* various issues

Liaisons Sociales, *Droit syndical: le délégué syndical,* February 1995

Liaisons Sociales, *Elections des représentants du personnel,* November 1994

Liaisons Sociales, *Législation Sociale,* various issues

Mémento Practique Social. Paris, Editions Francis Lefebvre, Paris, 1995

Ministry of Labour, national collective agreements for: chemicals, banking, metalworking (Paris region), road haulage

RIOUX, OLIVIER. 'Vacances des CE: c'est comme vous voulez'. *Liaisons Sociales,* 15 June 1993

5

Germany

German industrial relations are characterised by a high degree of statutory regulation, complemented and developed by a large body of case law which is decisive on some major issues, such as the lawfulness of industrial action. Employee interests are represented through a dual system of statutory works councils at workplace level and free collective bargaining, mostly on an industry basis, between trade unions and employer associations. Both structures are highly interrelated in practice, although the formal separation of pay bargaining from workplace issues is a key feature of the system, allowing for workplace exigencies to be addressed within an overarching framework. In addition, there is a structure of statutory board-level representation, which although having less impact on day-to-day industrial relations is an important 'political' component of the overall system.

Employer and trade union organisations remain strong, representative, centralised and fairly disciplined – although both sides, and in particular during the 1990s the employers, have begun to exhibit less cohesiveness than in the past. Increased pressures on the system – from unification, intensified international competition, changed relations between suppliers and manufacturers in industry, and a severe recession with associated job losses in 1993/94 – have all contributed to greater pressures on negotiators, occasionally culminating in industrial action, and raising concern about the long-term prospects for the present pattern of mostly industry-level bargaining. Proposals arising from different strands of thinking among employers range from reform to the effective dismantlement of the system.

Nevertheless the day-to-day conduct of industrial relations, especially at workplace level, remains consensual and, for the most part, rooted in 'high trust' relationships between the players – although it is a consensus which has been tested severely on several occasions during the mid-1990s. The relative stability of the system, at least hitherto, has also been rooted in a degree of mutual respect by trade unions and employers' assocations for each other's strengths, exhibited, for example, in the trade unions' continuing ability to win overwhelming support in ballots for strike action when they call for it.

New management initiatives, such as Total Quality Management, have generally built on existing arrangements for employee representation. And although employees have extensive statutory rights in the workplace, managers are held to exercise greater control over production processes, for example, than their United Kingdom counterparts have traditionally been able to do. However, contrary to popular stereotypes, German management styles have also been found to be more collegial, informal and participatory than those in the United Kingdom and France. Both managerial control and pragmatic informality are also fostered by broader features of the industrial culture, in which a highly skilled workforce, mostly directly managed by technically qualified supervisors, has been willing to recognise corporate objectives in return for institutionalised rights and economic participation in the international success of the economy. This mutual accommodation could be threatened were technical innovation to falter, as some fear, or through the widespread relocation of high value-added operations to foreign sites on grounds of cost.

Pay determination for the vast bulk of employees is carried out through a moderately centralised and co-ordinated structure of industry collective bargaining which sets minimum pay levels and basic provisions on allowances and premium pay. This system of collective bargaining, estimated to embrace around 85–90 per cent of employees, is complemented by a second tier of pay-setting at company level. In larger concerns this typically involves discussions and negotiation with elected employee works councils. In smaller organisations, unilateral management decision may prevail. Works councils enjoy statutory rights of co-determination on a number of basic issues connected with pay, although their right to negotiate on basic pay or grading is circumscribed by industry collective agreements which have legal precedence.

Although the basic contours of the system have shown great continuity over several decades, decentralisation within companies – at least of line functions – has shifted the balance towards the workplace as the key locus of employment regulation. This trend has put pressure on trade unions to match it with a new relationship between industry agreements and local provisions, and maintain their *de facto* strength in works councils.

The main players

Freedom of association

The right to form and join a trade union (or employers' association) is guaranteed under the 1949 Basic Law, which grants 'the right to form associations to safeguard and improve working and economic conditions . . . to everyone and to all trades, occupations and professions'. Any agreement which seeks to limit that right is null and void. The principle has been interpreted by the courts as meaning equally that individuals have a right not to belong to a trade union: the closed shop is therefore illegal.

Trade unions have a right to recruit in the workplace by distributing trade union literature outside working hours, using any notice boards intended to inform employees. However, there is no guaranteed right, for example, to hold shop stewards' elections at the place of work should the employer refuse.

The courts have developed the principles embodied in the Basic Law into a body of case law on what type of employer or union organisation can legitimately claim to be an association, enjoy constitutional protection, and participate in collective bargaining. For example, associations must be voluntary, must operate above the level of the individual enterprise or establishment, and must represent a genuine opposition to their counterpart (ie no company unions). They must fulfil certain minimum standards of democracy, respect the law on collective bargaining, and have as their objective the conclusion of collective agreements. Importantly, and ironically, given the country's reputation for industrial peace, they must be both willing and able to back their claims with collective pressure in the form of strikes or lockouts.

Trade unions

Trade union structure   There are four union confederations – the DGB (Deutscher Gewerkschaftsbund), the white-collar DAG (Deutsche Angestellten-Gewerkschaft), the civil service DBB (Deutscher Beamtenbund) and the Christian CGB (Christlicher Gewerkschaftsbund) – of which the DGB is by far the most important.

The DGB (German Trade Union Federation) was established as a non-political grouping based on industrial unionism in 1949. In 1994 the DGB had a membership of some 9,770,000 and accounted for 97 per cent of all blue-collar and 75 per cent of all white-collar union members. It represents employees in both the private and the public sectors, and includes some 800,000 established civil servants (*Beamte*) in its membership. Just over 25 per cent of the DGB's membership is in the eastern *Länder*. Although the overwhelming support of most of the DGB goes to the Social Democrats, its political independence – a product of the political divisions seen in the latter years of the Weimar Republic – is symbolised by the fact that the deputy general secretary has traditionally been a Christian Democrat. Moreover the relationship between the SPD and DGB is not without its tensions: there have, for example, been serious disagreements over the issue of working time, where some leading SPD figures have advocated a much greater degree of flexibility than is currently acceptable to most DGB unions.

The DGB is organised along industrial lines, with 13 affiliated unions, of which the largest is the general engineering union IG Metall, with 2,995,000 members in 1994. This principle means that one trade union represents all organised employees at a workplace, irrespective of their individual occupation. Although it has proved a very effective instrument for avoiding demarcation problems in the workplace, it is based on a subdivision of the economy that is being superseded by the growth of the service sector and the blurring of traditional industry boundaries. Employers are also challenging the system by breaking up their operations into their component parts and reassigning them to a variety of industrial branches. On these, and on cost, grounds there has been a series of actual or planned mergers between industry unions – but as yet no comprehensive service sector union has emerged.

The DGB does not negotiate with employers. It represents the trade union movement on the national stage, provides a range of services both to individual union members and to unions, and seeks to co-ordinate approaches to collective bargaining – although this latter element is often overrated by outside observers. The DGB is passing through a period of organisational debate and policy reappraisal, and expects to have a new strategic programme during the course of 1996. The main issues are the division of labour between the DGB and its affiliated unions, the viability of the existing branch structure of the DGB's constituents, and its basic policy objectives.

The German Salaried Employees' Trade Union (Deutsche Angestellten-Gewerkschaft, DAG) represents white-collar employees across industry boundaries, and in 1994 had some 520,000 members. It negotiates direct with employers, both at industry and at company level, although where other unions are represented there will ultimately be only one collective agreement covering an industry or enterprise. Although not part of the DGB, the DAG is a member of the European Trades Union Confederation (ETUC). The Christian Trade Union Federation (Christlicher Gewerkschaftsbund, CGB) has 300,000 members.

The German Civil Servants' Federation (Deutscher Beamtenbund, DBB), represents established civil servants (*Beamte*) and had approximately 1,100,000 members in 1994. Civil servants' pay is set directly by government, not negotiated collectively, usually closely in line with the main public sector settlement. Although civil servants are not allowed to strike, they enjoy the right of association. A large section of the DBB's membership is also in areas, such as the postal service or the railways, where pay is negotiated collectively by other unions.

The Union der Leitenden Angestellten (ULA), with about 40,000 members, represents senior executives and managerial staff but has no role in pay determination. Terms and conditions for such employees are laid down in individual contracts of employment, and so the ULA does not bargain on their behalf but represents their interests.

Union density   The main four organisations – DGB, CGCB, DAG and DBB – had a total combined membership at the end of 1994 of 11,685,000, equivalent to 37 per cent of the dependent workforce in 1994, although this figure is slightly inflated by retired trade union members. Based on 1993 labour force figures and DGB membership only, union density was just over 50 per cent in east Germany and 28 per cent in west Germany (compared with some 33 per cent during most of the 1980s). Union density initially rose sharply after German unification in 1990, reflecting the higher level of union organisation in east Germany. The collapse of manufacturing in east Germany took a heavy toll of the new – boosted – figures, compounded by recession in the west in 1992–93. However, there are signs that the rate of decline slowed considerably in 1994. Some 50 per cent of all manual workers are trade union members, 97 per cent of them in DGB unions: 24 per cent of white-collar employees are in unions, of whom 77 per cent are in DGB unions, 14 per cent in the DAG, and the rest in the DBB or CGB.

Although the unions suffered some membership losses during the 1980s, these were nowhere near the decline seen in countries such as the United Kingdom. Counting west Germany only, DGB membership, for example, peaked at 7,960,000 in 1981, dropped to 7,500,000 in the mid-1980s, and recovered back to 7,940,000 in 1989 – immediately before unification. However, the early 1990s have seen a more marked fall, primarily as a result of the 1992/93 recession, when DGB membership fell back to 7,383,000 in west Germany – although this is still at the levels of the mid-1970s.

The average rates of union density cited above mask substantial variations. Whereas 85–90 per cent of workers in large engineering plants may be union members, union organisation is low in the private service sector. Women are under-represented, and a fall has been recorded in the number of young people joining trade unions.

Membership of a trade union is entirely voluntary, and dues are relatively high, with members paying about 1 per cent of gross pay.

Workplace organisation and rights   Trade unions as such are generally weakly rooted in the workplace, and most union concerns are advanced through the statutory system of employee representation at the place of work, the works councils (see below). Nevertheless, works councils' rights on appointment mean that trade union membership can be 'encouraged' when employees are hired. This relative weakness, combined with the limits on works councils' right to take industrial action, could prove a problem for the trade unions should there be a large-scale devolution of bargaining to workplace level. At the same time the unions as organisations have undoubtedly benefited from the relationship they enjoy with works councils and from the integration between works councils' rights and collective bargaining.

Some unions, notably IG Metall, sought to set up a shop stewards' structure in the 1950s and 1960s to offset what they saw as the harmful impact of the original works council legislation on union rights and membership. The union built up a substantial shop steward presence, whose primary task became that of recruitment and of maintaining a union bridgehead at workplace level. However, in the early 1970s, partly in response to the greater scope for union activity under the 1972 Works Constitution Act (see below), the decision was made to concentrate on gaining influence on works councils, leaving shop stewards mainly concerned with representing the union rather than acting as a vehicle of employee representation *vis-à-vis* management.

Employers' organisations

Employers' associations are organised along industrial lines on a regional basis, with a national body, the Confederation of German Employers' Associations (Bundesvereinigung der deutschen Arbeitgeberverbände, BDA), which embraces some 700 employers' organisations represented through 46 industry and 12 regional groups. In contrast to many other EU countries, employer interests, both nationally and at industry level, are represented through a dual structure, with trade organisations attending to business, economic and technical matters, whilst employer bodies are responsible for collective bargaining and social issues. There is also virtually compulsory membership of chambers of trade and commerce, which play a key role in training.

Like the DGB, the BDA itself does not conclude collective agreements; that is a matter for the national or regional industrial affiliates. Member organisations of the BDA generally have a high degree of representativeness of employers in their industries. For example, some 75 per cent of all employees in the engineering industry work in firms affiliated to the Metal Trades Employers' Associations (whose central federation is Gesamtmetall).

Although the BDA does not negotiate, and lacks formal central powers, it does try to exercise some influence over the conduct of industry negotiations (see below). Its annual report customarily features a section on 'co-ordination of bargaining' in which the federation's views on the coming pay round are set out, reflecting the discussions held by its Pay and Collective Bargaining Committee. However, the BDA does not publicly set out pay recommendations, and its role as a co-ordinating body should not be overestimated, and is customarily downplayed by employer representatives.

Despite this attempt at co-ordination, it is the industry associations – which are coalitions of businesses of various types and interests – which undertake the actual bargaining, and the BDA's 'line' can be weakened or partly abandoned during negotiations. As discussed below, the vast bulk of employees are covered by multi-employer agreements: only 6 per cent fall under individual company agreements.

The presence of so many different types of company within the industry associations itself provides fertile ground for problems in maintaining cohesion and discipline. Tension can develop within industry associations between the interests of smaller and larger concerns, between regions, and between the central organisations and the regional bodies on which local employers are directly represented; such tension usually becomes most evident during a difficult pay round. In general, however, the need to retain marginal firms in industry organisations and confront generally strong industrial unions has, as yet, enforced both discipline and a broad averaging of interests.

On the other hand, there have been evident problems in maintaining employer cohesion in recent years, most notably in engineering and printing. They have been most dramatically evident in the number of companies leaving their industry association altogether, or switching to one in a different industry (this remains fairly unusual, though) and in manifest discontent within employers' associations over policy. As in the United Kingdom, a number of employers' associations have toyed with 'non-complying' membership, under which companies are not bound by the industry agreement.

National-level co-operation and consultation

There is no formal national tripartite or bipartite forum for consultation or negotiation on pay or industrial relations issues. There is however much informal exchange and an official ideology on both sides of 'social 'partnership' commanding broad allegiance. 'Concerted Action' – a tripartite process of assessing economic developments and shaping pay bargaining as part of the economic stability law introduced under the 1966–69 'Grand Coalition' of Social Democrats, Liberals and the two Conservative parties – was abandoned by the trade unions in 1977, ostensibly because of employer attempts to have industrial participation declared unconstitutional. A role in the end of Concerted Action was also played, however, by the growing strains on union cohesiveness of implied wage norms – highlighted by the oil crisis and a series of wildcat strikes in the period 1969–73. Nevertheless, a form of Concerted Action – as it is called – has continued as a forum for discussion in the health service.

During 1995–96 Federal Chancellor Kohl held a series of tripartite discussions on employment issues, such as long-term unemployment, fostering the creation of small businesses, and training, in an effort to generate consensus on policy in the wake of unification and concern about German competitiveness. In November 1995 the engineering workers' union IG Metall offered wage concessions in return for an employer commitment to create jobs and the abandonment by the government of some welfare cuts; the tripartite meetings with the Chancellor were expected to be important for discussing these proposals.

Consultation at regional/industry level

Consultation is well developed in some industries, of which the chemical industry offers the most publicised model – cemented through a number of non-binding accords between the BAVC employers' association and the union IG Chemie. The accords cover such matters as training, equal opportunities, employment promotion and employee consultation and European works council contacts: this latter agreement, concluded in 1990, played a major part in shaping voluntary practice in the industry and has had an impact on how the EU directive on European works councils is being implemented (see below).

There are also a number of 'round tables' in the engineering industry. In Baden-Württemberg, for example, there is a group embracing local government, employers, the union, and suppliers and manufacturers in the automotive and machine-tool industries.

Employee representation

Employee participation, which covers a variety of degrees of involvement ranging from information to co-determination, takes place via two institutions:

employee-only works councils (*Betriebsräte*) at workplace, company or group level, and employee representation on the supervisory boards of companies. Of the two, the most directly and practically relevant – for both managements and employees – is the works council system.

There is no formal involvement by trade unions in the day-to-day operation of works councils, though the informal and practical links are extensive, and the chairs of the works councils of large firms usually sit on unions' collective bargaining committees. Trade unions have a right of access to company premises, and may attend works meetings. Employers and works councils must co-operate with both unions and employers' organisations. A trade union is also entitled to take an employer to court and obtain a court order under the 1972 Works Constitution Act should the employer grossly violate his obligations under the act. Trade unions do, however, have representation rights at supervisory board level under the 1976 Co-determination Act, which applies to large public companies (see 'Employee participation at board level', below). There is also usually a direct link between works councils and supervisory boards in that the chair of a company's works council will also usually have a seat on the board.

The system represents an exchange of powers between a generally well organised workforce – especially in larger organisations – and management: managers give up certain prerogatives, at least as regards the speed with which decisions are implemented if not their strategic direction, gaining in return acceptance of their right to manage once agreement has been reached. Moreover the guiding philosophy of workplace participation, enshrined in the 1972 Works Constitution Act, is that works councils must accept the company's business exigencies. In practice the issue is less clear-cut, but those are the essentials.

Workplace employee representation

Works councils are one of the most characteristic features of German industrial relations and constitute one arm of the 'dual' structure. Originally a product of the factory council movement of the 1918 revolution, they became a core element of the institutional structure of the Weimar Republic (1919–33). They were revived and given a new statutory basis in 1952 by the Adenauer government, although opposed in that form by the Social Democrats and Communist Party on the grounds that the new system conferred insufficient rights and sought to weaken trade unionism at plant level by establishing all-employee bodies obliged to maintain industrial peace and co-operate with the employer.

Works councils' rights were considerably strengthened by the Social Democrat government under Willy Brandt in 1972, and it is that year's Works Constitution Act (*Betriebsverfassungsgesetz*), subsequently amended by the Conservative–Liberal coalition in the 1980s, which governs the current structure and powers of works councils.

Works councils are employee-only bodies, directly elected by the workforce, for an individual establishment (*Betrieb*): 'establishment' may be the same thing as a company but could mean an individual plant within a multi-plant firm, one department store within a chain, or a distinct works on a single site characterised by several types of operation. Where a company consists of several establishments, each with its own works council, a works council for the company as a whole (central works council, *Gesamtbetriebsrat*) can be formed of delegations from individual works councils. Similarly, if the company is part of a group, a group (or combine) works council (*Konzernbetriebsrat*) can be set up by delegation.

Works councils are not mandatory, but may be elected by employees in any establishment with at least five eligible employees. Once elected, they must be recognised by the employer. The law requires the employer and the works council to meet at least monthly.

Costs of the system   The costs are borne by the employer. They include office space and facilities, office personnel and travel costs, consultation with a lawyer or other experts, the costs of printing literature (although not a regular publication), buying in specialist literature, and the cost of hiring an interpreter for works meetings if necessary.   The employer may be obliged to pay for training courses run by trade unions for works council members: however, any such courses must be relevant to the exercise of the members' statutory duties. According to research carried out by the employers' economics institute, the IdW, the average annual cost per employee of running works councils in 1992 was DM 306 (£137).

Size of the works council   Where the establishment employs five to 20 employees, only one representative may be elected. The size of the works council then increases with establishment size, ranging from five members in establishments with 51–150 employees, to 15 members where there are 1,001–2,000 employees, and to 31 members for workforces between 7,001 and 9,000. Where the establishment has more than 9,000 employees, two more members can be added for each additional 3,000 employees.

Establishments mainly concerned with charitable, political, scientific or cultural activities, or which serve to express opinions or which are engaged in journalistic reportage are not covered by the 1972 law if the character of the establishment makes it inappropriate: in German they are collectively referred to as *Tendenzbetriebe*. The public sector is covered by separate legislation.

All blue- and white-collar workers employed by the establishment are eligible for membership, together with trainees. The definition of eligibility excludes the firm's management board, the owners, and 'executives' (*leitende Angestellte*), who since 1989 have been able to elect their own representative institution (see below). In practice, as we shall see below, DGB-affiliated trade unions supply the bulk of the candidates for works councils, usually in the form of approved slates. In the 1994 elections DGB candidates won two-thirds of all seats, and accounted for three-quarters of all chairs of works councils – a figure broadly stable over the past two decades. The number of independent non-union works council members has risen from 17 per cent to 25 per cent since the mid-1970s, largely at the expense of the DAG union.

Coverage and effectiveness   Coverage of the labour force by works councils is limited by a number of factors. Firstly, around a quarter of the labour force work in establishments which are too small to meet the size threshold, or which are excluded because of the nature of their activities (the *Tendenzbetriebe*), or which are in the public sector. Secondly, the fact that works councils are not mandatory leaves scope for employees to exercise their free will (and for employers to create a climate which is either hostile or which seeks to make statutory representation superfluous). Estimates of coverage vary: according to most, some two-thirds of private sector employees work in establishments with a works council. However, the incidence of works councils varies markedly by size and location, with many smaller establishments outside larger cities and towns operating either without a works council or with one which is handicapped by isolation and lack of internal support. Only some 20 per cent of small companies theoretically qualifying for a works council are thought to have one.

Although, by and large, the works councils' rights (set out below) are respected by employers, on pain of financial penalties, there are instances of flagrant breaches, and there is some evidence to show that these may have increased in recent years. The main culprits appear to be companies led by individual, sometimes flamboyant, entrepreneurs.

Status of workforce representatives   Works councillors are elected for four years. Above 300 employees, depending on the size of establishment, the employer must release a certain number of council members, on full pay, for works council activities either full- or part-time, again depending on establishment size.

Works council members also have a right to continuing access to vocational training, and training relevant to their duties – at a minimum three weeks off during their period of office to attend approved courses.

Works council members are protected against ordinary dismissal while in office and for a year after. Any application for the summary dismissal of a works councillor requires works council approval, although the employer may go to the courts with the object of getting a works council objection overruled. Candidates too are protected against ordinary dismissal from the date of nomination until six months after the outcome has been made public.

Duties of the works council   One major difference between statutory employee representation through works councils and bargaining or representation by trades unions is the requirement on works councils to co-operate with the employer 'for the good of the employees and the establishment' and for both employer and works council to refrain from acts of 'industrial warfare . . . or activities that imperil the smooth running of the establishment'. However, although works councils are formally subject to this absolute peace obligation, cannot call a strike, and in practice and for the most part function on a basis of co-operation with employers, they do possess informal sanctions based on their statutory powers. The mere existence of such negative powers, matched by employers' ability to grant or withhold a variety of concessions, creates the basis for informal resolution of conflicts in which full-time works council members, especially the chair, play a major role.

Works councils are statutorily enjoined:

- To ensure compliance with the law, with collective agreements and with works agreements for the benefit of employees.
- To make recommendations to the employer on action to benefit employees and the establishment.
- To promote the rehabilitation and integration of people with disabilities, older workers, and foreign workers.

The works council must also call a meeting of employees, either of the whole establishment or at department level, at least once a quarter, to which the employer is invited. The employer has to be given a copy of the agenda, and is also entitled to address the meeting. At least once a year the employer must present a report to a workforce meeting on staffing and social matters, together with a presentation on the business situation of the firm. The works council must notify any trade union represented in the plant of proposed works meetings, and union officials are entitled to attend in an advisory capacity.

Confidentiality   Both during and after their period of office, works council members may not disclose outside the works council, or make use of, any genuine trade or business secrets which are expressly identified as such by the employer, or confidential information about individual employees. This could, for example, include information on pay and labour costs. How the case of a proposed closure or merger might be treated would depend on case law and the specific circumstances.

Rights and powers of the works council   Works councils have a panoply of rights, ranging from information, through participation in decisions, to joint decision-making ('co- determination' – in German, *Mitbestimmung*), depending, formally, on the size of establishment and the issue. The principal rights are:

- *The right to be heard (Anhörungsrecht).* Works councils have a right to express an opinion on issues as well as to initiate proposals in some areas.
- *Information.* Works councils have a general right to be informed 'comprehensively and in good time' on any matters necessary for them to exercise their tasks. Information must precede any employer decision and cannot be a mere formality.

- *Consultation* (*Beratungsrecht*). The final decision remains with the employer, but employers must seek the works council's views, identify issues for possible negotiation, and balance their own interests with those of the workforce.
- *Co-determination* (*Mitbestimmung*) takes place through the exercise of various rights, including a works council's right to object to an employer proposal: that is, the employer may not proceed with a course of action without the assent of the works council or a decision from a labour court or conciliation committee in its stead.

Conciliation committees (*Einigungsstelle*) – somewhat of a misnomer in that they can issue binding rulings – may be set up as and when required, or on a permanent basis, and typically consist of equal numbers of employer and employee representatives, chaired by an independent figure – usually a local labour court judge. In general, recourse to this machinery is rare, and the parties prefer to keep negotiating with at least the prospect of shaping the outcome. Conciliation committees cannot decide on matters of law.

In some instances, both parties are required, or may choose, to come to a formal written agreement termed a 'works agreement' (*Betriebsvereinbarung*). Under the Works Constitution Act 'works agreements shall not deal with remuneration and other conditions of employment that have been fixed or are normally fixed by collective agreement' (*Tarifvertrag*) unless a collective agreement expressly authorises it. Works agreements therefore represent a tier of collective provision which is, in theory, one rung below that of collective agreements negotiated between trade unions and employers or employers' associations. Nevertheless, works agreements are mandatory and directly applicable, and rights granted under them are indefeasible: unlike collective agreements, they can be tested in the courts on grounds of equity. Also, unlike collective agreements, they can be terminated at any time upon three months' notice.

As well as regulating the matters identified below, works agreements can also cover such issues as pensions, financial participation by employees, the introduction of team-working, environmental matters, social benefits and equal treatment programmes.

Co-determination on social matters   The strongest set of rights – co-determination – apply in the area of 'social matters'. Co-determination here means that the employer and works council *must* come to an agreement on the following issues, unless the issues are already exhaustively governed by law or collective agreement. Where no agreement is possible the matter is settled by a binding ruling from a conciliation committee. That is, no unilateral management decision is valid in these areas. The main social matters are:

- The start and finish of daily working time, breaks and shift patterns, holiday arrangements
- Overtime and short time

- The timing and form of payment of remuneration
- The use of technical devices designed to monitor the behaviour and performance of employees
- Health and safety arrangements
- The 'form, structure and administration' of company benefits
- 'Remuneration arrangements', including the 'principles of remuneration' and the 'introduction and application of new remuneration systems'
- The fixing of rates under payment-by-results systems.

Job design and the work environment   Works councils must be informed of and consulted about plans concerning changes to premises, plant, work processes or jobs, and must be given scope to make suggestions and express reservations. Works councils have a right of co-determination on measures to mitigate, obviate or compensate for any burden imposed on employees as a result of changes in jobs, work processes or the work environment which 'are clearly at odds with the accepted findings of ergonomics'.

Personnel matters   Works councils can exercise considerable influence over personnel management, often impinging on areas customarily viewed as the prerogative of the employer in the United Kingdom. In many respects the influence of works councils is strongest in this field. First, the rights acquired can give works councils considerable leverage in both this and other areas of workplace relations. Second, not only can works councils shape internal labour markets, but, by institutionalising the power of 'insiders', they can also affect the broader labour market. Rights, set out more specifically below, can be exercised in the areas of: personnel planning, vacancies and recruitment, transfers and regrading, and individual dismissal.

- *Personnel planning.* There is a right to information and to make recommendations on personnel planning, including forecast personnel needs, any staff changes or movements, and vocational training, together with a right of consultation to avoid employee hardship.
- *Recruitment.* Works councils can ask for vacancies to be advertised internally before external recruitment begins, although both sides may agree to exclude some categories of employee from this provision. Failure to advertise internally may give the works council grounds for withholding consent to an appointment (see below). Any application forms, or staff questionnaires, require approval, and the employer must obtain a ruling from a conciliation committee if consent is not granted. Guidelines for selection, transfer, regrading or dismissal drawn up by an employer require works council approval.
- *Engagement, transfer, regrading.* In establishments with more than 20 employees the works council must be told of any proposed engagement or movement of staff, and must be shown any application and selection documents. A works council may refuse to approve the proposal on a number of

grounds, such as breach of existing guidelines, disadvantage to existing employees, failure to advertise internally, or fears that the individual might be disruptive of social and industrial harmony in the establishment. The employer must obtain a decision from a labour court to override any withholding of consent.

- *Individual dismissal.* All dismissals must be notified, with the reasons for dismissal, to the works council, which has a right to object on a number of pre-stated statutory grounds. Any dismissal which is not notified is null and void. The works council has a week to respond in writing to an 'ordinary dismissal' (that is, with notice) and three days to respond to a summary dismissal. (See *Contracts and Terms and Conditions of Employment* in this series.)

Works council opposition to a dismissal cannot stop the action as such. However, should the employee seek to contest the dismissal through the courts with the support of the works council, the employer must offer the employee work on unchanged terms until settlement of the case.

Financial and business matters In all *companies* with more than 100 permanent employees a sub-committee of the works council known as the Economic Committee (*Wirtschaftsausschuß*) may be established to deal specifically with information from the employer on the state of the business. Employers are required to give information on the financial state of the business 'in full and in good time', supported by appropriate documentation, as long as it does not compromise business secrecy, and spell out the implications for personnel planning. Issues on which information must be given include:

- the economic and financial situation of the company
- the product and marketing situation
- investment, production and rationalisation plans, including new work methods
- reductions in activities, closures, or transfers of operations.

Employers must also inform employees direct on the state of the business: in companies with more than 1,000 employees, this has to happen in writing at least once a quarter; in firms with more than 20 employees, information can be presented orally.

Redundancies In companies with 20 or more employees the employer must inform the works council of, and consult it on, any changes to the business which may entail 'substantial disadvantages' for the workforce, or a large proportion of it. The employer and works council must seek to reconcile their interests, and can express any agreement on the general principles attached to the proposed changes. The works council has also an enforceable right of co-determination in the negotiation of a 'social compensation plan' (*Sozialplan*) to compensate employees for any financial loss.

Works councils and the trade unions German trade unions are not based in the workplace as of formal or legal right, and trade union plant representatives (*Vertrauensleute*) do not have a recognised role in bargaining or representation comparable with that of British shop stewards. Rather, they act as a local base for their trade union, and serve as a two-way transmission mechanism between the union and its membership on issues such as pay claims. Since works councils are forbidden to initiate industrial action, shop stewards often take responsibility for co-ordinating official strikes at plant level, as well as occasionally being a catalyst for more 'spontaneous' – but technically unlawful – action. In practice, shop stewards work closely with works councils, reflecting the fact that most works councillors are union members. In large plants, shop stewards may establish a formal shop stewards' committee with a convenor (*Vertrauenskörperleitung*). Around 70 collective agreements and works agreements make provision for either dismissal protection or facilities for shop stewards; the main areas covered are engineering, printing, the clothing industry and the postal service.

Executive representation committees

There is separate statutory provision for the representation of executives. Under a law introduced in 1988 executives – who account on average for 2–3 per cent of the workforce – can establish executive representation committees (*Sprecherausschüsse*, ERCs for short) in any establishment with at least 10 executives. There is provision for setting up ERCs at company or group level. In 1994 elections a total of 540 committees were elected, a drop from the 568 in 1990: 400,000 managers participated in elections – with over 80 per cent of eligible managers voting, in some industries. Around half of all seats were taken by independent candidates, and around half by the ULA. The DGB has only a marginal presence, although it did win 10 per cent of seats in some traditional areas of manufacturing.

ERCs have rights to information, and individual executives have a right to inspect their personal files and append their own observations. ERCs and employers can agree binding guidelines for the commencement and termination of managers' contracts. The ERC must also be informed of any appointments, dismissals or changes in the employment of executives. The employer must inform the ERC about changes in remuneration systems, employee appraisal, or other general conditions of employment.

Employee participation at board level

The supervisory board   Participation at board level is effected through the two-tier board structure which characterises public joint-stock companies (*Aktiengesellschaft*, AG) incorporated under the 1965 Joint Stock Companies Act. This structure consists of a supervisory board (*Aufsichtsrat*) and a management board (*Vorstand*). The management board is responsible for conducting the business operations of a company, represents the enterprise legally, and is formally the employer, whereas the supervisory board is legally required to appoint the management board (in an AG) or the managing directors (in a GmbH or a private limited company) and oversee its/their activities. Employee representatives sit on the supervisory boards of companies, which meet between two and four times a year. Only joint-stock companies (AG) are required to have two boards as a matter of course. Other types of company are required to create a two-tier structure only if they are large enough to qualify for inclusion in one of the co-determination systems.

As members of the supervisory board employees have the same rights and duties as shareholder members. Trade union members are expected to transfer any directors' fees to the Hans Böckler Foundation, which researches co-determination and industrial relations issues. Moreover, following the resignation of the former General Secretary of IG Metall, Franz Steinkühler, on grounds of alleged insider dealings in the shares of companies on whose board he sat, IG Metall banned its officials from owning shares in companies they are involved with as supervisory board members. The supervisory board has a right to request information from the management board on all aspects of the business, and this right extends to the individual member, provided the request is supported by another member. Information which must be provided as a matter of course includes:

● Proposed corporate policies and other fundamental issues related to the management of the business
● The profitability of the business, especially the return on equity
● The general course of the business, including sales
● Operations which might be of considerable importance to the profitability or liquidity of the enterprise.

Considerable controversy surrounds the issue of how much information employee members of the supervisory board may receive. The law requires supervisory board members to behave with the due diligence of a manager, and not to divulge confidential information acquired as a result of their activities. However, some authorities contend that this does not preclude informing works councils, who themselves are covered by confidentiality requirements.

The models   There are three forms of board-level participation:

● In joint-stock (AG) and limited liability (GmbH) companies and limited partnerships based on share capital (KgaA) with more than 2,000 employees, under the 1976 Co-determination Act. In 1993 some 710 companies were covered by the act, including 100 in the former GDR *Länder*, compared with about 480 when the law first came into effect. The supervisory board consists of equal numbers of shareholder and employee members, with the size of the board varying according to the size of the company. Some seats on the employee side are reserved for representatives of trade unions with a presence in the enterprise. The remaining seats are allocated to employees, with a guarantee of at least one seat for each of the groups of blue-collar, white-collar and managerial employees. Election is usually direct, by employee groups, in enterprises with up to 8,000 employees, and by electoral college in larger firms. In 1995 the government issued proposals to reduce the size of supervisory boards – although the idea has met with stiff union opposition.

The most important single activity of the supervisory board is to elect the management board. In this the chair of the board, who is a shareholders' representative, has a casting vote in the event of a tie. (The deputy chair is an employees' representative.) The 50–50 composition of the board is also weakened, from the trade union point of view, by the presence of managerial staff on the employees' side, who may typically be expected to support the shareholders' view on major issues. The board also elects a so-called Labour Director to the management board with special responsibility for personnel and social matters: although the employee side has no veto over the appointment (see below), this manager is expected to enjoy the confidence of employee members.

- In enterprises with more than 1,000 employees engaged in the coal, iron and steel industries (the so-called 'Montan' industries), under the 1951 Montan Co-determination Act, broadly extended in 1956 to holding companies controlling enterprises in those industries, the supervisory board consists of an equal number of employee and shareholder representatives. The difference from the 1976 act is that the chair must be a neutral member, and the Labour Director cannot be appointed against the wishes of the employee representatives. (Deadlock is rare.)

  The number of companies covered by the act has fallen from around 100 at its inception to about 30 in west Germany and, in 1993, 18 in the former GDR *Länder*. A succession of statutory interventions have taken place, designed to maintain the system in the face of the decline in these basic industries – reflected in the diminishing share of the turnover of many of the companies and conglomerates accounted for by such 'smokestack' operations below the 50 per cent required by law. In 1981 a law ruled that any company which no longer met this criterion would remain covered by the act for a period of six years thereafter. In 1988 a new amendment was passed which provides for the controlling companies in industrial groups to remain subject to the act as long as 20 per cent of their turnover is accounted for by those industries, or the subsidiary active in those industries employs at least 2,000 workers. (In practice, most individual companies which have fallen out of the scope of the act in the past did so through merger or complete abandonment of that type of activity, hence the recent legislation focuses on the nature of controlling groups in conglomerates rather than on individual enterprises.)

- In companies with between 500 and 2,000 employees, under the 1952 Works Constitution Act (the predecessor of the 1972 act but still applicable in this area) one-third of the members of the supervisory board must be employee representatives.

Whereas external commentators have often focused on the special role of 'workers on the board' under the German system, and in particular its contribution to a 'stakeholder' model of corporate governance, in Germany itself board-level co-determination is overshadowed in practice by the works council system, with its clearly delineated employee rights.

'New industrial relations'

Initiatives in the field of 'new industrial relations' and human resource management are widespread and growing. Both trade unions and sectoral employers' associations produced discussion and policy documents during the 1980s. In 1986, for example, the chemical employers' association, the Bundesverband Chemie, issued a discussion document on team-working, and Gesamtmetall, the central employers' organisation in metalworking and engineering has also produced recommendations on the implementation of small groups in industry. Quality circles and continuous improvement programmes, TQM, team-working – often all subsumed under the rubric of 'lean management' – have all grown in significance during the early 1990s, with the pace of introduction of such approaches tending to speed up since the 1992/93 recession. As yet the new approaches have been overwhelmingly concentrated in production activities.

In general, new personnel approaches have been introduced through dialogue with existing channels of employee representation – works councils – although formal agreements tend to be in the minority. As a rule, however, the initiative has lain with management, and implementation has tended to be top-down, with formal observation of works councils' rights. Companies with very formal internal structures, often built around works councils, may have had more difficulty carrying sweeping organisational change through and shifting the balance of participation closer to the team or the shop floor. The role of the works council is subject to two contrary forces. Whereas the individualisation of employment relationships, or negotiation of output and quality between teams and team leaders in the immediate workplace, could erode the traditional powers and culture of the works council as a representative body, the need for a negotiating partner at the workplace level to resolve a host of new technical and organisational problems – in the absence of trade unions – is actually raising works councils' status. Moreover the changing nature of supplier–purchaser relations is beginning to lead to some co-operation and exchange of information between works councils in different firms in the supply/production chain. As yet there is no definitive resolution of the relationship between established statutory representative rights, the rights allotted to individuals and teams under new arrangements, managerial prerogatives, and the overarching framework of industry collective agreements which set crucial issues such as working time.

Trade unions have broadly favoured this type of management innovation. Unions such as IG Metall produced consultative documents on team-working in the early 1980s and fused ideas from this approach into its strategy document on bargaining, *Tarifreform 2000*. IG Metall has actively promoted group working since the 1980s. In this respect, ideas of group working, quality control, and enhanced training and development accord with features of German industrial culture and traditional labour movement objectives such as workplace co-determination and enhanced individual employee participation. According to one survey, carried out among manufacturing companies in Baden-Württemberg (see Howaldt, 1994), there was widespread employee support for such initiatives, with around 60 per cent of surveyed employees favouring innovation and only 10 per cent opposed. However, there is employee concern about job losses and work intensification which has been heightened as corporate change has been most rigorously pursued as a result of the recession. In a number of large firms, such as Mercedes-Benz, the introduction of team-working and changes in remuneration patterns to raise the performance element has gone hand in hand with 'concessions bargaining' over established terms and conditions in exchange for new investment commitments. This may have compromised some of the values previously associated with the prospect of enhanced employee participation through TQM and team-work.

Employee suggestion schemes have long played an important role in personnel management, and such schemes have often been incorporated into subsequent TQM and team-work programmes, yielding a growing number of suggestions. According to a 1994 survey carried out by the Deutsches Institut für Betriebswirtschaft, nearly all companies covered – which employed 3 million employees in all – recorded a big increase in the number of suggestions submitted, with 544,000 submitted in 1994, compared with 480,000 in the previous year. The companies paid out DM 180 million (£80 million) to employees to achieve savings put at DM 880 million (£392 million).

Implementation of the EU works council directive

Both practitioners and the legislature enjoy the advantage that steps to implement the EC Directive on Works Councils can build on many years of practical and legal experience with the highly developed national systems of employee participation and co-determination. In practice, European works councils in Community-scale enterprises headquartered in Germany will be an extension of their existing works council, usually at company level (*Gesamtbetriebsrat*). Indeed, in formulating German legislation to implement the directive, there will be no provision for the constitution of a European works council outside the domestic works council system. This will mean that German companies will not have to organise separate elections for European works council representatives, and will not be confronted with problems, at least within Germany, related to the representativeness of employee delegates.

One concern about this raised by employers is that the administration of the European works council could become too closely intertwined with that of the domestic system. For example, European works council representatives could seek the same rights as works council members on issues such as time off, training, foreign travel and language courses, effectively establishing a semi-permanent apparatus to administer the employee side of European works councils. However, employers who have already operated international consultation forums have not accepted the argument, often heard from British employers, that cost is a decisive factor; indeed, emphasising the cost aspect has been seen as impairing objective discussion of the advantages and disadvantages of the proposal.

Moreover the very fact that the German works council system is so well developed and established has raised a number of problems for the introduction of the directive. For example, the directive requires European works councils to cover all employees: German law excludes executives from works councils, and assigns them a separate vehicle, although the two groups are integrated at board level. In addition, any European works council in a German multinational, about 150 of which are expected to be affected by the directive, is likely to be dominated by procedures and forms developed through the works council system.

The national employers' confederation, the BDA, is keen to encourage companies to develop their own models using the voluntary option prior to formal implementation, based on their distinctive structure and needs, and has not recommended a single approach.

Some companies, notably in the chemical industry, were pioneers of international consultation mechanisms. The chemical employers' association, the BAVC, and the IG Chemie union concluded a non-binding accord on guidelines for works council contacts in Europe in 1990, and in the early 1990s a number of chemical companies established forums for information exchange: among them were Hoechst, Schering, BASF, Bayer, Henkel and Continental.

Collective bargaining

Pay determination through collective negotiation takes place on the basis of free collective bargaining, rooted in the Federal Republic's 1949 constitution, the so-called Basic Law. This grants the right to form trade union and employers' associations, to bargain collectively, and to be able to back up bargaining, if necessary, with industrial action, including lockouts.

The right to take industrial action in support of an industrial demand is one fundamental line of demarcation between 'collective bargaining' in the full and formal sense (termed *Tarifverhandlung*, literally, negotiations over 'lists of prices'), in which employees' interests are represented by trade unions, and bargaining at establishment level within the system of statutory representation, the works council system. Works councils, and employers when dealing with works councils, are required to refrain from 'acts of industrial warfare', and works councils must co-operate with the employer 'for the good of the employees and the establishment'. Although collective bargaining between trade unions and employers' associations or individual employers has legal primacy and establishes the context within which establishment-level bargaining takes place, both levels are integral to the overall mechanism of pay-setting, and works councils are by no means powerless in their dealings with the employer, as we indicate below. In most industries there is, in practice, a dual structure for the determination of contractual pay, with works councils exercising formal rights under the law, powers granted under collective agreements, and some bargaining strength anchored in the level of union organisation and circumstances in local labour markets.

The sometimes complex interplay between the two levels has been an important factor in maintaining the institutional stability of the system, at least up to the present. The system of industry-level bargaining, especially where industries are very broadly defined, inevitably means that unions must average interests out during negotiations: employees in companies which can pay above the 'going rate' accept a lower agreed increase – in return for the broader protection offered by an industry agreement. This creates scope for considerable wage drift, which is evident in many larger flourishing companies, which may pay on average 20–30 per cent above the industry minimum. The conceding, or winning, of such supplements at workplace level is a matter between managements and works councils: discussion of more plant-based bargaining was rejected by the unions in the early 1970s, worried that industry-level agreements might be fatally undermined. Local deals offer advantages to both management and unions. Managers are eager to exercise discretion over at least a portion of the pay packet which they can tie in to company objectives or simply use as a recruitment tool in boom periods. Unions can sustain their desired broader social role of representing employee interests on a larger scale without coming under pressure to engage in leapfrogging. During recessions the ability to cut into plant-based pay without encroaching on the minimum provisions of legally enforceable collective agreements offers scope to local managements and employee representatives to negotiate on employment levels or crisis packages – however unpalatable such concession bargaining may be.

Moreover the removal of bargaining over basic pay increases from the workplace takes out one potential source of conflict at local level – a fact often stressed by employer advocates of industry-level bargaining.

Collective agreements

Collective bargaining can take place only between trade unions and individual employers or employers' associations. Collective agreements negotiated between employers and trade unions take precedence over other forms of industrial accord, such as works agreements, or individual contracts, unless the latter

diverge in favour of the employee. Collective bargaining in the formal sense cul-
minates in a collective agreement whose status is regulated by the 1969
Collective Agreements Act. Agreements:

- *apply to members of the contracting parties.* In practice, employers will apply
  the terms of an agreement to all employees, whether they are members of a
  signatory trade union or not. An agreement will continue to apply even to an
  employer who withdraws from a signatory organisation until the agreement
  expires.
- *apply directly and with binding force.* That is, collective agreements are not
  only enforceable as civil contracts but are also deemed to have the force of
  law, and take precedence over works agreements and individual contracts
  except where the latter are more favourable to the employee. Deviations must
  be regulated by the agreement itself, and rights under a collective agreement
  may not be waived.

The provisions of a collective agreement continue in force until it is replaced
by another agreement of equivalent legal force (*Nachwirkung*). This means, for
example, that a company cannot simply withdraw from an employers' association and propose a change in individual employment contracts to lower provision. However, it can switch to another sector, either wholly or partially by
dividing the business up into its constituent parts, especially by separating out
services from manufacturing, and placing the individual new entities under separate industry agreements – taking advantage of the differences between industry
minima. Out-sourcing to small firms which may not be covered by collective
agreements is also eroding the impact of such agreements, even within larger
firms.

Collective agreements also include a 'peace clause' forbidding industrial
action during the lifetime of the agreement and for a period thereafter, usually
one month, during which negotiations over a new agreement can get under
way.

Directly or indiretly, collective agreements cover industries employing
85–90 per cent of the total workforce. Indirectly, in this context, means that
employers who are not members of employers' associations frequently adopt
the essential provisions of the agreement governing the industry they are in.
The only areas not covered are those with employers who do not traditionally
have collective agreements, such as lawyers' chambers. Single-employer bargaining is relatively rare, and covers only some 6 per cent of the labour force.
(Volkswagen, the oil companies and some firms in publishing are the major
examples of employers which negotiate on basic terms direct with trade
unions.) There are some 800 bargaining units in all. Of these 800, however,
only a relatively small number set the terms of employment for a large proportion of the workforce, and an even smaller number shape the bargaining environment in the pay round (see below).

Although most collective agreements are regional there is a high degree of centralisation within trade unions and employers' organisations. Minimum pay rates may vary a little from region to region, but most other terms will be common to all regions.

Extension of collective agreements

The 'extension' of collective agreements by the Ministry of Labour is a procedure that allows an industry agreement to be applied to employers who are not members of signatory employers' associations and who have not concluded a company agreement with a trade union. The system of legally enforceable and extendable collective agreements constitutes the mechanism for guaranteeing minimum conditions and pay levels.

Some 5.4 million employees are covered by extended agreements, although only 1 million of them are covered by wage provisions: most extended agreements cover issues such as working time or industry pension and disablement benefit schemes. Extension is most common in construction, textiles and small firms in the metalworking trades.

Under the 1969 Collective Agreements Act (*Tarifvertragsgesetz*) the Federal Minister of Labour can declare an agreement 'generally binding' (*allgemein-verbindlich*) throughout an industry, in consultation with a committee of three representatives each from the central employers' organisation and the trade unions, provided that it is requested by employers or unions who are signatories to the industry agreement, that employers bound by the existing agreement employ at least half the employees in the industry who either are who would be covered by the agreement, and that extension is in the public interest. These conditions may be relaxed in order to remedy social distress.

The issue of extension became the focus of great controversy during 1995 in connection with government proposals for a measure (the Posted Workers Law, or *Entsendegesetz*) to ensure that foreign workers on German building sites were not paid below the agreed minimum rate in the construction industry. Under the proposal the mechanism for ensuring that the agreed rates applied to all employees in the sector, irrespective of the nationality of the employer, was to extend to the construction industry agreement. However, the national employers' confederation, the BDA, and two industry associations, whose vote on the Ministry committee to implement the procedure is needed to enable the industry's provisions to be extended, refused their support – indicating a hardening of employer attitudes towards the mechanism, especially among larger employers, and with particularly strong objections from the engineering employers. The BDA argued that the bill violated the principle of free collective bargaining, and represented an unwarranted exemption: other industries were exposed to low-wage competition in product markets without protection.

The pay round

There is no formal structure of tripartite consultation on pay: a programme of consultation on the economy, including pay, termed 'Concerted Action', which was introduced in 1966 during the Grand Coalition of Social Democrats, Liberals and Conservatives, was abandoned by the unions in 1977. The ostensible reason was employer attempts to have legislation on employee co-determination declared unconstitutional. However, the feeling that consultations on pay were getting too close to 'pay norms', weakening collective bargaining and causing tension within unions, also influenced the DGB's decision.

Although the government formally, and mostly in practice, respects the principle of free collective bargaining, there have been episodes in the 1980s and early 1990s when politicians have sought to influence bargainers through exhortations to pay moderation – most notably in connection with German unification. The government as employer also has a potential impact on the pay round, but in general it has not been used to influence private-sector bargaining. In fact the government has been seeking to import ideas of performance-related pay from the private into the public sector.

Bargaining takes place throughout the year, but with a concentration of key settlements in the late winter and early spring (metalworking, chemicals, construction, printing, the public sector). The 1994/95 pay round saw a number of settlements of uneven duration, with 13 or 14 months in a number of industries. One effect will be to bunch pay negotiations even more closely in the future, with the banking and insurance settlements now also falling due for renewal in spring.

By far the most important single settlement is that for the 4 million or so employees in the metalworking industry negotiated between the union, IG Metall, and the regional metal trades employers' associations, co-ordinated nationally by Gesamtmetall. Traditionally the lead settlement in the metalworking industry has been in the North Baden/North Württemberg area around Stuttgart, although in 1993 and 1995 other regions were chosen for the 'pilot settlement' (see below, 'Challenges and reform'). The pay leadership exercised by the metalworking settlement reflects a consensus that pay bargaining should be shaped by the private sector and, moreover, by an industry heavily engaged in foreign trade.

In the past the range of settlements has tended to be narrow, reflecting both the influence of the metalworking settlement and other institutional forces which compress the 'going range'. However, although the range is small, especially between major sectors, this factor should not be exaggerated, and there is some evidence to suggest that bargaining outcomes may be becoming slightly more differentiated. Moreover, there are substantial differences in the *absolute* levels of pay and other provisions between industries.

Co-ordination between different regional bargaining units of a single industry is very strong: there is virtually total convergence of regional settlements within industries. The trade unions are centralised organisations, and although regional offices and branches may propose figures for pay claims, ultimately it will be the central Executive Committee which decides the claim, often in the light of macro-economic developments and discussions with other unions. In formal terms one region may still be the pacesetter for the industry, as agreements are signed by the regional industrial employers' organisation and the regional officials of the union. There may also be deliberate devolution of this role to a region providing the most favourable conditions for the union.

At the level of the economy as a whole the degree of active co-ordination is weaker and more informal but nevertheless exercises an influence. The BDA seeks to co-ordinate collective bargaining quite explicitly: its annual report contains a section entitled 'Co-ordination of collective bargaining'. It is difficult to assess how much individual employers' associations accept the recommendations and prohibitions of the BDA. The BDA itself does not claim to offer effective and rigorous co-ordination; individual associations are jealous of their bargaining prerogatives and emphasise that they merely 'inform' the BDA of the course of negotiations.

The autumn sees the publication of two important forecasts: that by the Council of Economic Advisers (*Sachverständigenrat*) and the joint forecast of the six main independent economic forecasting institutes. (The latter also publish another forecast in the spring.) The Council of Economic Advisers was set up in 1963, and its five principal members are academics appointed by the federal President, from among the federal government's nominees, for a period of five years. Its forecasts, which have customarily included a plea for wage moderation, are not viewed as offering a basis for consensus on the part of the trade unions but are looked upon more favourably by the employers. The unions have a research institute, the WSI, which functions as a section within the Hans-Böckler-Stiftung and which draws together and interprets bargaining data. Industry unions also have economic departments which produce sectoral data for bargaining purposes. The employers have a research institute, the IdW. The six institutes, whose policy outlooks encompass the range of central opinion, are also influential, but their occasional public pleas for wage moderation make it difficult for them to function as an assessment on which trade unions, at least in public, could base their bargaining perspective. However, German unions do acknowledge that external forecasts influence the climate within which they have to operate and recognise that, since bargaining outcomes are a major economic variable, with potential impact on employment and competitiveness, their claims must take into account the state of the economy as a whole.

This acknowledgement also takes place against the background of German membership of the exchange rate mechanism of the European Monetary System (EMS), and the Bundesbank's publicly stated readiness to counter high settlements with a rise in interest rates, albeit somewhat muted because of domestic recession and the strong DM. The role of the Deutschmark in the EMS, and hence in shaping interest rates throughout Europe, has led to the German pay round having a unique effect on the broader European economy. Trade union movements in countries with close economic ties with Germany acknowledge this. For example, fellow negotiators in Benelux have dubbed IG Metall, the metalworkers' union, the 'Social Bundesbank'.

Recent trends

Pay   Settlements ran below inflation in 1993 and 1994 under the pressure on unions both of the recession and of a sustained employer campaign to cut labour costs. However, 1995 saw a bounce-back and a more conventional pay round, accompanied in some cases – notably metalworking and retailing – by industrial action in support of pay claims. 1993 and 1994 also saw a number of concessions at company level on bonuses – in some cases in return for an employer commitment to new investment. There were also a number of initiatives at company level towards the introduction of an element of performance-related pay for manual workers (BMW, VW, Mercedes-Benz).

Working time   As noted below (see 'Main agreed provisions'), around a quarter of the workforce are covered by agreements providing for the introduction of a 35 hour week. The beginning of the 35 hour week in the metalworking industry on 1 October 1995 prompted a major debate on working time flexibility and Saturday working, with companies often agreeing to some new models of flexibility at workplace level. Probably the most common has been a shift to annualised hours, following the 1994 metalworking agreement, which allowed them for the first time.

Employment creation   The 1993/94 pay round saw a major trade union emphasis on employment conservation and creation via collective bargaining in the face of the major job losses, especially in manufacturing, seen during the recession. Two major initiatives took place. In the chemical industry it was agreed that companies could hire new starters at 95 per cent of the usual agreed rate, reduced to 90 per cent for the long-term unemployed. And in the 1994 metalworking agreement provision was made for cuts in weekly hours with loss of pay in return for employment commitments by companies. The pioneer role here had been played by the November 1993 agreement at Volkswagen, where the company had agreed a four-day week with loss of pay with the union IG Metall, in return for a commitment to retain 30,000 jobs endangered by rationalisation and the collapse of the car market.

The Volkswagen agreement was renewed in 1995, with the addition of extra provisions on hours flexibility and scope for performance-related bonuses. At its November 1995 conference IG Metall produced a new proposal for an 'Alliance for Jobs', to be negotiated in the 1997 pay round. Under the proposal the union would agree a pay increase no higher than inflation and, in a reversal of its previous policy, conceded the principle of special rates for new starters. In return the government would have to abandon plans to cut unemployment benefit and the employers would need to commit themselves to creating 300,000 jobs in the metalworking sector during 1996/97.

Employees outside collective bargaining

Collectively agreed pay scales extend some distance up the managerial/specialist ladder. In the metalworking industry, for example, employees on the top grade of the white-collar scale in 1994 earned a minimum of DM 6,717 (£2,998) a month, or around £38,000 a year, including annual agreed bonuses, with additional company supplements in many cases.

Managers and specialists outside collective bargaining (known as *'außertarifliche Angestellten*, or 'AT' employees) are estimated to make up around 2 per cent of the workforce in private industry, ranging from 3.5 per cent in chemicals to 1.7 per cent in metalworking. There are several convergent definitions as to who is exempt from collectively agreed pay. The 1972 Works Constitution Act, amended on this issue in 1989, offers a definition of 'executive' for the purpose of elections to works councils. Collective agreements usually also contain a line of demarcation either by level of responsibility (or prospective responsibility, in the case of management trainees) or by salary. For example, some agreements rule that employees are not counted as falling within the scope of an agreement if, on average, they earn a set percentage – typically 15–25 per cent – above the highest agreed grade. Definitions of responsibility are often ascertained at plant level through job evaluation, and the excluded employees agreed with works councils.

Pay for this group may be set through individual negotiation, although in larger concerns this is unlikely to be the case. In many companies, pay scales for AT employees, often determined by job evaluation, are added on to to the collectively agreed rates, albeit with a larger salary range and with the individual's position more subject to appraisal than to seniority. The variable element of pay is also likely to begin to grow at this level (see 'Top pay' below). The grades may be set out in a formal agreement with works councils. There is some legal debate as to the entitlement of this group to regular pay reviews, and how much discretion the employer has in granting differential awards. In law an employer may not treat employees differently except for a material reason: a merit system would be justified, if it was aimed at a clearly stated objective. However, if one AT employee was granted a general increase to offset higher living costs (or to maintain the contractually stipulated difference in agreed pay), in theory that would mean that all AT employees would be entitled to a general increase. Nevertheless, there is some evidence that pay for this group as a whole tends to lag during periods of economic downturn.

Challenges and reform

Challenges　The system of industry-wide bargaining has come under increasing pressure since 1990, in part because of the challenges posed by German unification but also because of a series of longer-term trends which have had a cumulative impact and which may have now attained sufficient mass to augur major reforms, or even a profound transformation, of the existing system.

Following German unification in 1990, the pattern of industry bargaining was extended, virtually unaltered, to the territories of the old German Democratic Republic, which had joined the Federal Republic. Collective agreements were negotiated in the two years or so following unification which provided for gradual convergence on pay over a five or six-year period. The collapse of manufacturing in the new *Länder* put great strain on these agreements, and in 1993 the engineering employers abrogated their contract, arguing that further swift convergence would merely multiply the number of business failures. Following a strike, the employers conceded the principle of further pay convergence but with a longer-drawn-out timetable and with scope for agreeing exemptions in the event of corporate hardship.

Moreover, many companies in the new *Länder* have not joined employers' associations, and some companies which are covered by collective agreements through association membership in west Germany (such as Opel, the GM subsidiary) have chosen to remain outside them in east Germany. According to estimates by the German Confederation of Industry (BDI), only a third of employers in the new *Länder* have joined employers' associations. There is also widespread infringement of the terms of collective agreements, either unilaterally by employers or with the tacit or explicit agreement of works councils, where elected.

Parallel processes are on the increase in west Germany. Although it is difficult to gauge their quantitative importance, they are eroding the symbolic as well as actual significance of collective bargaining. Examples range from corporate restructuring to enable some operations to be withdrawn from their former sectors and placed another – more favourable – collective agreement (IBM, Drägerwerk) to outright breaches of agreed terms. As noted above, out-sourcing, especially of service tasks in manufacturing, is also eroding the effective coverage of collective agreements. West German employers' associations have also seen some membership losses – although the prospect tends to be played up before pay rounds. In order to retain membership some employers' organisations have begun to experiment with the idea of 'non-complying' membership, allowing companies exemption from collective agreements. Trade organisations, such as the automotive association VDMA, have also expressed discontent with bargaining outcomes by threatening to establish themselves as employers' associations for more narrowly defined sectors.

There has also been a progressive tendency to decentralise employment regulation from industry level to company or workplace level. The process was given considerable impetus with the 1984 agreement on shorter working hours in the engineering industry, which allowed the implementation of working time cuts to be decided at establishment level between local management and works councils. Personnel policies such as TQM or group work – usually introduced through established consultative mechanisms, but occasionally in circumvention of them – have also added to the issues often most effectively organised in detail at the workplace. This shift is challenging the established role of industry-level agreements, and confronting trade unions and employers' associations alike with the need to find a new equilibrium between industry-level bargaining and the local setting of pay and conditions.

Some – but by no means all – employers have come to view the existing system of industry-level bargaining as a major threat to competitiveness and a barrier to job creation, arguing that it sets too high a minimum level and is too inflexible. This view is rooted in a number of processes which have put pressure on individual companies, and at the same time have created more scope for them to escape the constraints of industry bargaining. New supplier–purchaser relations, which are imposing greater cost disciplines on component suppliers under the threat of losing business, are squeezing medium-sized businesses, the *Mittelstand*. Many large final assemblers in manufacturing have decided to purchase a growing proportion of their inputs abroad, a process which the United Kingdom and Italy have benefited from at the expense of German suppliers. German companies looking for markets in the Americas or Asia have also begun to locate production where the market is rather than rely solely on exports from Germany: such corporate internationalisation is weakening the hold of German industrial culture on personnel practices and business organisation.

All these factors have tended to weaken traditionally strong employer cohesion, and have led to a more combative stance in collective bargaining (see 'Recent trends' above).

Threats to relocate production or establish fresh operations outside Germany have been an important factor in the granting of concessions – some entailing a watering down of collectively agreed conditions, others a partial withdrawal of unilaterally granted benefits – by workforces. Such competition to win investment can serve to weaken the effectiveness of industry-level collective agreements, one of the main roles of which has historically been to prevent product competition between companies turning into undercutting on wages and conditions.

Finally, all these factors, plus manifest employer discontent about recent bargaining outcomes, have spilled over into an intense debate within a number of employers' associations, but most dramatically amongst the engineering employers, about the tactics and strategy of bargaining. In most industries, collective bargaining has always been formally carried on at regional level, with very strong co-ordination between regional outcomes usually exercised by national unions and central employer confederations. Given the strategic role of the leading settlement for each industry, it was important that each side was strongly represented and that the regional outcome constituted a generalisable and sustainable outcome.

This pattern has broken down somewhat in recent years. In the past, unions would announce their claim and in effect choose the region for the initial settlement by terminating the current agreement there. In the engineering industry, for example, it was usually Baden-Württemberg, where both sides were strongly organised. However, in 1993 the central employers' confederation Gesamtmetall under pressure from its small- and medium-sized members – announced its own set of demands for the bargaining round ahead of the union, and succeeded in winning a very low basic pay award. The same approach was tried in the 1995 pay round, though with different results. The IG Metall union chose to negotiate initially in Bavaria, where the employers were less cohesive. When the employers refused to make a pay offer without a prior promise of concessions, IG Metall called a selective strike at a number of manufacturers – though they were deliberately chosen not to have major knock-on effects elsewhere. Given their opening position, the employers should 'theoretically' have responded with a lock-out: however, local support was lacking, and the union was able to win a pay award above inflation for 1995/96.

The 1995 engineering settlement, widely seen as reflecting a tactical miscalculation on the part of the employers, raised a number of issues. First, is regional bargaining a favourable strategy for the employers, given the fact that the unions effectively select the region for the initial settlement, which then sets a pattern for the whole country? Second, and related to this, are employers' associations and individual employers in a position to use the lockout as an effective counter-weapon in industrial disputes?

Reform proposals   As yet there is no consensus between the trade unions and employers about reforming the structure of bargaining, in part because there is no agreement on the character of the problems, and there are widely differing constellations of interests as to solutions. However, some broad positions can be outlined.

- Some employers and industry organisations have argued for the almost complete dismantling of the existing system, with wholesale devolution of bargaining to company-level – or no bargaining at all. That remains a minority view, espoused most publicly by the chair of the BDI and former managing director of IBM Deutschland, Hans-Olaf Henkel. It has only a small toehold amongst the main employers' organisations.
- A redefinition of the relationship between industry bargaining and workplace provision. This is the view held by most of the industry-level employers' associations and the BDA. Although the precise relationship between industry-level and workplace-level regulation remains unspecified – and open to negotiation – such an approach sets out to reduce the amount of detailed regulation in collective agreements, create greater scope for workplace-level agreements, and allow flexibility on issues such as hours and, in the event of hardship or to create employment, on pay.
- Centralisation *v.* decentralisation. The issue of centralisation of bargaining needs to be separated from the centralisation of the actual regulation of pay

and conditions. In some respects, as the debate in the engineering industry has illustrated, the most effective way for the employers to win a devolution of pay-setting to workplace level might be to centralise the process of negotiation and offer a more effective counterweight to IG Metall's national strength. Overall the past 20 or so years have seen an increase in the degree to which industry-level negotiations have been centralised and co-ordinated by the national bodies.

The commitment of the main employers' organisations and most large-scale firms to a reformed version of the current arrangement means that shifts towards greater workplace bargaining will probably take place, but in an evolutionary and and negotiated fashion, especially where works councils are active and subject to trade union influence. However, outside this core, especially in the service sector, more and more firms could drift out of the system of industry bargaining. What remains uncertain is whether such erosion could so fatally weaken industry-level agreements that they increasingly lose their regulatory role.

Main agreed provisions

Pay and grading   Industry agreements provide for minimum rates by grade, and usually contain provisions for grading or approved job evaluation systems. The actual grading of employees on appointment is undertaken at workplace level in conjunction with works councils.

Industry pay agreements are generally concluded for 12 months, but the period can vary from round to round. During the 1993/94 recession there were a number of pay pauses, of up to five months, which in some cases were associated with lengthening the overall contract period. The 1995 pay round also saw a number of longer-term agreements running for up to two years.

Some agreements have included clauses allowing the employers' side to renegotiate the implementation date of an agreed term. In west Germany this figured in the metalworking agreement on working time, under which the industry moved to a 35 hour week from 1 October 1995. In east Germany reopener provisions are included in a number of pay agreements which provide for convergence on minimum rates with the west by a set date. However, the effective use of these clauses depends on union willingness to sanction deferral. No deferral was agreed on the 35 hour week in west Germany, and few exemptions have been granted in east Germany.

The fact that employees' basic pay at company level exceeds agreed minima provides employers with some scope for offsetting increases in agreed minima, which must be implemented, against overall remuneration, allowing firms in economic difficulties to make a lower total pay award than the minimum or implement a pay freeze by eating into company-based supplements. Whether such offsetting is possible, and what rights works councils have to object or be consulted, depend on the nature of company supplements and the terms under which they have been granted.

Merit pay for blue-collar and administrative white-collar employees is typically included in collective agreements in manufacturing industry. However, the underlying philosophy is primarily that of offering incentives to workers not on payment-by-results systems, rather than as performance-related pay. Nevertheless, a number of companies have begun to explore more performance-based payment under team-working arrangements: BMW, for example, introduced such a system in 1995.

Single-status pay   Employees in Germany are still formally divided into blue-collar (*Arbeiter*) and white-collar (*Angestellte*), depending on the type of work undertaken, for social insurance purposes. However, differences of substance on issues such as holidays are generally less marked than in the United Kingdom. A number of sectoral agreements, though still a minority, now provide for single-status agreements in which employees are nominally put on the same scale, in some cases following a formal job evaluation exercise. The most notable example was the 1987 pay agreement in the chemical industry. Volkswagen (which has a house agreement), Audi and BMW (which are covered by an industry agreement) have also introduced single-status agreements. Negotiations are either in hand or expected in a number of industries, although progress remains halting partly because of the technical problems of resolving long-standing differences in grading.

Earnings protection   A number of collective agreements include clauses which protect employees' incomes in the event of regrading because of technological changes in the work process, or loss of performance through age. The metal-working agreement in north Baden/North Württemberg, for example, has a built-in mechanism designed to maintain previous earnings levels for older workers through a guaranteed minimum income for all employees aged over 54 with at least one year's service. Earnings protection is also provided for 18 months for employees who have been downgraded.

Holiday pay and bonuses   Most full-time employees are entitled to between five and six weeks' agreed paid annual leave. In west Germany around 80 per cent of employees have at least six weeks; in east Germany, just under 90 per cent have at least five weeks.

The vast majority are also entitled to additional holiday pay (*Urlaubsgeld*) from their employer. In the private sector this usually forms part of what is termed the 'thirteenth-month salary': the rest consists of year-end or Christmas bonuses. These may be calculated as a lump sum or as a proportion of agreed monthly pay, and both together may exceed an actual month's pay. These bonuses are often added to at company level, giving some scope for the single employer to tie extra elements to company objectives. A number of firms have sought to do this in the case of absence control.

Problems can arise if the employer grants a bonus payment unilaterally and then wishes to withdraw it, or pays a bonus to some employees but not to others. A bonus which has been paid regularly cannot be withdrawn unless the employer expressly reserved this right when the bonus was granted.

Working time   During the mid-1980s and early 1990s achieving cuts in working time was a major focus of collective bargaining for the trade unions. A staged reduction to 35 hours from 1995 was achieved in steel, metalworking and printing. Further moves to 35 hours will follow in a number of other industries by 1998. In all, around a quarter of the labour force are covered by agreements with an actual or prospective 35 hour week.

Among employers the pursuit of greater working time flexibility has accompanied this movement, and by the mid-1990s had become the major determinant of change against the background of shorter hours. From 1 July 1994, new legislation, the Working Time Act (*Arbeitszeitgesetz*) came into force, with changes in health protection for shift workers, new scope for collective bargaining, and scope for greater flexibility.

The working hours of most employees are set by collective agreements, typically negotiated at industry level, against the background of the statutory provisions (see *Contracts and Terms and Conditions of Employment* in this series). Such agreements specify the length of the working week, shift arrangements, and any provisions on annual hours or other forms of flexibility. In many instances the implementation of agreed provisions at workplace level is settled between managements and works councils, which have a statutory right to conclude agreements on the start and finish of daily working hours, breaks, and any temporary lengthening (overtime) or shortening of working hours (see above).

The 1994 Working Time Act also allows some derogation from statutory provisions provided it is by collective agreement (not simply a works agreement) and keeps within certain prescribed limits. For example, the statutory start of 23.00 can be put back or brought forward an hour. Collective agreements can also set a longer reference period for the achievement of the average normal working week without a maximum limit, allowing fully annualised hours or longer reference periods for project-related activities, as in the three-year period allowed under the chemical industry agreement.

In 1994, according to a survey of collective agreements conducted by the Ministry of Labour, average agreed hours in western Germany were 37.7, and 39.7 in eastern Germany.

Industrial disputes

Germany has a reputation for relative industrial peace, with some 40 days lost in industrial disputes per 1,000 workers in the period 1984–93, compared with 240 in the United Kingdom and 310 in Italy. However, the course of industrial relations has often been determined by set-piece conflicts, such as the 1984 engineering strike over shorter hours. The 1995 pay round saw industrial action in the engineering industry and in retailing, as well as other smaller industries, on such a scale as to suggest that claims that pay strkes had become obsolete may have been overstated. The mid-1990s have also seen some increase in white-collar militancy, evidenced in industrial action in banking and in the retail sector in 1994/95.

The law on industrial action has evolved almost entirely on the basis of court interpretations of the constitutional guarantee of freedom of association. This sanctions both strikes and lockouts, subject to a number of criteria. Striking suspends and does not breach the individual contract of employment and does not, therefore, constitute grounds for dismissal provided the action is lawful.

Freedom to take industrial action is, in the first instance, constrained by 'peace clauses' in collective agreements which outlaw industrial action during the lifetime of the agreement and for a period thereafter. In the metalworking industry procedure agreement this period extends for four weeks after the expiry of the agreement. In the chemical industry the parties undertake not to engage in industrial action until conciliation machinery is exhausted. A peace obligation is deemed to be an implicit term of collective agreements as regards disputes over rights, although agreements may also contain a written commitment to refrain from all forms of action.

Full-scale strikes are permissible only when negotiations have broken down: that is, a strike must be the last resort (the *ultima ratio* principle). The issue of token strikes of short duration during negotiations – termed 'warning strikes' (*Warnstreik*) – is more complex. Trades union officials can usually call such strikes without the need for a ballot, and their use seems to have grown in the 1990s.

During the 1980s the unions – especially IG Metall – developed the tactic of selective 'mini-max' strikes, as they were called, intended to put pressure on the employers by calling out members at strategically important suppliers in order to disrupt vulnerable supply chains. The effect on employers could also be magnified without the need for the union to pay strike pay by the fact that strikes were normally confined to one bargaining region: shortages of components at plants in other regions, resulting in lay-offs, would create additional pressure on the employers directly affected, with laid-off workers entitled to unemployment benefit. This tactic was successfully used in the 1984 strike over working hours. However, the prospects for using this approach again were severely curtailed by a change in the law in 1986, which now states that if laid-off workers are engaged in negotiations on a similar claim – and could therefore be seen as potential indirect beneficiaries of a pacesetting settlement elsewhere - they are not entitled to unemployment benefit, and would in practice call on the union for strike pay. Although challenged by IG Metall, this change in the law was upheld by the Federal Constitutional Court in 1995.

For a strike to be lawful, according to the case law developed by the Federal Labour Court:

- It must be the last resort, and must not be out of proportion to its objectives; it must be 'fairly conducted' and must not seek the destruction of the opponent. Nor should it prevent essential maintenance work required to keep equipment in good working order.
- It must be officially called by a trade union and must be supported by a duly constituted ballot: the constitutions of trade unions typically require a 75 per cent vote in favour of any proposed action. However, a union can make an unofficial strike official. In practice, most strike ballots win 90 per cent-plus support – although there have been rare occasions when members have not wholly endorsed a decision to end a strike.
- It must have as its aim matters which can be governed by a collective agreement. In theory a political strike aimed at exerting pressure on the legislature would be unlawful. Opinions differ on the lawfulness of sympathy action: while some authorities claim that such action is unlawful, as the employees concerned would not be seeking to affect their own terms and conditions, some court rulings appear to uphold sympathy action in support of a lawful strike in another part of the country, or where the employer may not be wholly disinterested in the outcome.

Unions, though only rarely individuals, have been fined for engaging in unlawful industrial action.

Lockouts

Lockouts are lawful, subject to certain conditions, and have featured in industrial disputes, notably in printing and metalworking. Case law has been decisive in regulating the permissible scale of a lock-out, through court decisions determining the extent to which employers could respond to a series of official but selective strikes. These decisions ruled that where a trade union was concerned to keep strike action as selective as possible, in order to minimise the outlay on strike pay whilst inflicting maximum economic harm on employers, employers' associations had a legitimate interest in widening the dispute to impose additional costs on the union. In 1980 the Federal Labour Court ruled that lockouts were in general lawful but had to meet a number of criteria. They must:

- fulfil the 'last resort' requirement, and not aim to destroy the other party
- be confined to the collective bargaining region in which the dispute is taking place
- be 'in proportion' to the trade union action. This was quantified by the court in the following terms. If fewer than 25 per cent of the employees in a region are on strike, the employers' side may lock out a further 25 per cent of the relevant workforce; if more than 25 per cent of the workforce are on strike, the employer may lock workers out, provided no more than 50 per cent of the workers in a region are either on strike or locked out.

In its 1995 ruling on employees' right to unemployment benefit in the event of a strike-induced lay-off, the Federal Constitutional Court noted that efforts by employers deliberately to cause lay-offs by an aggressive lock-out strategy could be unlawful.

A strike in the Bavarian engineering industry in early 1995 was marked by a change in union strategy which triggered a new wave of discussion amongst the employers about centralisation *v.* decentralisation of bargaining, and the ability of the employers to mount an effective response to IG Metall. Effectively prevented from using the 'mini-max' approach, the union decided to pick on a small number of end-producers – leaving component manufacturers untouched – who then urged a local settlement. The outcome caused great tensions within the employer camp because the logic of the employers' negotiating approach, which was to insist on a number of concessions from the union before making an offer, led most observers to conclude that the employers would have to respond to selective strikes with a lockout – and thus raise the cost of the dispute to the union. In the event, employer cohesion was not strong enough to enable a lockout to be imposed, triggering argument, as yet inconclusive, within employers' organisations about how to sharpen their own industrial tactics.

Strike pay and unemployment benefit

Strike pay, usually worth around two-thirds of earnings, is paid in the event of official disputes to workers directly engaged in industrial action. Strike pay is tax-free.

Strikers cannot claim unemployment benefit. As noted above, workers affected by lay-offs as a result of a strike in another collective bargaining region are not entitled to unemployment benefit if they work in the same industry, and if the union's demands in their region are 'equivalent in scale and character' to those in the region on strike, although they do not have to be identical to them, and the outcome of bargaining in the region on strike would be adopted in substance by the affected region.

Conciliation

Conciliation procedures for pay bargaining are provided for in collective agreements, on the basis of a model agreement between the BDA and DGB. There is no compulsory state conciliation or arbitration. In order for conciliation to be activated, one party must declare the negotiations to have formally broken down. The conciliation and arbitration agreement for the metalworking industry provides a typical example. Conciliation can be invoked jointly within two working days following the breakdown of talks, or unilaterally by one party within a further day. However, the consent of both parties is needed for conciliation to go ahead. Conciliation boards consist of two representatives of each side, plus a neutral voting chair and a non-voting independent member. The boards are often chaired by prominent current (or former) politicians, acting as honest brokers. Decisions are then made by simple majority. The board must submit a proposal for a settlement within five days, should no agreement be reached between the parties: if the negotiations are particularly difficult, this period may be extended once only for a further five days. The proposal is not binding, but the parties can agree in advance to accept it. Special provisions apply if there is a strike or lockout in progress. Under the agreement, there is also an arbitration procedure to settle disputes which arise out of the functioning of conciliation: under it, the parties agree to forgo resort to the courts. In some industries, such as chemicals, the parties agree not to undertake industrial action, or hold a strike ballot, until conciliation has been tried and failed.

Organisations

Federal Ministry of Labour
(Bundesministerium für Arbeit und
Sozialordnung)
5300 Bonn 1
Postfach 14 02 80
Rochustraße 1
Tel. + 49 228 5271

Federal Employment Institute
(Bundesanstalt für Arbeit, BfA)
Regensburger Straße 104
8500 Nürnberg 30
Tel. + 49 911 170
Fax + 49 911 17 21 23

German Employers Confederation
(Bundesvereinigung der Deutschen
Arbeitgeberverbände, BDA)
Gustav-Heinemann-Ufer 72
50968 Köln
Tel. + 49 221 37950
Fax + 49 221 3795 235

Federation of the Metal and Electrical
Industry and Employers' Associations
(Gesamtmetall)
Volksgartenstraße 54a
Postfach 25 01 25
5000 Köln
Tel. + 49 221 33 99 0
Fax + 49 221 33 99 233

Chemical Industry Employers' Association
(Bundesarbeitgeberverband Chemie eV)
Abraham-Lincoln-Straße 24
6200 Wiesbaden

Tel. + 49 611 71 90 16
Fax + 49 611 71 90 10

German Society for Personnel
Management (Deutsche Gesellschaft für
Personalführung eV, DGFP)
4000 Düsseldorf 1
Niederkasseler Lohweg 16
Tel. +49 211 59 78 0
Fax +49 211 59 78 505

Federal Association of German
Management Consultants (Bundesverband
Deutscher Unternehmensberater eV, BDU)
Friedrich-Wilhelm-Straße 2
5300 Bonn 1
Tel. +49 228 23 80 55
Fax +49 228 23 06 25

German Trades Union Confederation
(Deutscher Gewerkschaftsbund, DGB)
Hans-Böckler-Haus
Hans-Böckler-Straße 39
4000 Düsseldorf 30
Tel. + 49 211 43011

Union of Executives and Senior
Management (Union der Leitenden
Angestellten, ULA)
Alfredstraße 77–79
4300 Essen 1
Tel. + 49 201 78 20 35–6
Fax + 49 201 78 72 08

Main sources

BISPINCK, REINHARD (ed.). *Tarifpolitik der Zukunft*, Hamburg, 1995

BUNDESARBEITGEBERVERBAND CHEMIE. *Außertarifliche Sozialpartner-Vereinbarungen*, Wiesbaden, 1994

DEUTSCHE GESELLSCHAFT FÜR PERSONALFÜHRUNG. *Personalführung*, special issue on quality management, October 1994, and employee suggestion schemes, April 1993

HOWALDT, JÜRGEN. 'KVP. KAIZEN auf Deutsch', *Mitbestimmung*, November 1994

INSTITUT DER DEUTSCHEN WIRTSCHAFT. *IW-gewerkschaftsreport*, various issues

KELLER, BERNOT. *Einführung in die Arbeitspolitik*, 3rd edition, Munich, 1993

KITTNER, MICHAEL (ed.). *Gewerkschaften heute*, Cologne, 1995

LECHER, WOLFGANG. 'Betriebliche Interessenvertretung und direkte Partizipation. Vier Fallbeispiele', *WSI-Mitteilungen*, May 1995

SCHAUB, GÜNTER. *Der Betriebsrat*, Munich, 1988

THELEN, KATHLEEN. *Union of Parts: Labor Politics in Postwar Germany*. Ithaca, NY., and London, 1991

Collective agreements for the engineering industry, chemical industry, banking industry and Volkswagen AG.

6

Greece

Industrial relations and collective bargaining in Greece are showing signs of transformation from a culture rooted in political conflict, with the focus on an interventionist state, to greater autonomy and responsibility on the part of the negotiating parties. It has been fostered by the perceived need for institutional change as a result of growing European economic integration and a new legislative framework which has extracted the state from its former role in mediating between unions and employers in the private sector. This shift of emphasis has yet to be matched by any major shift in forms of workplace representation, despite legislation enabling works councils to be established. However, a more performance-oriented, though not participatory, culture has taken root in many foreign-owned businesses which exercise a leading role in private manufacturing and services.

The main players

The 1975 constitution enshrines the right and freedom to work, with equal pay for work of equal value, and safeguards collective rights of association.

Trade unions

Economic and political development in Greece has generally not been favourable to the growth of independent trade unionism. Agriculture, handicraft production and small traders in services account for a much larger proportion of the work-force than the European average, reflecting the weakness of industry – with a substantial foreign stake in the most developed sectors, often able to offer high wages based on better than national average productivity. Large-scale domestically owned industry is primarily extractive. In 1992 agriculture employed some 22 per cent of the total labour force, compared with an EU average of 6 per cent, and manufacturing 25 per cent, compared with the EU average of 33 per cent. Employees accounted for only 53 per cent of the labour force, with 35 per cent employers and the self-employed, and 12 per cent family workers (compared with an EU average of 3 per cent).

The public sector has also exercised a major influence over the economy in general and over industrial relations in particular. In the past, the state sector, both in its administrative and in its trading branches, provided a source of stable employment and political patronage. However, in recent years pressure on public finances, in part the result of EU financial assistance, which led to stringent pub-lic-sector incomes policies and the privatisation of a range of public services and formerly state-run enterprises, has generated industrial conflict among public employees.

The initial period of trade union formation lasted from 1880 to 1936 – that is, from the beginnings of industrialisation to the Metaxas dictatorship – and includes the crucial years 1909–36, when the foundations of the trade union structure, labour legislation and industrial relations arrangements were laid.

The GSEE (the General Confederation of Greek Labour) was founded in 1918, and enjoys a formal continuity to this day although its political make-up and functioning have been subject to a number of convulsions. This period also saw the establishment of a large number of locally based trade unions. The basis of present-day labour legislation was laid from 1909 to 1922 through a progressive body of law and government decrees which included statutory time off on Sundays (1912), regulation of working hours (1912), women and child labour (1912), the payment of salaries and wages (1914), industrial accidents (1915) and extensive regulations on unfair dismissal (law 2112/20). The same period also saw the laying of the foundations of state paternalism and government inter-vention which have left indelible imprints ever since.

Trade union activity was heavily restricted during the dictatorships of 1936–41 (the Metaxas dictatorship) and 1967–74 (the military government), went completely underground during the occupation in 1941–45, and was allowed only to non-communists during the 1945–67 period, when the Communist Party of Greece (KKE) was outlawed. Legal freedom of organisation has applied since the restoration of democracy and the legalisation of the Communist Party in 1974, although state interference in the internal affairs of unions, primarily through financial support and the nomination of union officials, continued to overshadow the movement into the 1980s.

Legislation has always played a central role in the regulation of industrial rela-tions and wage determination. Between 1955 and 1990 industrial relations were dominated by law 3239, which created the institutional framework of collective bargaining and defined the levels, units, forms and scope of collective bargain-ing. Formal collective bargaining could not take place at any level without for-mal procedures that involved the Ministry of Labour and the courts. Private-sector enterprise bargaining did not exist.

The formalisation and institutionalisation of collective bargaining through law 3239 significantly influenced the structure of trade unions. Employees seeking lawful collective activity were obliged to conform to bargaining levels, units, forms and procedures defined by the legislation, which left no scope for the con-clusion of valid collective agreements at enterprise level. One legacy of this was the weak development of enterprise bargaining, the lack of effective links between enterprise unions where these have developed, and the emphasis on cen-tralised negotiations and occupational trade unionism.

Trade union law   The sources of law on employment in Greece are the constitution, international labour conventions ratified by parliament, EU directives, and statute law, including the Civil Code. Labour legislation covers all employees regardless of the size of the employing organisation. However, certain categories of employees are excluded from the provisions of labour law: seamen, agricultural and fisheries workers, domestic servants and home workers, among others.

Although the full development of free collective bargaining has been held back by the high level of state intervention, in the form of compulsory arbitration, and weaknesses in trade union organisation at national level, there is evidence to suggest that legislation passed in 1990 (law 1876) may have begun to foster greater autonomy in negotiations and the normalisation of relations between employers and trade unions (see below). In particular, those aspects of the 1990 legislation which provided for new conciliation, mediation and arbitration procedures – introduced with the aim of avoiding the compulsory intervention of the state in the bargaining process – appear to have gained wide acceptance. The legislation paralleled moves towards greater bipartite discussion of industrial issues between the GSEE and the main employers' organisation, the SEB. For example, under the 1991 national agreement provision was made for joint consideration of major national economic issues, such as employment growth, productivity, industrial relations and training, to lay the basis of more detailed studies and appropriate responses. This followed a national agreement on joint health and safety discussions concluded in 1989.

Management is obliged by law to recognise all unions functioning in the firm, but has the right and obligation to negotiate in good faith with the most representative one, as determined by the number of union members voting in the most recent trade union elections. (Ascertaining which is the most representative union may entail recourse to the Ministry of Labour.)

A minimum number of 21 persons can apply to the Court of Common Pleas to form a union by submitting the proposed constitution of the organisation: the same procedure is followed for any form of association. Legal status is acquired upon the certain approval of the court, based on the constitutional guarantee of the freedom of association. As noted below, this procedure has given rise to a proliferation of union organisations, many of which – in the past particularly – had a primarily political role.

Structure and organisation   Greek trade unions present a complex picture, partly because of the proliferation of individual unions, partly because of the various levels of union organisation, and, in addition, because of the presence of formal political factions, which often leads to parallel structures existing alongside formal union organisations. The structure of trade unions can be represented as a pyramid with three tiers:

● *Primary trade unions* exist at local or enterprise level. There are over 4,000 such unions. In general, the number of such organisations has fallen as 'paper unions' have been wound up. At the same time there has undoubtedly been some growth in genuine workplace unions as a result of the devolution of collective bargaining. Many are not involved in pay negotiations but may represent employees on other issues and can cover employees up to middle management level.

● *Secondary trade union organisations* are higher-level organisations: they are either federations of two or more primary unions into a sectoral or craft federation (of which there are 116), or constitute 'regional labour centres', which group sectoral or craft federations within a specific area or city. There are 113 of the latter.

● *Tertiary trade union organisations* are the central confederations, which consist of associations of federations and labour centres. The main confederation, deemed competent to bargain, as representative of organised workers in the private sector and in public enterprises, is the GSEE (General Confederation of Greek Labour). In the public sector the dominant confederation is ADEDY.

However, this formal arrangement does not mean that every 'primary' union belongs to a federation, or that every federation is a member of the GSEE. Organisational problems, including the links between the various levels, have held back the development of effective and autonomous union organisation, although there have been phases of attempted reform such as the enterprise–union movement of the late 1970s/early 1980s, and some current aspirations to establish industrial unionism.

Although direct state interference weakened after the fall of the military regime in 1974, the continued hold over the GSEE of officials enjoying government patronage in the period 1974–80 encouraged the growth of political tendencies – in part an expression of pluralism within a unified movement but also an expression of faction-based office-seeking which led to overpoliticisation of the GSEE. The main executive board of the GSEE is still constituted along factional lines.

Membership and density   According to the most recent survey by GSEE, the rate of unionisation in the private sector is 31 per cent, while in the public sector it is about 78 per cent. Union membership is substantially higher in larger companies. In firms with more than 100 employees the unionisation rate is 64 per cent, falling to below 25 per cent in firms with fewer than 10 employees. Unionisation rates also tend to be higher among better-paid employees below management level. For example, among employees with salaries of up to Dr 100,000 (£278) per month the unionisation rate is 15 per cent, while the highest rate (68 per cent) is among employees with monthly salaries of Dr 200,000 (£557) to Dr 250,000 (£695).

Union membership in large Greek-owned and multinational enterprises varies considerably. In some enterprises trade unions may be quite active, while in others they may exist purely for historical reasons. Union appeal among younger members of staff has decreased considerably. According to local managers, no more than 16 per cent of employees were active trade union members in a multinational bank, dropping to 12 per cent in the subsidiary of a major multinational pharmaceutical company.

Trade union rights   Trade union rights and freedoms, internal union democracy and administrative regulations, together with the law on industrial action, are governed by law 1264, passed in 1982. Employers must not hinder trade union organisation, require employees to join or not to join a particular union, intervene in the administration of unions or support unions financially unless the expenditure is deemed to support socially beneficial goals for primary unions.

Dismissal on grounds of trade union activity is invalid and union officials enjoy protection against dismissal during their period of office and for a year after. The number of protected employees depends on the size of the union. However, dismissal is possible on grounds of serious misconduct such as disclosure of company secrets, injury to or serious insult on the employer or the employer's representative, persistent refusal to carry out contractual work, or unauthorised absence.

Under laws 1264/82 and 2224/94 employers must grant unpaid leave of absence to any employee who is a member of the executive board of a trade union, or a delegate to a different tier of a trade union, to enable them to carry out their duties. The amount of paid leave to be granted varies according to the size and status of the trade union:

- Executive members of 'the most representative' national trade union federation, as well as presidents and general secretaries of labour centres and federations of the 'second tier', are entitled to paid leave of absence for their whole period of office.
- Presidents of labour centres and federations with 1,501–10,000 voting members are entitled to paid leave of absence for the whole period of office.
- Presidents of labour centres and federations with less than 101 voting members are entitled to 15 days per month paid leave.

Members of executive boards of unions may take varying amounts of time off, depending on their position and the size of the union. Employees are allowed paid leave lasting no longer than 14 days per year in order to participate in trade union education programmes, provided the leave does not account for more than 1 per cent of a company's workforce.

Delegates to conferences may take unpaid time off to attend. Trade union leave is regarded as employment for the purpose of qualifying for any entitlement arising from employment, or of fulfilling the qualifying period for benefits paid under social insurance. However, the trade union itself is responsible for covering the social contributions of any its officials on leave of absence. Primary unions at the workplace are entitled to a notice board each and, if there are more than 100 employees, to suitable office space for the most representative union in the enterprise.

A union dues check-off system can be negotiated and included in a collective agreement. Before the change in the law in 1982 unions were financed largely through a system of levies on employers, compulsory dues collected from employees, and a state contribution, with money administered and channelled through the social insurance system via an organisation known as Workers' Hearth. Changes in the system of union financing, which curtailed state contributions and allowed check-off, were introduced in 1982, with further reforms in 1990, effective from 1992, intended to bring an end to state financing of unions altogether.

Employers' organisations

The four main employer organisations are

- SEB (Federation of Greek Industries)
- GSEBEE (General Confederation of Greek Tradesmen and Craftsmen), representing small trades
- EESE (Union of Commerce and Trade)
- EEE (Union of Shipowners).

By far the most influential organisation is the SEB, which – along with GSE-BEE and EESE – negotiates centrally with the GSEE on the National General Collective Bargaining Agreement (EGSSE), an agreement which sets minimum pay and other conditions for the whole private sector. The SEB groups some 40 sectoral industrial employers' organisations, eight local industry associations and over 300 directly affiliated individual companies. It supplies research and information to affiliated companies, undertakes research into and analysis of economic and social issues through its Institute of Economic and Industrial Research (IOBE), and lobbies on behalf of Greek business in national and international policy-making forums. The SEB is a member of UNICE and maintains an office in Brussels.

Despite the decisive role the banking sector plays in economic developments in Greece, no employers' federation exists. Collective bargaining is occurring by proxy. Authorised representatives of individual banks bargain with the OTOE trade union federation. The agreement is legally binding, even on banks that do not participate in the process (private, Greek or foreign-owned). Recent years have seen increasing resistance from non-participating banks to being subsumed into the agreement.

Consultation at national level

During the 1980s, under earlier PASOK (Pan-Hellenic Socialist Movement) governments (1981–89), a number of attempts were made to inaugurate tripartite consultation, on occasion with an aspiration to economic planning: all failed to take root. Following the re-election of a PASOK administration in October 1993, a fresh initiative has been undertaken which, combined with the bargaining reforms of 1990, may benefit from the generally better climate of industrial relations.

The Economic and Social Commission (OKE), established in 1994, is an independent body for social dialogue at national level. Its opinion is obligatory for the government on issues of labour relations, social security, taxation, socio-economic policy, local development, investments, exports, consumer protection and competition. The OKE is made up of 48 members and a president. Twelve members belong to the three main employers' organisations: the Federation of Greek Industries (SEB); the General Confederation of Artisans and Handicrafts of Greece (GSEBEE); and the Federation of Commercial Associations of Greece (EESE). Twelve members represent the private-sector trade union federation, the General Confederation of Labour of Greece (GSEE), four the Civil Servants' Federation (ADEDY), five the Federation of Agricultural Co-operatives (PASEGES) and the remainder representing each of various professional associations. The president is appointed by the Minister of Economic Affairs for a three-year term from two candidates proposed unanimously by the OKE. Its first and current president is Professor John Koukiadis, a respected employment lawyer, and also head of the new mediation body, OMED (see below). The first meeting of the OKE, on 19 January 1995, was opened by Prime Minister Andreas Papandreou and representatives of all political parties, with the exception of the Communist Party, indicating the wide acceptance of the new institution.

Since 1991 there has also been greater national-level dialogue between employers and the GSEE on a range of industrial and social issues specified in the national collective agreements (see below).

Workplace/company employee representation

Employees are represented in the workplace through local trade union organisations, through works councils, and on health and safety committees.

Works councils

Legislation on works councils (law 1767/88), which ratified the 1971 International Labour Convention No. 135, was introduced in 1988. Under law 1767/88 employees in enterprises with at least 50 employees, or with between 20 and 50 employees if there is no workplace trade union, have the right to elect works councils at a general meeting of all employees at the place of work or elsewhere. ('Enterprise' here also means branches or separate operations of a company.) The management and the relevant trade unions must be notified of the elections. The law does not cover the public sector or shipping companies.

The size of the council varies in accordance with the number of employees in the enterprise, with three members in firms with fewer than 300 employees, five in those with 301–1,000, and seven in firms with over 1,000 employees. During their two-year term of office members enjoy the protection granted by law 1264/82 to union officials. The chair of the council can have two hours' a week paid time off in order to perform official duties. Works council members have a right to 12 days per term of office in which to attend training programmes organised by the relevant top-level trade union organisation (see above). The cost of operating the system, including the provision of office space, is borne by the employer.

The function of works councils is 'participatory and consultative'; they are not intended to prejudice or displace trade unions, whose negotiating role to safeguard employee interests is expressly recognised in the 1988 law. Councils are required to co-operate with unions and provide them with any information which falls within their competence. However, agreements between works councils and managements do not bind the unions in their pay or other claims.

Councils may not act in ways which do the firm harm. They should confer with management every other month at least, and management must provide the information necessary, together with any other reasonable help, for them to carry out their duties. The information to be given (and the observance of confidentiality by council members) are specified in detail by law. Information to be provided by management includes

- any change in the legal status of the enterprise
- a total or partial transfer, expansion or reduction of its installations
- the introduction of new technology
- changes in staff organisation, a reduction or increase in the number of employees, proposed overtime and any lay-offs or rotation of workers
- annual plans for investment in health and safety
- business plans, balance sheets and accounts, the scheduling of production.

Works councils may also jointly decide a variety of issues not already regulated by collective agreement or where there is no trade union organisation in the enterprise. Under law 2224/94 works councils 'decide in conjunction with the employer' on issues including: internal works regulation; health and safety policy; the scheduling of the training or retraining of employees, particularly with the introduction of new technology; the scheduling of annual leave, the appearance and behaviour of employees in the media; the reassignment of injured employees; and the scheduling of social, cultural and entertainment activities. The works council is also the body which employers must consult over collective dismissal if no trade union organisation exists in the workplace.

Works councils have not yet made any substantial progress and considerable trade union suspicion about their role persists. According to a Ministry of Labour survey, in 1990, out of a total of 3,883 enterprises nationwide, only 80 had established works councils. In the Greater Athens area, out of a total of 1,702 enterprises, only 40 had works councils in operation.

Employee participation usually takes place in a small number of generally large and well managed firms. Local human resource managers have shown very little interest in establishing works councils, while the national employers' federation, the SEB, has reported a low level of awareness of the implications of the European Works Council Directive among its members. The SEB estimates that 61 firms, including subsidiaries of foreign parents, will be affected by the directive (37 manufacturing, 17 banks and seven insurance companies), although only one or two Greek-owned companies in banking will be directly obliged to establish European works councils themselves.

Health and safety committees

Law 1568/85 makes provision for the establishment of health and safety committees, consisting solely of employees, in all private and public companies with more than 50 employees. In enterprises with between 20 and 50 employees, workers elect a single representative.

The size of the committee varies from two members (51–100 employees) to seven in enterprises with more than 2,000 employees. The committee members, elected or appointed by the works council, consult the employer on health and safety issues, and are entitled to time off for training.

The health and safety committee has the right to be informed about

● industrial accidents and occupational diseases
● the introduction of new technologies, new production processes and substances, in so far as they affect health and safety conditions
● any harmful agents the workers are exposed to.

The committee has the right to propose measures for the improvement of working conditions and for the prevention of occupational and other work-related accidents and to call upon the employer to take all appropriate measures in the event of imminent or serious hazard, including stopping the operation of machinery, installations or production processes.

On building sites and in shipbuilding and ship-repairing establishments joint inspection committees have been introduced by ministerial decision. They consist of two trade union representatives, the labour inspector, a representative of the Technical Chamber of Greece and a port police officer where appropriate.

Firms employing more than 50 employees must appoint a safety officer (usually an engineer) and an occupational health officer.

At national level the main organisation is the Council on Health and Safety at Work (SYAE), while the Prefecture Health and Safety Committee (NEYAE) operates at prefecture level. The parties participating in the SYAE include the social partners (the SEB and GSEE), government representatives from the Ministries of Labour, Industry and Health, and scientific bodies such as the Pan-Hellenic Medical Association, the Technical Chamber of Greece and the Association of Greek Chemists.

The 1991–92 national agreement established the Greek Institute of Health and Safety at Work (ELINYAE) to provide the social partners with documentation, research and consultation.

Employee involvement and HRM

Certain aspects of a human resource management (HRM) culture in private-sector organisations (especially with an international culture) have been successfully implemented. Performance-related pay schemes linked with individual performance review for white-collar employees have gone from being virtually non-existent to widespread acceptance in the course of the last few years. The previous and continuing problems in implementing such strategies can be attributed – at least in part – to the strong individualism that characterises Greek culture.

On the other hand, despite enabling legislation, little has been achieved in practice in terms of co-operative and participative schemes. In contrast to most other European industrial relations systems, no sustained tradition of workplace employee representation exists. Managerial prerogatives are still highly regarded and strongly safeguarded, especially in the extensive small or medium-sized, usually family-owned and -run, private sector. Family ownership is a decisive element in management practice: more than 90 per cent of companies employ fewer than 10 persons, and paternalistic forms of management are common.

Legislation passed in the 1980s on works councils has generally not succeeded in implanting a new culture at workplace level, and such changes as have occurred have tended to be confined to large or multinational enterprises. Without a more concerted trade union willingness to support workplace-level forms of representation, and greater employer willingness to surrender some prerogatives, both predicated on a more stable set of national institutional arrangements between the two sides, works councils are likely to make only slow progress.

Collective bargaining

Industrial relations arrangements are based on

- the 1975 constitution, which guarantees freedom of association
- legislation, in particular the 1982 law on union organisation and industrial action (law 1264/82) and legislation passed in 1990 on collective bargaining, mediation and industrial action (laws 1876/90 and 1915/90)
- collective agreements.

In the past Greece had a weakly developed tradition of collective bargaining. Central agreements were frequently concluded through direct state intervention, and bargaining at workplace and company level lacked a legal framework. The trade unions were marked by a high degree of organisational fragmentation combined with political interference and control.

The formal system of wage determination has been described as 'bounded collective bargaining', a hybrid form of collective bargaining subject to direct state regulation. Since the end of the civil war the institutional framework of collective bargaining (reinforced by law 3239/55) established institutionalised state intervention through compulsory arbitration, which effectively set a framework of permanent incomes policies. In the 1950s and 1960s incomes policies were used to guarantee a supply of cheap labour, which was perceived as a prerequisite of rapid industrialisation. Since 1974 incomes policies have been used as an important weapon to control inflation and form economic policies, especially during the period 1974–78. From 1974 to 1985, even with pro-government GSEE leaderships, national agreements were reached only twice (1975 and 1977): the rest were settled through compulsory arbitration. In the 1970s and 1980s 'tight' incomes policies have been succeeded by more 'relaxed' versions, especially before crucial elections or after major political changes. Thus the first democratic conservative government in 1974, like the first socialist one in 1981, awarded, by fiat, wage increases in order to restore the purchasing power allegedly hit by the policies of their predecessors.

However, legislation passed in 1990 (law 1876/90) during the short-lived 'Ecumenical' coalition of the three main political parties in March 1990 marked an important step in efforts to create a new legal and institutional framework for collective bargaining in the private sector. It has been heralded as marking a breach with the preceding centralised pattern, by extending the scope of full collective bargaining to company-level agreements and by providing a new system of mediation to replace the previous focus on the state. The legislation took full effect only in 1 January 1992.

The 1991 national agreement between the union confederation GSEE and the employers (led by the largest federation, the SEB) was seen as a breakthrough in the conduct of bargaining and the broader range of issues placed on the agenda by protagonists and commentators.

Under the previous legislative framework of 1955 (law 3239/55), collective bargaining was seen essentially as a procedure for resolving disputes, a state of affairs reflected in the title of the law, the Collective Disputes Resolution Act. This philosophy, subscribed to by both sides, combined with state and political intervention in bargaining, meant that the law served as a mechanism for implementing government wage policies, weakening the status of unions as bargaining agents, and restricting (and often criminalising) individual union members' rights and resort to industrial action.

Until 1974 the Minister of Labour had the power to alter or reject an agreement or arbitration decision which increased pay above government guidelines. Industrial action was heavily circumscribed, and employers were able to make extensive use of the courts to stop industrial action and resolve disputes by court ruling. Enterprise bargaining and bilateral agreements between the employer and workforce were not allowed; the signature of a representative of the Ministry of Labour was required on what was, in effect, a collective agreement but in formal terms a private contract under civil law, known as a 'protocol of tripartite co-operation'. Mediation, when sought, was provided by the Ministry of Labour and interest arbitration by the civil courts.

The system put in place by law 1876, passed in 1990, marks a major departure from this tradition. The new law, which did not come fully into force until 1992, was specifically intended to foster a culture conducive to dialogue and negotiation rather than conflict. Employers are required to bargain with representative unions, and unions enjoy a right to greater information during negotiations. In return, and in contrast to the past, both sides have to take public responsibility for settlements. Of paramount importance in the new law is the abolition of compulsory arbitration and the creation of a new body for conciliation, mediation and voluntary arbitration (OMED), the first such institution in Greek industrial relations.

Nevertheless, the post-war legacy of permanent incomes policies has remained. Law 2025 forbade any wage, salary or benefit increases in the wider public sector in 1992 (including highly profitable state-controlled banks).

Levels of bargaining

The 1990 law established five levels of bargaining, each of which may lead to the conclusion of a legally binding collective agreement. This arrangement allows access to mediation and conciliation procedures in disputes arising during company-level bargaining. Agreements may be extended to cover non-signatory employers (see below).

Under law 1876/90 the parties entitled to conclude collective agreements are trade unions, employers' organisations and individual employers with at least five employees. Only the most representative union (as defined earlier) in the sector/occupation/enterprise may sign agreements. The same law specifies five types of agreement:

- National general collective agreements (EGSSE, originally introduced in 1935) are negotiated between the central organisations and apply direct to all employers without need for ministerial extension. They set the minimum working conditions applicable to all employees nationally in the private sector, including the national minimum wage, in public enterprises and in local government bodies and are concluded between the GSEE and the SEB–GSEBEE–EESE. Agreements are usually negotiated in early spring, to run for up to two calendar years.
- Sectoral agreements, applicable in a specific industry, either nationally or locally, are concluded by primary or secondary-level trade union organisations and by employers' associations. They are usually concluded for one year.
- National/occupational agreements are concluded between primary or secondary national union organisations (national occupational unions or national federations) and employers' associations in the relevant trades.

- Regional occupational agreements are concluded between primary or secondary local union organisations (local occupational unions or local federations) and regional employers' organisations.
- Enterprise agreements are concluded between primary trade union organisations (local or enterprise) and individual employers, provided they have at least 50 employees, and are applicable to all employees in the firm.

Individual agreements under civil law are also allowed and are common practice for higher and senior management positions.

There is a formal right and duty to bargain which can be triggered by either party. Negotiations must be conducted in good faith and each party must provide the other with reasons for its proposals or counter-proposals. Under law 1876 employees are entitled to 'comprehensive and precise information' from the employer which might be of relevance to negotiations, including information on the financial situation, business policy and personnel policy of the enterprise.

Where an employment relationship is covered by more than one agreement (eg individual–enterprise–sectoral–occupational), the one most favourable to the employee will prevail, with enterprise and sectoral agreements taking precedence over occupational agreements. A firm may find itself covered by a company and a sectoral agreement as well as by the generally binding national agreement.

Non-signatory parties, either unions or employers' organisations, can accede to an agreement by private contact if they wish. However, this cannot happen in the case of an enterprise agreement.

There is a legally binding minimum wage which is negotiated nationally and embodied in the national General Collective Agreement. This minimum applies in the private sector, in public-sector enterprises and in local government. Separate national minimum rates are specified for salaried employees and for wage-earners, with additional amounts according to marital status and years of employment in the same occupation. For example, the additions are 10 per cent for salaried employees and 5 per cent for wage-earners for every three years of experience, up to nine years, and 10 per cent 'marriage benefit', all based on the basic rate.

The Ministry of Labour can extend an agreement to non-signatory parties in a sector or occupation on its own initiative or upon application by an employers' or trade union organisation, provided the agreement is already binding on employers' employing 51 per cent of those employed in that sector or occupation, and that employers and employees to whom the agreement was extended could potentially have been affiliated with the organisations that signed the agreement.

A collective agreement cannot have a duration of less than one year but can be denounced by either side if the underlying conditions have changed considerably since signature. An agreement concluded for an indefinite period may be denounced by either party after the lapse of one year.

The terms of the agreement are valid for six months after its expiry or denunciation and are applicable to new employees entering the firm during that period.

Once the six-month period has elapsed, the underlying terms of employment remain valid until the termination or amendment of the individual contract of employment.

Peace clauses may be freely agreed by the parties.

The 1990 legislation both reflects and encourages a change in the pattern of bargaining, towards greater company bargaining, already a *de facto* reality in larger companies, and is intended to foster industry bargaining at the expense of national occupational agreements. Overall, the aim is to align the determination of pay more closely with decision-making on ability to pay.

This long-term change, which reflects aspirations on both the employer and the union side, could have profound implications for industrial relations, in particular for the structure of the GSEE should a transition to industry unions move ahead. One response by the GSEE has been to step up training for negotiators and to seek to raise the quality of its own research, both into general issues of competitiveness and inter-sectoral issues and on pay questions such as the impact of individualisation. GSEE is also actively participating in the new conciliation arrangements (see below).

Bargaining at company level

The past proliferation of national or regional occupational agreements combined with sectoral agreements means that a single, fairly large, undertaking may be affected by up to 20 collective agreements. Many of these will relate only to small groups of employees, perhaps reflecting the economic (or political) power of an occupational category in an entirely different sector. Where there is an enterprise union, there may be a single deal and its terms will take precedence. Occupational collective agreements involving usually a couple of occupational unions are very common.

However, the precise pattern of bargaining is variable, and depends on the structure and history of the industry and the individual enterprise. In well developed industries there is often a basic industry agreement on pay, backed up with plant or enterprise bargaining on non-pay issues. There is virtually universal support among employers for a shift from occupational to industry bargaining.

At company level, management may choose to develop its own pay policies and structures unilaterally, and is free to do so provided it pays at least the agreed minima for each occupational group, or the industry minimum if applicable.

The pay round

Central bargaining between the SEB and GSEE in the private sector takes place in the early spring. The agreements signed in March 1991 and 1994 lasted for two years (for the calendar years 1991–92 and 1994–95) and set an important benchmark through the rate of increase in the agreed minimum wage. In the past, national agreements have included provision for a mid-year review of the minimum wage, as well as an increase at the beginning of each year. For example, the 1994–95 settlement provided for a 5 per cent increase on 1 January, a 6.5 per cent increase on 1 July and two increases of 4 per cent in 1995, again on 1 January and 1 July. There are no leading sectors as such, but the banking sector agreement, following the national agreement, is viewed as a good indicator of collective bargaining trends. In broad terms it is the national general agreement, together with market forces, which set the pay environment for lower-level negotiation and pay-setting.

In the past the – then annual – central agreement and the pay awards in the public sector were followed by a round of company bargaining (or unilateral awards), with actual rates adjusted typically by a little more than what was agreed centrally. Although many company agreements run from December to December, both sides may delay negotiations until after the central agreement is reached. Company negotiators also await economic parameters, as well as any official forecasts on inflation.

Companies can determine their own pay structure and practice to a considerable extent, with more discretion the greater the divergence between company rates and collectively bargained rates. For example, local firms paying nearer the agreed minima are much more subject to the complexities of being covered by several agreements, including occupational agreements for some employees which can cut across company grades.

In the very recent past, high rates of inflation led companies to institute two reviews a year, with a general-plus-merit increase as from 1 January and the balance of the general increase paid from 1 June. Recently many large companies have opted for a general increase to be paid at the beginning of the year, that is, before the national agreement has been concluded, reflecting the lack of linkage in some cases between high-paying multinational firms and national collective bargaining, and also the decreased levels of inflation. The forecast level of inflation for 1995 envisaged in the national agreement was 8 per cent, the first single-digit figure for 23 years. Should levels of inflation decrease further, in line with the Maastricht convergence criteria, company as well as national pay increases are expected to be commonly awarded once a year.

Nevertheless, for most large and multinational employers national minima tend to be rather irrelevant – in any event, only some 20 per cent of the workforce, at most, are on the national minimum. Employees in such firms may often receive an annual one-off increase at the beginning of the year, well before the conclusion of the national round, at a rate substantially higher than that of the national agreement and the rate of inflation. During the last few years pharmaceutical firms have been awarding the highest rates of salary increase. For example, in March 1993 Glaxo Hellas AEBE increased pay by 15 per cent ahead of the collective bargaining round, and in 1995 Bianex AE awarded a one-off 13 per cent salary increase, well above the expected rate of inflation of 8 per cent for 1995.

Recent trends

The 1991 agreement between the GSEE and the SEB was regarded as a break-through both in collective bargaining and in the overall climate of industrial relations in the private sector. Bargaining in the public sector remained difficult, in part because of the government's determination to impose low (or no) increase in pay as part of its programme to curb public spending, and in part because of privatisation plans. The importance of the 1991 GSEE–SEB agreement round lay not only in its pay accord and the more constructive manner of negotiation but also in the number of other issues, such as training, health and safety, and social security, on the agenda over which agreement was reached. The agreement initially exposed the leadership of the GSEE to internal criticism, much of which subsequently abated given the agreement's protection against inflation and the fact that public-sector employees were given a zero pay increase.

As noted above, the 1994–95 agreement provided for staged increases in the minimum wage over the two-year life of the contract. Increases in 1994 equalled 11.5 per cent, compared with consumer price inflation of 10.9 per cent. The two 4 per cent increases payable in 1995 seemed likely to be offset by forecast price inflation of some 9.5 per cent.

Although the statutory system of pay indexation for the public sector was abolished in 1991, the two two-year national collective agreements in the private sector for 1991–93 and 1994–95 included an indexation mechanism to deal with any consumer price inflation above that allowed in for the settlement.

The 1994–95 agreement also provided improvements in severance pay and a number of non-binding declarations of intent in areas such as child care, parental leave and training. A number of working parties were also envisaged, complementing those already in operation, and covering topics such as employee protection and social exclusion, productivity, the environment and drug abuse.

Pay agreements

Basic pay   Pay is built up on the base of the national minimum wage, or any applicable occupational or sectoral minima. Most companies in developed sectors will be paying considerably above that level, as noted above, and have scope to structure company-based supplements either unilaterally or in negotiation with enterprise unions.

In addition to basic pay, employees also receive a plethora of allowances, many by local agreement. Many large companies have consolidated these allowances into basic pay in order to simplify pay structures.

Other common benefits and allowances include family, marriage and child allowances, staff Christmas parties and presents for employees' children, subsidised meals and presents upon marriage (usually a lump sum) and on the birth of a child (such as jewellery and flowers). Some firms also organise free weekend trips for employees' families and provide low-interest or interest-free loans.

Service increments and merit pay   Service increments are an important part of pay. This is reflected, for example, in the fact that the national minimum wage itself (see above) is structured in terms of years of employment. Industry agreements provide for a series of increments encompassing the employee's whole working life, with a total range of maybe 40 per cent for employees in the same grade. In addition to normal service increments, many companies also pay a loyalty allowance, with an increment awarded for each three-year period in service and consolidated into pay.

The element of seniority in pay structures, and the employee expectations deriving from them, raise a number of difficulties in the implementation of merit pay. Such schemes are much easier to introduce where pay levels are well above agreed minima, enhancing employer discretion. This applies particularly in multinational firms, which enjoy this structural advantage as well as being able to recruit suitably motivated staff by virtue of their reputation and above-average working conditions and pay. Local practitioners working in such enterprises indicate that performance-related pay and individually based reviews have gained acceptance among employees. Successful schemes have been based on close consultation and training. In some pioneering cases, merit reviews are being extended to blue-collar employees, although this is still a novelty.

The problems of building a merit element into normal salary progression have been solved in some cases through the expedient of moving above-average performers more rapidly through the seniority structure, with average performers going up one increment a year.

Family allowances   The national agreement provides for at least 10 per cent of the minimum salary or wage to be paid to married individuals, regardless of sex, including divorced or widowed persons with custody of children and single mothers, and extra allowances are paid for each child, either as a percentage of basic salary or as an annual lump sum. Industrial collective agreements and individual employers may pay even more.

Bonuses and supplements   The law provides for certain annual bonuses to be paid to all employees, leading effectively to salaries being paid 14 times a year. They are

- a Christmas bonus of one additional month's salary (or 25 days' pay for blue-collar workers)
- an Easter bonus of half a month's salary (or 15 days' pay)
- a holiday bonus, also of half a month (or 13 days), paid when the employee takes annual holiday.

Framework agreements

Working time   The legal maximum working week is 48 hours – based on six-day working – with a daily maximum of nine hours. In practice, most of industry works a 40 hour week, the normal maximum as set since the 1984 national collective agreement. Some service industries work 38 or 39 hours, and the banks 37. Under the 1990 development law (law 1892) the normal working week can be extended to 48 hours for a period of three months, provided it is allowed for in a collective agreement. This law also allows employees to be hired to work two 12 hour shifts at weekends only, with social insurance cover provided as if for full-time employees.

Since 1989 average operating hours in industry have increased substantially, while part-time work, despite enabling legislation, has decreased. Most firms have opted to increase flexibility in their internal organisation of work by adopting or extending shift work, night work or Saturday and Sunday working. The number of firms operating shifts has increased from 52 per cent in 1989 to 86 per cent in 1994, well above the EU average of 71 per cent. Similarly, average weekly hours of operation have increased from 64 in 1989 to 88 in 1994.

Annual leave and public holidays Any employee with one year of service with the same employer is entitled to annual paid leave plus a holiday bonus of half salary, or 13 days' pay for daily-paid workers. Holiday entitlement starts at 20 days after the first year and rises to 22 days for three or more years' service. Employees with 25 years of employment in all are entitled to 23 days' leave in the first year of employment with a new employer, rising to 25 days after three years' service or more. This entitlement is often increased in company agreements or by unilateral company decision, with additional holiday according to grade and length of service.

In the private sector, obligatory public holidays consist of Christmas Day, 25 March (Independence Day), the second day of Easter, 1 May and 15 August (Assumption). Other customary public holidays are 28 October (National Day) and the 'half-holiday' of Good Friday (starting at 11:00 am). Banks, public enterprises and civil service departments also take New Year's Day, Epiphany, the first Monday in Lent, Good Friday, Easter Saturday, the Day of the Holy Spirit, 17 November and Boxing Day.

Other leave Maternity leave and parental leave are regulated by statute law, supplemented by the national collective agreement. The basic maternity leave entitlement is 16 weeks on full pay, half of it payable by the employer and half by the state social security fund. Mothers are also entitled to paid nursing leave of one hour per day for up to two years (or two hours per day for one year). Under law 1483/83 and the 1993 General Collective Agreement, either parent, provided they have at least one year's service, may apply for unpaid parental leave of up to three and half months. The company must have at least 50 employees, and no more than 8 per cent of the workforce are eligible in any one year.

Leave for marriage and the birth of a child Under law 1483 employees in the private sector with dependent children are also entitled to apply for unpaid leave of up to six days per year to look after a sick child or spouse. The leave may be extended up to 10 working days where the employee has more than two dependent children. Parents of children with a chronic disability working in enterprises employing at least 50 workers may also apply for a reduction of one hour per day in their normal working hours, subject to a corresponding reduction in pay. Parental leave of up to four working days per calendar year may also be taken for visits to the schools of children below the age of 16 years. Larger companies may also provide, either by agreement or on a unilateral basis, leave for other family events, such as the death of a close relative.

Under the 1993 General Collective Agreement employees who marry are entitled to five days' paid leave, exclusive of their annual leave. In the case of a birth the father is entitled to one day's paid leave per child.

Sick leave   Under law 4558/30 absence through certificated illness for a relatively short period of time is permissible without prejudice to the employee's contract of employment. Such absence ranges from one month for employees with up to four years of service to three months for those with four to 10 years, four months for those with 10–15 years and six months for those with more than 15 years of service. These periods of absence are not deducted from annual leave; but any extra leave is deducted. Sickness benefit is paid out by the state scheme (IKA) for employees with qualifying service. The rate is equal to 50 per cent of normal earnings, plus 10 per cent of that sum for each dependent, up to a maximum of four. Benefit is reduced by one-third where there are no dependants. Benefit is initially payable for 180 days for the same illness, rising to 720 days, depending on the length of qualifying service. Under article 658 of the Civil Code the employer must pay the difference between the daily rate of the state benefit and the usual daily wage for a period of 15 days in the case of employees with more than 10 days' but less than one year's service and up to 26 days' in that of employees with at least one year's service. There are three waiting days before the state benefit is paid, although the employer is obliged to pay half the daily wage during that period. On 1 July 1993 the maximum amount of sickness benefit became Dr 2,450 for the first 15 days and Dr 4,550 per day thereafter.

Industrial conflict

During the 1980s and early 1990s Greece was one of the most strike-prone countries in Europe. Between 1984 and 1993, according to figures prepared by the UK Employment Department, 3,750 working days were lost per thousand employees each year: this compares with 240 for the UK and 40 for Germany. However, industrial conflict in the private sector has been subdued in recent years, primarily as a result of unemployment and agreed increases in real pay, in contrast to the more troubled public sector, where real wage cuts and privatisation have prompted many disputes. The new mediation arrangements (see below) have also undoubtedly led to an improvement in the industrial climate.

The right to strike is guaranteed by the constitution and statute law but courts can judge whether the right is being exercised within the limits or the practice of any other right specified by the constitution and civil law, and by laws 1264/82 and 1915/90. Industrial action must be conducted in good faith, in an ethical way and in accordance with the social and economic aims appropriate to that right.

Permitted and unlawful industrial action

A strike can be decided by the most representative trade union or by any other trade union. To be lawful a strike must be carried on in pursuit of industrial demands (including trade union rights) or in solidarity with employees in another undertaking provided that the interests of the strikers are affected by the outcome of the action and that it has been called by the most representative tertiary trade union organisation. Courts have judged political strikes (any strike with only political demands or under the pretext of employment issues) unlawful.

Strike action requires a 24 hour period of notice and must be preceded by a set of written demands, authorised by a recognised union and subject to a secret ballot. Other forms of industrial action are regarded as strikes and subject to the same legal requirements.

Before or during a strike either the union or the employer can request public dialogue on the demands presented by the other side under law 2224/94. The dialogue is chaired by a mediator from OMED. Public dialogue is obligatory for public utilities.

For the duration of the strike the union must ensure that a skeleton staff is maintained for safety reasons. Law 1915/90, as amended by law 2224/94, also requires essential public services to be maintained. Under the new regulations all matters related to the procedure for selecting security personnel and the maintenance of vital services to the public are the subject of collective agreements, primarily at enterprise level.

Law 1915/90, passed in the teeth of strong opposition from the unions, also stipulates that employers have the right to dismiss (including trade union officials)

- employees who remain on strike if the courts have declared the strike an abuse of the union's power, within 24 hours of the court ruling
- employees who prevent others going to work, occupy the premises or in any other way prevent the enterprise from functioning smoothly
- those who by law or collective agreement must work during a strike but do not follow management instructions
- employees who, during the course of a strike, by force, threats or other illegal act, prevent other employees from working or deliberately destroy or damage the installations or equipment of the enterprise.

In the latter case criminal charges may also be brought against the employees. Severance pay is obligatory for the employer in all such cases of dismissal as well as in the case of an unofficial strike. However, the employer need not pay severance pay where criminal charges have been brought against an employee.

Employees who are on strike cannot be sacked if the decision to strike was reached through legal procedures and the strikers have not broken the law. Even when the strike is over, sacking employees who took part in it could be judged by the courts an abuse of power.

Lockouts

Lockouts are illegal under law 1264/82. Employers can, however, take legal action if the law is broken by the strikers or by employees who, for safety or other reasons, must not participate in the strike.

Mediation and arbitration

Law 1876/90 established a new legal and institutional framework for conciliation, mediation and arbitration procedures to replace the 35 year-old state-controlled scheme of compulsory arbitration and state intervention in the bargaining process. The negotiating parties can resort either to mediation or to arbitration when an impasse occurs in the negotiations. Under the new system the state will no longer provide interest arbitration but will be available to provide rights conciliation (for example, in contested dismissals).

Mediators and arbitrators are provided via a new organisation, the Organisation for Mediation and Arbitration (see below).

Either party can request mediation. The mediator is selected by the parties from a special list of mediators or (when no agreement can be reached) by drawing lots. The mediator invites the parties to discussions, interviews them in private, examines individuals or makes any other enquiries regarding working conditions or the financial situation of the undertaking. Public organisations have to provide any relevant information that may be requested.

If, despite the efforts of the mediator, the parties fail to reach agreement within 20 days the mediator submits his or her own proposal. Should the parties fail to indicate their acceptance within five days the proposal is considered rejected and the mediator may publish it in the daily press. If accepted by the parties, it is signed and has the same standing as a collective agreement.

Under an amendment to the legislation (law 1915/90), in the face of an imminent strike either party can ask for a public discussion of the dispute under the supervision of a mediator chosen under the new system. If no settlement is reached within 48 hours the mediator can publish his or her own proposals. A settlement, if reached, has the status of a collective agreement. Otherwise, trade unions retain the right to take industrial action during mediation/arbitration unless they have already waived the right in an earlier collective agreement.

Arbitration can be initiated at any stage of the negotiating process by mutual agreement, unilaterally by either party if the other side has rejected mediation, or unilaterally by the union if it has accepted a mediation proposal which has been rejected by the employer. In the latter case the union must suspend any industrial action for 10 days. The arbitrator is chosen in a similar way to the mediator, operates in a similar manner, and has to assume his or her duties within five days. The law does not provide for a panel of arbitrators (either all neutral or tri-partite), only for a single, neutral arbitrator.

The arbitrator's award must be issued within 10 days of assuming his or her duties, if mediation has already taken place. Otherwise the award must be issued within 30 days. Interest arbitration in Greece takes the form of conventional arbi-tration; the arbitrator is free to fashion any award he or she deems appropriate. The award has the status of a collective agreement. Mediators and arbitrators form an independent body, affiliated to the Organisation of Mediation and Arbitration (OMED). They are appointed for a three-year renewable term and must be above 30 years of age, with considerable experience in employment relations and preferably relevant postgraduate qualifications as well as publica-tions. OMED is responsible for staffing the body of mediators and arbitrators but does not offer mediation or arbitration itself.

The Organisation of Mediation and Arbitration is governed by an 11 member executive board consisting of two academics, three trade union representatives from the GSEE General Confederation of Labour, one representative of each of the three main employers' organisations, a representative of the Ministry of Labour and a recognised authority in the field of industrial relations who is elected by the other members. The organisation is financed by employee, employer and state (Ministry of Labour) contributions as well as by the fees charged for its services.

From 1992 until the end of 1994, OMED handled 472 cases of mediation and arbitration. The breakdown for each year is shown in Table 3. Although it is involved in the new machinery, the SEB views OMED with some scepticism, and employers remain opposed in principle to any obligation to negotiate and reach a settlement.

Table 3 *Cases handled by OMED, 1992–94*

Applications for	1992	1993	1994	Total
Mediation	99	128	115	342
Arbitration	40	48	42	130
Total	139	176	157	472

Organisations

Official Manpower and Placement Agency
(OAED)
Thrakis 8
166.10 Glyfada
Tel. + 30 1 993 2589
Fax + 30 1 993 7301

Ministry of Labour
40 Piraeus Street
Athens
Tel. + 30 1 523 2110

Federation of Greek Industries (SEB)
5 Xenofontos Street
105 57 Athens
Tel. + 30 1 323 7325

Greek Personnel Management Association
3 Karitsi Street
105 61 Athens
Tel. + 30 1 322 5704

British–Hellenic Chamber of Commerce
25 Vas. Sofias
106 74 Athens
Tel. + 30 1 721 0361
Fax + 30 1 721 8571

General Confederation of Greek Labour
(GSEE)
Patision and Pipinou 27
112 51 Athens
Tel. + 30 1 883 4611
Fax + 30 1 822 9802

Organisation for Mediation and Arbitration
89 Patision Street
10434 Athens
Tel. + 30 1 881 4922
Fax + 30 1 881 5393

Main sources

BANOUTSOS, I., and THEOCHARI, C. *Industrial Relations and the Environment in Greece. National report.* Dublin, European Foundation for the Improvement of Living and Working Conditions, 1992

Deltion Ergatikis Nomothesias (Index of Employment Law), Athens, various issues

HARILAOS, GOUTOS, and LEVENTIS, GEORGE. *Ergatiki Nomothesia* (Labour Legislation). Seventh edition. Athens, Deltion Ergatikis Nomothesias, 1988

IOANNOU, CHRISTOS. *Salaried Employment and Trade Unionism in Greece.* Athens, Foundation for Mediterranean Studies, 1989 (summary in English)

KATSANEVAS, THEODORE. *Trade Unions in Greece.* Athens, 1984 (in Greek); based on a 1981 Ph.D. submitted at the London School of Economics

METROPOULOS, A. 'The Future of the trade unions', in *Positions,* 1987 (in Greek)

7

Irish Republic

An essentially voluntaristic system of industrial relations operates in the Republic of Ireland, which shares a common tradition with the British system, reflecting the fact that the republic secured independence from Britain only as recently as 1922, and reflecting also the two countries' traditionally close historic and cultural links. In recent years, negotiating arrangements have begun to diverge significantly, as successive Irish governments have consolidated collective bargaining through national corporatist agreements with the 'social partners', in contrast to the UK government's priority of liberalising the labour market and encouraging the devolution of collective bargaining.

Until recently the same piece of legislation (the 1906 Trades Disputes Act) governed industrial conflict in both countries. But in Ireland it has been superseded by the 1990 Industrial Relations Act, while in Britain successive acts of legislation have been introduced during the 1980s bringing fundamental changes in the conduct of industrial relations.

The most significant development in Irish industrial relations in recent times has been the negotiation of new corporatist-style agreements covering not just levels of pay increase but also broader socio-economic policies linked with the state's desire to exert control over public finances. These agreements are not legally binding, but compliance with the pay terms has been consistently high. The main dispute-settling agencies, the Labour Court and the Labour Relations Commission, have played an important part in ensuring that the agreed pay increases are not exceeded.

These agreements, beginning with the Programme for National Recovery in 1988, have contained voluntary industrial peace clauses aimed at ending attempts to improve on nationally agreed terms and conditions. The agreements have coincided with most significant decline in the number of days lost owing to strike action in the history of the state.

One distinctive feature of the Irish economy is the share of employment accounted for by the subsidiaries of foreign multinational companies. In 1994 they employed over 90,000 people out of a total employed labour force of 1.4 million. This reflects some years of national development policy aimed at attracting foreign direct investment, especially in high-tech manufacturing. One associated phenomenon has been the emergence of a significant non-unionised sector, particularly among newly established multinationals operating on greenfield sites. Research undertaken at the University of Limerick has established that over half the 53 greenfield operations established in Ireland from the mid-1980s to 1992 and employing more than 100 people opted not to recognise trade unions for collective bargaining purposes. Country of origin was the critical explanatory factor: of the 27 US-owned companies, 23 were non-union, whereas over 80 per cent of newly established Irish companies decided to recognise unions. This trend has continued in recent times and presents an important new dimension of Irish employee relations.

Another significant feature of employment is the rapid growth in atypical employment – part-time, temporary and fixed-term contract workers. As part of a Europe-wide survey in 1990, it was found that there was a relatively low incidence of part-time work, fixed-term contract work, Saturday and evening work, compared with the major EU countries. However, data from the Industrial Development Authority (IDA) show a sharp rise since the 1980s in the growth of 'atypical' employment in state-assisted companies. Between 1987 and 1994 part-time, temporary and subcontract employment increased by 121 per cent in companies assisted by the state's industrial development agencies, while over the same period permanent employment in those firms rose by just 10.5 per cent. Of the total of 20,700 'atypical' jobs among these state-assisted companies at the end of 1994, 60 per cent were in indigenous firms and 40 per cent in foreign-owned companies.

The rate of growth in atypical employment since 1992 in foreign-owned firms supported by the IDA was around 100 per cent, while in indigenous firms it was 38 per cent. In 1994 almost 60 per cent of fresh employment created in foreign companies assisted by the IDA was due to new contract and temporary jobs. By the end of 1994 such jobs accounted for 10 per cent of all employment in foreign-owned companies and 9 per cent of total employment in foreign and indigenous companies assisted by the state's industrial support agencies.

The recent economic background has shown rapid growth and low inflation, albeit combined with sustained and high unemployment. The economy has also benefited from substantial inflows of EU funds. Economic growth has been running at around 5 per cent since the early 1990s, and fast growth is forecast for the next years – with some impact on unemployment, now standing at 15 per cent. Inflation is running at 2.5 per cent. After peaking at 116 per cent of national income in 1986, gross public debt fell to some 88 per cent of national income by 1994.

The main players

The system of employee relations is founded on a pluralist tradition. Recently the state has become more directly involved in employee relations and joined the trade unions and employers in centralised, all-encompassing collective bargaining. The state also has an important part to play in supporting dispute resolution agencies such as the Labour Court and the Labour Relations Commission as well as the quasi-judicial Employment Appeals Tribunal. The system of Joint Labour Committees which sets legally binding minimum wage rates following negotiations between employer and trade union representatives also provides for enforcement by state inspectors.

The state also plays an important role as a legislator on the conduct of industrial relations. Largely as a consequence of EU membership, the state has introduced considerably more legislation in recent years which has contributed to greater regulation of employment. It has diligently introduced legislation giving effect to the various EU directives in the area of social policy. Lastly, the state plays an important role in its capacity as employer of 270,000 workers in a total employed workforce of just under 1.2 million, and given that half of all current government expenditure is accounted for by pay and pensions.

The main employer and trade union confederations are well established as 'social partners' and can be said to be representative of both sides of industry, given the numbers and the spread of their membership. The emphasis on centralised collective bargaining has merely reinforced the central role played by these organisations in the consensual approach to economic management favoured by the majority of political parties.

Trade unions

The most up-to-date (1993) official figures suggest total trade union membership of 485,700, equivalent to 47 per cent of all employees at work. After considerable growth in trade union membership, from 312,600 in 1960 to 527,200 in 1980, the 1980s saw the greatest decline in union numbers since the 1930s. Total membership fell by over 51,000 members, almost 10 per cent, between 1980 and 1985. The fall was arrested in 1988, when the total stood at 470,000, and since then most years have seen a slight rise in overall numbers.

The reverse in the decline of union numbers is thought to reflect growing recruitment of women and significant recruitment among the 42,000 now employed on state-sponsored community employment programmes, introduced as part of the 1987 Programme for National Recovery.

The contrast in levels of trade union representation among employees (excluding the self-employed) in the private and in the public sectors is striking. In 1993 the number of trade union members in the private sector stood at 220,300 representing just under 36 per cent of all private-sector employees, while in the public sector union membership levels of 200,600 represented a density level of 76 per cent. A growing number of trade union members are unemployed. Of the 485,700 trade unionists in 1993, just under 48,000 were unemployed.

The overwhelming majority (over 97 per cent) of trade union members belong to unions which are affiliated to the main national union confederation, the Irish Congress of Trade Unions (ICTU). The ICTU was established in 1959, ending a rift within the trade union movement, largely revolving around personality differences and tensions between Irish and British-based trade unions. Today around 40 staff are employed in servicing the activities of ICTU.

The fact that more than half its members are employed in the public sector is also reflected in the composition of the 29-strong executive council of ICTU, which oversees the implementation of policy decided at the biennial delegate conferences. A general purposes committee deals with urgent business between executive council meetings. A number of subcommittees perform important functions within the ICTU. They include the industrial relations committee, which deals with applications for 'all out' pickets, the disputes committee, which considers inter-union membership disputes, and the demarcation committee, which deals with inter-union differences over work organisation and boundaries.

The function of the ICTU is to 'represent the collective will and purpose of the trade union movement'. Its main task is to co-ordinate trade union activity by representing the unions in national collective bargaining, overseeing inter-union relations, representing the unions on various national agencies and to act as the voice of the trade union movement internationally through membership of the European Trade Union Confederation and involvement in the work of other international institutions. The presidency and vice-presidency of ICTU alternate in two-year terms between officials from Northern Ireland and officials from the Republic of Ireland.

Today a total of 69 trade unions belong to the Irish Congress of Trade Unions. Individual trade unions retain a considerable degree of autonomy. The structure of the Irish trade union movement is unusual in that it includes unions which organise only in the Republic of Ireland, Irish-based unions which organise in both the Republic of Ireland and Northern Ireland, British-based unions which are affiliates of the British TUC and organise in both the Republic of Ireland and in Northern Ireland, and British-based unions which are affiliates of the British TUC and which organise in Northern Ireland only. In fact, of the 69 trade unions belonging to the ICTU, 29 have their headquarters based outside the Republic of Ireland. The Irish sections of British-based unions have virtual autonomy in decision-making.

Ten of the trade unions affiliated to the ICTU are also affiliated to the Irish Labour Party, including SIPTU, and many of the larger British-based unions such as the AEEU, GMB, MSF and UCATT, which are also affiliated to the British Labour Party.

According to the ICTU membership returns at 31 December 1994 the total affiliated membership of 678,392 was composed of 473,743 employed in the Republic of Ireland and 204,649 in Northern Ireland.

Considering union members in the Republic of Ireland only, the largest unions were: SIPTU (190,501 members); IMPACT (27,210); MANDATE (27,048); TEEU (23,269); the primary teachers' union, INTO (20,861); the white-collar union, MSF (21,000); the postal and telecommunications union, CWU (19,600); and the general union ATGWU (17,514). As can be seen, the largest union, SIPTU, accounts for just over 40 per cent of all trade union membership in the Republic of Ireland.

Freedom of association and trade union law

In article 40.6.1(iii) of the 1937 constitution the state guarantees liberty for the exercise, subject to public order and morality, of 'the right of the citizens to form associations and unions'. The Supreme Court has since ruled that the constitution also guarantees, by implication, the right of citizens not to join a trade union if such is their desire. As a result pickets cannot be mounted on employers in a bid to compel non-union employees to join a trade union. This also makes it unlawful for an employer to dismiss an employee for refusing to join a trade union. The Unfair Dismissals Act 1977 deems that the dismissal of an employee for trade union membership or activity is one of a number of grounds which makes such a dismissal automatically unfair.

The constitutional status of closed shop agreements remains very unclear, though it has been held that the legal status of such agreements probably depends on whether they are pre-entry or post-entry agreements. In a pre-entry closed shop a worker cannot apply for a job unless he or she is a member of a relevant union or unions; in a post-entry closed shop the employer can select any applicant but the selected employee must join a union on taking up employment or soon after. It would appear from the Educational Company *v.* Fitzpatrick judgement of 1961 that post-entry closed shop agreements are suspect constitutionally, while pre-entry closed shop agreements would appear to conform with the intentions of the constitution according to the judgement in the 1981 case of Abbott and Whelan *v.* Transport & General Workers' Union and Southern Health Board.

The main legislation dealing with the formation and operation of trade unions are the Trade Union Acts of 1941 and 1971 and the Industrial Relations Act 1990. In order to register, a union must apply to the Registrar of Friendly Societies, who will inspect the union's rules, objects and procedures. The conditions to be met before a union can gain a negotiating licence from the Minister for Enterprise and Employment have most recently been amended by the Industrial Relations Act 1990.

Trade unions must have a minimum membership of 1,000 and must place a minimum deposit of £20,000 with the High Court – the amount to be deposited rises in accordance with the size of the union's membership to a maximum of £60,000 for those with over 20,000 members. Deposits are not required where a new union is formed by the amalgamation of two or more unions. Trade unions with headquarters outside the Republic of Ireland are not required to register on this basis but must be legally recognised trade unions in their country of origin and must meet some prescribed guidelines in relation to their controlling authority. The Minister for Enterprise and Employment has discretionary power to allow what are termed 'exempted bodies' to participate in collective bargaining: such bodies are not required to hold a negotiation licence to engage in collective bargaining. Such 'exempted bodies' are few in number and of lesser importance in the greater scheme of collective bargaining. Examples would include in-house or staff associations and some civil service associations; the most important 'exempted body' is probably the Irish Hospital Consultants' Association.

Employers' organisations

There are three main employers' organisations: the Irish Business and Employers' Confederation (IBEC), the Construction Industry Federation (CIF) and the Society of the Irish Motor Industry (SIMI). The newly formed Irish Small and Medium Enterprise Association (ISME) is also a significant employers' representative but it has yet to secure a negotiating licence and cannot engage in collective bargaining.

According to the 1941 Trade Unions Act, employers' organisations are obliged to register as trade unions to gain a licence to engage in collective bargaining. All the employers' organisations, bar ISME, which was a break-away from IBEC, have a negotiating licence and can engage in collective bargaining.

By far the largest and most representative is IBEC, which represents 3,700 firms in both the private and the public sectors, employing in the order of 300,000 workers, some 20 per cent of the workforce. IBEC was formed in January 1993 following the merger of the Federation of Irish Employers (FJE, formerly the Federated Union of Employers) and the Confederation of Irish Industry (CII). Primarily the FIE acted as an employee relations confederation of employers, while the CII was a trade and industry lobbying organisation. The merger of the two has given Irish industry a single influential voice in dealing with the state, trade unions and international institutions.

IBEC is funded by members' subscriptions and is politically independent. A general council of 250 members, which meets twice a year, is the overall policy-making body. The council is made up of representatives from the confederation's 12 regions, 12 sectors and over 50 industry consultative groupings. The national executive council is the body which formulates policy within the confederation's overall objectives and supervises the implementation of policy.

The Construction Industry Federation (CIF) has over 2,000 affiliated firms, employing around 50,000 workers, or 75 per cent of all workers in privately owned construction firms. The CIF represents the industry in representations on trade and commercial matters as well as employee relations negotiations. The CIF has a branch network and a national council which formulates and monitors policy – the national council is representative of various specialist associations such as home builders, electrical contractors and general contractors.

The Society of the Irish Motor Industry (SIMI) performs a similar role in the motor industry, engaging in lobbying on trade and commercial matters as well as employee relations negotiations on behalf of 1,200 member firms.

Consultation at national level

Tripartism and the role of the state

The tradition of collective bargaining is strong and has been increasingly associated with centralised tripartite bargaining between employers, trade unions and the state. In 1987 the state introduced a new dimension into centralised collective bargaining by joining with the employers and trade unions in a more concerted corporatist approach to managing the economy. What followed were three-year tripartite agreements revolving around voluntary incomes policies but also containing an agreed approach to all aspects of social and economic development.

Through their representative organisations the employers and trade unions enjoy unprecedented influence in shaping a broad span of socio-economic policies. While the pay agreements are seen as the glue which holds these arrangements together, there is no doubt that a new sense of social consensus prevails or that it has played an important role in turning the economy round since the mid-1980s and contributed to relatively harmonious employee relations.

The three agreements since 1987 – the Programme for National Recovery, the Programme for Economic and Social Progress and the Programme for Competitiveness and Work – were concluded on an entirely voluntary basis, in keeping with the voluntarist approach which pervades employee relations, and are not in any sense legally binding. In spite of this, adherence to the pay terms has been remarkably high and has contributed significantly to low and stable rates of inflation, consistently high economic growth and some measure of control over public finances. Implementation of these agreements is overseen by what is known as the Central Review Committee, which meets monthly and is composed of representatives of the state and each of the social partners.

Voluntary social partnership

The voluntarist approach to employee relations is reflected in and enhanced by these new forms of centralised collective bargaining. Consequently the employers and trade unions actively participate as the main social partners in a broad range of state agencies regulating industry and employment. Both IBEC and ICTU have representatives on numerous tripartite bodies. Examples of institutions to which the employers and trade unions have nominated representatives include the National Economic and Social Council (an advisory body which reports on all aspects of economic and social policy), FAS (the state training authority), the Labour Court and the Labour Relations Commission (the state's main dispute-settling agencies) and the Industrial Policy Review Group.

Incomes policies

According to the 1981 Commission of Inquiry on Industrial Relations the Irish system of industrial relations reflects the view that collective bargaining and not the law should be the primary source of regulation in the employment relationship. Collective bargaining in Ireland is firmly rooted in the pluralist tradition, with a strong tendency towards centralised bargaining involving the state, employers and trade unions.

After the Second World War there were 12 distinct wage rounds up to 1970, eight of which were negotiated at industry or company level and four of which were negotiated nationally between the employers (FUE) and the unions (ICTU). State involvement in collective bargaining was minimal during this period but centralised wage rounds set permissible increases. Only in 1964 did the national wage recommendation for the first time set a pay increase for a fixed term of 30 months; all the others had been open-ended. Overall, the wage round system was very loose, with increases passing on to some groups faster than others and with lengthy gaps over time in the finish dates for particular wage rounds across different sectors, groups and individual employments. Certain groups such as maintenance craft workers set the pace in negotiations because of their bargaining strength and this had the effect of contributing to considerable wage inflation, especially in the late 1960s.

In the wake of a number of major strikes during the 1960s, support grew politically for a new form of incomes policy in the hope of controlling inflation and restoring 'order' to industrial relations. When the National Industrial and Economic Council (a body set up in 1963 and composed of employer and employee representatives, civil servants and academics) suggested in 1970 the establishment of a new bipartite body to interpret national policy guidelines for wage increases, the government responded by reviving the Employer–Labour Conference. This was to be a joint forum of unions and employers (with representatives of the state in its capacity as an employer) with an independent chair.

Following the breakdown of negotiations on a national agreement at the Employer–Labour Conference that year, the government introduced a Prices and Incomes Bill and threatened statutory control of pay unless a national pay norm could be agreed in voluntary negotiations. Faced with a statutory incomes policy, the employers and trade unions concluded the first national agreement in six years and between 1970 and 1980 eight further (voluntary) central agreements followed; four emerging from bipartite negotiations (between 1972 and 1976) and four from tripartite negotiations (between 1977 and 1980). The latter two agreements were termed National Understandings; they saw the first move to broaden the agenda of negotiations and were precursors of the type of agreements to come at the end of the 1980s.

A feature of the agreements between 1970 and 1980 was the addition of tax reform to the agenda and the linking of state budgetary policy with national pay determination. The agreements of the 1970s tended to have three main pay elements: provision for basic pay rises; provision for above-the-norm increases in order to allow the negotiation of 'productivity' deals and, from 1972 onwards, provision for below-the-norm increases.

Attempts to negotiate a further national agreement in 1981 broke down in the face of resistance from employers and the state, which was concerned at mounting problems with public finance. Between 1981 and 1987 free collective bargaining returned and the state withdrew from the increasingly prominent role it had played in national pay negotiations during the previous decade. In this period there were five pay rounds which differed substantially from those that had gone before. Levels of wage rises within individual pay rounds varied significantly and higher rates tended to be paid in foreign-owned, high-technology firms and in the manufacturing sector compared with companies in the distribution and services sector. The public sector fell still further behind. Pay rounds *per se* almost disappeared during this period and the termination dates in different sectors and employments for 'round' agreements stretched from three months to 21 months between 1982 and 1985. Company-level bargaining became more popular and sectoral-level bargaining became less common.

The return to power of a minority Fianna Fáil government in 1987 prompted renewed interest in concluding new corporatist-style agreements. The trade unions were supportive of such a move, as their bargaining power was being eroded during free collective bargaining, they were losing numbers as unemployment grew and they feared that an Irish government could be tempted to follow the lead set by the Thatcher government in Britain in isolating trade unions. The new government saw benefits in controlling the public finances, a large portion of which are still accounted for by pay and benefits, and had to address a spiralling public debt in order to remain within the European Monetary System and aspire to economic and monetary union. In spite of initial reluctance, the employers were tempted to look again at centralised bargaining.

What followed was a new concept of centralised agreement, much more comprehensive in scope than any previous centralised agreement. The Programme for National Recovery concluded in 1987 was a three-year agreement which set modest pay increases but also contained commitments on a broad range of economic and social policies. Central to the success of the agreement was the willingness of the employers and the trade unions to embrace in a new consensus with the state in aiming to tackle the economic crisis by meeting stated economic targets and, in particular, the stabilising of the debt–GNP ratio.

The agreement had four main objects: the creation of a fiscal, exchange and monetary climate conducive to economic growth; movement towards greater equity and fairness in the tax system; the reduction of social inequalities; and greater practical measures to generate employment. Unstated commitments were made to introduce legislation for part-time workers and to reform trade disputes law.

A separate public-sector agreement concluded in 1987 provided for the phased payment of 'special pay awards' handed down by the public service arbitrator mainly to compensate public service workers whose pay had fallen behind that of similar workers in the private sector. The basic pay terms of the Programme for National Recovery applied equally to the public and private sectors.

A parallel agreement also provided for the reduction of the working week from 40 to 39 hours, thereby ensuring an increase in the hourly rate of pay and greater overtime earnings in return for productivity concessions. In spite of the fact that the agreement was voluntary, adherence to the pay terms was almost universal. The pay increases set out in the agreement made no allowance for 'above the norm' increases and the Labour Court refused to support claims for such increases as a matter of policy. Neither was there provision for below-the-norm increases, although subsequent agreements made provision for employers who could reasonably plead 'inability to pay' the agreed increases. No further cost-increasing claims could be served, a proviso that continued with the following agreements, the PESP and the PCW.

The agreement was generally regarded as successful in meeting its stated objectives. The debt–GNP ratio fell from 131 per cent in 1987 to 111 per cent in 1990. Wages increased in line with the terms set out in the agreement and net earnings increased on account of reform of the income tax system. Economic growth of more than 4 per cent annually reflected growth in manufacturing output and exports. Inflation fell to its lowest level in decades and significant net job creation was achieved. The first noticeable decline in strike activity was also evident.

In spite of changes in governments which saw various coalitions emerge involving the five main political parties, the state continued to participate in these new-style agreements. After the Programme for National Recovery there followed two more agreements of the same nature, the 1991 Programme for Economic and Social Progress and the 1994 Programme for Competitiveness and Work.

The 1991 Programme for Economic and Social Progress was even more expansive in the breadth of socio-economic reforms it contained in addition to the pay increases which act as the cohesive force of these agreements. Its overall aim, set out in grandiose terms, was 'the development of a modern efficient market economy in Ireland, with innate capacity for satisfactory, sustainable growth and discharge of the obligations of a developed social conscience'. The agreement explicitly linked its own fate with achieving fiscal, monetary and exchange rate improvements. In pursuing macro-economic stability, the programme set an explicit target for the reduction of the debt–GNP ratio (100 per cent by 1993).

The programme contained commitments to reform of the income tax system and also addressed the issues of indirect taxation, company taxation, the taxation of capital, tax collection and enforcement and the black economy. On social welfare, the agreement provided for continued protection of welfare rates against inflation and eventually to increasing welfare rates in line with the recommendations of the tripartite Commission on Social Welfare. In employment terms the programme set targets of 20,000 new jobs each year while reform of industrial policy was also agreed. Area-based projects to tackle long-term unemployment were to be developed. The programme included a commitment on the part of the state to introduce legislation covering part-time workers, payment of wages by non-cash means, unfair dismissal and equality legislation as well as reviews of public holidays, employment agencies and general conditions of employment (see *Contracts and Terms and Conditions of Employment* in this series).

In addition to three annual pay increases, the agreement provided for a local bargaining clause in the second year of the agreement where increases of up to 3 per cent could be paid in 'exceptional cases' in return for productivity changes. This was the only time provision was made for such a local bargaining increase among the three agreements – the PNR, the PESP and the succeeding PCW. The agreement also saw a subtle but significant change when it was decided that commercial semi-state companies should be bracketed with the private sector for the purposes of pay policy and that the same 'local bargaining' rules should apply to both sectors – slightly different provision was made for local bargaining in the public sector.

The PESP also allowed claims for the introduction of pension or sick pay schemes where none existed, having regard to the capacity of the employer to absorb the costs and, in the case of sick pay schemes, the implications for attendance.

The Programme for Competitiveness and Work (PCW) was agreed in early 1994. Reduction of the debt–GNP ratio to 95 per cent by 1996 and annual employment growth of 2 per cent were among the more important economic objectives it detailed. Overall the agreement was not as comprehensive as its predecessor, perhaps reflecting the weaker commitment of the government of the day under a new Prime Minister, Albert Reynolds, to this type of all-embracing deal with the social partners. In political circles concern had begun to be expressed about the power of this new fifth estate – the social partners – and, ironically, the presence of the Labour Party in the new coalition may have contributed to official scepticism, given the uneasy relations Labour has had with the trade unions when in government. Another factor was the absence of the previous Prime Minister, Charles Haughey, who has been credited as the political force behind the new concept of centralised agreements.

Separate pay agreements were concluded for the private sector and the commercial semi-state companies on the one hand and the public service on the other. The agreement for the private sector and commercial semi-states provided for four increases over three years (the final increases coming at six-month intervals in the final year). The public service pay agreement provided for the same total of pay increases but spread over a three-and-a-half-year period and with an initial five-month pay pause. Slight amendments to the private-sector terms were also agreed for the construction and motor industries. As there was no agreement on local bargaining increases in the public service (commercial semi-states apart) during the PESP, provision was made in the PCW for continued attempts to 'restructure' work practices in the public sector – the main aim of which, for the state, was to break the formal pay links with private industry and among key grades within the public sector.

Workplace/enterprise employee representation

Statutory provision

For the vast majority of Irish workers effectively the only opportunity for employee participation is through the collective bargaining process. There is legislation governing board- and sub-board-level participation in semi-state companies but there is no statutory provision for employee participation *per se* in the private sector. Health and safety legislation is the only statutory impetus to employee representation in the wider range of workplaces. EU legislation requires information and consultation on the transfer of an undertaking and on collective dismissal.

Private-sector employers, represented by IBEC, remain adamantly opposed to the notion of legislation for employee participation and there seems little willingness on the part of any of the political parties to consider legislation, a move which could seriously jeopardise the social consensus, given the strength of employer feeling.

A general joint declaration on employee involvement between the employers and trade unions in 1991 has proved the most significant development for the private sector so far. The first study of joint consultation in industry was undertaken by the independent Irish Productivity Centre in 1976. It found that about one-third of the 183 firms surveyed had some form of consultative procedure. It was found, however, that joint consultation had a negligible effect on absenteeism and discipline problems, while consultation mechanisms had little or no effect on productivity, the acceptance of new work methods, or the quality of work.

Ten years later the majority of an Advisory Committee on Worker Participation, comprising representatives of the FUE (now part of IBEC) and ICTU, came out in favour of legislation on employee participation, though the employers insisted that voluntarism was essential, as firms forced to introduce employee participation would feel 'straitjacketed'. The committee estimated there were only 50 works councils, or their equivalent, in the private sector at the time.

In line with a commitment in the PESP, the FIE (now IBEC) and ICTU produced a joint declaration in 1991 on employee involvement. This rather bland document avoided any mention of participation and avoided the issues of board-level participation and the development of employee shareholding and profit-share schemes such as had been demanded at the ICTU delegate conference in 1990. The declaration surveyed international practices and noted that in private-sector companies in Ireland a significant number of enterprises were developing 'a range of relevant practices and procedures'. These were characterised by their voluntary nature and were designed to relate to individual circumstances such as the size of the organisation, the nature of the business and the level of development.

An appendix to the declaration listed the various forms of employee involvement which could be used – including team briefing, employee reports, newsletters, notice board and attitude surveys – and the kind of issues on which consultation might take place: health and safety, plant layout, incentive schemes, grading, the state of the firm, market performance, personnel practices, technological change and equality issues. With regard to information-sharing, communications and consultation practices, it emphasised confidentiality requirements in regard to commercial sensitivity, contracts, company law and regulations as well as personal privacy.

The declaration emphasised the need for appropriate training and suggested a role for the Employer–Labour Conference in monitoring employee involvement in the private sector and for the Irish Productivity Centre in supporting organisations seeking to introduce employee development schemes.

The declaration noted the wide variety of financial participation schemes in place: 90 approved schemes covering 80,000 workers introduced since the enactment of the enabling legislation, the 1982 Finance Act. Both the employers and the trade unions agreed to recommend to government that further improvements in fiscal incentives should be introduced as a means of encouraging voluntary initiatives. Ironically, the government's reaction in the following year's budget was initially to remove the tax incentives for employee share ownership schemes entirely but after extensive lobbying by both employers and the trade unions it was decided simply to lower the limit for tax relief from Ir£5,000 to Ir£2,000. However, in the 1995 budget the concept of share ownership was given a major boost when the limit for tax relief was increased to Ir£10,000.

Safety representation

The Safety in Industry Act 1980 provides for the establishment of safety committees, delegates and representatives to ensure that health and safety standards are complied with. Safety committees may be established in factories with more than 20 workers, while workers have the right to safety representatives in firms with fewer than 20 workers. Where workers fail to elect a safety committee or representatives within six months the employer is entitled to select the safety committee or representative, having consulted the workforce. These posts have three-year terms of office. Safety committees and representatives are entitled to make representations on behalf of the workforce to the employer, who must pay due regard to their views, and to be consulted by employers with regard to appropriate health and safety questions. Meetings of the safety committee may take place within working hours without loss of pay, provided the meetings are not more frequent than once every two months (emergency meetings apart), do not last for more than two hours, do not cause major problems for production and have a quorum of not less than three members. Safety committees may have between three (in firms with between 20 and 60 employees) and 10 members (firms with over 180 employees); the number of worker representatives can range from two to seven, according to company size, while the number of company representatives can range from one to three.

EU statutory consultation rights

Employees also have the right to be consulted under law where collective redundancies are planned (covered by the Protection of Employment Act 1977) or where a business or part of a business is being transferred (Transfer of Undertakings Regulations 1980) and through the various elements of the framework EU directive on health and safety (enacted in Ireland through a series of statutory instruments).

Workplace developments

In spite of what may appear to be the limited extent of formal employee participation structures, evidence is emerging of an increasing preference by employers for new employee involvement strategies. A recent Europe-wide study by the European Foundation for the Improvement of Living and Working Conditions concluded that overall the Irish were 'broadly in line with the general European average for the planning stage of technological change'. The Irish appeared to employ greater levels of participation in the implementation stage.

The same survey showed that Ireland was among the top five European countries in terms of employee participation in product and service quality. The study concluded that 'the most positive employee representatives in Europe can be found in Ireland', which the authors took as another indication that Irish industrial relations are increasingly diverging from the British tradition.

Irish workers' representatives and unions were much more positive about participation than their UK counterparts, the authors added. This claim is borne out, to an extent, by the adoption of an important new policy document adopted by the ICTU entitled *New Forms of Work Organisation – Options for Unions*. The report, presented at the 1993 ICTU conference, found that the extent of new work organisation initiatives in Ireland was similar to, if not ahead of, the position in other European countries, mainly because of the presence of a large number of US multinational subsidiaries. The unions decided that outright opposition to change or the development of their own approach by employee representatives or local officials was not the best response. Rather, policy choice should be based on a minimalist approach involving a floor below which the unions would not be prepared to go; a pro-active approach so as to have as much input as possible, and the active promotion of initiatives with the unions' agenda.

One very successful experiment in the semi-state sector has been the introduction of autonomous work groups in the peat production company Bord na Móna. Other semi-state companies, including the forestry agency, Coillte, have also taken steps towards the introduction of similar autonomous work groups.

Employee participation at board level

Board-level participation by employees is almost entirely confined to the semi-state sector, with no known evidence of such practice in the private sector.

Legislation rather than managerial initiative has proved the spur to board-level participation in the semi-state sector.

The Worker Participation (State Enterprises) Act, 1977 introduced board-level participation to seven semi-state companies. The Worker Participation (State Enterprises) Act 1988 was concerned primarily with sub-board arrangements but also provided for the extension of board-level participation to a greater number of semi-state companies.

The 1977 Act provided for the direct election of full-time employees to one-third of the seats on the board of directors in seven state-controlled companies (subsequently extended to a total of 35 companies by the 1988 legislation). Subsequently it was stated that the level of representation in non-commercial state companies should be dictated by the need to maintain the balance of representational interests and to ensure that the board remained an effective body. Each case is to be considered on its own merits and the Minister of Enterprise and Employment can vary the number of worker directors below the one-third arrangement by order, subject to a minimum of two worker directors.

Candidates for election can be nominated only by a trade union or any other body such as a staff association which is recognised for collective bargaining purposes by the company concerned. The electorate has been broadened to include employees of subsidiaries in certain circumstances, though such extensions of the electorate have to be cleared by the Minister responsible for the company as well as the Ministers of Finance and of Enterprise and Employment. The franchise extends to all full-time employees and regular part-time employees with at least 13 weeks' continuous service and expected to work at least eight hours per week. The term of office of elected worker directors is four years. Worker directors hold the same status as any other director and are entitled to the same rights and to assume similar responsibilities. Worker directors who cease to be employees of the state enterprise concerned must give up their board membership or resign from the enterprise. By 1994, the ICTU estimated, the number of state companies with worker directors stood at 19.

Sub-board participation

The 1988 act aimed to establish sub-board participation in semi-state companies. The act states that it is up to management and employee representatives to devise mutually acceptable arrangements for employee involvement following a request from a majority of employees. A range of options from direct to indirect forms of participation and from highly structured to relatively informal initiatives are accommodated within the legislative framework. Three basic requirements arise from the legislation:

- the exchange of views as well as the exchange of clear and reliable information between the enterprise and its employees
- the communication in good time to employees of information likely to have a significant effect on their interests

- the distribution to all employees of views and information arising from the participative process.

A number of state financial institutions were excluded from the sub-board consultation provisions of the 1988 act, reflecting concern about the confidential nature of their business. By 1994 about 28 companies had established sub-board structures.

The EU works council directive

Opposition to the European works council directive was as pronounced among Irish employers as in Britain, though the presence of so many subsidiaries of (particularly American) multinationals meant that the opposition expressed through the main employers' organisation, IBEC, was possibly even more trenchant.

On the basis of the number of workers employed in companies likely to be covered by the directive, Ireland would appear to be the member state where the directive will have the greatest impact. At present information and consultation mechanisms at workplace level are rare. IBEC estimates that as many as 100,000 workers (around 12 per cent of total private-sector employment) are employed in companies likely to be covered by the directive. Over 250 operations are likely to be affected: fewer than 10 Irish-owned multinationals are of sufficient size to qualify in their own right. The vast majority of workplaces to be affected will be subsidiaries of foreign multinationals.

The Irish Congress of Trade Unions launched a campaign aimed at raising awareness among union officials and activists about European works councils in early 1995. Until then there was little apparent urgency on the part of the unions to secure agreements establishing works councils.

The possibility remains that a national framework agreement will be concluded between the employers and trade unions, given the strong preference by the employers for flexibility in implementing the directive and the unions' wish to see its widespread application.

Collective bargaining

The status of collective agreements

Collective agreements are not legally binding contracts but, where workers sign a statement accepting that collective agreements contain their terms and conditions of employment, the collective agreement is said to be incorporated into their employment contract. However, the incorporation of agreements is unrelated to the enforceability of the agreements. Indeed, there is some doubt whether collective agreements are legally enforceable.

Provision is made for registering legally binding collective agreements at the Labour Court but this seldom happens. The agreements concluded by the Joint Labour Committees are also legally binding when ratified by the Labour Court as employment regulation orders (see below).

By law, collective agreements cannot contain discriminatory pay rates on the basis of an employee's gender. The Anti-discrimination (Pay) Act 1974 provides that a man and a woman doing the same or like work should earn equal pay. Equality officers at the Labour Relations Commission issue recommendations on claims for equal pay and these can be appealed to the Labour Court. Successful claims for equal pay can mean up to three years' retroaction of the difference in the pay rates. Determinations issued by the Labour Court can be appealed on a point of law to the High Court.

Levels of bargaining

In spite of the fact that tripartite agreements have operated since the end of 1987 company-level bargaining has continued to prevail above industry- or sectoral-level bargaining. For the most part company-level bargaining takes place within the framework of these nationally negotiated agreements. The agreements have a strong moral force within Ireland's industrial relations culture and the state's dispute-settling agencies will recommend adherence to the pay terms as a matter of policy. Each of the national agreements has had a three-year time span and apart from the second agreement, which contained provision for a further local bargaining increase to be paid in exceptional cases, the agreements have tended merely to set out increases to be paid at 12-month intervals.

The increasingly important non-union sector tends to take note of the increases specified in these national agreements and build their remuneration policies for non-managerial employees around the increases. Research undertaken for the independent Economic and Social Research Institute in 1987 suggested that workers in large (employing over 100 workers) non-union firms received net hourly wages 7.3 per cent in excess of the rates paid to their counterparts in large unionised firms. In small unionised firms (employing fewer than 20) workers' pay was 19 per cent ahead of that earned in non-union firms. The larger non-union companies tend to be subsidiaries of multinationals, while small non-union firms are typically Irish-owned.

Statutory pay determination

There is no statutory minimum wage but legally binding minimum rates of pay are negotiated through a system of Joint Labour Committees (JLCs) for workers in traditionally low-paid industries. The JLCs are serviced by staff employed at the Labour Relations Commission. Employer, trade union and independent representatives on the JLCs determine wages and conditions for almost 100,000 workers in various industries where collective bargaining structures have traditionally been weak. The sectors covered are predominantly service industries such as the retail trade, catering, contract cleaning, hairdressing and law offices but also include manufacturing sectors such as textiles, mineral water production and agricultural workers.

Following negotiations between representatives of employers and trade unions, as well as independent members, wages and conditions are published by the Labour Court as legally binding registered employment agreements. These orders are enforced by the Department of Enterprise and Employment. The rates are commonly seen as a floor and in many cases those paid are well in excess of the rates stipulated in the orders.

Coverage by collective bargaining

The extent to which pay is determined by collective bargaining remain unclear. Nevertheless the fact that union density has remained around the 50 per cent level suggests that collective bargaining plays an important part in pay determination. Apart from the system of Joint Labour Committees, another important industry-level system of bargaining is that of the Joint Industrial Councils. These are permanent voluntary negotiating bodies whose object is to facilitate collective bargaining in certain industries – employer and trade union representatives sit on the councils, which are chaired by an agreed, independent facilitator. At present there are three councils registered with the Labour Court, for the footwear and construction industries and for wholesale fruit and vegetable trading in Dublin.

There are, in addition, 11 unregistered councils: these cover bacon curing, the bakery and confectionery trade, banks, electrical contracting, flour milling, the grocery provisions and allied trades, hosiery and knitted garment manufacture, the printing and allied trades in Dublin, state industrial employees, woollen and worsted manufacture and employees of Telecom Éireann – the state-owned telecommunications company.

The main forums for settling pay disputes among 'white collar' grades in the public sector are the various conciliation and arbitration schemes for areas such as the civil service, education, health services and local government. Those with access to a conciliation and arbitration scheme are not entitled to pursue pay claims to the Labour Relations Commission or the Labour Court. Within the public sector, about half the 270,000 workers have access to an appropriate conciliation and arbitration scheme and the other half – mainly industrial workers – have access to the Labour Relations Commission and the Labour Court. Pay rates in the public sector have traditionally kept in line with pay for comparable work in the private sector. The conciliation and arbitration schemes have been used by public service unions to keep pay rates in line with developments in the private sector – this is in addition to public service workers receiving the increases set out in the various national pay agreements. Failure to agree at the conciliation stage means referral to the arbitration board, chaired by an independent arbitrator, whose awards have to be approved by the parliament. The state is attempting major reform of the various conciliation and arbitration schemes amidst growing criticism that the public-sector pay bill has risen much faster than pay in the private sector over recent years. However, pay movements in both sectors have moved broadly in parallel since 1975 and the recent acceleration in the public service pay bill reflects growing employment numbers and the payment of increases which were deferred with the agreement of workers in the mid-1980s.

Pay rounds and negotiating procedures

With the advent of centralised collective bargaining the pattern of pay settlements has changed. Increases agreed in the national pay agreements are rarely exceeded, and in fact the majority of deviations from those terms come where firms face financial difficulties and seek to alter the phasing of payments. No longer are increases in the national agreements seen as minimum rises which can be built upon by the trade unions – the Labour Court and the Labour Relations Commission have a policy of not recommending increases in excess of those embodied in the national pay agreements and they also uphold those agreements' restrictions on other cost-increasing claims apart from provision for agreed changes such as the introduction of pensions and sick pay schemes.

The only industrial sector where unionisation is high and where the pay terms of the national agreements are regularly exceeded is the chemical and pharmaceutical sector, where employers have had a traditional policy of paying in excess of national norms, a policy which stretches back to the days of free collective bargaining. In part this reflects the 'dangerous' nature of the work involved but it also reflects a deliberate pay strategy on the part of companies, aimed at securing production and limiting turnover. The sector, which is largely based in Cork, employs over 15,000 nationally and pay rates are among the highest in industry generally.

In the first two tripartite agreements it was implicitly agreed that self-financing productivity agreements could take place, thereby allowing greater scope for company-level collective bargaining on other than the basic increases set out in the national agreements, but such flexibility does not appear to have been provided in the PCW. It should be stressed that the agreements are voluntary and nothing can prevent an employer concluding an entirely separate deal, though where talks break down the state's dispute-settling agencies will be reluctant to recommend the granting of increases at variance with the rates agreed in the national pay agreements.

The increasing non-union sector is also associated with pay rates and increases ahead of industrial norms, and this is also seen as a deliberate management strategy aimed at keeping trade unions outside the factory gates. Performance-related pay is also more commonly found in non-union companies.

The National Economic and Social Council (NESC) and the Economic and Social Research Institute (ESRI) have an important role to play in producing economic forecasts which provide the backdrop of national level pay negotiations. Prior to each of the last three tripartite agreements the NESC (a tripartite body) produced medium-term strategic economic analyses which have been largely accepted by the main social partners as representing the likely economic environment. The independent ESRI produces quarterly economic commentaries and longer-term economic forecasts on a regular basis.

Wage movements are monitored by the Central Statistics Office, with separate reports for manufacturing, construction and the financial services sectors produced quarterly. Between 1987 and 1993 average weekly earnings for the 192,000 workers employed in the manufacturing sector increased by just over 29 per cent, while real weekly earnings (taking account of inflation) rose by just under 10 per cent.

Collectively agreed provision

Company-level collective bargaining tends to concentrate on basic pay rates, premium payments, shift patterns, employment structures, holiday entitlement and fringe benefits. For the most part, pay increases agreed in national-level talks are almost always passed on as a matter of course, though companies in financial difficulty may seek productivity trade-offs. The presence or otherwise of a local bargaining clause in the national agreements determines whether bargaining for more than the basic increases will be likely.

Research undertaken at the University of Limerick as part of the Cranfield/Price Waterhouse Project on HRM in Europe estimated that fringe benefits (both statutory and voluntary) constitute an additional 25–30 per cent on top of the basic weekly pay for manual grades. An extra 15–35 per cent should be added in the case of clerical, administrative and managerial grades.

Industrial conflict

Traditionally Ireland has been grouped among those European countries with higher than average days lost to industrial conflict. However, in the last five years the numbers of days lost in strike action has dropped dramatically, so much so that 1994 saw the lowest total of strike days lost since the foundation of the state in 1922. A total of 25,500 days were lost owing to strike action in 1994, reflecting the involvement of 5,000 workers in 29 disputes. Days lost per thousand workers were more than halved in the period 1987–91 compared with 1982–86. In terms of international comparison, Ireland lost 186 working days per thousand employees in the period 1987–91, compared with 275 in Italy, 126 in the UK and six in Germany.

Since 1960 the pattern of strike activity has changed profoundly. While strike activity increased in the 1960s and 1970s, it slowed in the 1980s and fell to record low levels in the 1990s. In the 1960s an average 60 days were lost annually per hundred workers in the private sector while 53 days were lost annually in the public sector. Between 1990 and 1992 these figures fell to 17 and 16 days respectively.

Unofficial action has declined and strike activity in the private sector in particular has declined considerably since the 1960s. The public sector now has greater strike frequency, involving considerably more workers, though strikes are of shorter duration than in previous eras. Large strikes have a disproportionate impact on the overall pattern, and a small number of organisations account for an inordinately large proportion of overall strike activity.

Disputes law

There is no positive right to strike in Irish law. The main legislation governing industrial disputes is the 1990 Industrial Relations Act, which repealed the 1906 Trade Disputes Act and reintroduced its provisions with amendments. The most significant of the amendments concern the requirement for and conduct of secret ballots and the curbing of the circumstances in which *ex parte* injunctions can be granted.

The 1990 act provides that trade unions and their members are immune from prosecution where an action is 'in contemplation or furtherance of a trade dispute'. Before the immunities apply a number of conditions must be met:

- There must be a trade dispute as defined by the legislation.
- The action must be of a type permitted by the legislation.
- The proposal to take action must not have been rejected in a ballot of the workers concerned.
- If the dispute concerns one individual worker, agreed procedures or procedures normally used in the employment must have been used and exhausted.

A trade dispute is defined as 'any dispute between employers and workers which is connected with the employment or non-employment, or the terms or conditions of, or affecting the employment of, any person'. This definition has been held to cover disputes arising from the dismissal of a worker, regardless of whether the dismissal was fair or unfair. Disputes between workers are not covered by the definition, but disputes arising from attempts by trade unions to secure recognition are.

Other issues which do not fall within the legislation's definition of a trade dispute concern disputes aimed at trying to enforce a closed shop agreement, disputes connected with a purely political issue, disputes concerning purely commercial issues which do not affect the interests of the workforce and disputes concerning an individual worker where agreed procedures or those which apply by custom and practice have not been used and exhausted.

The 1990 act contains definitions of both strike action and industrial action; both definitions are broad and comply with the usual understanding of the terms.

Strike action is defined as 'a cessation of work by any number or body of workers acting in combination or a concerted refusal under a common understanding of any number of workers to continue to work for their employer or to aid other workers who are compelling their employer to accept or not to accept terms and conditions of or affecting employment'.

Industrial action is defined as 'any action which affects, or is likely to affect, the terms and conditions, whether express or implied, of a contract and which is taken by any number or body of workers acting in combination or under a common understanding as a means of compelling their employer or to aid other workers in compelling their employer to accept or not to accept terms or conditions affecting their employment'. This definition covers activities such as working to rule, overtime bans and refusing to carry out certain duties.

Ballots   As a result of the 1990 act the rules of every registered trade union must contain a provision that the union will not organise, participate in, sanction or support a strike or other form of industrial action without a secret ballot of the members of the union who, it is reasonable to believe, will be called upon to engage in the strike or industrial action. The union must take reasonable steps to ensure that members are given a fair opportunity to vote without interference. As soon as is practical after the votes have been counted, the union must make known to the members entitled to vote in the ballot

- the number of ballot papers issued
- the number of votes cast
- the number of votes in favour of the proposal
- the number of votes against the proposal
- the number of spoiled votes.

The committee of management, or executive, of the union has full discretion in organising, participating in, sanctioning or supporting a strike or other industrial action so long as a majority of those voting favour such a course of action. The law also provides that an aggregate majority must support industrial action where more than one trade union ballots before any action can be sanctioned. The Irish Congress of Trade Unions must sanction a strike where an aggregate majority supports such action and where members of another trade union affiliated to ICTU have participated in the secret ballot and voted to support a strike organised by another union.

The decision on when and how to hold the ballot is decided by the union's own rules and the decision as to the question(s) asked is also left to the union. There is no stated limit on how long the mandate conferred by the ballot can last.

The act does not make 'unofficial' action unlawful. What is outlawed is action taken in disregard of or contrary to the outcome of a secret ballot. Immunities are still available to trade union members taking industrial action without a ballot but the restrictions on the availability of interim and interlocutory injunctions will not apply in such an event.

It had been assumed that employers could not take legal action against a trade union for failing to conduct a ballot prior to industrial action or strike action proceeding. However, doubts grew following the granting of an interlocutory injunction in a case in 1993 involving the state-owned rail company, Iarnrod Éireann, and the bus and rail workers' union, the NBRU, where the company sought an injunction in the belief that the dispute was a single worker dispute and not all procedures had been exhausted before industrial action began. While precedent was not established (no written verdict was handed down), concern emerged among unions about the judge's comments on the conduct of ballots when he granted the injunction. As bulwarks of democracy, he said, trade unions should be open to their members and be able to tell the court the exact details of the ballot. The judge found that the details required by the 1990 act were not forthcoming and he was dubious about the compliance of the union with the act's provision that unions should not participate in industrial action without a secret ballot subject to the act's provisions. Expressing concern at the judgement, ICTU officials pointed to the (then) Department of Labour's guide to the 1990 act, which states, 'any right of legal action against a trade union for failure to comply with the secret ballot rule is confined to the members of the union concerned'.

The legislation clearly states that a member of a trade union can apply for an injunction to force the union to comply with the balloting provisions. A union member can also seek to recover damages for any loss suffered as a result of the union's failure to comply with the balloting requirements.

The first authoritative interpretation of some of the key provisions of the 1990 legislation was handed down in the 1994 case of Nolan Transport (Oaklands) *v.* Halligan and others. The dispute arose when two employees at a haulage firm were dismissed after attempting to recruit other employees into the union SIPTU, which had been seeking recognition from the company. After a ballot of employees, which yielded a 20:3 majority for strike action, the company's premises were picketed. The High Court granted the company permanent injunctions restraining picketing on the grounds that the ballot had been falsified, and hence that industrial action had been initiated without following the procedures of the 1990 act. Importantly, the judgement ruled that a secret ballot can be investigated at the instigation of the employer. The judgement also established that a dispute between an employer and a trade union over a claim to represent an entire workforce, union and non-union, is not a trade dispute, and unions have no legal protection against a claim for damages – in this case Ir£400,000 for Nolan plus costs and other damages totalling Ir£2 million in all. The judgement has been appealed.

Injunctions   The 1990 act prohibits the granting of *ex parte* injunctions against workers and trade unions engaged in industrial action where a secret ballot has been held and at least one week's notice given to the employer. It also states that an interlocutory injunction will not be granted restraining a strike or industrial action where, in addition to holding a secret ballot and giving one week's notice, the union establishes a fair case that it was acting in contemplation or furtherance of a trade dispute.

Picketing   The 1990 act also introduced important changes in respect of 'secondary picketing'. Workers may picket any place where their employer works or carries on business. Where it is not practicable to picket the employer's place of business, pickets may be placed at the approaches to the employer's place of business. Otherwise secondary picketing is permitted only if it is 'reasonable' for the picketers to believe at the start and during the continuation of their attendance at the picket that the employer 'has directly assisted their [own] employer who is a party to the trade dispute for the purpose of frustrating the strike or other industrial action'. Any such action taken by an employer in the health services to maintain life-preserving services during an industrial dispute will not be deemed to be frustrating industrial action and secondary picketing will not be lawful in that event. The purpose of a secondary picket is restricted to obtaining or communicating information peacefully or peacefully persuading any person to work or to abstain from working.

Lockouts   The Unfair Dismissals Act 1977 defines a lockout as 'an action which, in contemplation or furtherance of a trade dispute . . . is taken by one or more employers, whether parties to the dispute or not, and which consists of the exclusion of one or more employees from one or more factories, offices or other places of work or of the suspension of work in one or more such places or of the collective, simultaneous or otherwise connected termination or suspension or employment of a group of employees'. Dismissal is deemed to be unfair if employees are locked out and not re-engaged or reinstated when work resumes. Accordingly, lockouts may be regarded as legal if all employees are reinstated.

Industrial peace clauses   A majority of collective agreements incorporate procedures to deal with discipline, grievances and collective industrial conflict. In recent years, industrial action has been curbed by the voluntary national agreements concluded by the social partners and commencing in 1988 with the Programme for National Recovery, followed by the 1990 Programme for Economic and Social Progress and the 1993 Programme for Competitiveness and Work.

The industrial peace clause in the PCW stated: 'this agreement precludes strikes or any other form of industrial action by trade unions, employees or employers in respect of any matter covered by this agreement, where the employer or trade union is acting in accordance with the provisions of this agreement'.

Dispute resolution agencies

In line with Ireland's voluntarist industrial relations culture, the official dispute resolution agencies operate, with infrequent exception, in a non-legally binding fashion. An important change contained in the 1990 Industrial Relations Act was the creation of a separate state-funded conciliation agency, the Labour Relations Commission (LRC). Both the Labour Court and the LRC are overseen by boards composed of nominated representatives of the employers, the trade unions and the government and which are chaired by representatives nominated by the Minister of Enterprise and Employment.

Previously the conciliation service came within the remit of the Labour Court, but the passing of the conciliation service to the Labour Relations Commission was intended to promote the resolution of disputes prior to any possible reference to the Labour Court. The related objective was to re-establish the Labour Court as the 'final authoritative tribunal in industrial relations matters' or court of last resort. Previously, the most trivial of disputes found their way to the court for a recommendation without any great effort being made to resolve the dispute in local negotiations, and this was especially the case in a small number of large employments.

The Labour Relations Commission has achieved notable success in resolving disputes since its establishment in 1991. Between 1990 and 1993 an average of 1,800 cases were handled at conciliation, 76 per cent of which were settled (covering 88 per cent of workers in cases referred) and with just under 17 per cent of cases referred to the Labour Court.

The Labour Relations Commission has the broad object of promoting good industrial relations through a range of services, including its conciliation service as well as a Rights Commissioner service, an equality service and an industrial relations advisory service, and by assisting Joint Labour Committees and Joint Industrial Councils.

Rights Commissioners deal mainly with disputes involving individuals or smaller groups of workers where the dispute is not concerned with rates of pay, holidays, working hours or times of work for a group of workers. Recommendations can be appealed, according to the relevant legislation, to the Labour Court or to the Employment Appeals Tribunal, whose decisions are legally binding. The quasi-judicial Employment Appeals Tribunal (EAT) hears cases concerning redundancy, minimum notice and terms of employment, dismissal, insolvencies, disputes involving part-time workers, the payment of wages, and maternity protection, all of which are covered by separate pieces of legislation. The EAT consists of one representative each from the employers' and the trade unions' sides and is chaired by an independent person, usually with a legal background.

For the most part, cases can be referred to the Labour Court only after they have been through the conciliation service of the Labour Relations Commission. Exceptions to this rule include situations where

- the court is informed by the chair of the commission that it has waived its function of conciliation in a dispute
- the court is asked to investigate a dispute which in the eyes of the Minister of Enterprise and Employment 'affects the public interest'

- the court decides after consultation with the commission that exceptional circumstances warrant a Labour Court investigation
- a recommendation by a Rights Commissioner or an Equality Officer is appealed
- either the union, or both parties, indicate in advance that they will accept the recommendation of the court in accordance with section 20 of the 1969 Industrial Relations Act. (This tactic is often employed by unions or individuals in employments where trade unions are not recognised and is often the recourse for unions seeking recognition. Of course a court recommendation in favour of recognition is not legally binding and can be ignored by an employer.)

Recommendations issued by the Labour Court are voluntary but carry strong moral authority. A survey of 75 recommendations from the Labour Court in the second quarter of 1994 found that 84 per cent were accepted by both sides to the dispute, 9 per cent were accepted by the employer only and 4 per cent were rejected by both sides.

Organisations

Department of Enterprise and Employment
Kildare Street
Dublin 2
Tel. + 353 1 6767571
Fax + 353 1 6762285

Training and Employment Authority
(FAS)
27–33 Upper Baggot Street
Dublin 2
Tel. + 353 1 6685777
Fax + 353 1 6682691

Industrial Relations News
121–3 Ranelagh Road
Dublin 6
Tel. + 353 1 4972711
Fax + 353 1 4972779

Irish Business and Employers'
Confederation (IBEC)
84–6 Lower Baggot Street
Dublin 2
Tel. + 353 1 6601011
Fax + 353 1 6601717

Irish Congress of Trade Unions (ICTU)
19 Raglan Road
Dublin 4
Tel. + 353 1 6680641
Fax + 353 1 6609027

Institute of Personnel and Development
35–9 Shelbourne Road
Ballsbridge
Dublin 4
Tel. + 353 1 6686244
Fax + 353 1 6608030

Labour Court
Tom Johnson House
Haddington Road
Dublin 4
Tel. + 353 1 6608444
Fax + 353 1 6685069

Labour Relations Commission
Tom Johnson House
Haddington Road
Dublin 4
Tel. + 353 1 6609662
Fax + 353 1 6685069

Main sources

Industrial Relations News, IRN Publishing Dublin, various issues

EUROPEAN FOUNDATION FOR THE IMPROVEMENT OF LIVING AND WORKING CONDITIONS. *New Forms of Work and Activity. A survey of experiences at establishment level in eight European countries.* 1992

EUROPEAN FOUNDATION FOR THE IMPROVEMENT OF LIVING AND WORKING CONDITIONS. *Workplace Involvement in Technological Innovation in the European Community.* Vols. 1–2, 1993

HIGGINS, EDDIE, and KEHER, NUALA. *Your Rights at Work.* Dublin, Institute of Public Administration, 1994

MEENAN, FRANCIS. *Working with the Law: A practical guide for employers and employees.* Dublin, Oak Tree Press, 1994

MURPHY, THOMAS, and ROCHE, WILLIAM K. (eds). *Irish Industrial Relations in Practice.* Dublin, Oak Tree Press, 1994

GUNNIGLE, PATRICK, MCMAHON, GERRY, and FITZGERALD, GERRY. *Industrial Relations in Ireland. Theory and Practice.* Dublin, Gill & MacMillan, 1995

GUNNIGLE, PATRICK, FLOOD, PATRICK, MORLEY, MICHAEL, and TURNER, THOMAS. *Continuity and Change in Irish Employee Relations.* Dublin, Oak Tree Press, 1994

8

Italy

Italian industrial relations are characterised by the prominent role of collective bargaining, many issues which are governed by law in other European Union countries being dealt with under collective agreements. For example, information disclosure at company and workplace level is regulated by agreement, not statute. The law, principally the 1970 Workers' Statute (*Statuto dei Lavoratori*), provides a broad framework of protective rights, leaving employers and employees a good deal of discretion as regards their organisation and mutual relationships. Such arrangements are frequently formalised in accords between the main unions on issues such as workplace representation, and between the unions and employers on pay bargaining. The accords often express broader political and social exchange between the two sides of industry and government which have served as a source of relative stability in the face of recent economic and political convulsions. Compared with the 1980s, the national employers and trade unions, together with a series of 'technocratic' administrations, have intensified their co-operation in the first half of the 1990s.

Employee representation at workplace level represents a hybrid arrangement between union organisations and all-employee bodies, rather than a clearly dual structure (as in Germany) or a monistic arrangement (as in Denmark and the United Kingdom). On the strength of rights acquired after the 'hot autumn' of industrial militancy in 1969, Italian unions were able to establish trade union organisations at workplace level. These meshed with the works councils (*consigli di fabbrica*), which often sprang up during industrial action, to create a unique pattern in which workplace bodies were elected by the whole workforce, usually based on the individual parts of the organisation, and acquired bargaining rights exercised through the trade unions, and increasingly specified in industry-level agreements.

Employers' associations and trade unions are *de facto* organisations and have no legal personality, and are subject to little outside legal interference. In law, employers and employees are not obliged to negotiate, or to sign contracts. The freedom to enter into contracts (*libertà di contrattazione*) implies complete freedom in the choice of mechanisms for the conclusion of any agreements considered necessary.

Compared with the 1970s, industrial relations in the private sector during the 1990s have been markedly less conflictual. For the first time ever, for instance, the leading national settlement – in the metalworking industry – was signed on time in 1994 and without a single hour lost through strike action. However, the public sector continues to be the subject of disruptive action by unofficial union organisations despite the passage of legislation to curb industrial action in the public sector. Much of this action is linked with attempts at reform and restructuring.

Three particular developments have been of key importance in the development of industrial relations in the early 1990s:

- New bargaining arrangements, agreed in July 1993, which establish a new pattern and rhythm of industry- and company-level bargaining, and formally tie bargaining more closely to inflation expectations, rather than, as in the past, compensating for previous inflation performance. The new system will raise the pressure on government to meet its side of the accord by taking vigorous action to contain inflation. In future, increases paid at company level must be tied to results or performance (see below, 'Collective bargaining').
- New arrangements on workplace-level employee representation, agreed between the three main national trade union confederations in 1991 and formally acknowledged by the national employers' organisation, Confindustria, in December 1993. The accord set out to respond to the 'crisis of representativeness' increasingly experienced by the main trade union confederations during the 1980s by widening the basis of nomination and election to workplace representative bodies, whilst seeking to consolidate the position of the main confederations and halting any further erosion of their position. The agreement has been undermined to some degree by the June 1995 referendums on industrial relations, but as yet no new legislative initiative arising out of the referendums has been successful (see below, 'Workplace employee representation').
- The political upheavals of 1992–94 saw the collapse and recasting of the political landscape, with the implosion of the Socialist Party (PSI) and the splintering of the Christian Democrats, the rise of Forza Italia under Silvio Berlusconi, the entry into government of the Northern League and the neo-fascist MSI, and the re-emergence of the Communist Party as the Party of the Democratic Left – with a left split in the form of the Party of Communist Reconstruction. All these changes have had profound implications for the main trade union confederations, each of which was broadly aligned with a political party. In some cases, although there are no official figures, membership is thought to have plummeted. The least affected has probably been the CGIL (see below) which was traditionally aligned closely with the Communist Party but which had considerable non-communist support. Of all the political forces in Italy, the Communist Party (now the PDS) has enjoyed the greatest continuity. However, all the trade unions now describe themselves as free of any political alignment and there has been discussion of closer co-operation or even merger – though that would be difficult, given the persistence of separate structures and loyalties. The collapse of the Berlusconi government and the emergence of a 'government of technocrats', with a mission to tackle deep-seated institutional and economic problems, also created space for the trade unions to intervene in the broader political sphere, and they played a major

role both in mobilising mass support to reject a proposal for pension reform and in negotiating a subsequent compromise.

Regional differences play a profound role in Italian society, and have recently found expression in a separate political movement for the highly industrialised and affluent north, the *Lega*. In contrast, southern Italy continues to struggle with high structural unemployment, poorly provided and poorly functioning public services, and the pervasive influence of organised crime in many areas of economic and public life.

The main players

Trade unions

Freedom of association and trade union law   Trade union, and employer, freedom of association is enshrined in the 1970 Workers' Statute, which defines those freedoms and outlines the sanctions which may be invoked in the event of infringement. The Workers' Statute guarantees the following rights:

- to belong to a trade union/association, and the right to engage in union activities at the workplace
- to meet during working hours without loss of pay for up to 10 hours a year.

Any agreement is null and void if it aims to:

- require workers to belong or not to belong to a trade union in order to carry on their occupation
- discriminate against them because of their union affiliation or because they have taken part in strike action.

Trade unions are not regulated by statute: the law simply gives them the freedom to organise themselves at their discretion. However, under the Workers' Statute, in order to be competent to sign a binding collective agreement, a trade union must be part of a nationwide organisation. In practice this right is extended to the three main official union confederations, the CGIL, the CISL and the UIL, and to one or two independent trade unions (see below).

Whilst the law recognises employees' rights to belong to a trade union, and through unions to set up bodies for workplace-level representation, as well as granting the right to strike, it does not require the parties to bargain or to sign agreements. In theory an employer could decide unilaterally what the conditions of employment should be, though the courts might refuse to ratify such an approach were it challenged. (See *Contracts and Terms and Conditions of Employment*, in this series, pp. 233 f.) Rather, the Workers' Statute should be seen as a law which facilitates a union's ability to negotiate and reflects the institutional and negotiating strength of the union movement at the time when the law was passed in the aftermath of the wave of strikes in 1969.

In practice, employers will typically recognise a trade union and negotiate with it at local level. However, problems have arisen in recent years where employee representatives have been elected by the workforce but do not come under the auspices of one of the recognised national union confederations. Such representatives enjoy none of the legal rights due to officially recognised representative bodies (see below) but have been able to cause widespread disruption, particularly in the public sector, through legal strike action in support of pay claims. In some cases these representatives have ultimately been allowed to sit at the bargaining table with the nationally recognised unions. For their part, the main trade union confederations have attempted to address the issue more fundamentally by changing the rules for the election of workplace representatives in 1991, primarily by altering nomination procedures and changing the established share of seats. The rules now state that employees may be nominated provided they can demonstrate the support of at least 5 per cent of the workforce eligible to vote (see below, 'Workplace employee representation').

Rights of trade union representatives   Trade unions have parallel rights at the place of work – as the force behind employee representation and as trade unions *per se*. Apart from the right to represent members in the workplace and to be involved in bargaining, members of works councils (*rappresentanti sindacali*) may not be dismissed, except for serious misconduct, and may not be transferred without the prior consent of the works council. In addition they are entitled to a certain amount of time off. The entitlement is usually at least eight hours per month.

In terms of representing the union itself, each trade union may have the following number of delegates with the right to time off in each workplace:

- one delegate in companies employing fewer than 200 employees in each unit for which the union branch was established
- one delegate for every 300 employees (or fraction of that number) in companies employing up to 3,000 employees in the unit for which the union branch was established
- in larger workplaces, one delegate for every 500 employees (or fraction of that number) in the unit for which the union branch was established, in addition to the minimum of one delegate per 300 employees.

The Workers' Statute also provides that lay union officials are entitled to unpaid leave of up to eight days a year to pursue union activities. Collective agreements may improve on the law's provisions. Employees elected to trade union office at national or provincial level are entitled, under clause 31 of the Workers' Statute, to unpaid leave of absence at their request at any time during, or for the entire duration of, their term of office.

Trade union structure and organisation   There are three major trade union confederations, plus a number of smaller political or occupational associations which have acquired greater importance in recent years.

The CGIL (Confederazione Generale Italiana del Lavoro), which claimed about 5 million members in 1993 (half of them retired) is the largest of the main union confederations. It is a left-leaning radical movement whose influence is mainly in engineering and heavy engineering but has recently gained a significant toehold in the public sector. Traditionally it was closely aligned with and led by the Italian Communist Party (PCI), now the Party of the Democratic Left (PDS), although the union always had a substantial minority of non-communist socialists. The CGIL has probably been least organisationally hit by the political upheavals of the past few years.

The CISL (Confederazione Italiana Sindacati Lavoratori), with 3.5 million members in 1993, was formerly aligned closely with the Christian Democrats. However, following the dispersal of the centre and right-wing forces over a number of organisations, and the collapse of the Christian Democrats as a mass party, the union has severed the political link. Nevertheless, it remains faithful to the values of the Catholic political centre.

The UIL (*Unione Italiana del Lavoro*) had approximately 1.8 million members in 1993 and its values are drawn from a reforming, lay tradition. Until 1993 it was aligned with the Italian Socialist Party (PSI), which disbanded in that year following a wave of corruption charges against leading politicians. It has been conjectured that the UIL's membership may have since collapsed, but there is no hard evidence or officially audited membership figures. The UIL tends to recruit from the higher grades in industry.

There are two trade unions representing managers, who are extensively covered by collective agreements. FNDAI is the largest association negotiating on behalf of Italy's estimated 90,000 industrial managers. It claims a membership of around 50,000, represents industrial managers across all sectors, and negotiates with employers' organisations in both the private and the public sector. FNDAC negotiates on behalf of some 18,500 commercial managers.

Outside the official structure there are a number of unaffiliated or 'autonomous' unions, some of which represent right-leaning or far-right political forces, whilst others represent sectional militancy or employees disillusioned with the 'reformist' turn of the CGIL. A number are now grouped under the umbrella organisation ISA (Istituto Sindacati Autonomi) but this has produced no results and its affiliates have pronounced it dead. CISNAL (once the trade union wing of the fascist Movimento Sociale Italiano), concerned about its lack of growth and lack of support from the new right, has changed its name to UGIL (Unione Generale Italiana del Lavoro) and was relaunched, with a new strategy, in February 1996. It claims to represent 2,110,000 members in both the public and the private sectors and claims to negotiate and sign 300 industry agreements. After a long delay it finally signed the 1993 framework agreement on incomes policy.

The CISAL union confederation groups together 10 independent unions (of various political tendencies) and claims to represent six million members. (The official unions claim their membership is five times less!)

These groupings represent a challenge to the authority and legitimacy of the main confederations and have, on occasion, caused widespread industrial disruption, especially in the public sector. At the same time the growth of white-collar employment, with separate union structures, has added to the pressures on the claim of the main confederations to represent the entire workforce. As noted above, these pressures mounted as the political landscape began to change and traditional affiliations dissolved. At the workplace level the response of the official confederations has been to widen the basis of representation to include other unions while still retaining overall control and a fixed proportion – 30 per cent – of seats on workplace bodies. The ISA claims, however, that a system which guarantees seats at the workplace for the official trade unions is undemocratic and has refused to take part in workplace elections. At national level ISA and its components are not legally recognised. (See also below, 'Workplace employee representation'.)

In July 1972 the three main confederations came together in a 'United Federation' (Federazione Unitaria) which guaranteed each confederation's identity and independence but, at the same time, built a common structure for collective bargaining with employers and for negotiation with government, within a broad reference framework of united trade union action. In spring 1984, however, the Federazione Unitaria broke up, following disagreement among the union confederations over proposals by the Socialist Party-led coalition government to reform the system of pay indexation, the *scala mobile*. Whereas the CISL and UIL supported the proposals, the CGIL withdrew its support at the last minute and backed the Communist Party's opposition to the change – bringing to an end to the united trade union front.

Nevertheless close co-operation continued between the industry-level unions of the main confederations, and although the formal unitary federation of CGIL–CISL–UIL was not revived collaborative relations between the confederations were restored, and workplace relations were maintained. All three unions came to an agreement on workplace representation in 1991, ratified by the employers in 1993, and all three were parties to the national accord on bargaining in 1993.

Each of the confederations has affiliated unions organised by industry or sector. Within the engineering industry, these separate industry-level federations (*federazioni unitarie di categoria*) were further united in the Federation of Metalworkers (Federazione Lavoratori Metalmeccanici) from 1972, although inter-confederation co-operation within this particular industry federation has fluctuated. Similar national federations were formed for other sectors: for example, Fulta in textiles, Fulc in chemicals, and Fib in banking. Some of these industry-level federations remained active despite the break-up of the Federazione Unitaria at national level.

Organisations representing senior white-collar staff Senior white-collar staff with technical and managerial responsibilities (*quadri*) were for long denied recognition as a separate category of employee under Italian law. After much parliamentary lobbying, legal recognition was finally granted through an amendment to article 2095 of the Civil Code, passed by the Senate on 23 April 1985. Under the amendment employers are required, through collective bargaining, to establish which of their employees fall within this category. Although Italy's 700,000 or so *quadri* have been accorded legal recognition, the national organisations which represent many of them have no legal bargaining rights. These organisations do, however, act as pressure groups and have some influence on the bargaining practices of the unions.

Membership and density In the early 1990s some 40 per cent of Italian employees were organised in the three main trade union organisations. Compared with the United Kingdom or the Netherlands, however, much of the apparent ability of the unions to sustain their membership during the 1980s was attributable to the inclusion of non-active retired members. This effect has been reinforced by the operation of the unique Italian redundancy system, which has kept workers on the rolls of their industries who would have been dismissed in other countries.

Employers' organisations

Italian employers are organised by broad economic sector (industry, commerce, agriculture, crafts), according to whether they are in the public or private sector, and often according to size.

Confindustria, established in 1910, is the largest employers' organisation in the private sector. In the early 1980s it embraced over 100,000 companies employing about 3 million people. As well as co-ordinating employers' action at local and regional level, Confindustria represents private-sector industry in national talks with the unions and with government, and signs national-level agreements with the main trade union confederations. It has a special internal body representing the interests of smaller companies, and is thought to embrace around half of all small firms. Confindustria is divided regionally and provincially into smaller units, such as Assolombarda in the Milan area of northern Italy – the largest of the regional bodies. In addition, it counts among its members over 100 national professional or national industry federations such as Federmeccanica in engineering, Federchimica (chemicals) and Federtessile (textiles) which bargain with their trade union counterparts. Federmeccanica, for example, was set up in 1971 to enable specific sectoral negotiations to be detached from the broader social role then being pursued by Confindustria: it represents employers in the private sector of the engineering industry, is the largest employers' federation belonging to Confindustria, and represents over 10,000 companies employing around 1.2 million people.

Confapi represents small and medium-size companies in the private sector, sharing representation with Confindustria, and has a strong influence locally among the highly developed small business networks in Emilia Romagna

(Bologna, Modena). It was set up following the creation during the 1950s of a provincial organisation representing small employers.

There are a number of separate federations for publicly owned commercial organisations. Intersind represents publicly owned companies in the engineering industry. It was set up in 1958 following a government directive providing for separate employer representation in the public and private sectors. ASAP represents employers in publicly owned companies in the petrochemical industry.

Consultation at national level

Bipartite and tripartite talks

There is no formal institutional mechanism for tripartite negotiation, but there is extensive and continuous tripartite discussion on fundamental economic and social issues. The economic and political crises of the early 1990s, with the ejection of the lira from the European Monetary System in 1992, the collapse of the established party structure, and the need to pursue the Maastricht convergence criteria for European Economic and Monetary Union, have served to revive national-level discussion and negotiation, leading to a number of important accords – on workplace representation, on collective bargaining and on pension reform. Partly prompted by a need to shore up their own weaknesses and partly spurred by the need to take a grip on events and establish some stability, the state (under 'technocratic' administrations where the main posts are occupied by 'neutral' prominent ex-public officials), the employers and the three main union confederations have combined to play a crucial role in setting the economic framework in a period during which the party political landscape has been in a state of flux. This has been an important but hazardous enterprise for the trade unions, which have taken on a wider social role but risked alienating some of their core and most committed members by settling for national compromises – for example, on pensions.

There is a well established practice of bipartite bargaining at national level between employers' confederations such as Confindustria and the three trade union groups, the CGIL, CISL and UIL. Occasionally the government will become involved in negotiations where issues of concern to all employees are at stake and the partners are looking for external mediation.

Agreements reached at this level often effectively replace legislation, and can eventually become law. For example, procedures on collective dismissal were governed by a national agreement, widely adhered to even by non-signatories, until legislation was passed in 1991. Moreover, collective bargaining at national level also often takes on the role of fleshing out and implementing statute law (so-called 'bargained laws'), as has happened on atypical employment.

In practice, both tripartite and bipartite talks often become intertwined, with compromises in one set being made conditional on – typically – government action in another. In addition, simultaneous bilateral discussions may also take place, with each of the three partners meeting one of the others in a cycle of meetings.

The National Economic and Employment Council (Consiglio Nazionale dell' Economia e del Lavoro, CNEL) is a tripartite body established in 1947 whose responsibilities include giving opinions on legislation, preparing its own proposals and suggesting draft legislation, and undertaking surveys. It has also been given the task of maintaining a database of collective agreements.

National 'incomes policy'

The 1993 national framework agreement on incomes policy and the reform of collective bargaining marked a turning point in the culture and conduct of industrial relations. While consultation between the social partners had always been a strong element at all levels it was often conducted in a confrontational atmosphere. The framework agreement sought to initiate a more co-operative approach and in this respect seems to have been successful so far, given that a period of greater industrial peace has followed.

The agreement was important in three respects. First, it pegged increases in pay minima to projected inflation at a rate agreed between the social partners. Second, it introduced a 'peace' clause preventing any form of industrial action pending the outcome of negotiations. (Significant penalties are incurred for infringement.) Finally, it attempted to address the issue of workplace representation and 'wildcat' action by calling for legislation to endorse new arrangements allowing greater participation to unofficial union organisations. (Further details are given below under 'Collective bargaining'.)

Workplace employee representation

There are no statutory mechanisms for employee participation in the form encountered in countries such as Germany, France or the Netherlands. Rather, the 1970 Workers' Statute offered a framework of protective rights for trade union organisation, which effectively ratified forms of representation forged during the 'hot autumn' of industrial conflict in 1969. In effect the three main unions used their rights under the Workers' Statute to take over these spontaneous forms, in a joint agreement concluded in 1972, enabling them to overcome some of their weaknesses at plant level. Institutions for employee representation at the workplace are a product of these trade union rights, rather than wholly independent forms of representation.

During the 1980s the representative cartel established by the three main confederations came under increasing pressure. New groups of employees, such as specialists and technicians (*quadri*), were organised outside the ambit of the main unions. Other union confederations, representing occupational interests or other political currents, were striving for influence in a process which gained ground as the old political landscape began to break up. In an effort to stabilise their position, in part by giving some ground to the new forces, the three main union confederations changed the arrangements for workplace representation in an agreement between themselves in 1991. The agreement was recognised by the national employers' federation Confindustria and embodied in a new national-level agreement in December 1993. Confindustria was also interested in stabilising workplace representation, especially as the new arrangements for collective bargaining agreed in July 1993 put a new onus on company-level negotiations.

These new arrangements themselves were then challenged by smaller right- and left-wing organisations in a referendum held in June 1995 which overturned some of the agreed provisions (see below). As yet no action has been taken by the legislature to translate the referendum results into a new statutory provision which would overturn the basis set out in the Workers' Statute.

According to section 19 of the Workers' Statute, employees have the right to set up representative bodies at all units of production, provided three conditions are met. The three conditions are:

- there are at least 16 employees in the unit of production
- the representative body is set up on the initiative of the employees themselves
- it is set up under the auspices of the one of the trade unions at national level which meet the criteria of being 'most representative' – in practice, so far, the CGIL, CISL and UIL – or unions not affiliated to these confederations but which sign national-level industry collective agreements. These criteria of 'representativeness' were successfully challenged in a referendum held in June 1995 which lifted the requirements for the right to establish workplace bodies and to enjoy the rights for representatives granted by the Workers' Statute – with, as yet, uncertain results.

The formal name of such workplace union representative bodies was initially *rappresentanze sindacali aziendali*, or RSA. In practice they became known by the titles of the actual bodies with which they merged or whose existence they formalised – that is, works councils (*consiglio di fabbrica*). The precise term varied by sector. Under the 1991 agreement these bodies were given a new formal name: *rappresentanze sindacali unitarie* (RSU), unitary union representation.

Under the 1993 agreement, which effectively supersedes the previous system, employee representative bodies can be established in any workplace with at least 16 employees. The initiative can be taken either by one of the three main confederations (CGIL, CISL, UIL) or a properly constituted workplace union, a union which has signed a national agreement covering that workplace, which can present a list of candidates backed up by the signatures of at least 5 per cent of the eligible workforce, and which agrees to abide by the regulations contained in the 1993 agreement.

Two-thirds of the seats are directly elected by the whole workforce eligible to vote, with the remaining third reserved for representatives of unions which have negotiated the national agreement – in most cases the three main union confeder- ations – regardless of the actual support the organisations may command in the workplace. This provision provoked considerable controversy and prompted the move to the June 1995 referendum which overturned some of the formal require- ments for submitting candidates by allowing local unions, even if they do not meet the national criteria for being 'most representative', to put forward nomina- tions. As yet no legislation to give effect to the referendum result has been enacted. In general, the main unions have been able to hold on to their position in the private sector under the new arrangements.

The minimum size of the representative body is determined by the number of employees: three members in workplaces with 16–200 employees, three addi- tional members for every 300 employees above 200, up to 3,000 employees, and an additional three members for every 500 employees where the establishment has more than 3,000 employees. Separate representation within the overall body can be provided for blue-collar workers, white-collar workers and middle man- agers and specialists.

Members are elected (or in the case of the reserved seats possibly appointed) for three years. Rights to time off and to convene works meetings are provided through the Workers' Statute. The role of workplace representative bodies in the bargaining system is regulated by the 1993 agreement on bargaining, together with any sectoral provisions. They have no statutory consultation or co-determi- nation rights. Rather, their right to information is regulated by industry- level collective agreement (see below). The relationship between employers and works councils at company level is a function of the strength and leverage of the trade unions represented in the workplace. In large to medium-size companies works councils play an active role and cannot in practice be circumvented.

Rights under collective agreement

Employees have information rights under industry agreements rather than under the law. The metalworking agreement, for example, makes the following provi- sion, based on an underlying recognition of managerial prerogatives.

At central level a joint commission exists to monitor new technology, employ- ment trends (with particular reference to non-EU workers and those employed by quotas), investment trends in the industry, labour costs compared with other OECD countries, changes in actual hours worked, actual earnings, training.

Similar commissions and information rights are envisaged both at regional level (designed to cover groups of companies employing under 200 people) and at company level for larger organisations. According to these arrangements, employer organisations or the employer must provide trade unions and/or work- place representatives with information on issues such as any significant changes in the production process or the technology being used; changes in the overall organisation of work which might impinge on employment levels; decentralisation of production, and large-scale permanent transfers of employees; training programmes; and equal opportunity policies.

Implementation of the EU works council directive

At the time of writing, few Italian companies had moved to set up a European Works Council. Overall, some 30 companies with their headquarters in Italy are expected to be directly affected by the directive.

The first Italian company to establish a European Works Council under the provision for voluntary agreements was Merloni Elettrodomestici SpA, which manufactures domestic appliances, followed by ENI in the chemical industry. The Merloni agreement lays down an information and participation procedure which is sketchy but appears to build on existing practice, at least for its Italian employees. It does not define how representatives will be drawn from the different European plants. The ENI agreement, however, specifies that representatives will be nominated according to the law and/or custom and practice of the country from which they are drawn.

Interestingly, the current metalworking industry agreement also mentions the EU directive. Article 8 states that employers and trade unions will set up a joint working group to examine the industrial relations and information systems at European level so that they may make a valid contribution to the debate prior to the directive being enacted into national legislation.

Employer and trade union views on the EU Works Council Directive have provoked lively debate, given the current challenge to the representativeness of existing trade union structures. However, the line which is emerging is that European representatives will be drawn from a system which builds on existing representational arrangements.

Collective bargaining

Collective bargaining is passing through a period of transition, following the abolition of automatic pay indexation in 1992, the new arrangements for workplace employee representation, and the July 1993 central agreement on bargaining which commits the parties to a form of incomes policy and the introduction of more results-based pay at company level.

Status of collective agreements

National industry agreements are binding on all employers in a sector, whether or not they are members of a signatory organisation. Two mechanisms ensure this. First, should a non-signatory employer implement one term of an agreement in its industry, the company is deemed to have accepted all its terms. Second, the social security organisation INPS requires employers to indicate the collective agreement to which employees are subject when making returns for compulsory social insurance contributions. Section 46 of the constitution also provides that 'The worker has the right to a payment which is proportional to the quantity and quality of his work and which in any case is sufficient to ensure for himself and his family an independent existence without loss of human dignity.' The civil courts (*preture*), which have come to exercise some of the functions of labour tribunals, have interpreted the phrase 'payment . . . to ensure . . . an independent existence without loss of human dignity' as the basic rate established by collective agreement in the relevant industry. In this the civil courts have always been supported by the appeal courts (*cassazione*). In consequence, employers are seen as obliged to pay the basic rate even if they themselves are not party to the agreement. The courts have interpreted the 'basic rate' as including 'thirteenth month' payments, which are now virtually universal, but not fourteenth, fifteenth or sixteenth month payments.

In contrast, civil servants' and other public employees' organisations negotiate with the government and local authorities. Agreements must be ratified by parliament or local government before they acquire the force of law.

There is, therefore, no single minimum rate of pay for the whole country, but rather a series of minima for different industries. These minima are revised each time an industry agreement is renegotiated. Workers then bargain at plant or company level for improvements on the basic agreements which equally have the force of law once negotiated.

Duration of agreements

Under the July 1993 central agreement on collective bargaining, concluded between the employers' association Confindustria (together with Intersind, Asap and Confapi) and the three main union confederations, with the government playing an active role in mediating and brokering the deal, a new pattern was established for industry- level and company bargaining.

In future industry-level agreements will run for two years on pay matters and for four years as regards other issues, such as working time. Company-level agreements, to be negotiated between local/corporate management and workplace representative bodies elected under the terms of the 1993 agreement (see above), will also have a duration of four years, with company-level bargaining following industry-level bargaining after a preordained gap.

Levels of bargaining

National agreements are occasionally negotiated between Confindustria and union confederations. Examples include the agreement of 25 January 1975 which reformed the wage indexation system and the July 1992 agreement which abolished indexation altogether. Very occasionally, also, agreements are negotiated between Confindustria, union confederations and government. Such tripartite agreements are rare, however. By far the most significant in recent years is the current tripartite central agreement on incomes policy and industrial relations signed in July 1993, and that on workplace representation, signed in December 1993.

Industry/sector level

Sector-level bargaining is important, as it is the level at which minimum wage rates are established for each industry. There is no national minimum wage. For each sector – such as engineering, construction, textiles, and so on – there are usually three sectoral agreements. They cover:

- the private sector
- publicly owned companies (*a partecipazione statale*)
- the small business or craft sector (*artigianato*).

There is sometimes more than one agreement in the small business sector. With around 25 major industries in the economy there are a total of 100 or so national industry agreements.

There is no regional or provincial bargaining, and the regional bargaining area (*gabbia salariale*) was abolished in 1966 except in agriculture, where regional differences in rates are still permitted. Regional differences may, however, be established through company or plant-level agreements. There is some debate about whether the *gabbie salariali* should be reinstated in order to promote employment in depressed areas.

Company/plant level

In the year following the conclusion of an industry-level agreement, or at any other time should the industry agreement set a different timetable, employee representatives in companies have customarily negotiated at company or plant level for improvements on the minima laid down at industry level. These improvements (*superminimi*) then form the basic rate from which bonuses, overtime rates and so on are calculated. Hundreds of such company-level agreements are in existence.

Under the 1993 agreement the latest company bargaining round was scheduled to begin in 1995 with pay rises payable only from 1996. Company increases should now be tied to performance, broadly defined as the results of agreed plans to raise productivity, quality, overall corporate competitiveness, and general economic performance. Company bargaining is not intended to offset any settlement at industry level which fell below the actual inflation out-turn. However, this aim may be difficult to enforce if inflation strays above forecast levels, and it presents new challenges for many companies and local negotiators on how to measure and implement such performance-based pay increases. For larger companies, with developed personnel strategies, this is likely to be less difficult, as evidenced in some company agreements in 1995.

Collective agreements at company or plant level are between employee representatives (*rappresentanze sindacali unitarie*, RSU) and the company or plant management. As well as supplementary company pay, they cover issues such as the grading structure, health and safety, production bonuses, and information on company plans affecting investment and employment. Company or plant agreements generally seek to improve upon terms and conditions laid down in national industry agreements or at the very least to ensure that the basic terms and conditions set at industry level are currently implemented. They also seek to work out specific applications of any general provisions laid down by national industry agreements (such as flexible working time arrangements). However, in law there is no hierarchy of agreements, and company agreements could theoretically introduce a worsening of terms and conditions as easily as an improvement, provided it did not break the law. Under the new arrangements issues to be covered in company agreements are laid down in national industry agreements.

The pay bargaining system, therefore, is based on a network of national agreements fixing minimum rates, plus company and plant agreements which improve on these minima to varying degrees. The difference between minimum and actual rates varies considerably, according to the industry, the type of company and even the region: large factories in the north may pay up to 30 per cent above the minimum national rates as a result of local bargaining.

Employees outside collective bargaining

Officially no employees are left outside collective bargaining except those in the 'black' economy. The importance of collectively agreed pay, however, varies according to job category. As a rule it is far more important for blue-collar workers than for managerial staff.

The pay round and negotiating procedures

There has never been an annual pay round. Since July 1993 bargaining rounds have operated on a two- or four-year cycle at industry level (depending on the issue) and on a four-year cycle at company level. The 1993 agreement introduced a number of innovations to help speed up negotiations and bring them to a conclusion. In the past, negotiations could often last months, with employees being compensated for inflation through the operation of the *scala mobile* system of pay indexation. First, the parties are now under a 'peace obligation' during the negotiating period. Trade unions must present their demands three months before the current agreement expires in order to allow time for bargaining to begin: no industrial action is permitted for either side during this period. Second, if no agreement is reached within the three months following the expiry of the agreement, employees are entitled to interim payments as compensation for the lack of an agreement (*indennità di vacanza contrattuale*). These payments are initially equal to 30 per cent of the expected inflation rate, rising to 50 per cent if no agreement is concluded within six months.

The 1993 tripartite framework agreement between government, trade unions and employers set up a system whereby the social partners would reach agreement on a figure for projected inflation. This figure serves as a guide in industry-level negotiations. Inflation predictions tend to come from several authoritative forecasting organisations rather than from a single widely accepted assessment. The new system worked well for the 1994/95 industry bargaining round, with industrial disputes at their lowest ever. However, the system could come under pressure should inflation significantly exceed the forecast, putting particular responsibility on the government to create a non-inflationary environment.

Settlements in the major industries tend to be bunched at the beginning of the round, with metalworking, in particular, chemicals and textiles being the pacesetters. The existing trade union and employer organisation structures strongly favour a great deal of co-ordination between different union confederations and between employers on the preparation of claims and employer responses within the same industries. For example, the metalworking unions Fiom, Fim and Uilm, affiliated to the trade union organisations CGIL, CISL and UIL respectively, meet in talks to agree their claim before submitting it to the employers. Employers, similarly, respond in a co-ordinated fashion through their federation, Federmeccanica. United trade union federations also exist in a number of industries, notably chemicals.

This highly co-ordinated approach between regions and different union organisations at industry level does not extend downwards to company bargaining. Pay awarded at company level, where it exists at all, is settled in accordance with market factors and depends on the company's size, its ability to pay, its location, the local labour market, and workforce organisation – although in future these factors should, theoretically, yield to the performance measures set out in the 1993 agreement.

Serious differences during negotiations which lead to a breakdown of talks tend to be resolved by strike action (except where governed by law). In some cases, where the dispute is protracted, the Minister of Labour may step in and mediate.

Recent trends

There have been several significant changes to past practice in the pay rounds of major industries and firms. Perhaps the most important in recent times was the abolition of pay indexation in July 1992, given the longevity of the system and the considerable weight attached to it by the trade unions. Increases in industry minima are now tied to projected inflation in line with the 1993 agreement. In addition, the 1993 framework agreement regulates company bargaining by stipulating its scope and timing, as well as requiring company pay rises to be linked with agreed objectives. In this way, employers have acquired greater control than ever before over their direct labour costs as the 'automatic' elements have been removed or qualified. In fact, rises in industry minima have been below inflation since May 1992, although actual earnings in large-scale manufacturing have managed to keep ahead of prices, possibly reflecting the buoyant export sector.

Agreed provisions

Basic pay   The average pay packet is made up of a number of components – agreed minimum pay under national industry agreements, frozen indexation payments from the period prior to 1992, agreed bonuses – such as seniority increments and production bonuses – and any supplements paid under company agreements, some of which may have a performance element.

Service increments are very common for both blue- and white-collar employees and managers in most sectors. They are also criticised as an element of 'automaticity' in Italian pay determination, though employers may be able to live with them, given the development of greater flexibility in other elements of the pay packet. Typically, incremental scales for blue- and white-collar workers have five points for each grade, with movement up the scale every two years. Around 4.7 per cent of a skilled blue-collar worker's average monthly earnings are accounted for by seniority payments. For managers, flat-rate seniority payments are also triggered every two years, up to a maximum 20 years' seniority.

Bonuses and supplements
Holiday pay and bonuses   All employees have an indefeasible right under the constitution to an annual holiday and are entitled to be paid at the normal basic rate during their leave. Some agreements provide for a holiday bonus, payable prior to annual holiday leave. Others provide for the payment of company supplement pay (*superminimi*) in two lump sums, prior to annual holiday leave and then before the Christmas break.

Annual or other bonuses   A thirteenth-month bonus is universal. It is normally paid in December. Some agreements provide for fourteenth- and sometimes fifteenth-month bonuses. Collectively agreed length of service bonuses may also be paid in some industries.

Production bonuses (premi di produzione)   may be laid down under collective agreement whether at national or at company level and may take the form of collective rather than individual payments. While originally intended as a form of incentive payment, production bonuses have now become an item of basic pay. In engineering they make up around 2 per cent of a salaried worker's pay, rising to about 11 per cent (and now frozen at that) in the chemical industry.

Other types of allowance, for example for attendance (linked with the number of hours worked, excluding overtime), dirt or danger, and canteen allowances, are often found in company agreements. Sometimes a company will combine several of these smaller items of pay to make one larger supplementary payment.

Financial participation   There is no specific legislation on the granting of share options or offering a special tax regime for employee profit-sharing. However, there was reported growth in employee shareholdings in the late 1980s, much of it attributed to the long upward movement of the Italian stock market. Studies have found, however, that shares distributed to employees rarely exceeded 5 per cent of the employer's total share capital, and were often non-voting. Where shares are allocated to employees, and held in trust for two years, the employee is not taxed on them. Nor is capital gains tax payable if shares are acquired at below market price and then disposed of, provided the shares do not exceed a threshold proportion of the total share capital (2 per cent of a listed company and 5 per cent of a private company). No capital gains tax is payable if shares are held for at least five years. Fully fledged share option schemes are a rarity, however.

Similarly, employer-financed savings schemes are unusual. The national agreement of managers in retailing, distribution and services does provide for a provident fund, the Fondo Mario Negri, which is financed mainly by the employer.

Working time   The statutory maximum working day is eight hours, with a maximum working week of 48 hours based on a nominal six-day working week. These maxima were established by decree 692 (15 March 1923) and became statute law with law 473 (17 April 1925). In practice, hours of work are governed by collective agreement. In 1994 average agreed weekly hours in manufacturing stood at 40 a week, or 1,744 on an annual basis. A large number of collective agreements either express or manage hours of work on an annualised basis, with cuts in hours in recent years generally taken in the form of additional days off rather than a shorter working week.

This applies, for example, in the engineering industry. Under the terms of the current agreement the basic week has been fixed at 40 hours since the mid-1980s. However, 16 hours were taken off the working year from 1987, and a further 16-hour reduction was agreed in 1991. By 1992 agreed annual hours stood at 1,709.

In the private-sector chemical industry the basic working week is 40 hours for day workers and 37.5 hours for shift workers. To cater for flexible hours of work arrangements, the normal working week may, with the consent of the works council, be arrived at by averaging out the total number of hours worked weekly over a reference period to be agreed at company or plant level. Hours worked above the statutory maximum week as part of these flexible arrangements are paid at rates higher than normal.

Holidays   The constitution guarantees workers the right to paid annual holidays which they may not surrender (though no penalties are laid down for infringement). If, in exceptional circumstances, employees have to work during their leave they are entitled to double time. Entitlement to leave is acquired following the successful completion of a probationary period. If an employee falls ill while on leave the holiday entitlement may be suspended for the period of illness. There are currently no general legal provisions relating to the length of annual leave, which is determined by collective agreement. Agreements may link holiday entitlement with job grade – or, more often, with length of service. (However, from November 1996 the European Union's working time directive will require three weeks' paid leave, rising to four from 1999.)

Basic leave entitlement ranges from four to six weeks a year. The bulk is almost always taken during August, when most factories in manufacturing, for example, shut down. Industry-level agreements usually provide for a basic annual leave entitlement of four weeks, but an additional week is often allowed to compensate for the abolition in 1977 of five state and religious holidays.

In engineering a basic annual entitlement of four weeks is increased by one day for employees with between 10 and 18 years' service and by six days (calculated on the basis of a six-day working week) for those with 19 years' service or more. The number of weeks taken off together may not exceed three, unless a company-level agreement provides otherwise. Companies may improve on the agreed arrangements. Fiat, for example, adds five days to be taken individually to offset the past cut in public holidays. Moreover, any Christmas shutdown is not taken out of employees' holiday entitlement.

Public holidays   There are 10 public holidays (*giorni festivi*). In addition to the national holidays local saints' days are also observed as public holidays in certain cities (such as 24 June in Turin and 7 December in Milan). Employers are obliged to pay normal pay on a public holiday – that is, what employees would have earned had they been at work. Article 2 of law 90 (31 March 1954) requires the employer to pay even if the employee would have been off work in any case – because of illness, injury, maternity leave, annual holiday, etc. Where an employee has to work over a public holiday (*lavoro festivo*) – for example, on shift work or some other agreed exception – collective agreements lay down special supplements in addition to a day off in lieu.

Maternity leave   Mothers are forbidden to work during the statutory period of maternity leave, which runs from two months before the expected date of the birth to three months after the actual date. In certain jobs – laid down by ministerial decree – the period begins three months before the expected date of birth.

Maternity benefit during statutory maternity leave is equal to 80 per cent of normal pay. The cost of the benefit is borne by the social security organisation. Maternity benefit is payable to the employee with the first month's salary or wage following resumption of work. However, the employer must pay an amount in advance which is normally laid down by collective agreement, but which in any case may not be less than half of previous monthly pay. Some collective agreements provide for maternity pay at 100 per cent of normal pay, payable on a monthly basis during the period of leave.

The law also prohibits women from doing dangerous, unhealthy or heavy work from the beginning of pregnancy until the seventh month after the birth. During that period a woman normally on such work has to be assigned to other duties without loss of pay.

Time off for breast-feeding   During the first year of a baby's life the employer must allow the mother two special breaks during the day (one break if her working hours are less than six) to breast-feed her baby. These breaks must each be of one hour's duration (half an hour if the mother has the use of a room for the purpose, or of a creche provided on the premises by the employer). The breaks are counted as normal working time and are paid.

Optional parental leave   In addition to maternity leave, a woman may choose to take a further six months' leave during the first year of the baby's life. Her job is protected until the baby is one year old. She is entitled to payments from the sickness benefit fund equivalent to about 30 per cent of normal salary. Payment is made by the employer, who recovers the amount by offsetting it against social security contributions.

A woman is also entitled by law to time off in order to nurse a sick child if the child is under three years old. She must present a medical certificate to her employer. Such leave is normally unpaid.

Rights to special leave can also be exercised by the father should he replace the mother or have primary responsibility for the child.

Periods of optional absence from work are counted as periods of employment for the purpose of calculating length of service.

Other time off
Educational leave   The Workers' Statute gave all employees in companies employing more than 15 people certain rights to facilitate study. Article 10 distinguishes between employees attending university (where attendance at lectures is not compulsory) and workers enrolled and regularly attending classes at primary, secondary or vocational schools which are public, state-approved or authorised to award legally recognised qualifications. The latter – but not the former – are entitled to have their hours of work arranged to facilitate attendance at classes and preparation for examinations. In addition, they may not be compelled to work overtime or during weekly rest periods.

All employees, including university students, are entitled to paid leave in order to sit examinations.

Many collective agreements contain additional provisions on study leave. The national engineering agreement specifies that workers wishing to attend approved courses of study for personal or professional improvement are entitled to total paid leave of up to 150 hours over a three-year period (this leave can be used up in any one year by an individual) provided the paid leave is matched by a similar period of unpaid leave. The allowance increases to 250 hours for workers completing their basic education or attending literacy courses. Workers must furnish certification of registration and regular attendance at courses. The agreement also stipulates, however, a maximum total number of hours available for educational leave, generally based on a given formula. It states that no more than 2 per cent of the workforce may be absent on study leave at any one time and that the absences must not interfere with normal production.

Similar agreements exist in most sectors, although the number of hours' leave and the limitations may vary slightly from sector to sector. Sector-level agreements along these lines are aimed at improving the educational standard of workers in general. Other provisions may exist at company level, or may be worked out on an informal basis for individual workers following courses other than the approved ones.

Trade union activities   Under section 3 of the Workers' Statute all employees are entitled to 10 paid hours' time off per year to attend trade union meetings in the workplace. Trade union delegates are also entitled to paid leave of absence for the performance of their duties. Entitlement is usually at least eight hours per month. The number of delegates entitled to leave of absence depends on the size of the company.

Trade union officials are also entitled to unpaid leave of up to eight days a year in connection with union responsibilities. Collective agreements may improve on the law's provision.

Employees elected to trade union office at national or provincial level are entitled to unpaid leave of absence at any time during, or for the entire duration of, their term of office.

Family leave   Most industry-level collective agreements provide for employees to take paid leave if they get married. Entitlement ranges from 10 to 30 days, starting on the wedding day. All white-collar employees are entitled by law to at least 15 days.

Many collective agreements provide for a short period of leave to be allowed on the death of a close relative, for attending a funeral or for other family reasons. A typical allowance would be up to 24 hours, or three working days, per year. Many companies also grant short spells of leave for personal reasons on an informal basis.

Military service   Employees called upon to undergo compulsory military service are entitled to have their job protected for the duration of the service – that is, to unpaid leave. (For the army and air force, service lasts 12 months; in the navy it lasts 18 months.) On completion of military service the employee must present himself for work within 30 days, otherwise the employment contract may be terminated automatically. In the case of recall to the reserve for any reason an employee is entitled to paid leave. The amount of pay or benefit is laid down by special laws or may be determined by collective agreement.

Leave for public duties   Under the Workers' Statute an employee elected to the national parliament, to a regional parliament or to other public office is entitled to unpaid leave at any time during, or for the entire period of, his term of office. The period of elected office must, if the employee so requests, be taken into account for the purpose of calculating pension rights. Employees elected to public office who do not wish to be granted unpaid leave are entitled, upon their request, to leave of absence with full pay for the time strictly necessary to carry out their official functions.

An employee who is elected mayor or deputy major, chairman or vice-chairman of the provincial council is likewise entitled to unpaid leave not exceeding 30 hours a month.

Employees carrying out election duties are entitled to three days' paid leave over and above their normal leave entitlement.

Industrial disputes

By tradition Italy has been, and has been seen to be, a country with a high incidence of industrial conflict, especially in the public sector. According to figures provided by the UK Employment Department, some 250 days per 1,000 employees were lost as a result of industrial action between 1989 and 1993, compared with 70 in the United Kingdom and 20 in Germany. However, the character of disputes has changed markedly since 1980 – the year of a major union defeat in a strike at Fiat. Industry or company-level disputes aimed at influencing pay negotiations in the private sector, especially in manufacturing, have declined, with a very low rate of conflict in the 1994/95 pay round. During the 1980s there was a significant increase in disputes in the public sector, culminating in legislation to restrict industrial action in 1990 (see below). There has also been an increase in the early to mid-1990s of large-scale demonstration strikes against government policy, notably over pension reform.

No formal procedures exist for handling the breakdown of talks. *In extremis*, where an important national industry agreement is being negotiated, the Minister of Labour will step in and mediate. With the exception of what is laid down in self-regulatory codes and in law 146 of 1990 (see below) on strikes in essential public services, employees do not have to give notice of their intention to take industrial action unless the safety of persons or plant is endangered. In that case the length of notice should be sufficient to allow adequate safety measures to be taken.

Ballots are not required before strike action is called. Italian law grants all employees a positive right to strike, with any kind of industrial action permitted. Even political strikes are legal, provided they do not aim to overthrow the constitution.

Strike action in essential services

In June 1990 the government introduced a new law to regulate strike action in essential services, overwhelmingly provided by the public sector. Provision for such a law had always existed under the constitution but had never previously been enacted. However, frequent disruption of public services and the reaction of public opinion finally forced the government's hand. For many, however, the new law does not go far enough and they claim it has no teeth. Law 146 provides:

- a non-exhaustive list of essential services (those deemed necessary 'to guarantee the basic human right to life, health, liberty, security, welfare, education and freedom of communication'), where the right to strike is limited in order to guarantee users a minimum level of service
- regulations governing *la precettazione* – legal notice served on individual workers requiring them to present themselves for work – in existence since the 1930s
- the formation of a commission to ensure proper implementation of the law.

The minimum level of service is defined by national industry collective agreements, which must identify essential services in their sectors both in the public and in the private sector. Disputes are referred to, and on request arbitrated by, the commission, which consists of nine members appointed by both houses of parliament. Workers are required to give employers 10 days' notice of strike action and of its duration, and organisations affected must give the public five days' notice. To ensure a minimum level of service, workers may be ordered to present themselves for work. Failure to comply with such an order entails a fine. The order can be challenged in a court of law within seven days of its receipt.

Infringement of the law will attract sanctions, which can apply to individuals (though not dismissal) as well as to organisations. They include fines, withdrawal of paid leave and suspension.

Union codes of conduct

To avoid legal intervention on the right to strike, the three main trade union confederations, the CGIL, CISL and UIL, drew up voluntary codes of conduct to be followed prior to strike action. The codes, however, applied only to their members and were not respected by independent organisations. For this reason the traditional unions gave their support to law 146 of 1990, particularly as it refers the minimum level of service to be provided to the collective bargaining process.

Employers' industrial action

As with employees, so the law permits employers to undertake industrial action, in the form of a lockout, provided it is not in response to trade union strike action. In such a case a lockout would be considered anti-union behaviour, under article 28 of the Workers' Statute.

Conduct during industrial action

Peaceful picketing is legal provided force is not used against those wishing to work and no damage is done to the plant. If either should occur, the individuals concerned would be held liable.

Consequences of lawful industrial action

During strike action an employee's contract of employment is deemed suspended and therefore employees are not entitled to payment for the period during which the strike takes place.

However, the employer must pay all social security contributions as usual, and periods of strike action do not affect length of service payments. Workers who take strike action are protected from dismissal or disciplinary action under sections 15, 16 and 28 of the Workers' Statute. Under the law sacked workers can be reinstated and/or the employer fined.

Consequences of unlawful strike action

Strike action is unlawful only if it infringes the provisions of law 146 of 1990 governing strike action in essential public services. In such a case individuals or organisations can be sanctioned according to the severity of the violation. Measures which terminate or alter the employment relationship, however, are excluded. Sanctions can include a fine, the withdrawal of paid leave or suspension.

Settling disputes

There is no formal procedure for settling disputes. Disputes are settled mainly by strike action, followed by collective bargaining. In serious cases government Ministers will mediate.

Conciliation and arbitration

Conciliation and arbitration are not widespread, and in all cases consist of a voluntary procedure laid down – if at all – by collective agreement. Conciliation may normally take one of two forms:

- in civil courts (*conciliazione giudiziaria*), once a problem has arisen
- through the provincial conciliation commissions (*commissioni provinciali di conciliazione*), which were set up under law 533 of 11 August 1973.

These commissions are based at the headquarters of each provincial labour office (*sede provinciale dell'Ufficio del Lavoro*). They are chaired by the labour office, presiding over a panel of employers' and union representatives. Sub-committees may also be set up as appropriate.

Under article 4 of law 533 of 1973 arbitration may be undertaken only if explicitly referred to in a collective agreement and is an uncommon procedure.

Organisations

Labour Ministry (Ministero del Lavoro e della Previdenza Sociale)
Via Flavia 6
00187 Roma
Tel. + 39 6 4683

Confederation of Italian Industry
(Confindustria)
Viale dell'Astronomia 30
00100 Roma
Tel. + 39 6 59031

Publicly owned companies in engineering
(Intersind)
Via Cristoforo Colombo 98
00147 Roma
Tel. + 39 6 51751

Engineering employers' federation
(Federmeccanica)
Piazza Benito Juarez 14
0144 Roma
Tel. + 39 6 59 25 44 6

Employers' confederation for small
businesses (Confapi)
Via della Colonna Antonina 52
Roma
Tel. + 39 6 67 82 44 1

General Confederation of Italian Labour
(Confederazione Generale Italiana del
Lavoro, CGIL)
Corso d'Italia 25
00198 Roma
Tel. + 39 6 84761

Confederation of Italian Trade Unions
(Confederazione Italiana Sindacati
Lavoratori, CISL)
Via Po 21
00198 Roma
Tel. + 39 6 84731

Italian Labour Union (Unione Italiana del
Lavoro, UIL)
Via Lucullo 6
00187 Roma
Tel. + 39 6 49731

National Federation of Industrial
Management (Federazione Nazionale
Dirigenti Aziende Industriali, FNDAI)
Via Palermo 12
00184 Roma
Tel. + 39 6 47 40 35 1–4

National Federation of Commercial
Management (Federazione Nazionale
Dirigenti di Aziende Commmerciali,
FNDAC)
Via Nazionale 163
00184 Roma
Tel. + 39 6 67 81 49 8

Main sources

Durante, Bruno and Filadoro, Camillo. *Enciclopedia dei diritti dei lavoratori*. Milan, 1991

Maggioli Editore. *Codice Civile a leggi complementari*. Rimini, 1991

Volpini, Franco (ed.). *Agenda per l'Amministrazione del Personale delle Aziende Industriali 1994*. Rome, 1993

Collective agreements including: *Contratto di Lavoro, Industria Metalmeccanica Privata* (engineering); *Contratto Collettivo Nazionale di Lavoro – Industria Chimica* (chemicals); *Contratto Collettivo Nazionale di Lavoro – Industria Tessile* (textiles); *Contratto Collettivo Nazionale di Lavoro per i dipendenti da aziende del terziario: distribuzione e servizi* (commerce and services); *Contratto Collettivo Nazionale di Lavoro per i dirigenti di aziende commerciali* (commercial managers); *La contrattazione sindacale collettiva per i dirigenti di aziende industriali* (managers in industry)

9

The Netherlands

The Netherlands has a long history of consultation and consensus politics. This tradition also characterises the formal institutions of the system of industrial relations. The regulation of labour affairs in the post-war period has been highly institutionalised and centralised, although the period since 1980 has seen greater decentralisation and differentiation in the pattern of industrial relations. Immediately after the Second World War collective bargaining was highly centralised and under the control of the government, which laid down improvements in terms and conditions after consultation with both sides of industry. In this field, decentralisation initially meant a shift to industry level, then, over the past decade and a half, increasingly to company-level bargaining.

The formal institutions of employee representation and bargaining have remained intact through the 1980s and early 1990s, but their relevance has arguably been transformed – as evidenced by the substantial drop in the number of trade union members in the 1980s, the rise of company bargaining, and the weakening of the legal distinction between the powers of workplace works councils and those of industry-level trade unions. Steps to 'modernise' and consolidate the powers of central tripartite bodies are also in hand, possibly weakening the influence of tripartite consultation on legislative matters.

Collective agreements set pay and other terms of employment for some 75 per cent of employees in the private sector and virtually all employees in the public sector. Whilst decentralisation to company-level bargaining has begun to fray the edges of industry-level collective agreements, steps taken at national level since the election of a Labour–Liberal coalition in May 1994 have sought to streamline the operation of national tripartite and bipartite organisations which have customarily formed the institutional superstructure of collective bargaining and industrial relations. The government has maintained that the plethora of consultation requirements merely slow down the process of political decision-making. Steps are also under way to separate decision-making from the implementation of policy.

The two main national bodies of the industrial relations system – the Labour Foundation and the Social and Economic Council (see below) – are to be maintained, but their functions are being slimmed down.

The main players

Trade unions

A notable feature of both employers' organisations and trade unions is that, like the major political parties, they have traditionally been divided along religious lines, although some have merged in recent years. The trade unions therefore have no political factions, and do not make electoral recommendations. However, some unions' stated aims may correspond with those of political parties (for example, the FNV and the Labour Party).

National confederations   There are three fully recognised central trade union confederations:

- *Federatie Nederlandse Vakbeweging* (FNV) is the largest, with a total of 1.1 million members at the end of 1994 – some 80 per cent of all trade unionists. The FNV was created through a merger of the Socialist Confederation (NVV) and the Catholic Confederation (NKV), which began in 1976 and was completed in 1982. The FNV now consists of twenty sectoral and occupational affiliate unions, the largest of which are the public-sector union AbvaKabo (309,174 members); the industrial union Industriebond FNV (239,757 members) and the construction workers' union Bouw- en Houtbond FNV (163,091 members).
- *Christelijk Nationaal Vakverbond* (CNV), the Protestant trade union confederation, which has some 339,000 members (1994 figure), 23 per cent of the workforce. Like the FNV it consists of sectoral and occupational affiliates.
- *Vakcentrale voor Middelbaar en Hoger Personeel* (MHP) represents the interests of white-collar and management staff through its three member unions. It has a total of 155,800 members (1994).

A fourth centre, Algemene Vakcentrale (AVC), was set up in May 1990 and now has some 111,000 members, drawn largely from the civil service and other service sectors. In 1994 the AVC was deemed sufficiently representative to be admitted to the Social and Economic Council (see below) but has not – yet – been recognised as such by the Labour Foundation. As a result the AVC has been seeking closer co-operation with the FNV, and may yet merge fully with the larger union.

Freedom of association   There is little statutory regulation of trade unions as such, and trade unions may be established by employees under the general principles of freedom of association. However, if they are to enter into collective agreements unions must have a legal personality, as well as specifying in their own rulebooks that they may bargain collectively. Only a trade union, as opposed to a works council (see below), can negotiate a formal collective agreement (although works councils are increasingly involved in setting primary terms and conditions – see below). Unions also enjoy some rights in the area of collective dismissal.

Trade union density has stabilised at around 25 per cent after a dramatic drop from 40 per cent in the mid-1970s to a low point of 24 per cent in the mid-1980s. Overall membership of the FNV, for example, fell from 1,078,000 in 1980 to 893,000 in 1986 but has since recovered to 1,119,000 (October 1994). However, the make-up of membership has shifted somewhat. Many new members have been recruited in sectors where employees feel insecure because of the impact of recent job losses, as in banking and insurance. According to the FNV union confederation, union density in these sectors rose from 10 per cent of the workforce in 1989/90 to approach 23 per cent by 1994.

On the other hand, unions concentrated in manufacturing industry have continued to lose members as a result of company failures, new technology and a broad push for rationalisation involving workforce reductions. Nevertheless, Industriebond FNV retains its prime position as one of the most powerful unions, and has largely clung on to a share of around one-fifth of total FNV membership.

Company-level representation and influence remain a problem for the trade unions. Although works council representatives are also frequently trade union members and are elected on a union ticket, the extent to which this guarantees influence over policy and decision-making in works councils is open to debate (see below).

A number of union rights and concessions, such as workplace facilities, notice boards and time off for meetings, are regulated by collective agreement. For example, the insurance industry agreement provides for rooms to be available for meetings, notice boards, internal mail facilities, room on the employers' premises outside office hours for members' meetings and a guarantee that no employee will suffer as a result of carrying out the duties of a trade union representative.

Trade unions draw up their own rules and regulations for elections and voting procedures on industrial action, a freedom from statutory intervention which continues to be fiercely defended. In contrast to members of the works councils, official trade union representatives, registered as such with the company management, enjoy no specific legal protection against dismissal. However, there may be provision in collective agreements for their rights and status. Unions have been pressing for legislation and have been engaged in discussions with the government on the possibility of introducing statutory dismissal protection along the lines of that granted to works council members.

Trade union representatives at company level may be called into collective bargaining at company or sectoral level, but their prime responsibility is to attend to the needs of the individual members and act as a workplace base for the union. In practice about 70 per cent of all works council places are occupied by trade union candidates.

Employers' organisations

As with trade unions, employers' organisations consist of a central confederation with sectoral affiliates. The two main organisations – the Confederation of Dutch Enterprises (Verbond van Nederlandse Ondernemingen, VNO) and the Christian Employers' Organisation (Nederlands Christelijk Werkgeversverbond, NCW) – agreed in December 1994 to unite their operations, although they have not abandoned their separate identities. As of March 1995 each organisation took on the title of VNO-NCW.

The old VNO was the largest employer body, with about 10,000 companies with more than 10 employees affiliated to its 100 member federations. The two most important are the FME, representing employers in the general and electrical engineering industries, which includes large concerns such as Hoogovens and Philips, and the AWV, a general organisation of some 360 firms, including Shell and Unilever. The NCW has four member categories, the largest being the 100 business associations with a membership of thousands of companies.

The interests of small and medium-sized enterprises were represented by two organisations which have merged their operations to form the Midden- en Kleinbedrijf Nederland (MKB-Nederland). All these employers' organisations are in turn members of the umbrella association, the Raad van de Centraale Ondernemingsorganisaties (RCO). The RCO is located at the VNO's administrative headquarters.

The main employers' organisation, the VNO-NCW, conducts a certain amount of debate internally on a common position *vis-à-vis* the trade unions in preparation for the collective bargaining round. Although no document or official recommendation is produced, and guidelines are not legally binding on members, it does give an indication of the direction to be taken. For example, in late 1991 a public statement issued by the two major employers' organisations (then still operating separately) urged members not to yield to union demands aimed at compensating for proposed government reductions in long-term disability benefit. However, in the 1992 and 1993 round this position was not sustained at company level when the subject became one of the major negotiating issues. No sanctions can be imposed on an employer for failing to adhere to the guidelines.

Consultation at national level

The Social and Economic Council

The role of the SER   The tripartite Social and Economic Council (Sociaal-Economische Raad, SER) is the major advisory and consultative body on social and economic issues at national level. Until the beginning of 1995 the government was under a statutory obligation to consult the SER on all major socio-economic issues. Legislation introduced in 1995, but awaiting final Senate approval at the time of writing, amended this to a consultation requirement on the 'main principles' affecting social and economic legislation. Despite the change the SER none the less remains the main national body for debate, information exchange and consultation on employment issues generally, but only very rarely on pay issues.

The SER was set up in 1950 and is composed of representatives of employers and trades unions in equal numbers, plus independent advisers appointed by the Crown (*kroonleden*) – making 45 members in all. It has an administrative structure, with specialist departments dealing with individual issues. Its formal advice reflects the different interests of its member groups and does not have to be unanimous. However, a unanimous or majority recommendation (*advies*) inevitably carries more weight. In most cases the unions and the employers tend to vote *en bloc*, with the independent members (who usually also vote together) having the casting votes. Two-thirds or more of the SER's recommendations are unanimous. However, unusual alliances of employers and unions can sometimes occur, as, for example, over the question of abolishing the requirement of authorisation for all dismissals – a move not favoured by the unions or the organisation of small and medium-sized companies and agricultural employers. The SER usually produces some 35 advice papers per year.

The functioning of the SER Proposals submitted to the SER by the government are referred to specialist committees for initial debate. Each committee can request the attendance and advice of experts in a given field. The committees are always chaired by a representative of the Crown. The 1995 regulations shortened the time scale for submitting a report to two or three months, which some members of the SER feel is not long enough for the more complex issues. The SER itself wants a three-month minimum, with extensions for the more complex queries. Once a preliminary position (*wit stuk*) has been reached within the committee, the trade unions and employers' organisations have to circulate it to their members for debate and comment. In theory the report is not in the public domain at that stage; in practice, however, the debate becomes public at that point. All committee meetings are held behind closed doors, but more general sessions may be public. Once the respective memberships have been consulted, comments and reactions are incorporated as necessary into the paper for debate at a full council meeting, which agrees the final form of the report to be submitted to the government. The Crown members hold a separate debate on a given issue, outside the council. They are very keen to be seen as independent members and individual experts. They are usually academics (legal or economic) and in appointing them an attempt is made to maintain a political balance.

The issues that most commonly come before the SER are

- social security
- legislation, including the most appropriate level of decision-making
- interpretation of the law, including European law

- company-level issues (but pay only in the broadest terms)
- job creation and labour-force participation (especially for the unskilled)
- the minimum wage and the link with social benefits (see *Contracts and Terms and Conditions of Employment* in this series).

However, the SER may also consider such issues as infrastructure, the environment, education, technological developments, EU integration and Eastern Europe. The SER may also look at issues on its own initiative. In the past, for example, it has investigated shop opening times, government deregulation programmes and flexible hours.

The Labour Foundation

The other main forum for national consultation is the bipartite Labour Foundation (Stichting van de Arbeid, STAR). It was set up in 1945, and was originally concerned with the operation of the highly centralised pay-setting mechanism which prevailed in the Netherlands until the late 1970s. Its task was to prepare a pay recommendation which was subsequently adopted and implemented by government. More recently it has prepared non-binding accords on a range of aspects of industrial relations. The last one of these to cover pay was the November 1982 framework accord on pay indexation and cuts in hours, agreed in the face of a possible statutory pay freeze. This marked the beginning of a definite move away from government interference in collective bargaining and wage policy, and towards more sectoral and company agreements – although it was a government threat of intervention in late 1992 that induced the social partners to agree to delay the 1993 bargaining round, effectively creating a two-month pay pause. Since 1982 the STAR has not concluded any agreements, although it produces two consultation documents a year. The autumn one may include a discussion of pay. In addition the STAR advises the government on aspects of industrial relations. It has, for example, produced an influential code of conduct on recruitment practices (see *Recruitment, Training and Development* in this series).

The role of the STAR, which celebrated its fiftieth anniversary in 1995, is now under scrutiny. In particular it is perceived to have lost some of its role through the delegation of functions to industry-level meetings between employers and trade unions, on the one hand, and to European-level consultations on the other.

Government intervention

The Wage Determination Act of 1970 (*Wet op de loonvorming*) sets out the conditions under which the government may intervene in free collective bargaining. This may occur if sudden unforeseen changes create an emergency in the national economy requiring a reduction in wage costs, provided these are taken in conjunction with other measures of economic restraint. In effect the Minister of Labour may intervene to suspend clauses of collective agreements for up to six months (renewable for a further six months). Certain groups of employees may be excluded from this suspension and an 'adequate standard of living' must be maintained for all employees. The government used these powers on three occasions in the early 1980s to introduce a general pay policy. Since then there has been no direct intervention.

However, the government did threaten to intervene in the 1993 pay round in order to limit pay rises as the economy moved into recession at the end of 1992. In response the social partners agreed to delay the beginning of the bargaining round by two months, effectively creating a two-month pay pause. No agreements were signed until 1 March 1993, although pay rises could be backdated to 1 January. For its part the government agreed to reduce certain taxes and premiums in order to ensure that employees would be assured of an increase in purchasing power equivalent to a 1.25 per cent pay rise. Measures taken by the government in relation to pay policy relate equally to employees covered by collective agreements and to those not so covered.

Regional and industry consultation

Numerous bodies exist to act as forums in which employers and unions meet at regional and industry level, offering a means to anticipate and possibly avert conflict during pay negotiations. Some industries, such as shipping and agriculture, have independent bodies or individuals to preside over collective bargaining. Others have bipartite industrial boards. In the engineering industry, for example, a consultative body, the Raad van Overleg in de Metaalindustrie (ROM), consists of 12 members, with six from the employers and six from the three main unions. Its brief is to look at a wide range of industrial issues, including training and job creation. The presidency alternates between the employers' organisation, FME, and the largest union concerned, the Industriebond FNV.

At regional level employees are represented in chambers of commerce (*kamer van koophandel*). One-third of the chambers consist of employees, one-third of employers in small and medium-sized enterprises and one-third other employers, as well as the regional arms of the SER.

Workplace employee representation

Works councils

Although trade unions have been seeking to establish union delegations in the workplace, and to obtain more rights for workplace union representatives, the dominant form of employee representation at the place of work is the statutory system of works councils. Recent debates at SER and government level have sought to clarify the scope of works council rights and powers, and legislation was expected to detail the position during 1996.

The statutory system of works councils has been developed through a number of legislative steps, beginning in 1950 and evolving, via important amendments in 1971, 1979 and 1981, into employee-only bodies embracing a large spectrum of companies. The current position is governed by the 1979 law on works councils (*Wet op de ondernemingsraden*), last amended in 1990. It defines works councils as employee-only bodies which must be set up by the employer at enterprise level as soon as certain size criteria are met (see below). One of the major changes embodied in the 1979 legislation was to remove the employer from the role of chairing the works council. The 1990 amendments were in part a response to a recommendation from the Social and Economic Council for a clarification of the differences between trade union and works council tasks.

Employers in any enterprise (*onderneming*) employing

- at least 100 employees, or
- at least 35 employees working more than one-third of normal full-time hours

are required to establish a works council (*ondernemingsraad*). Employers who have two or more enterprises which meet these criteria may establish a joint works council where it is deemed appropriate to facilitate the application of the law. Conversely the employer may also establish individual works councils for parts of an enterprise employing 100 or more employees. 'Enterprise' is defined as any 'organisation operating . . . as an independent unit' and could therefore be taken to mean an individual workplace, office, shop or institution providing a service. The employer and the works council must meet at least six times a year, and discuss the operation of the enterprise in at least two of those meetings.

Special regulations apply to enterprises with fewer than 100 employees in respect of employees' eligibility for election, right to information and consultation, and the need for prior agreement (see below).

The cost of operating the works council is borne wholly by the employer. The expenses may include, if the works council wishes, and provided the employer is notified in advance, the cost of obtaining expert advice and any costs incurred in legal proceedings taken by the works council.

Composition and election   Works councils consist solely of employees from the enterprise to which they relate, and are directly elected by all employees with at least six months' service (one year's where fewer than 100 employees are employed). Any employee with at least one year's service is eligible to stand for office. The size of the council will vary according to enterprise size, with three members where there are fewer than 50 employees, five members for 50–100 employees, seven members for 100–200 employees, and up to 13 members for enterprises with between 600 and 1,000 employees. An additional two members may be elected for each additional thousand employees, up to a maximum works council size of 25.

Elections are held every three years on the basis of lists of candidates, although the works council itself may pass regulations varying the period of election to anything between two and four years, or allowing half the council to step down every two years. Lists of candidates may be submitted by trade unions represented in the enterprise, or by non-unionised employees provided they account for a third of the workforce and that a minimum quorum of 30 signatures is obtained. In practice, on average some 70 per cent of works council members are union-nominated. Provision may be made for separate lists for different groups within the workforce, to ensure that the works council reflects different occupational groups, or other subdivisions of the workforce deemed to be relevant.

Status and rights of works council members   Works council members may not be disadvantaged on account of their candidacy for or membership of a works council. Special dismissal protection also applies. Works council members' employment cannot be terminated except:

- by mutual written consent
- for an urgent reason which must be notified to the employee without delay
- where the enterprise or department in which the employee works ceases operations
- for an 'important reason', provided it is submitted to a cantonal court.

Protection for candidates and works council members lasts for two years after their candidacy or membership: any termination of employment requires the permission of the cantonal court, which may consent only if it concludes the dismissal is unrelated to the employee's candidacy: the same provisos, including the possibility of termination of employment for 'an important reason', apply as in the case of current works council members.

Works councils meet during normal working hours, and members are entitled to paid time off to attend the meetings. Time off is also allowed for participation in any other discussions required for the council to perform its duties or obtain information about employment conditions in the enterprise. The employer must also allow paid time off for works council members to attend training courses, the precise amount of time off to be settled jointly between the works council and the employer. Time allowed off for consultation may not be less than 60 hours a year, with at least five days annually for training.

Works council members, and any experts they consult, are bound by a requirement of confidentiality on business and industrial secrets as well as any issue which the employer or works council deems confidential. In general, a matter must be identified as confidential before it is submitted for discussion, and where possible the precise scope of secrecy and the duration of confidentiality should be stated. Works council members continue to be bound when their period of office has expired.

Right to information   The employer is obliged to supply the works council with as much information as can reasonably be required for it to carry out its tasks, in writing if requested. Specifically, this includes

- the legal form of the employing organisation, its articles of association, the board members and the parent company – together with details of its owner-ship and control should the enterprise be a subsidiary or part of a group
- twice annually a report on the general conduct of the business, and specifically those matters on which the works council has a right of consultation or where its prior agreement is required (see below); they include the employer's expec-tations for the future, and investments undertaken, both at home and abroad
- annual accounts, backed up where appropriate by financial information on the individual enterprise if it is not readily identifiable from the published accounts
- at least annually, a report on employment trends in the enterprise and social policy in the preceding year, together with the employer's expectations for the coming year.

Consultation with the works council   Any consultation between the employer and the works council must take place at a time which allows the works coun-cil's opinion to have a 'significant impact' on any decision. Employers must pro-vide information backed up by reasoned argument, along with an assessment of the implications of any decision for the workforce. The main issues on which the employer is required to consult the works council are

- transfer of control of the enterprise or any part of it
- acquisitions, joint ventures, divestments
- closures or relocation
- significant reductions, expansion or other changes in the enterprises' activities, including major investments and loans
- recruitment of employees or the hiring of temporary staff
- commissioning of external expert advice by the employer, and the terms of reference of any consultancy hired.

Where the advice or the stance of the works council is accepted, decisions can usually be expected to be implemented smoothly and effectively. However, should the employer decide to reject the works council's position, the employer must set out the reasons in writing and may not proceed with the proposed action until after a delay of one month, unless the works council agrees otherwise.

In cases of disagreement the works council has the right to lodge an appeal with the Companies Chamber of the Court of Appeal in Amsterdam. The cham-ber may examine the issue and, if it deems the employer to have behaved unrea-sonably – for example, by acting in breach of statutory consultation procedures – may enforce a rescindment of the decision and prohibit the employer from pro-ceeding further. Delays in the legal process are substantial and the costs of the case have to be borne by the employer, including the cost of the works council's legal representation. In practice this latent power forms the basis of negotiations between works council and employer, although in law works councils have no formal right to negotiate as such. The law was due to be revised in 1995 in order to clarify this aspect.

Works council prior agreement   The agreement (*instemming*) of the works council is required in the event of any employer decision to make, amend or withdraw provision in the following areas, provided they are not already regulated by a collective agreement (see also below):

- works regulations
- any arrangement on hours or holidays
- a pay or job evaluation system
- a pension, profit-sharing or savings scheme
- regulations on health and safety
- regulations on recruitment, dismissal, promotion, training and employee appraisal
- grievance procedures
- policy towards young employees.

The employer must submit the proposed decision in writing, together with the reasons and any implications for the work force. The employer may appeal to a cantonal court if the works council withholds approval: the court will override the works council's refusal only if it is held unreasonable or if the employer can adduce 'important reasons'. Any decision taken without works council approval is null and void, provided the works council appeals against it within one month.

Works councils and collective agreements   No works council decision may contravene the provisions of a collective agreement, and works council approval is not required in areas already regulated by collective agreement. Some firms, such as Philips, which is covered by a company collective agreement, prefer to detail as much as possible in their collective agreement, although others, Royal Dutch Shell being one example, opt for a less specific collective agreement and more consultation with the works council at establishment level. Moreover, additional powers may be granted to a works council under the terms of a collective agreement, although not in respect of terms and conditions set out in that agreement.

Works councils cannot, by law, negotiate collective agreements – a prerogative reserved exclusively to trade unions. However, the rights accorded to works councils mean that they are being increasingly involved in the determination of primary terms and conditions of employment. A 1993 court ruling found that under article 32 of the act, which allows extra powers to be granted to works councils either by collective agreement or by the employer with the consent of the works council, works councils could in fact negotiate with employers on primary terms. Although very few works councils are in a position to undertake such negotiations, which are usually left to the trade unions, the whole question of the division of responsibilities between trade unions and works councils is becoming more difficult. In 1994 the Social and Economic Council issued advice on the role of the works councils regarding bargaining, and legislation is pending: it is expected to give works councils more powers to determine primary terms and conditions. One of the main problems identified in the SER recommendation was the safeguarding of employee negotiating powers at company level. Works councils would, for example, find it difficult to call a strike, as they have no strike funds. Works councils are not bound by a formal peace obligation, but are required to contribute to the 'proper functioning of the enterprise', although this would not, in law, necessarily prevent them from initiating industrial action.

Rights in smaller enterprises   Different provisions apply where the enterprise employs between 35 and 100 employees. A works council may be set up on a voluntary basis in enterprises employing between 10 and 35 employees. However, if no works council is set up the employer must allow the workforce the opportunity to meet at least twice a year, and report annually on the business. The main differences as regards works councils' powers in enterprises with 35–100 employees are

- no right to commission expert advice without prior permission, unless the cost is met by the works council from its regular budget
- no specified minimum time-off requirements
- consultation has to take place only if the proposed change might lead to job losses or a major change in conditions of employment affecting at least a quarter of the workforce; the obligation to defer implementation of a decision is restricted to closure, a significant reduction or expansion of activities, or relocation
- information may be presented orally.

Employee involvement

Employee involvement is seen in two respects: first, initiatives towards employee consultation (termed *werkoverleg*), job enrichment and job enlargement many of which date back to the late 1970s, and secondly more employer-initiated human resource management techniques such as TQM and team working. Whereas many of the earlier initiatives petered out in the 1980s, there has been a steady, if unspectacular, increase in the application of quality management, spurred on by the adoption of ISO standards by companies.

The use of quality circles, company councils and teamworking tends to be highest in US-owned multinationals, but even then is not very widespread.

According to an estimate by the union Industriebond FNV for an EU-sponsored study (see below), some 5 per cent of Dutch industrial companies had introduced autonomous work groups by 1994, and a further 30 per cent were expected to do so shortly. Quality initiatives were especially developed in the engineering sector.

A recent study of direct participation in Dutch companies carried out under the auspices of the European Foundation for the Improvement of Living and Working Conditions showed an ambivalent attitude on the part of employers and unions alike towards a number of these new strategies. Unions were concerned that new approaches would weaken traditional avenues of representation, as already evidenced in many foreign-owned companies, and often viewed quality management and 'lean production' simply as productivity offensives that undermined the objectives of early initiatives in the field of direct participation. Employers noted that although there was a movement towards greater team working and the devolution of responsibility, management structures, with their traditional hierarchies and functional separations, and the structures of employee representation at plant level could make such initiatives difficult to operate.

US and/or Japanese-owned firms tend to have a lower incidence of trade union representation, with management effectively negotiating direct with works councils, although such negotiations do not constitute formal collective bargaining. Staff associations may also bargain, as has happened at the furniture retailer IKEA. However, such companies remain a minority (see below).

A survey carried out by the Hugo Sinzheimer Institute (part of the University of Amsterdam) showed that in large companies with a central works council which are outside industry bargaining 95 per cent still negotiate terms and conditions with the trade unions, and the majority expect to continue to do so.

Employee representation at board level

Since 1971 all public limited liability companies employing at least 100 workers and with a balance sheet total of Fl 22.5 million (£9.1m) must establish a supervisory board (*raad van commissarissen*). It will comprise shareholders, management and some form of employee representation. The role of the supervisory board is to oversee the general direction of the company and approve the annual report and accounts. Its precise powers may be subject to decisions taken by the management board (*raad van bestuur*).

In the event of a vacancy these three groups can put forward candidates who are then chosen by the board itself. In other words, works councils have a limited influence on the selection of candidates but do not have the final say. Moreover, candidates proposed by works councils are not seen as representing the council if selected to the board. Indeed, supervisory board members need not be current employees of the company or a subsidiary, nor an official of a trade union involved in determining pay and conditions at the company. (Typically, employee candidates are former trade union officials or sympathetic experts.)

Works councils also have a right to object to an appointment to the supervisory board, with disputes resolvable through the courts if necessary.

The EU works council directive

The European works council directive will arguably have a fairly limited impact on the conduct of industrial relations and communication inasmuch as employers are very familiar with statutory forms of employee representation, and the national system of works councils offers a framework for the selection of representatives to European representative bodies. The Netherlands does, however, have a fairly large number of multinational companies headquartered on its territory, and in some cases could also provide an 'agent' for companies which might be subject to the directive but which have their head office outside the European Economic Area.

Many companies are expected to take little action until domestic law implements the directive in September 1996. However, there is mounting pressure from the unions to act quickly and conclude voluntary agreements, especially in view of the threat to their role in the final legislation. The ultimate impact of the directive is still something of an unknown. Figures as to how many companies will be affected remain uncertain, but estimates are between 30 and 40. Nor has the final form of the implementing legislation solved for good the question of whether works councils or trade unions – or both – will be involved. The division of labour between European works councils and national works councils has not yet been settled either.

At present, employers and unions both maintain that the directive could be a positive development but there are still many conflicts of interest in the details.

Collective bargaining

Since the early 1980s there has been a marked shift away from centralised national agreements and towards industry-level, and beyond it to company-level, bargaining. Companies subject to industry agreements have also allowed scope for a second tier of pay-setting, typically involving discussions – though not necessarily formal negotiations – with works councils.

As in most other European countries, the content of collective agreements has broadened to embrace issues beyond pay and hours. Coverage of the workforce remains high, at 70 per cent of private-sector employees and almost all employees in public administration and in the so-called 'G&G sector', which covers hospitals, libraries and other public services.

Industry-level bargaining still predominates, although there has been an increase in the number of company agreements signed: there are now over 650 company agreements covering 550,000 employees – some 8 per cent of the employed labour force. Company agreements of this formal type are not intended to complement but take the place of industry-level provision. Industry agreements are normally signed by affiliates of the two main union confederations and the relevant employers' bodies or individual companies (see below). They are then frequently fleshed out by the employer at company level, often following discussions with the works council. The councils, in consequence, are becoming increasingly involved in setting primary terms and conditions. Many of the companies whose terms and conditions are exclusively determined by a domestic collective agreement are to be found in the chemical sector, where no industry agreement exists: among them are major employers such as Akzo, DSM Limburg and ICI. Large conglomerates whose activities straddle more than one industry may also prefer company agreements; examples include Royal Dutch Shell, Hoogovens and Philips.

Status of collective agreements

Two main acts regulate the status and practice of collective agreements: the 1927 law on collective agreements (*Wet op de collectieve arbeidsovereenkomst*) and the 1937 law on the extension of collective agreements (*Wet op het algemeen verbindend en het onverbindend verklaren van bepalingen van collectieve arbeidsovereenkomsten*, AVV). The first defines collective agreements, sets out what may and may not be included in an agreement, and establishes the statutory rights and obligations attached to a collective agreement. The second lays down criteria and procedures for extending collectively agreed provisions to non-signatory parties in an individual industry. The so-called AVV law has been the target of a good deal of criticism in recent years, and there have been frequent calls for the amendment, if not abolition, of the law. In the current redrafting of the Civil Code the law on collective agreements is to be incorporated almost wholesale under Book 7, Title 11.

Collective agreements are defined as 'agreements, entered into by one or more employers or one or more employers' organisations with the full legal rights of employers, and one or more organisations with the full legal rights of employees, which primarily or exclusively govern terms and conditions of employment which must be taken into account in employment contracts'. Collective agreements may also cover the contracts of groups such as freelance or temporary and agency workers, and can exclude certain employee categories such as senior managers.

An organisation can be party to a collective agreement only if its articles expressly authorise it. The law on collective agreements does not specify how an organisation may acquire the capacity to bargain collectively or what internal regulations it must have, for example on balloting to accept a settlement. The signatories to collective agreements are trades unions (the appropriate affiliates of the FNV or CNV) on the one hand and employers' associations or individual firms on the other. In a fairly recent development, staff associations – established to represent workers to an individual employer – have been recognised as having the capacity to conclude a formal collective agreement. One example is at the retail company IKEA, where in April 1995 the staff association (*werknemersv-ereniging Ikea-medewerkers*) concluded a formal pay agreement with provision for performance-related increases. There are thought to be another three or four similar examples.

It is also possible for a ruling to admit to collective negotiations a party representing a given group of workers which is not strictly entitled to bargain collectively. (This area remains somewhat unclear and the provisions are in any case seldom used.)

Collective agreements must be in writing, and signatory parties must ensure that copies of the agreement are made available to their members. Many agreements stipulate that employers shall make the text available to their workforce. Minimum conditions in collective agreements can be improved on, but may not be curtailed, in individual contracts of employment. Standard conditions may not be departed from at all.

Most collective agreements (*collectieve arbeidsovereenkomsten,* CAOs) are integrated – that is, they lay down terms and conditions of employment, including pay, for both blue- and white-collar staff in an industry, regardless of occupation. A collective agreement may be confined in its application to a particular region or to a stipulated level of seniority (either by job classification or level of income). Some collective agreements may apply only to more senior white-collar and lower managerial staff (*hoger personeel*) but very rarely affect more senior management.

Agreements cover the whole range of terms and conditions of employment, including basic pay, bonuses and supplements, pay indexation, hours of work, holidays, the rights of union representatives, and special concessions for certain groups. Terms laid down in a collective agreement may be changed before expiry only if all the signatory parties agree to the change. They seldom do, and then usually only in the face of severe economic conditions.

The provisions of agreements are divided into two main types. Normative clauses cover the employment relationship between individual employers and employees, and set out specific terms and conditions. Obligation clauses set out the mutual rights and duties of the contracting parties in relation to the implementation of the agreement, and parallel the procedure agreements found in the UK, though they are legally enforceable in the Netherlands and establish a contractual relationship between unions and employers. One of the most important provisions is the 'peace clause' which forbids industrial action during the lifetime of the agreement. The difference is relevant not only in relation to which parties are bound by which clauses of an agreement; it also affects the practice of 'extending' agreements (see below).

Under the terms of the law on pay (*Wet op de loonvorming*) all draft agreements must be lodged with the Ministry of Labour for registration (*verplichte aanmelding*) and do not come into force until that has been done. Most collective agreements will specify the date when the agreement comes into force and the length of time for which it will run. Most collective agreements are concluded some months after the previous agreement has run out, and therefore are applied retrospectively. Collective agreements may be signed for a maximum of five years, but the vast majority are valid for one or two years. Often a particular clause or clauses will be dated for a longer period, such as pension or early retirement provisions. Unless otherwise specified, a collective agreement is deemed to last for one year, with the option of a further year's extension. Moreover, agreements frequently contain a clause to the effect that if neither party calls for it to be renegotiated the agreement will automatically be renewed for another year.

The rules applying to individual companies in sectors for which national agreements have been concluded are:

- if the employer and the employees are affiliated to the contracting parties (employers' association and unions) the agreement is binding on all parties
- if only the employer is affiliated, the employer must apply the agreement even to employees who are not union members
- if neither the employer nor the employees is affiliated, an agreement will be binding only if extended by the Ministry of Employment (see below).

Agreements are legally binding once registered.

Extension to non-signatory parties

The Minister of Employment may declare an agreement 'generally binding' (*algemeen verbindend*) on all companies in a sector, at the request of one or more of the signatory parties. In that case a distinction is drawn between the normative clauses and the obligation clauses. Normative clauses, such as those on pay, hours, terms and conditions, may be extended to non-signatory parties in a sector. However, obligation clauses, for example the peace obligation limiting industrial action during the lifetime of an agreement, cannot be extended. In addition, the extension of an agreement is not retrospective: clauses apply only from the date when the agreement is made generally binding. Agreements which have been extended may be enforced by the courts and infringements penalised.

Extension often increases the number of workers covered by an agreement very considerably: the construction industry agreement, for example, applied to 120,000 employees before extension and to 180,000 afterwards.

During 1994 and 1995 there was much debate over the question of declaring agreements generally binding, with moves to amend the law and enable the Minister to make only certain elements binding, specifically excluding pay. The Minister threatened not to declare agreements generally binding in 1996 unless agreed minimum pay levels were brought more into line with the statutory minimum wage. Although current rates are unlikely to be lowered, this had the effect, in a number of negotiated agreements, of giving rise to new – lower – entry-level grades. (Currently, agreed minima are on average 12 per cent over the statutory minimum.) The aim is to encourage the employment of people with low occupational skills who may have little work experience.

The pay round

Trade unions usually present claims at the beginning of the year: most agreements expire at the end of February or March, and negotiations begin between December and February. The majority are settled by the end of April, generally well after the previous collective agreement has expired, and the new ones are therefore implemented retrospectively. Should a common position or recommendation be reached at national level, whether formally or informally in the SER or the STAR, there is less likelihood of protracted conflict at industry or company level. However, there has been no truly central pay agreement since 1982.

Although there is no single leading settlement, agreements in the engineering industry, which covers some 220,000 employees, at Philips, which has a company agreement, in the port of Rotterdam and at Akzo and Hoogovens play an influential role – with the exception of Rotterdam, all agreed by the union Industriebond FNV.

Company-level pay, set either by a specific domestic agreement or by management-determined topping up of an industry agreement, tends to be 10–15 per cent above that settled in an industry collective agreement. Some agreements may limit the amount of additional pay in order to combat wage drift. For example, companies in the light engineering sector may not pay more than 10 per cent above the agreed minimum scale.

Economic forecasts

The most important economic forecasts recognised and used as a framework for the bargaining round are those produced by the Central Bureau of Statistics (CBS) on a monthly basis, and the annual forecast (*Macro Economische Verkenning*) from the Central Planning Bureau (CPB). The latter is published in time for the opening of parliament in September each year, and is widely accepted by both sides as an authoritative basis for negotiations.

Recent trends

The scope of collective bargaining has been widening in recent years, with the focus on agreed cuts in working hours in particular in the 1980s and again in 1993 and 1994. In the early 1980s unions found that their members were willing to negotiate hours cuts of some 5 per cent in exchange for pay rises. This was achieved through pay freezes and the effective abolition of the price indexation clause. Unions are now pushing for job maintenance and creation measures, with hours cuts viewed as one aspect of this. Members who in the late 1980s and early

1990s were reluctant to pursue hours cuts at the expense of pay are now keener to hang on to employment, even where hours cuts result in a corresponding loss of pay.

The 1980s saw an increase in the incidence of extra payments in the event of sickness, disability or unemployment from around 50 per cent of employees covered by collective agreements in 1984 to almost 70 per cent by 1989. Despite government exhortations for this coverage to be reduced, paralleled by official efforts to curb disability benefit, the unions have managed to resist any major change in the spread of such payments. Payments generally top up sickness and disability benefit to 100 per cent of pay. In the case of unemployment some agreements require the employer to top up statutory unemployment benefit for a period, usually related to age and length of service.

Pay rises in 1994 averaged 0.9 per cent, with a number of cuts and freezes in some sectors and companies, notably the chemical industry, hospitals and at Akzo. The increases at Philips, which is covered by a company agreement, ranged from +5.5 per cent to −2 per cent because of the effects of pay pauses and freezes in benefits. Initial agreements in 1995 saw increases of 2.0–2.5 per cent over the year, with two industry agreements providing for some 5 per cent over two years. Consumer price inflation in 1994 was running at 2.7 per cent, and at 2.3 per cent in 1995. The restraint in real pay growth in 1993/94, in exchange for job creation initiatives which proved less effective than hoped, is likely to give way to greater determination on the part of the unions to recover lost ground.

Main agreed provisions

Pay agreements As indicated above, collective bargaining has become increasingly decentralised over the past 20 years, with the number of industry and company-level collective agreements rising. The last central agreement on pay was settled in 1982, since when bargaining has been left to take place at industry level, without the direct involvement of the state. None the less the 1993 bargaining pause was introduced under government pressure (see above).

Most minimum levels of pay are laid down in industry collective agreements which reach approximately 75 per cent of the private-sector workforce and 100 per cent of the public and semi-public sector. Figures for coverage vary widely: 94 per cent of employees are covered in construction but only 40 per cent in some service sectors.

The number of company agreements has risen steadily over the last few years and they now affect 15 per cent of the workforce.

Basic pay Agreed basic pay at industry level is usually improved on by 10–15 per cent at company level, depending on the size and profitability of the individual firm. Increments are normally geared to age (especially for those under 23) and/or length of service. The number of increments varies with the level of the job. In the textile industry, for example, semi-skilled workers will have one or two increments, while skilled staff and technicians have five or six and those at the top of the scale eight or nine. Most collective agreements specify that pay rises must relate to actual pay in order to prevent companies offsetting their bonuses and other payments against the industry-agreed minima.

Bonuses   Employees have a statutory right to paid holidays and an additional holiday bonus (*vakantiebijslag*). The latter is set at 7.5 per cent of annual basic pay. However, most collective agreements improve on this and pay around 8 per cent of total earnings. The bonus is usually paid in May or June. Some agreements specify a minimum cash payment to heads of households and employees with children.

The vast majority of collective agreements also award a thirteenth-month payment (*jaarlijkse extra uitkering*). It may be conditional on length of service. In the banking sector, for example, all those with at least one year's service are entitled to such a payment. As a result most salaries represent payment for twelve months plus the holiday bonus plus the thirteenth month. Staff on four-weekly pay scales (still common in many collective agreements) would receive their thirteenth month as a fourteenth payment.

Other bonuses laid down by collective agreement include: supervisory responsibility payments; performance bonuses; supplements for dangerous or dirty work; on-call payments and skill acquisition supplements. For example, under the 1993/94 printing industry agreement supervisors in certain departments are entitled to between Fl 1.12 and Fl 2.66 per hour extra, depending on the number of staff for whom they are responsible. At DSM Limburg work under difficult conditions is specified on a scale agreed separately with the trade unions and attracts additional monthly payments of between 2.5 per cent and 17 per cent of basic pay.

Financial participation   Voluntary *profit-sharing* schemes are quite widespread, particularly among larger companies. Most schemes apply to all employees. However, the definition of profit share (*winstuitkering*) is often unspecific and the bonus may not always be linked strictly to company performance. Tax benefits for profit-share schemes are at present limited, although the system is expected to be reviewed.

There are two basic types of *share option* schemes – approved and non-approved. In both cases, share options are taxed as income and the benefit to the employee is valued at the time the option was granted. An approved scheme must be open to 75 per cent of the workforce and detailed in a written scheme, approved by the works council (see also *Contracts and Terms and Conditions of Employment* in this series).

A growing number of companies are introducing *savings schemes* for their employees, encouraged to some extent by recent national pay moderation policies. The introduction of such schemes also attracts considerable tax advantages.

Schemes may take one of two forms: the *premiespaarregeling*, where a set percentage of net pay (up to a ceiling) is paid into the scheme for four years, with the employer matching the sum; or the *spaarloonregeling*, where a set percentage of gross pay is paid into a scheme and can be reclaimed after four years free of tax and social charges. There is no employer contribution, but a 10 per cent tax is levied on the employer for the amount.

Working time

New legislation came into force on 1 January 1996 and will take effect at company level as current collective agreements expire during 1996, but will supersede all existing arrangements from 1 January 1997. The new law lays down two forms of statutory control: *standard regulation*, which provides a basic protective framework for all employees, and *maximum regulation*, which sets absolute upper limits that may be taken advantage of provided this is set out in a collective agreement. The standard regulation provides for a nine-hour normal maximum working day, with a 45-hour week allowed, provided an average of 40 hours is achieved over a 13-week reference period. However, by collective agreement the daily maximum can be extended to 10 hours, with no specified weekly limit but an average maximum of 50 hours over four weeks, and 45 hours a week over 13 weeks. Companies not covered by a collective agreement can vary from the standard regulations by agreement with workforce representatives, such as works councils or others. However, an agreement with a works council cannot diverge from the terms set out in a formal collective agreement. In practice, working hours are set by collective agreement, and the average working week laid down by collective agreement is about 37 hours. Actual weekly working hours may be longer than the agreed average, however, especially for shift workers, with extra hours translated via 'time banking' into additional free days (*roostervrije dagen*) to be taken throughout the year. In the textile industry agreement, hours for shift workers are specified for a variety of reference periods: 85 hours' maximum for two-shift workers over two weeks; 128 hours over three weeks for three-shift workers.

The agreement of works councils is required if companies wish to change their hours of work, including shift work, flexible working hours and short-time working, unless there is specific provision otherwise by collective agreement.

Holidays   The Civil Code provides for annual leave of at least four times the number of days regularly worked per week: employees working a five-day week are entitled to 20 days. Collective agreements may increase this and often stipulate a period during which at least 10 consecutive days must be taken, usually between April and September. Length of service and/or age often entitle an employee to additional days' holiday. In the textile industry, for example, the standard leave of 25 days increases to 26 for those aged over 40, to 28 for those aged 50–54 and increasing to 30 days for those over 60. Some collective agreements grant younger workers extra days' leave.

Time off   Leave of absence (*georloofde verzuim*) is governed by the Civil Code, which specifies an employee's entitlement to paid time off over and above paid holiday. It includes two days for the birth of a child or up to four days for the death of a close relative. Collective agreements generally extend the list of acceptable reasons and may include wedding anniversaries, weddings and the ordination of a relative. In addition, paid time off is allowed for dental and medical appointments, job-hunting (for those made redundant) and examinations. The right to unpaid leave for such things as military service, training, public office and works council or trade union duties is laid down by statute.

Industrial conflict

There is no legislation governing industrial action. The rights of association and assembly are laid down in articles 8 and 9 of the constitution, and the right to strike is based on article 6 of the European Social Charter, ratified by the government in 1980, and on the courts applying and developing legal principles through rulings on individual instances. (The Netherlands has one of the lowest strike rates in Europe: between 1989 and 1993 only 10 days were lost per year per thousand employees. This figure compares with an annual 586 days per thousand employees in Greece over the same period, 70 in the UK, 36 in France and three in Japan.)

Strikes

Strike action directed at the terms of an existing collective agreement is unlawful. Most collective agreements contain a so-called peace clause (*vredesplicht*) restricting the use of industrial action by employers and employees during the lifetime of the agreement over issues covered by the agreement. The courts have also inferred a peace clause even where no such provision has been expressly stated (*stilzwijgende vredesplicht*). However, action may be taken over other issues, or if the employer should breach the contract, or over working conditions not detailed in an agreement.

Unofficial strikes – that is, strikes not sanctioned by a ballot – are not automatically unlawful but may be ruled so by the courts. Wildcat strikes are often taken over by the unions in order to protect their members; this is particularly true in the ports and in the construction industry. Trade unions can be held liable for damages awarded in compensation for illegal industrial action.

Other action

There are no statutory definitions of permitted or prohibited industrial action: strikes are seen by trade unions as a last resort. Go-slows, working to rule (*stipheidsactie*) and sit-ins (*bedrijfsbezetting*) are the most common alternatives. Purely political strikes are not protected under the charter and are illegal. Action such as a blockade or occupation runs the risk of being declared illegal by the courts on the grounds that it infringes the rights and freedoms of others. Sympathy action may also founder, as it affects the rights of a third party. However, sympathy strikes are allowed in so far as terms and conditions of employment in one sector could affect those in another. Port blockades may be ruled illegal on the grounds of the national interest – the most recent blockade was in the port of Amsterdam in February 1995.

An employer has the right to seek a court injunction to prevent a strike, but as long as a strike falls within the terms of the charter an injunction is unlikely to be granted. However, the courts can, and do, impose restrictions on strike action. This is possibly more evident in the public sector but has occurred in the private sector. The main criterion in such a decision is whether the adverse effects on a third party are 'out of proportion to the reason for the strike'. The question of balance and proportion – *evenredigheid* – is central in the courts' deliberations, although its definition and use as a criterion have been questioned. For example, a bus strike in February 1995 was permitted between 10.00 and 15.00 but not during the rush hours, as the court ruled that then it would have had a 'disproportionate effect' on commuters. The trade unions appealed against the decision and it still awaits final clarification by a higher court.

Participation in a strike suspends the contract of employment, including the payment of wages. However, it does not constitute grounds for dismissal. Disciplinary action against striking employees is deemed illegal unless the strike has been ruled illegal in court. Case law indicates that, during go-slows, or working to rule, the employer may reduce the workers' pay for the period of the action. In cases of unlawful action a trade union can be held liable for damages if a strike is ruled to be illegal and the union none the less proceeds with the action. It is not clear from case law whether this would apply in retrospect to an action already begun but then ruled illegal.

Lockouts

Lockouts (*uitsluiting*) are an extreme rarity, and under the Civil Code an employer would have to continue paying employees if work were not possible owing to action of his own.

Arbitration and conciliation

There are no official arbitration or conciliation bodies in the private sector. In 1986 a number of independent experts were nominated by the Labour Foundation to a 'STAR list' to whom disputes may be referred to on a voluntary basis. The list is not comprehensive and has not been updated since.

If talks on a new collective agreement collapse an ultimatum is usually given by the trade union with the threat of industrial action, which will often push the employers back to the negotiating table. A voluntary process of arbitration may be instigated, with both sides agreeing to abide by the decision of an independent arbitrator (from the STAR list) or of the courts. Agreements or arbitration decisions may not be accepted by all the trade unions involved, in which case the agreement is usually applied regardless to all employees and battle is delayed until the following bargaining round.

Should negotiations with a works council break down on issues where its agreement is required by law, the employer can go to the district judge (*kantonrechter*) for an adjudication. His ruling then takes precedence over the works council's agreement. However, such recourse is very rare.

The trade unions have called for a more explicit and formal system of resolving disputes, otherwise they are left with little else but the threat of strike action should negotiations break down. They tentatively favour the voluntary system of final offer arbitration, the Advies- en Arbitrage Commissie Rijksdienst (known as the Commissie Albeda), which operates in the public sector.

Where no new agreement is reached, even after arbitration, the employer usually extends the existing terms and conditions or imposes new ones unilaterally, as happened in the banking sector in 1994.

Organisations

Social and Economic Council (Sociaal-Economische Raad, SER)
Bezuidenhoutseweg 60
2594 AW The Hague
Tel. + 31 70 349 9499

Labour Foundation (Stichting van de Arbeid)
Address as for the SER

Ministry of Social Affairs and Employment (Ministerie van Sociale Zaken en Werkgelegenheid)
Postbus 20801
2500 EV The Hague
Tel. + 31 70 371 5911
Fax + 31 70 371 4555

Netherlands Trade Union Confederation (Federatie Nederlandse Vakbeveging, FNV)
Postbus 8456
1005 AL Amsterdam
Tel. + 31 20 581 6300
Fax + 31 20 684 4541

National Christian Trade Union Confederation (Christelijk Nationaal Vakverbond, CNV)
Postbus 2475
3500 GL Utrecht
Tel. + 31 30 91 39 11
Fax + 31 30 946 544

Federation of Netherlands Industry (Verbond van Nederlandse Ondernemingen, VNO)
5 Prinses Beatrixlaan,
Postbus 93093
2509 AB The Hague
Tel. + 31 70 349 7373
Fax + 31 70 381 9508

Federation of Christian Employers (Nederlands Christelijk Werkgeversverbond, NCW)
Postbus 93093
2509 AB The Hague
Tel. + 31 70 349 7373
Fax + 31 70 381 9508

Main sources

GIER, H. G. DE, *et al. Lexicon van arbeidsrecht en arbeidsverhouding*. Amsterdam, HSI Institut, 1994 (Dutch edition of proposed European Foundation European Employment and Industrial Relations Glossary)

JONG, E. P. DE, and ROOD, M. G. (eds). *Zakboek Arbeidsrecht*, Dordrecht, Kluwer, looseleaf

MECHÉ, PIETER VAN DER, *et al. Direct Participation in Organizational Change in the Netherlands*. Dublin, European Foundation for the Improvement of Living and Working Conditions, Working Paper No. WP/94/48/EN (November 1994)

Ministry of Labour. *CAOs in Nederland*, looseleaf collection, The Hague, SDU

Social and Economic Council, various reports

VISSER, J. 'The Netherlands: the end of an era and the end of a system', in A. Ferner and R. Hyman (eds), *Industrial Relations in the New Europe*. Oxford, Basil Blackwell, 1992

Wet op de collectieve arbeidsovereenkomst (Law on collective agreements), 1927

Wet op het algemeen verbindend en onverbindend verklaren van bepalingen van collectieve arbeidsovereenkomsten (Law on the extension of collective agreements), 1937

Wet op de loonvorming (Wages Act), 1970

Wet op de ondernemingsraden (Works Councils Act), 1979

10

Portugal

On the face of it everything on the political, economic and social scene has changed in Portugal over the past 20 years. Between 1973 and 1976 the country shed the shackles of dictatorship, overthrew the corporatist Caetano regime, dismantled its empire, saw enormous upheaval under the Armed Forces Movement government, and in 1976 embarked on the transition to democracy, with a socialist government returned in the first general election based on universal adult suffrage. This period of unprecedented change was swiftly followed by preparations for membership of the European Community, with the associated – and continuing – pains of economic adjustment, cushioned in some degree by new external sources of finance for social projects.

Despite these dramatic transformations, the pattern of industrial relations on the ground has not exhibited quite the same breathless pace. Twenty years after the establishment of democracy, and 10 years after joining the European Community, Portugal is still very much in the throes of transition. Industrial relations, for example, display distinct vestiges of the past: an unwieldy and overregulated system which discourages innovation and is often of peripheral importance to Portugal's many small firms, a strong role played by the state, and lack of autonomy on the part of the social partners, which narrows the scope for problem-solving via negotiation.

The institutions of the industrial relations system have arguably proved insufficiently adaptable and are in danger of losing touch with corporate realities. The crucial challenge for the main players over the coming years will be developing a response to change and acquiring the capacity to locate themselves in the mainstream of developments.

The main players

Trade unions

Freedom of association   The principle of freedom of association for workers and trade unions is enshrined in the constitution, as is the right to strike and a ban on lockouts. Under the impact of mass employee mobilisation at the time of the 1974 revolution, the constitution sought to establish workers' rights, the primary aim then (1976) being to establish a democratic and independent trade union movement, following the denial of rights under the Salazar dictatorship (1932–68) and the limited form of bargaining permitted during the Caetano years

237

(1968–74). Legislation on freedom of association for employers as well as unions was enacted in 1975 (see below).

Union density   Trade union density in Portugal rates about the middle of the European spectrum, higher than in Spain, Greece, France or the Netherlands. Precise data do not exist but the level has undeniably declined since the late 1970s, in part because of the increase in precarious forms of employment. A union density figure of around 30 per cent has been estimated by the OECD for the early 1990s, representing around 1 million employees out of a total work-force just exceeding 3 million. Given the scale of job losses arising since then from restructuring in sectors such as steel, shipbuilding and textiles, and the pri-vatisation of utilities, banking and insurance, together with a subsequent eco-nomic downturn, the current figure is likely to be somewhat lower. These changes have caused unions severe financial difficulties, reflected in the limited resources offered to members and the lack of trained staff. Collection of dues is regulated by law 57-77 and collection methods can be agreed between employ-ers' associations and trade unions. The most common is check-off, which requires the authorisation of the individual employee. Check-off arrangements are often sanctioned by collective agreement.

Membership density varies enormously according to sector, industries, occu-pations and company size. Density is highest in banking and insurance, transport and communications, public administration and the public sector (where check-off prevails), lowest in woodworking and construction.

Inter-union rivalry, employer attempts to marginalise workplace unions, and the development of multi-skilled jobs and greater autonomy in work organisation have all served to diminish union influence. Young recruits, a majority of whom are hired on fixed-term contracts, do not tend to rate unions highly in terms of effectiveness. Unions' links with political parties (representatives often sit on party bodies, although less so now than in the past) have not helped, either.

Trade union law, including workplace rights   Article 55 of the constitution recognises the right of workers to organise freely in trade unions in order to pro-mote and defend their interests. (It would not necessarily cover a situation where the self-employed or home workers wished to organise.) Specifically, union organisations can be set up at all levels, define the field of their activities (that is, in sectoral, geographical and occupational terms), constitute themselves as they wish and draw up their own rules within broad legal parameters.

Unions acquire a legal personality through registration with the Ministry of Employment, following which their statutes are published in the *Labour and Employment Bulletin* (*Boletim do trabalho e emprego, BTE*). Under article 56 of the constitution individual unions (not confederations) can engage in collective bargaining with the object of concluding binding agreements (see below) without having to establish their representativeness or clear any formal recognition hur-dles.

Workers have the right to engage in union activity at the workplace, with protection against dismissal being afforded to their representatives. Rights in the area of trade union organisation and activity in the workplace are fleshed out in decree-law 215-B/75. As noted elsewhere, in practice union bargaining at plant level is exceptional in the private sector, save in large companies.

Under the constitution no individual can be forced to pay subscriptions to a union of which they are not a member. Any agreement making the recruitment of a worker contingent upon union membership is therefore unenforceable. Prior to 1974 individuals were often constrained to pay union dues if they were employed in an area covered by a corporatist union, even if they had not opted to join.

The union confederations

An unofficial and underground union co-ordinating structure, the Intersindical, dominated by the Communist Party, was formed in 1970 during the Caetano years. It grouped two-thirds of unions at the time of the 1974 revolution. The confederation won a union monopoly under a 1975 law passed by the Revolutionary Council, despite objections from political parties other than the Communist Party, and became known as the Confederação Geral dos Trabalhadores Portugueses (CGTP-IN) in 1977. However, the 1976 constitution recognised the freedom to establish unions, which effectively ended the Intersindical's monopoly, although the formation of a second national union grouping, the União Geral de Trabalhadores (UGT), supported by the Socialist and Social Democratic Parties, occurred only in 1978. Both union confederations are now members of the European Trades Union Confederation (ETUC).

According to official figures, in 1993 there were 396 unions, over 200 of which are affiliated either to the CGTP-IN (around 150) or the UGT (60). Many represent occupational interests, despite attempts, particularly by the UGT, to strengthen vertical organisation. Non-affiliated (autonomous) unions are independent, tend to be small and represent particular occupational or even grade interests. These are especially concentrated in transport and public administration; their number increased in the 1980s, sometimes through breakaways from larger organisations. The CGTP-IN remains the most important confederation, with perhaps 60 per cent of total membership, compared with 35 per cent for the UGT and 10 per cent for the rest – although the figures are disputed.

CGTP-IN   The CGTP-IN claimed 877,000 members in 1993, 690,000 in affiliated trade unions and 187,000 in unions closely involved in its activities. It has 17 national branch federations, five national unions and 22 regional trades councils. The CGTP-IN used to be strongest in manufacturing, transport, utilities and parts of the civil service, and in blue-collar employment, but in some areas employers have started to disregard established arrangements and bargain with UGT unions, which they see as more compliant. In 1995 the CGTP-IN launched a drive to increase membership among young workers, and to streamline its structure in order to strengthen workplace organisation.

It has recently promoted improvements in the minimum wage (which has fallen behind increases in average earnings), real pay and pensions. The confederation also opposes reductions in the working week via flexibility, instead campaigning for a standard 40 hour week in 1995 through negotiations and in parliament, through Communist Party deputies. Its aims are often pursued by means of national actions. CGTP-IN has not signed any of the pay pacts agreed within the Economic and Social Council (CES).

UGT   The creation of the rival General Workers' Union, the União Geral de Trabalhadoes (UGT), in 1978 was a political act spearheaded by moderate unions in banking, insurance and office work, supported by the Socialist and Social Democratic parties. Strongest in white-collar employment in finance and public administration, but also with many technical and professional unions in services, the UGT has been working for some time to strengthen its federal structure of industry unions. Its official membership is just under a million. It is less cohesive than the CGTP-IN and its leadership's compromises with the government in power – manifested in accords within the CES – have often brought it into conflict with its grass roots.

Inter-confederation links   Relations between the two major confederations are often prickly and tend to get in the way of co-operation. However, a thaw in relations allowed the UGT to drop its opposition to CGTP-IN membership of the ETUC in 1994. Attempts to follow a broadly consistent pay strategy in the 1995 failed, and approaches to flexible working time have been divergent. It has been suggested that a merger between the two organisations would strengthen the union movement, but there seems no immediate prospect of this.

Other employee organisations

A confederation grouping technical and scientific staff (Confederação Portuguesa de Quadros Tecnicos e Cientificos) was set up in 1988 with 30,000 members in 18 unions. However, this body acts more as a professional lobbying organisation; it has no bargaining rights, or representation on the Economic and Social Council (CES). Several independent trade unions moved to establish a non-political trade union confederation in 1995; a number of others expressed interest and a constitution is being drafted. They seek to promote professional interests and to gain representation on the Economic and Social Council.

Employers' organisations

Role in bargaining   Decree-law 215-C/75 deals with freedom of association for employers, who may organise in associations with a federal, union, confederate or category structure in order to represent and promote their interests. Individual employers and associations may both enter into binding collective agreements, and the latter may render services to their affiliates. Like trade unions, they must register with the Ministry of Employment.

National and industry structures There are two main employers' confederations representing the interests of non-agricultural entrepreneurs: one represents industry and the other commerce, although they have overlapping memberships in manufacturing and services. The largest and most influential, the Confederação da Indústria Portuguesa (CIP) was founded in 1974 and represents employers grouped in 70 associations, both sectoral and regional, in 60,000 companies with some 750,000 employees in all the main industries in the private and public sectors. To date, it has not managed to secure a common bargaining structure for its area of influence. The CIP is a member of the International Employers' Organisation (IEO) and of UNICE.

The CIP has been a consistent advocate of privatisation, not excluding banking and insurance – the prime targets of the post-revolutionary nationalisation programme – and of strengthening the economy's competitiveness. It also supports deregulated labour legislation and more flexible working practices. For example, it argues for the removal of statutory limits on overtime, more restricted grounds of justifiable absence from work and greater dismissals deregulation. It has tacitly supported the national process of social dialogue.

At the end of 1994 the other main employers' confederation, the Confederação do Comércio Portugues, established in 1978, grouping employers in commerce, decided to change its name to Confederação do Comércio e Serviços Portuguesa (CCSP) and make organisational changes to widen its appeal among other service sector organisations and strengthen its lobbying. Now individual associations are directly affiliated to the centre, together covering around half a million employees. The CCSP launched an effective defence of small shopkeepers in 1995 when it persuaded the government to restrict the hours during which supermarkets could open on Sundays and public holidays. At the beginning of 1995 the CCSP concluded a bilateral pact with the UGT confederation, aiming at greater working time flexibility in retailing through the addition of enabling clauses to sectoral agreements.

The Confederação da Agricultura Portuguesa (CAP) represents medium-sized and family enterprises in agriculture.

Estimates of affiliation to employers' organisations among firms with at least 10 employees range widely between 30 per cent and 60 per cent. The main functions of the central employer bodies are to represent the voice of business nationally (and in the case of the CIP internationally), in tripartite national discussions (all three have seats on the Economic and Social Council) and on the various tripartite bodies. They disseminate research findings and provide member associations with information on economic, legal, technical and technological matters and on employment questions, including training. They also furnish support for collective negotiations. In 1990 the three main employers' organisations sought to establish a degree of co-ordination through the setting up of the National Council of Portuguese Enterprises (CNEP).

Consultation at national level

By law employers and unions have a right to be represented on social consultation bodies, to participate in the formulation of economic and social policy, to be consulted on draft laws and to be involved in joint management bodies in fields such as social security, equal opportunities and health and safety.

Portugal has only limited experience of consultation at national level, compared with other EU member states. Given the dramatic events precipitating the overthrow of the authoritarian, corporate Caetano regime, the 1974 revolution and the industrial upheaval which followed, it is not surprising that a further decade elapsed before a forum was established for tripartite social dialogue. The government's prime motive was to secure consensus for policies preparing the country for EU membership. Profound differences of view emerged between and among employers and unions on participation in the process.

Given the state's role in industrial relations under the pre-revolutionary corporate regimes, which stifled the development of free association between employers and unions, the state continued to act as a dominant force after 1974.

The CPCS and the Economic and Social Committee

The tripartite Permanent Council for Social Consultation (Conselho Permanente de Concertação Social) was set up by law in 1984 specifically to promote dialogue between the social partners on economic and social matters. Major areas of concern were modernising the economy, promoting industrial competitiveness and improving living standards to approach those of other EU countries.

As a result of an amendment of the constitution, an Economic and Social Council (Conselho Económico e Social) was created in 1991 with a much broader remit and membership than the CPCS, which has, however, remained a distinct section within this larger body, retaining responsibility for employment matters. The CES broadly deals with policy formation in a wide area, the use of EU structural funds, sectoral and restructuring plans, regional development, and the promotion of social dialogue. The CPCS section comprises six representatives from government, two each from the three national employers' organisations and three from each of the national trade union confederations.

National accords

Accords struck within the tripartite forum are not legally binding, nor do they require the signature of all the parties in order to become effective; the union confederation Confederação Geral dos Trabalhadores Portugueses (CGTP) has consistently refused to sign any pay agreements, as have individual employers' organisations from time to time. Nevertheless, some accords put forward proposals for legislation; after consultation with the social partners, they are submitted for parliamentary approval in the normal way. Agreements on health and safety and vocational training were signed by all parties.

Pay pacts

The CPCS is consulted on the national minimum wage, which is implemented each year by means of legislation (see below).

Four social contracts on prices and incomes have been signed since 1984: a 1987 Recommendation on Incomes, a 1988 Agreement on Incomes Policy, a 1990 Economic and Social Agreement (including a prices and incomes policy for 1991 and a package of draft legislation, see below) and a 1992 Incomes Policy Agreement. Negotiations on an accord for 1994 failed, as did an attempt at concluding a longer-term pact up to the end of the decade which included employment proposals. Nevertheless, these failed talks did result in a bilateral declaration by the union confederation UGT and the commerce employers' CCP on flexible working time schedules which is expected to filter through into negotiations (see below).

The prices and incomes section of the 1990 Economic and Social Agreement spelt out aims intended to achieve economic convergence, including reducing the budget deficit, bringing price inflation down to the EU average, improving pay gradually to approximate to EU levels and ensuring low unemployment.

The various national agreements on prices and incomes have played a part in curbing price inflation. As the rate of inflation has declined, so government inflation forecasts have become more accurate. The result has been a shift away from basing pay demands on past inflation to using inflation projections. Certainly there is greater consensus on the importance of lower inflation, although the unions still regard official inflation forecasts with some scepticism. However, it has been argued that voluntary pay restraint has mostly impacted on agreed minimum rates in the private sector, simply increasing wage drift.

Consultation on legislation

All new draft employment legislation must be subject to consultation. The 1990 Economic and Social Pact included a programme of legislation aimed at amending a number of laws as part of an overall strategy to modernise the economy. They included laws on early retirement, lay-offs, probationary periods, the reduction and adaptation of working time and dismissal on grounds of unsuitability for new tasks (see *Contracts and Terms and Conditions of Employment* in this series). These measures and others, such as social safeguards in sectors undergoing restructuring, were eventually implemented by individual laws or regulations.

Other agreements

Health and safety, and education and vocational training, were also discussed as part of the 1990 Economic and Social legislation package but became the subject of separate accords.

The 1991 health and safety agreement contained a draft health and safety at work framework law (later incorporated into decree-law 441/91) covering such matters as the prevention of occupational hazards, training, workplace improvements, and the organisation of prevention and monitoring services, including through tripartite national bodies. The extension of collective bargaining to issues which improve the quality of working life is anticipated in the agreement.

Legislation arising from the vocational training accord encompassed decree-laws in a framework for vocational training, vocational training within the labour market and the regulation on pre-apprenticeships. Provision was also made to ensure the input of the social partners on employment and vocational training policies.

In 1993 a pact aimed at restructuring the ports was agreed within the Economic and Social Council (*Pacto de concertação social no sector portuário*). It involved abolishing restrictive practices, shedding excess labour and streamlining negotiating procedures in the revamped sector.

Proposals for reform

Despite the positive role attributed by some to the CES in helping to create economic stability, curtail inflation, moderate pay and minimise conflict over reformed labour legislation, the social consultation process still displays some fundamental flaws.

Many commentators believe the process of dialogue is too political. On this view, there is too much emphasis on reaching agreements which lend credibility to the government of the day. In this context the government has been prepared in the past to offer concessions to both employers and unions (in the form of above-inflation pay rises, or tax reductions and subsidies) as an inducement to come to an agreement. It now has fewer instruments at its disposal, given the commitment to achieving economic convergence.

These developments are seen as detrimental to hopes of resolving some of outstanding problems of the economy, such as social security reform. There is little scope for a wide-ranging exchange of views. Talks are sporadic and tend to peter out in the run-up to a general election, for example. They can be bilateral.

The close links between the former ruling Social Democrats and the UGT union confederation have also created tensions within the latter, especially on matters of pay policy; this promises to continue with the new Socialist Party government (elected in October 1995). On one hand the unions cannot be seen to give way to official pressure too easily but on the other they have been accused of reluctance to criticise government.

The economic context has changed since the 1992 recession, giving employers the upper hand, temporarily at least, and reducing the need for a pay pact. In 1995 the government set a pay target of 4 per cent plus productivity gains. Attempts at concluding an agreement on employment failed.

Consultation on labour legislation

Under the constitution (article 56) trade union organisations must be given an opportunity to express their views on draft employment proposals under consideration by the national assembly or individual regional assemblies. This also applies to workplace workers' committees when the proposals concern an individual sector. The government is obliged to consult employers on these matters as well. Proposals are published in the official employment journal, *BTE,* and responses must be submitted within 30 days. Non-observance of these procedures would be a matter for the constitutional court.

Workplace employee representation

Dual structure of workplace employee representation

Workplace representation is based on a dual structure. The constitution establishes the right to set up enterprise workers' committees (*comissões de trabalhadores*) for consultative purposes, as well as granting unions the right to elect workplace trade union representatives or committees (*delegados sindicais, comissões sindicais, comissões intersindicais*) for the purpose of bargaining. The formal demarcation between bargaining and other functions was recognised by law in 1979, although in practice the distinction is often blurred.

Workers' committees

Article 54 gives workers the right to set up enterprise committees (*comissões de trabalhadores*), non-union bodies and employee-only, in order to defend their interests and to promote democratic participation in the workplace. Law 46/79 provides the legal framework for their establishment and functioning. Whilst committees are set up on the initiative of employees, the employer must ensure they are able to function properly once in existence.

Around 1,000 committees are registered with the Ministry of Employment, considerably less than the number of establishments entitled to set one up. Research conducted by the CGTP-IN union confederation has suggested that a majority are inactive, although those in the public sector and in large companies' committees tend to be operational. The economic crisis in traditional sectors, such as glass and textiles, has also reactivated some virtually moribund committees. Some commentators believe that in their present form the committees are an anachronism, and favour restructuring them along the lines of enterprise committees, initiated by the employer and jointly constituted. This would require a revision of the constitution, and could provoke resistance by some sections of the trade union movement, on the grounds that a review might diminish union influence and proscribe informal bargaining activity (see below).

Composition   In principle a committee may be set up in any enterprise. Its size is governed by law according to the number of staff employed, as follows:

- three members in firms with under 201 employees (two members if there are fewer than 10 staff and annual turnover is under Esc 30 million, about £125,500)
- between three and five members in firms with 201–500 staff
- between five and seven in firms with 501–1,000 staff
- between seven and 11 in firms with 1,000 or more staff.

There are distinct arrangements for sub-committees and co-ordinating committees in multi-plant enterprises.

Election   Candidates for office must be endorsed by 10 per cent or 100 of the firm's permanent workforce, all of whom have the right to stand for election. Unions are not permitted to draw up lists of candidates, although in practice they exert a lot of influence. Voting is conducted by secret ballot, and the procedure does not guarantee representation to any particular occupational groups. The workers' committee itself is responsible for drawing up standing orders on issues such as term of office and election arrangements which in turn must be approved by the workforce. The law provides guidance on these matters.

Committee members' rights and duties   Elected committee members enjoy the same job protection rights as workplace trade union representatives (see below). They are entitled to up to 50 hours' time off a month (in the case of a member of a co-ordinating committee in a large enterprise) to perform their duties. Meetings with management must take place at least once a month, usually on the committee's initiative. Members are bound by secrecy on matters which management has expressly indicated and justified as confidential.

Workers' committee rights on collective matters   In broad terms the committee is entitled to

- receive all information necessary to carry out its functions
- participate in the reorganisation of production
- manage the enterprise's social welfare fund.

Workers' committees also play a formal role, defined in law, in handling individual grievances.

Information   The law specifies the information to be supplied by management. It includes the overall strategy and budget, the profit and loss account and balance sheet, sales results and forecasts, the methods of financing the business, and tax liabilities. Details must also be provided of the organisation of production (notably the mix between capital and labour), internal works rules (including operating hours and working time schedules), the total wage bill, with a breakdown by grade, and productivity and absenteeism levels.

Consultation   The employer must seek the committee's views in writing and in advance when planning restructuring, closures, redundancies, worsening working conditions, drawing up holiday schedules, altering working hours for all or some employees, altering job grading or promotion criteria, and moving premises.

Supervision   Committees also have the right to supervise the management of the enterprise, although in practice it has become virtually a dead letter.

Informal consultation and bargaining   Following the 1974 revolution, some workplace workers' committees took on a consultative as well as bargaining role, often in direct competition with union organisation, which at the time was dominated by the Communist-leaning Intersindical. As already mentioned, a 1979 law recognised a demarcation of consultative and bargaining functions within the workplace.

Nevertheless some workers' committees and individual representatives continue to bargain or to be consulted informally at plant or company level. In some cases it is because workplace unions are weak or non-existent. In others it may be part of an employer strategy to keep unions at arm's length and reach informal understandings with workers' representatives which form no part of any written agreement. It has been argued that this type of arrangement minimises the potential for political conflict and is easier in practical terms: there is only one workers' committee per enterprise, or establishment, whereas there may be several union committees.

It is difficult to assess the extent and regularity of this informal activity; it is thought to be most widespread in engineering, chemicals and clothing – areas where unionisation is relatively strong.

Trade union committees

According to article 55 of the constitution, individual unions may exercise rights within an enterprise and enter into binding collective agreements; they do not have to establish their representativeness so long as they are duly registered with the Ministry of Employment. As might be expected, unions are most active in large companies. By law employers may not refuse to recognise a union and are obliged to answer a proposal for negotiations within 30 days (see below); otherwise the union can apply for official concliation at the Ministry of Employment.

In practice, employers have a degree of freedom to choose whether or not to engage in negotiations and with which unions. Unions frequently complain that employers either prevaricate or simply refuse to enter into negotiations.

Workplace unions function through individual delegates (*delegados sindicais*), a committee (*comissões sindicais*) or a joint committee (*comissões intersindicais*) of several workplace unions. There is no limit on the size of committee, although only a given number of representatives are allowed time off for trade union duties. It amounts to five hours per month (eight for members of joint committees). Internal union rules normally specify the procedure for electing representatives, whose names are then communicated to management. Like workers' committee members, trade union representatives enjoy enhanced job protection rights during and for five years following their term of office.

Since there are competing unions as well as autonomous unions, the management of a single large concern may have to conduct negotiations with more than one union committee. Co-operation between unions is the exception rather than the rule.

Health and safety representatives

The 1989 EU framework directive making provision for informing and consulting workers on health and safety matters was implemented in Portugal by decree-law 441/91.

Workers' safety representatives are elected by secret ballot of the workforce. Only candidates on lists presented by trade unions represented in the enterprise, or endorsed by 20 per cent of the workforce, may stand for election; reserves are also elected. The number of representatives is prescribed by law, ranging from one, in enterprises with fewer than 61 staff, up to seven for enterprises with 1,500 or more staff. Representatives have a three-year term of office and have five hours off per week to undertake their duties. Joint safety committees can be established by collective agreement.

Workers' representatives or, in their absence, the entire workforce must be informed about a number of health and safety matters (health risks, preventative action, action when danger is imminent, fire-fighting, first aid) and consulted about proposals with health repercussions and about training; they may be invited to make suggestions.

Workers responsible for aspects of health and safety must be properly trained and allowed time off for training (with or without pay) in cases where a specific subsidy is granted by another body (law of July 1992).

Since health and safety legislation is relatively recent, action to implement its provisions is only just getting under way. The election of representatives, for example, is being delayed for lack of specialised training facilities. Private specialist firms have recently become established in order to fill the gap.

Employee participation at board level

Other than in public companies, there is no provision in law for employee participation at board level.

Employee involvement strategies

One of the fundamental issues in Portugal is raising the general standard of education and training. Substantial EU funds finance many initiatives in this area.
Incoming companies usually find that employees are keen to upgrade their skills
and operate in a flexible fashion. The problem lies rather with small, domestically owned concerns, many of which are family-run, lack professional management experience and reject the erosion of traditional prerogatives. Much of the
country's industrial training effort is now being channelled into small and
medium-sized enterprises in an attempt to modernise them and increase their
productivity. This has triggered more experimentation with teamworking and
total quality management.

The EU works council directive

Since labour law is so extensive, virtually none of the EU directives dealing with
individual rights has imposed substantial additional requirements on the system,
except in the health and safety sphere. Given the small scale of Portuguese business, and its position on the periphery of Europe, there are few indigenous multinationals which will be affected by the European works council directive. As far
as electing delegates to councils set up by foreign multinationals is concerned, in
principle legislation capable of adaptation is in place (that is, the law providing
for workers' committees). Whereas the unions acknowledge the necessity for the
legislation, employers would prefer to be without it and believe the formulation
to be unclear.

Collective bargaining

One of the key features of the bargaining system is the extent of fragmentation,
both in terms of negotiating levels and in terms of forms of representation. All
unions are regarded in principle as representative and have the same right to bargain and enter into binding agreements. Unions can organise at any or all levels.
There is no structured interrelationship between one level and another and competing unions are divided along political lines.

Collective agreements are legally binding upon the signatories and upon
organisations affiliated to them. They are invariably extended by the Ministry of
Employment to non-signatories in a given sector. In addition to its powers of
extension, the Ministry of Employment can also regulate terms in unorganised

sectors. Moreover, either employers or trade unions may apply for employees to be covered by the terms of a published agreement, through the medium of an adherence agreement (*acordo de adesão*).

As a consequences of these various mechanisms, around 80 per cent (around 2 million) of Portugal's wage and salary earners, including those in public administration, are covered by some kind of agreement or employment regulation.

Sectoral agreements predominate, partly owing to the preponderance of small firms (75 per cent of enterprises employing staff have fewer than 10 employees) but also thanks to the pattern of 'negotiations' in the pre-revolutionary period. They increasingly set a minimum 'floor' of pay and conditions rather narrowly reflecting extensive and detailed statutory provisions.

Formal company bargaining is unlikely to increase greatly from its present low level, in part because of the practical difficulties entailed. Moreover it often suits employers to shelter under the umbrella of sectoral agreements and avoid engaging with unions in the workplace, where, in any event, the unions are weaker. Conversely, unions have not been actively pressing for a shift of activity to company level, since it would expose their membership weakness.

Labour legislation on terms and conditions is wide-ranging and has tended to act as a straitjacket on negotiations. The government has been considering an overhaul of the legislation, as in Spain, to allow more freedom for matters to be settled by collective negotiations, and proposals could emerge in the future. Unions are staunch in their opposition to deregulation, which, they argue, does not stimulate the creation of new jobs.

The status of collective agreements

Decree-law 519 C1/79, as amended by decree-laws 87/89 and 209/92, governs bargaining in the private sector and in publicly-owned enterprises. Bargaining is essentially voluntary, although, once the process is in train, detailed procedural rules apply. Once an agreement exists it remains in force until renewed.

Any organisation registered with the Ministry of Employment as a trade union or employers' confederation may negotiate an agreement, which must be in written form and signed by the parties. Agreements become legally enforceable once registered with the Ministry of Employment and published in its official bulletin, *Boletim do Trabalho e Emprego*. The terms of registered agreements are vetted only to the extent of ensuring that certain formalities are observed – for example, that the contracting parties are empowered to sign a collective agreement. An order extending a registered agreement to non-signatories (see below) often specifies that no clause which is in contravention of, or less favourable than, statute law can be extended. Agreements covering publicly owned enterprises require ministerial approval before entering into force.

Levels of bargaining and types of agreement

There are three forms of collective agreement, the difference between them being determined essentially by the identity of the negotiating parties and the scope of their coverage. There is no hierarchy of agreements or interaction between different levels. For example, company agreements are not bound by sectoral agreements covering their industry but in practice they invariably offer better terms and conditions.

The most predominant type of agreement by far is the *contrato colectivo de trabalho* (CCT), concluded between one or more employers' associations and a trade union (or trade unions) for a given sector, either on a national or on a regional basis. Four-fifths of employees outside public administration come under arrangements of this nature.

In the chemicals sector, for example, there are three national agreements: one covers managers, another covers stokers and firemen, and a third embraces all other occupational groups. In addition, there are a number of company agreements. In engineering, separate national agreements cover engineers, skilled craftsmen and all other groups. In commerce and retail there are dozens of sectoral agreements, mostly covering geographical districts, though some are national and cover distinct types of activity such as pharmacies or garages. Madeira and the Azores are often covered by separate agreements.

A collective accord (*acordo colectivo de trabalho*, ACT) may cover several companies either in the same region or in the same sector. Only 4 per cent of agreements are of this type.

Enterprise agreements (*acordo de empresa*, AE) are signed between union(s) and a single company. The companies are usually publicly owned companies or large private-sector firms. Formal company agreements affect only 7 per cent of employees in all (including semi-state enterprises), but a mere 1 per cent in private, companies.

Extension of agreements

Following consultations with the signatories, the Ministry of Employment has legal powers through an extension order (*portaria de extensão*) to extend an existing collective agreement (a CCT or an ACT) to firms in the same sector which are not affiliated to signatory employer bodies; the order may also include firms in a geographical area outside the scope of the original agreement. This device is also used to regulate terms in other sectors where conditions are similar but where there are no parties capable of negotiating. Where there is more than one agreement for a bargaining area the law gives no firm guidance on which one should be extended. The extension procedure is widely used.

Content of agreements and renewal

There are around 400 agreements in force, principally concerned with minimum pay rates for a range of occupations, premium payments and various allowances and grading issues, as well as many other terms which usually mirror statutory provisions. Hours of work, tasks and entry requirements tend to figure less prominently. By law, pay clauses in agreements cannot be revoked within ten months of registration with the Ministry. In practice this means that they remain in force for a year but in principle are valid until replaced by a new accord. Non-pay clauses in an agreement remain valid for at least two years. The law prevents a number of issues being determined by collective agreement; these include, for example, grounds for dismissal.

By law a new agreement cannot be 'globally' less favourable than the one it replaces. In many sectors companies pay far higher salaries than those set by the industry agreement, which gives them great flexibility in interpreting this clause. Examples of buy-outs of seniority bonuses, for example, are by no means unusual.

Most agreements, sectoral or company-wide, cover blue- and white-collar staff, often up to technician and middle management levels. However, there are also many agreements covering particular occupational groups.

Industry agreements have a limited impact on what happens on the ground within companies, both in terms of actual pay levels or on other issues.

Applicability of agreements

In principle, agreements apply to workers represented by signatory unions. Although separate agreements may have been negotiated by affiliates of the CGTP-IN and affiliates of the UGT, or even by an autonomous union for its own members, in a single workplace, only one agreement can apply to a given group of workers. By convention the accord supported by the union representing the largest number of employees in that bargaining unit will take precedence, even though that union may be in a minority position within the industry as a whole. When inflation was high, employees tended to endorse the agreement which gave the most recent adjustment in wages. In that way CGTP-IN affiliates have been displaced from some key companies in the textile and clothing sectors. UGT and independent unions have in the past been prepared to negotiate away long-standing terms in return for more frequent wage adjustments.

Acquisitions

Collective bargaining legislation requires that, when the ownership of an enter-prise or establishment changes, the acquiring entity is required to honour the existing collective agreement until it ceases to be valid. However, the law is less clear in the event of a merger where the merging companies each have their own agreement. The convention is that the agreement covering the largest number of employees takes precedence until a new accord is signed. However, the law is ambiguous. For example, the management of the newly formed Portugal Telecom opted to deal with the 'minority' union. Members of the former 'majority' union had either to consent individually to new terms, including wage increases, or forgo pay rises until their own union accepted a similar deal.

Regulating terms in unorganised sectors

The Ministry of Employment may occasionally, through a Regulation of Work Order (*portaria de regulamentação de trabalho*, PRT), decide to regulate terms and conditions in sectors which are unorganised and there are no obvious parties who can negotiate. Routine administrative staff, workers in the shoe repair trade and social workers in old people's homes are currently covered by a PRT. Such orders are no longer used as a device for resolving situations where the parties refuse to negotiate.

Employees not covered by bargaining

There remain a few small sectors which are not covered by any kind of collective agreement, extension or regulation of work order. As mentioned above, labour law provides a safety net for such employees in any event. As far as pay is concerned, minimum wage legislation is national in scope and therefore applies across the board. Senior executives are sometimes excluded from agreements and negotiate their own terms.

Negotiating procedures

The 1979 decree-law on collective bargaining also specifies the detailed procedure for negotiations. It starts with a written proposal, normally initiated by a trade union, addressed to the employers' side, requesting the negotiation or renewal of an agreement, specifying the clauses to be reviewed. The employer must respond within 30 days. Both proposal and response are submitted to the Ministry of Employment, together with the supporting information necessary for bargaining. Once the employer has replied, negotiations should commence within 15 days (unless a longer period is set by mutual agreement), otherwise the initiator may refer the matter to official conciliation. The first meeting must draw up a written negotiating timetable, and a formal exchange of powers of attorney takes place in order to ensure that negotiators have the authority to bargain.

Employers may not refuse to recognise a bargaining party if that party is duly registered. In theory, a refusal to negotiate allows the Ministry of Employment to issue a regulation of work order (see above), but in practice this is now rarely used. There are few effective sanctions that can force an unwilling party to negotiate or agree to mediation or arbitration.

The pay round

The vast majority of pay agreements are for one year, with most settlements reached between January and April. Increases are on agreed minima. Although most companies pay above the minimum it has a knock-on effect on the scales. The economic downturn of the mid-1990s has seen some delay in negotiations; in such cases, existing agreements remain in force until renewed, with some employers awarding increases in the interim.

Negotiations are often protracted. The social partners start preparing their bargaining platforms in the autumn. The three main employers' confederations consult through the CNEP (Conselho Nacional de Empresas Portuguesas). They publish no pay guidelines, although individual federations may issue guidance. No voluntary prices and incomes policies have been in force since 1992. Difficult economic conditions and a rapid rise in unemployment have since put a damper on pay awards. Formerly, pay outcomes in public administration, transport and banking and insurance served as benchmarks for deals elsewhere in the economy, including the private sector. All that may change, given the government's efforts to contain the public-sector wage bill and privatisation of the finance industry, leading to job cuts.

Recent trends in pay and working time

Pay negotiations in 1993 and 1994 delivered average awards of around and just below inflation, on a reduced volume of settlements, in contrast to previous years, where awards comfortably exceeded inflation. There was considerable variation across sectors, regions and skill levels.

Pay claims increasingly take account of official inflation forecasts rather than past inflation performance. Government attempts to curb inflation have proved broadly successful and therefore the gap between official forecasts and actual outcomes has narrowed, lending greater credibility to targets. Employers also look at the percentage increases in the national statutory minimum wage and industry agreed minima. Profitability and productivity have become more prominent elements shaping pay awards.

As for working time, Portuguese employees put in longer hours than most of their EU counterparts. The statutory working week was reduced to 44 hours (42 hours in offices) as part of the 1990/91 Economic and Social Pact; a further reduction to 40 by 1995 by way of negotiations was also anticipated. However, the issue of working time cuts has become linked, in many cases, with flexible hours. The somewhat ambiguous wording of the relevant clauses in the pact is partly responsible.

Legislation was amended in 1991 which in principle allowed employers to introduce flexible schedules, provided an enabling clause was inserted into the relevant collective agreement (in most cases at sectoral level).

The union confederation CGTP-IN has refused to accept agreements that include the flexibility option, arguing that working hours should be reduced in line with the levels prevailing in other EU countries. It launched a major campaign in 1995 to negotiate a 40 hour week across the board, with no strings attached. The issue has also been taken to parliament, although deputies from non-communist parties rejected a statutory 40 hour week. However, in early 1995 the employers' confederation for commerce and the UGT union confederation signed a bilateral pact on flexibility intended to guide negotiations in their areas, covering 500,000 employees in commerce. The aim is to cut hours to 40 a week, averaged out over three to six months by collective agreement, with an absolute weekly maximum of 50 hours.

In practice employees, particularly in small firms, often work flexibly and the recession has accelerated moves in that direction. There are examples of employees agreeing to take time off in lieu of overtime payments.

The rate of recorded unemployment remains one of the lowest in the EU, at 7 per cent in the second quarter of 1995, but it rose rapidly over 1993–94, with new young entrants and older workers most at risk. Yet job creation, including reducing hours to increase employment, has not been a major subject of negotiations. Instead the government has given employers incentives to recruit first-time employees and the long-term unemployed direct by reducing or waiving employers' social security contributions and lump sums. There is evidence that the take-up has been low, and in some cases legislation implementing some of the announced measures has not been forthcoming.

Agreed provisions and the objects of bargaining

All employees receive 13 monthly payments a year – one as a holiday bonus – and most receive a fourteenth month's pay, due at Christmas by agreement.

Statutory minimum wage legislation is national in scope, although the basic pay of most workers is related to binding pay minima established by sectoral agreement. Although the differential between agreed minimum rates and actual rates has widened over time, particularly in industries where white-collar, high-tech, highly skilled jobs are concentrated, negotiated minima are an important reference point for the lowest points on the pay scale and increases have a knock-on effect throughout a scale.

Premium rates for overtime and night work are specified by law, with some agreements allowing further enhancements. Shift payments are governed by agreement, as are bonuses related to the nature of the business or job or for working irregular hours. A particularly Portuguese concept is the 'exemption from working hours' allowance, in principle paid only to staff in positions of responsibility for working outside normal operating hours. Such staff may not wish to accept it, as many regard the allowance as a green light for employers to impose long hours of poorly remunerated overtime. Length of service payments feature in some agreements but are losing their importance.

Since most companies are small, and often family-owned, financial participation is rare. Multinational subsidiaries often include senior staff in share option-schemes based on parent company stock. Likewise, profit-sharing is not wide-spread.

Industrial conflict

Collective agreements and disputes over rights

By law every collective agreement must make provision for the establishment of a joint committee (*comissões paritárias de interpretação*) to monitor and inter-pret the implementation of the agreement's terms and to resolve disputes over rights. The committee comprises an equal number of employers and union repre-sentatives but may also include other experts. The parties may request the involvement of the Ministry of Employment, but it has no voting rights. This mechanism has not been very successful in resolving disputes, given the commit-tee's composition and the requirement of unanimous decisions. Resort to the courts, whose rulings are binding on disputes over rights, can entail delays of up to two years. Although there is no explicit peace clause in the law, industrial action would not normally be pursued on matters covered by an agreement dur-ing its lifetime or while a dispute was under consideration by the committee .

According to amendments of the collective bargaining law dating from 1992, agreements may also outline procedures for dealing with disputes arising from individual contracts and specify mechanisms for conciliation, mediation and arbitration.

The right to strike

The right to strike is guaranteed under article 57 of the constitution and applies across the public and private sectors. Decree-law 65/77 implements this principle and covers other aspects of industrial action. Special rules apply to public admin-istration.

Workers have the right to define the scope of the interests they choose to defend. To be regarded as lawful, a strike decision must be taken by a properly constituted body, defined in law, and the action must be taken in pursuit of socio-economic goals. A strike decision can be taken only by a trade union, in accor-dance with its own rules or, if no union exists, or it does not represent the majority of workers, by a meeting convened by 20 per cent of the workforce (or 200 employees) which a majority attend and where most vote in favour in a secret ballot.

Once a strike has been declared, advance notice must be given to the employer, the employers' association or the Ministry of Employment, as the case may be. The notice period was lengthened to five days (10 days in essential ser-vices) in 1992, a move fiercely opposed by the unions at the time. Notice periods are usually observed, since absence from work without justification (which could include failure to give proper notice in a strike) may constitute grounds for dismissal. General obligations to maintain the security of the workplace, and of essential equipment, apply during a dispute. Essential services are defined as mail and telecommunications, medical services, water supplies, fire services, funeral services and the transport of livestock or perishable foods. The government has emergency mobilisation and requisition powers.

Strikers must be represented by their trade union, or an elected strike committee, and the action ends when an agreement is reached between the parties in dispute. The labour courts have the responsibility of ruling on the legality of a strike, and there is a large body of case law in this field. Under the law fines may be levied on trade unions or employers for failure to observe strike procedures, or on an employer who imposes a lockout which is expressly forbidden by law.

Forms of industrial action

Employees are free to choose the particular form of industrial action they will take. Normally it will be regarded as lawful provided it is in pursuit of socio-economic objectives. The latter include action in protest against proposed labour legislation which could have a negative effect on the position of workers. The law is silent on the legality of action short of a strike; such action could in any event lead individuals to breach their employment contracts. Since most unions have no strike funds, tactics which minimise loss of earnings are preferred, as are short sympathy actions – sometimes on a national basis – against government policies. Financially well endowed unions with large strike funds, such as in banking or transport, have often used them to great effect.

A trade union or strike committee can organise pickets which, by peaceful means, persuade other workers to join the dispute. Non-participating union members would not normally be disciplined unless they were representatives.

Employers may not substitute other workers for those on strike. Returning strikers may not be discriminated against. The effect of taking strike action is a suspension of the employment contract and hence loss of pay, which may entail the loss of attendance bonuses in appropriate cases.

The level of strike activity has plummeted dramatically since the mid-1970s, hitting a low during the boom years of the late 1980s. It edged up again as the economy slid into recession. There have been some short (one- or half-day) general strikes, stoppages over arrears in salary payments (often accentuated by the difficulty companies have in declaring redundancies) and over the non-renewal of collective agreements or job losses. According to comparative figures prepared by the UK Department of Employment, an average 75 working days were lost per thousand employees per year in the period 1990–93, exactly the same rate as in the UK and well below the rates seen in other southern European countries.

Conciliation, mediation and arbitration

If negotiations fail to progress, voluntary conciliation is normally attempted before strike action is taken. Procedures may be outlined in collective agreements or, if not, in law. The services of the Ministry of Employment may be used by joint request or sometimes at the request of only one party; the process is triggered within 15 days of a request being lodged. The results are not usually very positive. As from 1992, collective agreements can also make arrangements to submit grievances arising from an individual employment contract subject to conciliation, mediation and arbitration.

A voluntary mediation procedure is set down in law. An outside mediator may be selected by the parties, who must submit a proposal within 21 days.

Conciliation and mediation services are available free of charge from the Ministry. This service gives it the opportunity to intervene in disputes.

Few disputes are referred to private arbitration. Since 1992, however, any dispute arising in connection with the renewal or signing of a collective agreement may be subject to compulsory arbitration if conciliation and mediation have failed. The use of this mechanism is at the discretion of the Ministry of Employment, either on request by both parties, or on the recommendation of the Economic and Social Council. The law outlines arrangements for nominating or designating an arbitrator. It is too early as yet to say how effective this device will prove in resolving disputes.

Organisations

Ministry of Employment and Social Security (Ministério do Emprego e da Segurança Social)
Praça de Londres 2
1000 Lisbon
Tel. + 351 1 80 44 60

Institute of Employment and Vocational Training (Instituto do Emprego e Formação Profissional)
11 Avenida José Malhoa 11
1100 Lisbon
Tel. + 351 1 726 25 36

Office of Technological, Artistic and Vocational Education (Gabinete de Educação Tecnológica Artistica e Profissional, GETAP)
Avenida 24 Julho 140
1300 Lisbon
Tel. + 351 1 395 34 07
A section of the Ministry of Education.

Directorate General of Occupational Safety and Health (Direcção Geral de Higiene e Segurança do Trabalho)
Avenida da República 84-5
1600 Lisbon
Tel. + 351 1 77 28 22

Association of Portuguese Human Resource Managers (Associação Portuguesa de Gestores e Técnicos de Recursos Humanos, APG)
Avenida do Brasil 194 7º
1700 Lisbon
Tel. + 351 1 89 97 66
Fax + 351 1 80 93 40

In Oporto
Rua Formosa 49 1º
Tel. + 351 2 32 32 34
Fax + 351 2 200 07 64

The professional organisation of personnel practitioners, with some 2,000 individual members and company affiliates. APG is a member of the European Assocation of Personnel Management and the World Federation of Personnel Management Associations.

Confederation of Portuguese Industry (Confederação da Indústria Portuguesa, CIP)
Avenida 5 de Outubro, 35 1º
1000 Lisbon
Tel. + 351 1 54 74 54
The central employers' organisation for industry.

Confederation of Portuguese Commerce (Confederação do Comércio Português, CCP)
Rua Saraiva de Carvalho, 1
1000 Lisbon
Tel. + 351 1 66 85 39
The central employers' organisation in trade and commerce.

Confederação Geral dos Trabalhadores Portugueses–Intersindical Nacional (CGTP-IN)
Rua Vitor Cordon, 1 3º
1200 Lisbon
Tel. + 351 1 34 72 181–8

União Geral de Trabalhadores (UGT)
Rua Buenos Aires 11
1200 Lisbon
Tel. + 351 1 67 65 03/5

Portuguese–British Chamber of Commerce (Câmara do Comércio Luso-Britânica)
Rua da Estrela 8
1200 Lisbon
Tel. + 351 1 396 14 86
Fax + 351 1 60 15 13

Main sources

BARRETO, J. 'Portugal: Industrial relations under democracy', in A. Ferner and R. Hyman (eds), *Industrial Relations in the New Europe*. Oxford, Blackwell, 1992

Chronique international, No. 30, Sept. 1994, IRES, France

NASCIMENTO RODRIGUES, H. 'Da luta de classes à concertação social', *Diário de Notícias-Empresas*, Lisbon, Oct. 1991

NETO, A. *Contrato de Trabalho: Notas Práticas*, 12ª Edição, 1993 for legal texts and case law

O Conselho Económico e Social, Lisbon, CES, 1993

Occupational Hygiene, Health and Safety Agreement, Lisbon, CPCS, 1991

Os Acodos de Concertação Social em Portugal (Estudos, Textos) Lisbon, CES, 1993

PINTO, M. 'Trade union action and industrial relations in Portugal', in G. Baglioni and C. Crouch (eds), *European Industrial Relations: the challenge of flexibility*. London, Sage Publications, 1990

Various issues *Boletim do Trabalho e Emprego 1ª Series*, for collective agreements and employment regulations

Vocational Training Policy Agreement, Lisbon, CPCS, 1991

11
Spain

Twenty years after the end of the Franco dictatorship, industrial relations in Spain continue to hinge on dismantling the institutional and cultural legacies of the corporate state. Reforms introduced in 1994, intended to replace the vestiges of legal regulation of employment by collective bargaining, should, in theory, broaden the scope of negotiations. However, the reform package – proceeded with by the government in the face of union opposition and employer scepticism – has been implemented only very slowly.

These developments are posing both challenges and opportunities for the trade unions. Trade union membership rose enormously after democratisation, as unions were seen as untainted, accessible democratic institutions, and bore popular hopes of political emancipation as well as economic improvement. Membership peaked in the late 1970s, and then went into severe decline, in part because of changes in the structure of the economy and rising unemployment, which militated against union membership, in part because of the massive growth of temporary contracts which now embrace nearly one-third of new hirings, but also because of the lack of deep roots for a culture of participation and negotiation strong enough to withstand the initial disenchantment of members after the short phase of intense mobilisation. Some observers have commented that Spain's trade unions are still struggling to move on from their past status as political (and often heavily politicised) institutions to the more humdrum business of collective bargaining, and they remain often only weakly implanted in the workplace.

Statute law provides the main underpinning for the structures of industrial relations, with statutory and constitutional guarantees of freedom of association and trade union rights, and statutory forms of employee representation at workplace level. Both trade unions and employer organisations must meet statutory criteria of representativeness in order to engage in collective bargaining.

The main players

Trade unions

The historical experience of the trade unions in Spain has shaped many of their current preoccupations. Their performance has often been highly politicised, and ideological considerations have played a major part in trade union policies.

Spanish trade unionism emerged in the late nineteenth and early twentieth centuries, principally in the form first of the socialist Unión General de Trabajadores (UGT) and then the anarcho-syndicalist Confederación Nacional de Trabajo (CNT). For much of the 1920s trade union activity was curtailed, in the putative corporate state controlled by General Primo de Rivera from 1923 to 1930. In the 1930s, during the Second Republic (1931–6) and the Spanish Civil War (1936-9) the UGT and CNT (with more than a million affiliates each) were prominent in the highly polarised struggles between left and right which culminated in the victory of General Franco. The bitter aftermath of that conflict was the outlawing of trade unions in the corporate state in which Franco tried to adopt many of Mussolini's policies. From 1939 to 1975, when Franco died, all employers and employees were obliged to belong to Franco's National Syndicate organisation, controlled by the government, through which all aspects of employment law and labour relations were rigidly controlled by central government dictat. Under Franco, those attempting to flout anti-trade union regulations were regularly imprisoned.

Whereas the CNT was virtually destroyed by Franco after the civil war, and the UGT all but disappeared, two new organisations emerged in the 1960s. Comisiones Obreras (CC.OO) – workers' commissions – developed clandestinely among the mineworkers of Asturias, the steelworkers of the Basque country, and in several other centres, led by a combination of communists, democrats and radical Catholics. During the 1960s and early 1970s they began to play an important role in articulating workers' interests at workplace level, and often entered into informal negotiations with employers as well as putting forward candidates for office within the institutions of the corporate state. Unión Sindical Obrera (USO) emerged as a semi-clandestine body, led largely by progressive Catholic militants.

Following Franco's death, there was no official infrastructure of trade union organisation, and while the UGT rapidly reformed, CC.OO rapidly expanded, and USO expanded briefly, there was an institutional and legal void. It was gradually addressed in the transition years between Franco's death and the 1978 constitution. In 1977 Spain legalised trade unions, along with political parties and employers' associations, and ratified ILO conventions 87 and 98, guaranteeing the right of association and protecting trade union activity.

Trade union law The present legal status of the unions was established with the 1977 law on freedom of association (*Ley de asociación sindical*), which permitted the formation of unions and employers' organisations. Article 28 of the 1978 constitution guaranteed basic democratic union rights, which were detailed in the 1980 Workers' Statute (*Estatuto de los trabajadores*): this also laid the basis for a range of other employee and representative rights. The reforms of the Workers' Statute in 1994 (*Reforma del Estatuto de los trabajadores*) marked a major step towards greater flexibility in the labour market, and in particular enhanced the scope of collective bargaining by providing for the repeal of the labour ordinances regulating employment which stemmed from the Franco era.

Specific legislation on the character and role of trade unions came in 1985 with the Law on Trade Union Freedoms (*Ley orgánica de libertad sindical*), which granted unions the right to establish workplace sections.

Trade unions have a legal personality and are answerable for acts carried out by duly established organs acting within their competence, but not for the acts of individual members unless they are acting on behalf of the union. In order to acquire legal standing, which also includes tax concessions and the capacity to engage in collective bargaining, unions must register with the authorities. This entails lodging a copy of their rulebook, which will be open to public inspection.

Union representativeness   In 1985 the Law on Trade Union Freedoms also established the concept of 'most representative union', by which the powers of the major unions to conduct collective bargaining at national and regional level are defined, and larger unions favoured. For bargaining at national level, only those unions which obtain 10 per cent of the elected members of works' councils or workers' delegates are empowered to negotiate. At regional level (principally the Basque country and Catalonia) the required figure is 15 per cent, with a minimum total of 1,500 elected in that region. The qualifying unions, which can also benefit from state subsidies, are the UGT, CC.OO nationally, the ELA-STV in the Basque country and the CIG in Galicia.

Structure and membership   Since the restoration of democracy the UGT and CC.OO have dominated union representation in a relationship marked, in the past, by competition and political rivalry. Although a large number of unions emerged in the late 1970s, most have remained small, with the exception of the USO, Confederación General de Trabajadores (CGT) (the successor of the old CNT), ELA-STV, the Basque trade union, and CIG, the Galician trade union.

The Unión General de Trabajadores (UGT) is by far the oldest established union, dating from 1888. It has always been the trade union wing of the Spanish Socialist Workers' Party (PSOE), closely supporting the party for most of its history, until the mid-1980s, when it distanced itself from PSOE government policies on industrial restructuring and reforming the labour market. Relations with the PSOE, in power since 1982, have been strained since, and the UGT was involved in organising general strikes (in 1988, 1992 and 1994) against the PSOE government. The UGT's public image has also been badly shaken by the collapse of its housing co-operative amid accusations of financial scandal, and by internal differences, culminating in an extraordinary conference convened to re-elect the union's head.

Comisiones Obreras (CC.OO) although originally composed of a wide range of dissident groups, including liberals and worker priests, has been mainly influenced by the Spanish Communist Party (PCE), now part of the united left movement Izquierda Unida. However, the CC.OO was never a mere agency of the PCE and continued to contain a number of political groupings and look for broader alliances. Differences of strategy between 'traditionalists' and 'modernisers' (embodied in the person of the current leader of the union, Antonio Gutiérrez) remain, however. On the strength of its origins as a grass-roots, workplace-based movement, CC.OO has continued to demonstrate a strong capacity for workplace mobilisation.

Union membership peaked in the late 1970s, with the UGT and CC.OO reaching a combined membership of some 2.6 million in the euphoria following the death of Franco and the rebuilding of democratic organisations. From that point on for many years the UGT and CC.OO were rivals, vying with each other for membership and influence with employers and government during the early 1980s, when Spain experimented with a series of social contracts. This competition abated in 1985, since when there has been increasing collaboration between the two organisations, culminating in jointly staged general strikes against the PSOE government in 1988 and 1994. These changed relations have developed in an environment of steadily falling membership, to the point where union density is down to some 12 per cent of the workforce – one of the lowest rates in Europe. However, unions enjoy broader support than their nominal membership through elections to statutory works councils and for other workplace employee representatives (see below). However, some recent research (see Jordana 1995) has suggested that the peak of union membership in the late 1970s was overestimated, that the trough was reached in 1985, and that since then – aided by a degree of *rapprochement* between the federations – union density may now have recovered to above 20 per cent of the workforce, (if correct) confounding long-held views about the evolution of trade unionism in Spain since the fall of Franco.

The UGT claims some 720,000 members, and gained 44 per cent of places in the elections for works councils and employee representatives in 1990, the last time elections were held simultaneously for all works councils: under reforms introduced in 1994, elections are now staggered (see below). CC.OO won 36 per cent of places in the same elections, and currently claims some 700,000 members. Following the shrinkage of other smaller unions, the UGT–CC.OO duopoly of representation grew during the 1980s. Up to May 1995 elections held under the new arrangements, totalling around 70 per cent of the number elected in 1990, indicated some loss of support for the UGT, which won 34 per cent of places, and sustained backing for CC.OO, which won 37 per cent. CC.OO has traditionally favoured a strategy of using elected works councils as a vehicle for representing employee interests: in contrast, the UGT has advocated independent workplace union branches, as permitted under the 1985 law on trade union freedoms (see below).

Union membership has remained most strongly concentrated among blue-collar workers in traditional industrial sectors, and in public-sector organisations. The trade unions have been notoriously tardy in improving their appeal to new occupations, to women and to young employees, and are seen largely as bastions of male employees on permanent contracts. Both the UGT and CC.OO have varying strongholds, with the UGT better represented in small and medium-sized companies, the CC.OO more strongly entrenched in larger-scale firms in manufacturing and the finance sector.

In the absence of an overall trade union organisation, each of the unions tends to follow independent policies, with joint activity happening only sporadically. The UGT and CC.OO leaderships have had close contact on several occasions, and have moved closer in recent years, but the leaders of the major unions have met only twice to discuss joint policy – in 1988 on the occasion of their one-day general strike, and again in 1992 to protest against the PSOE's labour market proposals.

Organisation   Each major trade union confederation consists of sectoral and regional federations, with national federal headquarters in Madrid. The UGT, for example, has 13 federations representing different sectors, each with its provincial structure in the 50 provinces of Spain. The general secretaries of each confederation (Antonio Gutiérrez of CC.OO and Cándido Méndez of the UGT) have considerable influence over union policies, and are treated as political figures of some weight. To some extent this also reflects historical precedent, rather than the current importance of their organisations: Gutiérrez's predecessor, Marcelino Camacho, served a long jail term under Franco, and Méndez's predecessor, Nicolás Redondo, after suffering persecution under Franco, became an MP for the PSOE for several years while also general secretary of UGT. Both men were significant participants in the construction of a consensus democracy in the 1970s, and their policies stamped the emerging trade union movement as a political and ideological force besides being an important social partner. One important legacy of the period of social contracts between 1980 and 1985 has been a marked centralisation of both organisations, with weak structures at workplace level – especially in small firms.

Union subscriptions may be deducted by the employer through a check-off system if the union requests it and provided the individual employee consents. In order to strengthen trade unions as bodies capable of regulating and organising industrial relations, the government has provided substantial funding over the past decade to finance their management and the training of union representatives. Some Pta 5,422 million (£23m) was paid to UGT and Pta 4,814 million (£21m) to CC.OO in the decade 1982–92.

Workplace rights   The Law on Trade Union Freedoms defines the unions' statutory sphere of activity in the workplace. Unions are entitled to be active inside and outside the workplace, to engage in collective bargaining, initiate individual or collective disputes, and to put forward candidates in works council elections. They have a right to establish workplace sections (see below), hold meetings (with due notice to the employer), collect dues, and distribute and receive union information.

Employers' organisations

Employers have had the right to form associations since the 1977 law on the freedom of association. Their role in bargaining is governed by legislation: an employers' association employing more than 10 per cent of employees nationally (or, at regional level, employing more than 15 per cent of the employees in the region) is entitled to negotiate with any unions which also fulfil criteria of representativeness. The Confederación Española de Organizaciones Empresariales (CEOE) is the largest employers' association, representing the vast majority of large companies in the private and public sectors, totalling some 10 million employees, and made up of 700 employer associations. Small and medium-size firms are represented by the Confederación Española de Pequeñas y Medianas Empresas (CEPYME), structured along similar lines to the CEOE. Employers are also organised in regional associations and associations in the large cities.

As with unions, employer organisations must meet criteria of representativeness in order to bargain: regional or national-level bodies are deemed to be 'most representative' where they represent at least 10 per cent of the employers covered by the agreement who also have to employ at least 10 per cent of the employees covered by the agreement.

Consultation at national level

Incomes policies

An important factor in the pattern in which collective bargaining evolved in the period immediately following the end of the Franco regime was that the arrival of democratic industrial relations coincided with deepening economic recession. Government priorities in the period 1977–85 were to reduce high inflation and tackle rising unemployment while making the economy more competitive in preparation for entry to the European Community. This, and the need to protect fledgling democracy, partly explains the prevalence of 'consensus' in industrial politics for much of the period, with corresponding effects on the pattern of collective bargaining. The first in 1977 was the Moncloa Pact, agreed between Adolfo Suárez's ruling centre-right union UCD (Unión Centro Democrático) government and the opposition parties. Pay curbs and a number of monetarist measures were agreed in exchange for a package of democratic reforms, social reforms and increased union rights. The unions, although not party to the pact, supported it. There followed a series of national framework agreements in the period 1980–86 involving employers, unions and on one occasion the government which laid down general principles for the role and recognition of trades unions as well as for issues such as productivity, working time, combating absenteeism, and health and safety measures. These principles were to provide guidelines for collective agreements at industry level. The last of these Economic and Social Agreements (AES) also involved government pledges on investment and training. Each of the agreements included pay restraint clauses. The agreements established the broad pattern of collective bargaining, which was largely adopted by sectoral, provincial or company agreements.

These agreements undoubtedly helped to maintain industrial stability and cut inflation during the period of substantial industrial restructuring in traditional industries. These framework agreements were

- 1980–1, the Acuerdo Marco Interconfederal (AMI) between the CEOE and the UGT
- 1982, the Acuerdo Nacional sobre Empleo (ANE) between the CEOE, UGT and CC.OO
- 1983, the Acuerdo Interconfederal (AI) between the CEOE, UGT and CC.OO
- 1985–6, the Acuerdo Económico y Social (AES) between the CEOE, UGT and the government.

The phase of consensus signalled by these agreements ended in 1986. Although in general terms the aim of reducing inflation was achieved, few of the other undertakings were translated into effective action. The result was scepticism among the unions about the worth of framework agreements. Another effect of these six years of framework agreements was that collective bargaining remained largely restricted to discussions about global percentage pay rises within a narrow band, and few initiatives were taken on other themes.

In 1992 the parties came together again voluntarily to agree a national vocational training programme which co-ordinates company training plans and government funding.

Following the elections in 1993, which saw the PSOE returned to power but as a minority government, talks began between the social partners as to the feasibility of a new social pact to tackle the recession, which hit Spain especially severely. However, no agreement could be reached and the government proceeded with its own labour market reforms, embodied in the 1994 amendments to the 1980 Workers' Statute.

Statutory forms of tripartism and the role of the state

The major forum for tripartite consultation is the Social and Economic Council (Consejo Económico y Social, CES), established in 1992, 14 years after being proposed in the constitution. The institution is essentially a policy forum, and has no statutory power to examine legislation. It consists of a council of 61 representatives, 20 nominated by the 'most representative unions', 20 nominated by employers' associations, 10 from farming, fishing and consumers' organisations, and 10 nominated by the government.

There are other regional forums which bring employers and unions together to debate similar agendas, notably the Consejo Vasco de Relaciones Laborales in the Basque country.

Labour ordinances

On one key long-standing issue the social partners have recently been required by statute to agree to the fundamental reform of basic employment conditions. In the 1994 reform of the Workers' Statute the government required the social partners by the end of 1995 to negotiate new sectoral accords to replace the outdated and obsolete labour ordinances (*Ordenanzas laborales*) which determined employment conditions in each sector under Franco, and which have been formally derogated by national bipartite negotiations in very few sectors, such as chemicals and construction. Such renegotiation of these fundamental conditions (which often shape the pay structure and pay elements of workforces) has been pending since the Workers' Statute in 1980.

In October 1994 the CEOE, CEPYME, UGT and CC.OO formally agreed to prepare replacement accords by November 1995. The importance of this step lies not only in removing the paradox of overlapping ordinances and modern collective agreements but also in the fact that repealing the ordinances will remove a modicum of employment protection from about 25 per cent of employees who have no collective agreement and where there is no employers' association capable of signing one. The UGT and CC.OO hope that in the process the large number of existing provincial collective agreements will be integrated into national sectoral bargaining.

Until this procedure is finally settled the issue of voluntary negotiation between the social partners is likely to remain unresolved. Indeed, the persistence of the ordinances is a major factor obstructing the modernisation of collective bargaining in general. The conversion of some of them into mere collective agreements in the 1970s helped to prolong arrangements designed for the 1950s or 1960s into the 1980s – with all the substantive obstacles to modernisation and rationalisation that implies. Some 70 ordinances were still in force in late 1995. In some cases there is simply no national employers' body to negotiate a national sectoral agreement to replace the ordinance. Another 14 sectors which do have national employer organisations have simply refused to participate in the process of abrogating the ordinance. On the other hand, another 20 sectors successfully negotiated agreements to replace their ordinance; these include major sectors such as banking, hotels and catering, cleaning services, woodworking, insurance and textiles.

Another feature highlighted by the concern to replace Francoist ordinances with national sectoral agreements is that the centralising tendency evident in labour relations since at least the 1920s, which Franco did much to reinforce, are still broadly supported by both the social partners. Neither the national employers' confederation, the CEOE, nor the major trade unions advocate decentralisation of bargaining to workplace level. The philosophy behind the reforms of the Workers' Statute is in large part to try to decentralise those relations, but in the absence of a well developed culture of local bargaining and negotiation (save in the Basque country) it may be difficult to achieve for some time.

Voluntary social partnership

For largely historical reasons there has been little tradition of voluntary co-operation between the social partners until recently. The general secretaries of the UGT, CC.OO and CEOE occasionally meet to discuss national issues but seldom conclude agreements.

There has been more voluntary co-operation in some of the regions. The Catalan employers' confederation, Fomento de Trabajo, has established voluntary agreements with the unions in Catalonia on such issues as arbitration, mediation and conciliation, and the Basque employers' and union confederations have co-operated on various issues, from arbitration and conciliation procedures to training and job creation, in their joint labour council, the Consejo Vasco de Relaciones Laborales.

Consultation at regional/industry level

Various agreements have been reached between the social partners and regional governments, notably the Basque government, to promote job creation, training and restructuring. Regional governments have separate budgets, allowing them to encourage these sorts of initiative. Also at regional level, the Catalan and Basque employers' confederations have reached similar agreements with the trade unions.

Some industry sectors have achieved voluntary national agreements. Banking, chemicals, construction, engineering and some food processing sectors have agreed national framework conditions which replace the Franco ordinance for their industry and which establish agreed minimum conditions applying to all companies in the sector. Representatives of the large number of companies which belong to the state holding company Instituto Nacional de Industria (INI) also reached an agreement in 1993, to run for three years, by which the UGT and CC.OO participate in strategic decisions affecting such issues as the introduction of multi-skilling, regrading, mediation and arbitration. The engineering employers' confederation Confemetal agreed with the UGT, CC.OO and CIG in 1995 to establish permanent joint committees to promote dialogue and reform the structure of collective bargaining in the sector.

Workplace employee representation

There are a number of forms of workplace employee representation. They encompass staff representatives in smaller establishments, works councils in larger organisations and rights of trade union organisation at workplace level. In addition, meetings of the whole workforce (*asembleas*) also enjoy some statutory powers. Although the pattern of workplace representation has features of a 'dual' system, the arrangement is more hybrid in that works councils have negotiating rights, with more restricted involvement by workplace trade union sections in bargaining. There is also a difference of view between the two main union federations about which form of employee representation should be supported.

The Workers' Statute established a system of employee representation in 1980. It was refined by the Law on Trade Union Freedoms and the 1994 reforms of the Workers' Statute.

Staff representatives (*delegados de personal*)

In smaller companies of 6–50 employees the law requires staff representatives to be elected, with one representative for up to 30 employees, and three delegates for 31–49 employees. Companies with fewer than 10 employees are not bound by statute to have an employee representative but may have one if a majority of employees so wish.

Works councils (*comites de empresas*)

The main features of works councils For companies with 50 employees or more the statute provides for works councils to be set up in every workplace with at least 50 employees. The number of members varies by workforce size as in Table 4. Above 1,000 employees there are two members per thousand (or less), up to a maximum of 75.

Table 4 *Membership of works councils, by company size*

Workforce size	No. of members
50–100	5
101–250	9
251–500	13
501–750	17
751–1,000	21

When a company has two or more workplaces in a province or in adjoining municipalities, each with fewer than 50 employees but with 50 between them, a joint works council is formed. When one workplace in this sort of situation has 50 employees but the others have not, then the workplace with 50 employees forms its own council and the others form one between them. It is permissible by collective agreement to form a joint works council linking several workplaces, with a maximum of 13 members, whose functions and administration are defined by the agreement.

Elections for employee representatives may be called by a majority of the employees, by the 'most representative' trade unions or by unions representing at least 10 per cent of the elected representatives. Elections were originally held every two years, then from the mid-1980s every four years. However, the coincidence of all works council elections at the same time led to the procedure turning into a high-profile competition, often politicised, between the two main union confederations, which soured relations – although recovery after the 1990 election was fairly rapid – and drained their resources. Under the 1994 reforms of the Workers' Statute the electoral arrangements were changed, and elections may now be held at one month's formal notice. Where the entire works council is to be replaced, one month's notice is also required; however, this also requires majority agreement between 'the most representative unions' or employee representatives. All employees with at least one month's service are entitled to vote. Candidates may be nominated by union branches, coalitions of union branches, or employee sponsors totalling at least three times the number of vacancies. In workplaces with more than 50 employees elections are based on separate 'electoral colleges' of technical and administrative staff on one hand and specialist and unskilled staff on the other.

Voting is by proportional representation for lists of candidates, with a minimum 5 per cent of votes necessary for approval. Candidates are elected for a four-year term. Detailed statutory election and monitoring procedures must be followed.

Votes in elections to works councils are an important index of support for trade unions, whose direct membership is low (see above).

Works councils' rights   The principal statutory right of workforce representatives is to information and to express an opinion on matters put before them. Works councils are also required to supervise employer compliance with labour, social security and employment legislation, and to oversee health and safety conditions in the workplace. The council is required to warn the employer of dangerous or unhealthy working conditions (in the absence of a health and safety committee), and may suspend work where necessary if working circumstances present a threat to health or life and the employer has not responded to earlier requests for action. Works councils and managements may also conclude agreements on any area they wish.

The main information and consultation rights are

- to receive quarterly information on developments in the economic sector the company is in, reports on production and sales plans, and news of likely employment trends in the company
- to receive company financial reports, annual reports and the same information as shareholders receive
- to express an opinion before the employer takes action on workforce restructuring, redundancies, short-time working, the total or partial transfer of a workplace, the implementation of time and motion studies, bonus systems and job evaluation, grading, flexitime arrangements and shift working
- to be informed of the type of employment contract the company uses and documents relating to termination of contract
- to receive quarterly reports on absenteeism, occupational accidents and sickness
- to be informed of all sanctions imposed for very serious offences
- to receive a copy of all fixed-term written employment contracts issued by the

employer, so as to monitor the use of temporary employment contracts
- to be informed of the company's plans for training young recruits on training contracts
- to be informed of the arrangements reached with INEM for work experience contracts
- to receive monthly reports of overtime worked.

The committee may convene workplace meetings out of working hours at least every other month and when one-third of members or a third of the workplace call for a meeting.

Collective agreements may enhance the council's functions: for example, more frequent meetings may be provided for, or arrangements agreed for councils to include specialist consultants in joint meetings.

The rights of workforce representatives

Elected workforce representatives enjoy a number of rights and guarantees. They are protected against dismissal or sanctions during the first year of office, and for one further year, where dismissal or sanction is connected with their role as an elected representative. There is also a right of appeal in the event of sanctions for a very serious or a serious offence, to be exercised in the presence of the works council or the other worker delegates.

Where redundancies are taking place on economic or technological grounds, elected representatives have priority as regards safeguarding employment and enjoy protection in the event of relocation for technical, geographical or organisational reasons.

Representatives are free to express their views on matters relating to their role as workers' representative, and to print and disseminate material of economic or social relevance, provided it does not interfere with normal working.

Each member of a works council or staff representative is entitled to paid time off to carry out their duties, with the amount of time off determined by the size of the workplace. The monthly scale is shown in Table 5. These hours may be pooled, to allow certain delegates or works council members to devote more time to representation. Collective agreements may improve on the arrangements.

Table 5 *Entitlement of works council members and employee representatives to time off, by size of workplace*

Workforce	Hours' leave per month
1–100	15
101–250	20
251–500	30
501–750	35
751+	40

The right of assembly

The Workers' Statute grants the right of assembly to a workforce (*asambleas de trabajadores*), irrespective of works council or trade union procedures. Workers have the right to call a meeting, for example to repeal the mandate of a works council (after due notice, when called by at least one-third of the workforce) or to take decisions which affect the workforce as a whole. Such an assembly will not prejudice the lawful working of the works council. The employer must be given 48 hours' notice of the meeting, and the meeting must be chaired by the works council, or by staff representatives, and must have an agenda. The employer must be informed of the agenda and of the names of any non-employees who will be attending. The employer is obliged to allow the meeting to take place in the workplace, provided lawful requirements have been met and that at least two months have elapsed since the last meeting. Any decisions taken by the meeting must be by secret ballot, including postal ballot, with a simple majority of the workforce deciding.

Workplace trade union branches (*secciones sindicales*)

Under the 1985 law on trade union freedoms, employees who are members of 'most representative unions' and unions represented on the works council have the right to form workplace union branches, which take part in collective bargaining, to use a notice board and to have their own office in workplaces with more than 250 employees. These powers were granted to unions some five years after the Workers' Statute established works councils, to quote the law, 'as vehicles of democratisation of labour relations within companies'. Traditionally the UGT has been the stronger advocate of workplace branches as a form of employee representation.

In workplaces with more than 250 employees, union members may also elect trades union delegates (*delegados sindicales*) according to the scale in Table 6. A single delegate may represent any trade union which did not achieve 10 per cent of the vote for works council members. Union delegates enjoy the same protection as elected staff representatives, including paid leave and the right of access to the same information. They also have a right to participate in meetings of health and safety committees (see below) and to express views on company policies which affect the workforce.

Table 6　*Number of union delegates, by size of workforce*

No. employed	No. of delegates
250–750	1
751–2,000	2
2,001–5,000	3
5,001+	4

Collective agreements may grant them extra powers. For example, Sociedad Española de Oxígeno allows its union branches to call weekly 15 minute meetings in working time during negotiations for the firm's collective agreement. Iberdrola has given union delegates extensive powers, effectively recognising them rather than a joint works council as the negotiating body.

Health and safety committees

New health and safety regulations were due to take effect from January 1996; previous legislation dated from 1971. Under the latter, each company or workplace with 100 employees (or fewer where dangerous activities are carried out) is obliged to have a health and safety committee. It consists of a chairperson appointed by the employer, a qualified health and safety technician and a qualified medical specialist, a member of staff qualified in first aid, the head of company safety, a number of elected staff representatives (three in companies with under 500 employees, four in companies of 500–1,000 employees or more) and a secretary appointed from the administrative staff. In workplaces with fewer than 100 employees, health and safety are the responsibility of the works council or employee representatives.

Employee participation at board level

There is no provision for statutory employee participation in the private sector. However, Spain has the best-known European example of extensive employee board-level participation in the Mondragón co-operative in the Basque country. Some 100 enterprises employing 25,000 employees have a sophisticated scheme of employee co-ownership which is centred on employee integration into the co-operatives' management structure. However, it is not typical of the rest of industry, where board participation is very rare.

The EU works council directive

The EU works council directive has generated little interest in Spain. Only a handful of companies have sufficient employees in other EU countries to qualify.

Collective bargaining

During the Franco regime, from 1939 to 1975, the determination of pay and employment conditions was highly centralised and rigidly controlled. Under the National Syndicalist State all employees and employers were obliged to belong to the one government-controlled national corporate organisation, *Movimiento nacional*. Industry, agriculture and services were subdivided into a number of economic sectors. Each sector had its basic conditions of employment prescribed under the labour ordinance (*ordenanza laboral*) for that sector. Pay at company level was determined by a joint employer–employee committee (*jurado de empresa*). A semblance of 'bargaining' was therefore provided, but in practice government intervention dictated compulsory arbitration settlements (*laudos*) in cases of disagreement. There were, of course, no free trade unions, although the CC.OO especially had substantially infiltrated the bargaining mechanism by the early 1970s.

During the transition to democracy, collective bargaining evolved away from government intervention. The present pattern of collective bargaining has been shaped by a mixture of laws, national framework agreements and collective agreements. Legislation, both international and national, has been used to provide a broad framework under the conditions of democracy.

In April 1977 Spain ratified two ILO conventions – No. 87, on the right of association of workers and employers, and No. 98, on union guarantees. On the same date Spain also ratified the International Treaty on Civil and Political Rights and the International Treaty on Economic, Social and Cultural Rights. In 1980 Spain signed the European Social Charter.

In 1977 the law on freedom of association allowed the formation of free trade unions and employers' associations, which could then engage in collective bargaining. The 1978 constitution (article 28) enshrined the principle of trade union rights. The 1980 Workers' Statute legislated on a wide range of employment conditions, including pay, working time, workers' representation and forms of contract, and set out detailed arrangements for the manner in which collective bargaining should be carried on.

The reform of the Workers' Statute in 1994 boosted the scope and importance of collective bargaining in several ways. Collective bargaining may now have more impact on pay structures, overtime and night-work rates, the extent to which fixed-term contracts should be utilised in a company or sector, job classification and relocation, and working time, among other matters. In many cases statute law formerly decreed fixed procedures. The new legislation also affects the status of collective agreements, which are no longer legally binding after expiry. Statute law allows provincial or sectoral agreements to establish exclusion clauses for firms in economic difficulties unable to meet pay demands. Separate bargaining in autonomous regions, especially Catalonia and the Basque provinces, and possibly Galicia, where there are 'most representative' regional unions, is now more freely permitted, leading to the possibility, for example, that in the Basque country there may be a different sectoral agreement to that agreed nationally for the whole of Spain.

It is possible to extend existing collective agreements in areas or sectors where employees have no suitable agreement of their own. On average 15 agreements per year are extended to groups which agree to adopt one, or for whom the Ministry of Labour agrees to extend an agreement 'where bargaining is especially difficult, or where there are very special economic and social circumstances'.

It is normal for collective agreements at all levels to restate in their agreed provisions elements which are determined by statute, thereby fixing a statutory element current at the time of the agreement as binding until the termination of the agreement.

Levels of bargaining

Notwithstanding the recent reforms, agreements are concluded at one of three levels: undertaking, province or national. In 1994 there were 2,890 agreements reached at undertaking level, covering 842,500 employees, while 1,191 agreements at other levels covered 5,584,000 employees. Formal overall coverage by collective agreements is high, at around 70 per cent, attributable to the binding effect of industry-level agreements. Despite aspirations to decentralise bargaining, the incidence of single-employer bargaining actually fell during the 1980s, from 16 per cent to 14 per cent.

Recent surveys suggest that coverage of employees varies greatly between sectors, ranging from 42 per cent in services to 95 per cent in industry. Within a sector, too, there may be wide variation: in the service sector, the largest employment sector, coverage of employees ranges from 89 per cent in financial services to 48 per cent in retailing and a mere 3 per cent in repairs and maintenance. It is estimated that some 3–4 per cent of employees in large companies are outside collective bargaining. This exempt group, largely comprising such specialised service activities as IT, marketing, public relations and advertising, account for 6.3 per cent of the national wage bill, and on average earn some 30 per cent more than employees covered by collective agreements. Executive personnel are excluded by statute from collective agreements.

The pay round and negotiating features

Most collective agreements last for one calendar year; a small number last for two years, and a tiny minority for three. Bargaining takes place in a bargaining committee which is limited to a maximum of 12 on each side, though at provincial or national level it may rise to 15. Many large companies are represented by labour lawyers in their bargaining sessions at company level, while the employees are represented by nominated members of the works council. Decisions are reached by a simple majority on each side. The employee side usually registers its intention to negotiate some time between October and December; formal notice must be given to the Ministry of Labour. Although agreements are usually dated from 1 January, in practice bargaining often does not start until February, when the official retail price index for the past year and the official inflation forecast for the new year will be known. Negotiations may go on for a couple of months; agreements become valid when they are published in the government official gazette, the *Boletín oficial del estado*, perhaps by June or later.

It is common to link the agreed pay rise with forecast inflation by means of a 'safeguard' clause, triggering a further rise if inflation rises above a forecast fig-ure. In mid-1995, for example, 70 per cent of agreements concluded for the year contained such a clause. Negotiators take their forecast inflation rates from a variety of sources, notably the government, the OECD, the EU and the Banco de Bilbao y Vizcaya (BBV), sometimes using an average of several of the figures. It is less common now than it was in recent years for the employers' CEOE and the major trade unions to issue guideline bands for negotiators, typically pitched above the forecast inflation rate by the unions and at the forecast rate by the employers.

Minor disputes about the application of a collective agreement are usually dealt with by a joint committee of representatives of both sides, or by the works council. More serious matters of dispute are handled by the courts. The govern-ment-run Mediation Arbitration and Conciliation Service (SMAC) was intended to deal with such disputes, but it has come almost exclusively to handle disagree-ments relating to individual dismissals.

For most of the 1980s, and the early 1990s, employers and union confedera-tions followed a regular annual procedure of recommending target bands for pay increases to be negotiated during the coming bargaining round. Typically the unions would propose a few percentage points above forecast inflation, and the employers approximately the forecast inflation rate. Such recommendations would be issued as circulars from the confederation executives to member feder-ations responsible for bargaining. The practice has diminished in recent years, but the CEOE has suggested taking Europe-wide inflation rates as a model, with the aim of cutting increases in costs to the level of the country's European com-petitors.

Recent trends

The most significant trend in collective bargaining has been the sheer growth in the number of agreements and the number of employees covered. In 1977, when modern democratic labour relations began, there were a total of 1,349 agree-ments covering 2,876,400 employees, which rose to a peak in 1992 with 5,010 agreements covering 7,921,900 employees. Since then there has been a down-ward trend in the number covered, largely because of the recession. In the same period, annual agreed pay rises fell from 25 per cent in 1977 to 3.4 per cent in 1994, and agreed annual working time fell from 1,877 hours to 1,760 hours. In recent years there has been a tendency to include clauses banning overtime work (44 per cent of sectoral agreements), to sustain manning levels (61 per cent of agreements), to curb temporary employment contracts (41 per cent of agree-ments) and to ensure continuing training (72 per cent of agreements). A small but significant number of agreements in 1994/95 traded job protection for pay cuts – a new feature of bargaining.

Agreed provisions

Pay agreements   The contents of collective agreements have a fairly standard structure. There may well be a difference between the few national sectoral agreements where an effort has been made to streamline the content and consolidate pay and benefit arrangements, and those which are still shaped by long-standing ordinances which allow a multiplicity of separate payments. However, most collective agreements share a common format.

To take the chemicals national sectoral agreement as a model modern agreement, the following components are negotiated:

- the organisation of work and systems
- employment contracts
- job classification
- regrading and multi-skilling
- recruitment
- promotion
- relocation
- pay policy, including the eight basic scales for the sector
- increments
- additional payments
- length of service
- absenteeism policy
- sick pay
- pay review clause
- bonuses
- incentives
- working time
- overtime
- vacations
- paid and unpaid leave
- expenses
- disciplinary procedures
- health and safety
- environmental policy
- canteens
- company shop
- workwear
- union and works council functions
- training
- shift work
- steering committee functions
- voluntary dispute resolution procedures.

Typically, in annual bargaining, of the above features only employment contracts, pay policy and working time would be the subject of negotiation each year. Other aspects may be dealt with periodically.

Basic pay   Spain has a statutory minimum wage, set by decree each year when the government considers inflation and consults the unions and employers' organisations. The wage is designed to be a subsistence one. In 1995 the minimum pay levels stood at Pta 877,800 per annum (£4,640) for 18 year olds (Pta 580,020 (£3,070) for 17 year olds).

Legislation defines pay as benefits in cash or kind for contractual working time, whatever the form of payment, including paid rest time. The reforms to the Workers' Statute also, for the first time, specifically charge collective bargaining with the responsibility for establishing an employee's pay as a function of his individual work. No more than 30 per cent of basic pay may be in kind (except for domestic servants, for whom it may rise to 45 per cent). For tax purposes, all remuneration except 'justifiable expenses' is considered as pay, including free meals, free train travel, coal, gas and electricity. Pay must be paid at least monthly, and employees have the right to receive 10 per cent interest on delayed payments.

The employer is required to deduct social security contributions, and legislation allows collective agreements to make provision for union dues to be deducted at source. Statute law requires employees to be paid at the level appropriate to the job classification they were allocated on recruitment. If required to do work of a lower level, they must continue to receive the higher level of pay. Equally, if required to do work of a higher level than their classification, they may appeal to be promoted after no more than six months' work in a 12 month period, or eight months in a 24 month period.

An employee's basic pay is established by reference to a job classification which carries with it a monthly or annual salary. Many job classifications are very long-established and complex, and the reforms to the Workers' Statute charged collective bargaining with establishing modern appropriate grade structures based on the professional skills, qualifications and working requirements of employees. This intended modernisation of grades is proving slow to achieve.

Social security classifications, used to establish bands for contribution purposes, distinguish 12 classifications of employee, ranging from first- and second-year apprentices at the lowest level, through clerical staff at level 6, to qualified engineers and graduates at the highest level. A great variety of grade structures are to be found in collective agreements, ranging from intricate multi-layered structures in the older agreements to the simple eight-grade structure of the chemicals national sectoral agreement, which is considered a model modern pattern.

A typical company's total pay bill consists of a number of elements:

● basic pay

- the *plus de convenio*, a collective agreement ratification supplement which can often amount to more than basic pay
- two extra statutory monthly payments in July and December
- increments
- bonuses
- incentive payments
- allowances of various kinds
- overtime
- profit-sharing
- commission
- expenses
- awards
- scholarships
- loans
- canteen and housing subsidies
- other social benefits.

Additional payments can often more than double 'basic pay'.

Bonuses and supplements The *plus de convenio* was traditionally a sweetener for signing a collective agreement. It has become consolidated into many agreements, and some modern agreements have moved to abolish it as a separate factor, but in some large company agreements it may still appear as a larger payment than basic pay. Statute law requires employers to make two extra monthly payments to employees, one at Christmas and the other at a time to be collectively agreed (usually July). Therefore, in practice, an employee's annual salary is divided into 14 payments, two of which are made in July and December. Several agreements take this further, and make up to 16 payments in total, spreading them through the year. The trend, though, is for these to be reduced and consolidated, as allowed by collective agreement, although the trend is not a very marked one.

Length-of-service increments are not statutory, and since 1994 there have been no restrictions on the proportion of an employee's pay they may represent. Typically, collective agreements establish service increments of around 5 per cent of basic pay for every three years' service, and 6 per cent for every four years. Long-service awards are fairly common in collective agreements. A typical award would be two to four months' pay after 25 or 40 years' service.

Punctuality and attendance supplements are fairly common in longer-established agreements, though newer ones tend to consolidate them. Where they still exist, they currently set a typical rate of some Pta 2,000 (£11) monthly. Special job supplements are not common, but can be important where particularly arduous work is involved. They can add 10 per cent to basic pay. Dangerous and noxious work supplements, on the other hand, are common, and can add between 10 per cent and 30 per cent on to basic pay in certain conditions. Shift-work supplements are common, and can add 10 per cent to basic pay, while 'on call' supplements are uncommon but add between 10 per cent and 30 per cent to basic pay.

Responsibility supplements are widely paid to employees with particular responsibilities, such as team leaders.

Social benefits are a widespread feature of collective agreements. They include housing and personal loans at favourable rates, life and accident insurance and survivor's benefit, family supplements for disabled children in lower-income families, children's educational allowance, benefit payments on the birth of a child or on marriage, a travel-to-work allowance, subsidised canteen payments and in rare cases a creche allowance.

Regional variation　　There is considerable variation in agreed regional pay rates. The highest-earning regions, such as the Basque country or Madrid, pay on average over 50 per cent more than the lowest-earning regions such as Murcia. Until the reforms of the Workers' Statute in 1994, however, it was difficult for major employers to take advantage of the difference by locating in lower-paying regions, since they were likely to be bound by the agreed rates of a national sectoral agreement. However, the reforms introduced an exclusion clause by which a company demonstrably unable to meet a nationally agreed pay award is relieved of the obligation to pay. This may have some effect on location.

Financial participation　　There has long been a component of many pay structures labelled 'profit-sharing' (*participación en beneficios*), but in practice the term has often been synonymous with 'fifteenth-month payment', not really related to profits. Indeed, loss-making companies were frequently seen to be making such payments as part of the standard collectively agreed pay package.

Employee share placement schemes have recently begun to emerge. Banks appear to be leading the way, and BBV has linked employee share participation in 1 per cent of the bank's capital with a targeted 20 per cent turnover increase and profits rise. A new development which is augmenting this trend is the privatisation of public-sector companies. Endesa has placed 1 per cent of its capital with the employees, and Repsol has done the same by making cheap loans available to them.

Framework agreements　　In the period 1980–6, as discussed earlier, a series of national framework agreements were concluded, covering all sectors, and detailing such aspects as annual working time, overtime limits, etc. The recent history of industry-level framework agreements has been obscured by the continuing existence of the labour ordinances also mentioned earlier. Dating in some cases back to the 1940s, these detailed codes established all aspects of working conditions for 38 sectors of the economy. While democratic labour relations and the Workers' Statute established a pattern of free collective bargaining to replace them, only a few sectors have substituted sector-wide agreements; the rest were due to do so by the end of 1995.

The sectors which already have framework agreements to replace the old labour ordinances are: chemicals, engineering workshops, insurance, banking, paper and board, construction, footwear, textiles, canned foods and fruit, fisheries, retailing, large stores, metal packaging, tanneries, perfumeries, glass and ceramics.

Working time By statute the maximum working week is 40 hours, which, since the reform of the Workers' Statute, may be averaged over a year. If the working day is more than six hours there must be a 15-minute break, which may or may not be paid, depending on collective agreement. Under-18 year olds must have a 30-minute break after four and a half hours' working time. A normal working day must not exceed nine hours' actual working time, unless otherwise agreed collectively, and there must be a minimum 12 hours' break between one working day and the next. Under-18s must have at least two continuous rest days per week. Effective working time does not include changing clothing, travel or clocking on. In cases of split-day working, which is still widespread, there must be a minimum one hour's break between working periods.

Most collective agreements now define working time in terms of annual hours. According to the Ministry of Labour the average collectively agreed working year in December 1994 stood at 1,760 hours. Since 1982 the average working year has fallen by 117 hours.

One special feature which distinguishes Spain from most European countries is the persistence of the siesta. Flexitime arrangements are not widespread, but they are often agreed in larger companies, allowing an hour's variation in starting and finishing times.

The reform of the Workers' Statute derogated the previous statutory guarantees on overtime payments. Now overtime hours are to be paid at agreed rates, which shall not be less than normal time rates. In the absence of agreement to the contrary, they can be compensated for by time off in lieu during the next four months. Statute law also limits the amount of overtime which may be worked to 80 hours per employee per annum. Overtime is prohibited to those under 18. Since 1980 collective agreements have consistently carried pledges to limit overtime, in the interests of job creation. In another measure to discourage overtime, social security rates distinguish between 'structural' and other types of overtime, structural overtime rates being half the amount levied for other types of overtime. Employers also have a statutory right to recover working time lost due to *force majeure* at a rate of no more than one hour per day.

Notwithstanding the removal of the statutory higher rate for overtime, collective agreements do still regularly enhance the minimum, by agreeing supplements of typically 75 per cent on normal time, rising to 125 per cent for weekend and holiday overtime.

Industrial conflict

Despite low trade union membership, Spain has been among the most strike-prone countries in Europe – illustrating the capacity of unions to mobilise beyond their immediate members, demonstrated most forcefully in the three general strikes of the last 10 years. According to figures prepared by the UK Employment Department, the average number of days lost through industrial action per thousand workers was 430 between 1988 and 1993, compared with 70 in the UK and 20 in Germany over the same period. The incidence was raised by the general strikes in 1988 and 1992, although in 1993 250 days were lost per thousand employees, compared with the much reduced UK rate of 30 the same year.

Industrial action is regulated by the 1977 Labour Relations Decree (royal decree 17/77), the 1978 constitution and the 1980 Workers' Statute. Statute law establishes that either side may initiate a dispute. Strikes must be notified to both the employer and the labour authorities, with at least five days' notice. The notice must be in writing, must set out the objects of the action, any steps taken to resolve differences, the dates of the proposed action, and the composition of the strike committee. In theory, under the 1977 legislation, which was drawn up in a period of institutional vacuum and mounting labour disturbances, the labour inspectorate may mediate to try and find a solution after receiving notification of strike action, and the government can intervene and propose arbitration. In practice these powers have seldom been used, and the government is generally unwilling to resort to forms of intervention so redolent of the Franco years. In 1994 some 2,085 collective disputes were dealt with by the labour authorities in this way, theoretically affecting come 85,000 companies. However, 73,000 of the companies were in Andalucia and Extremadura, and the procedures were used largely for resolving farm disputes.

The right to strike – and to lock out

The constitution guarantees the right to strike. However, in the absence of a long-promised 'strike law', the principal ruling on what is acceptable is a 1981 Constitutional Tribunal ruling (*sentencia* 11/81). It established that the decision to strike must be an express decision of the workforce. If the strike decision is taken by the works council, at least 75 per cent of its members must be present. If the decision is taken by a ballot of the whole workforce, at least 25 per cent of those eligible to vote must have participated. The decision may be made by the employee representatives, the works council, or established trade unions, or by the workforce in general, provided it is a majority decision. Due notice, as noted above, must be given.

The strike committee must establish the aims of the strike, the measures taken to try to avoid it, and the composition of the strike committee, which may consist of up to 12 members drawn from employees directly involved in the dispute.

Among its duties are co-ordinating essential services to ensure the safety of people and plant, adequate maintenance, and preparations for start-up later. When strikes are declared in the public services, or in other essential services, the government is empowered to order a skeleton service to be maintained but not necessarily to order a return to work.

Occupations of the workplace are unlawful, as are a number of types of strike action, including rolling strikes, strikes to interrupt production in strategic sectors, go-slows and working to rule, or any other form of collective action other than an all-out strike. Political strikes and disproportionately disruptive strikes are also excluded. Secondary action is permitted. Striking employees may not be replaced by other employees, and can publicise the strike and collect funds, but they are not allowed to intimidate non-strikers. Strike action suspends the employment contract but does not provide grounds for terminating it.

Lockouts by the employer are permissible, provided there is a threat of violence or a material disuption, an illegal occupation or an unlawful disturbance of work. The employer must notify the labour authorities. The lockout effectively suspends the employment contract, with no benefits for the employee.

There are no indications that 'peace obligations' clauses will be considered by collective negotiators; such clauses would probably be unconstitutional.

Conciliation and arbitration

There has been general disillusion with the functioning of SMAC and its predecessor, IMAC, and general discontent with the failure to develop effective national conciliation machinery. These bodies have served mostly to facilitate individual dismissal compensation. At the regional level the Basque government assisted the Basque employers' confederations and unions in establishing voluntary arbitration and conciliation mechanisms in 1984; these are considered to have worked well, and a decade later the Catalan employers' confederation concluded a similar arrangement with the unions in Catalonia.

Given these circumstances, one of the government's objectives in the reforms of the Workers' Statute in 1994 was to encourage collective negotiators to establish and develop their own procedures for resolving disputes. Article 85 of the reformed Workers' Statute specifically charges the social partners with establishing arbitration procedures which themselves would have the force of law if collectively agreed. It is too early yet to say how far these provisions will expand voluntary arbitration procedures; however, collective agreements do establish certain mechanisms already.

Some national sectoral agreements establish very detailed mechanisms, some none at all, and some company agreements establish the working of a joint committee (*comité paritario*) to oversee the implementation of the collective agreement. The chemicals national sectoral agreement provides a model: it establishes a national bipartite committee, consisting of six representatives from the UGT and CC.OO unions and six representatives from the employers' federation

FEIQUE, to adjudicate on disputes relating to the application of the collective agreement submitted to it. It may also devolve dispute resolution to decentralised mixed committees in five of the regions. Ordinary disputes are to be resolved within 15 days and extraordinary disputes within 72 hours. The agreement pledges that the joint committee will have full arbitration, conciliation and mediation powers, that it can be convened by either side, that it will receive regular wide-ranging social and economic reports on all matters affecting employment in the sector, and that it will present annual reports. The agreement also establishes detailed procedures for voluntary dispute resolution. Some company agreements establish brief procedures for dealing with disputes.

Organisations

Ministerio de Trabajo y Seguridad Social
(Ministry of Labour and Social Security)
Agustín de Bethencourt 4, Madrid
Tel. + 341 553 6278
Fax + 341 533 2996

Instituto Nacional de Empleo (INEM)
Condesa de Venadito 9, Madrid
Tel. + 341 585 9888
Fax + 341 268 3981

Instituto Nacional de Seguridad Social
(INSS)
Padre Damian 4, Madrid
Tel. + 341 564 9023
Fax + 341 564 7822

Dirección General de Inspección de
Trabajo y Seguridad (the labour
inspectorate)
Agustín de Bethencourt 4, Madrid
Tel. + 341 553 6000

Unión General de Trabajadores (UGT)
Hortaleza 88, Madrid
Tel. + 341 308 3333

Comisiones Obreras (CC.OO)
Fernández de la Hoz 6, 28010 Madrid
Tel. + 341 419 5454

Unión Sindical Obrera (USO)
Príncipe de Vergara 13, 7º, 28001 Madrid
Tel. + 341 262 4040

Confederación General de Trabajo (CGT)
Sagunto 15, 28010 Madrid
Tel. + 341 447 5769

Confederación Sindical Euzko Laguillen
Alkatasuna–Solidaridad de Trabajadores
Vascos (ELA–STV)
Euskalduna 11, 1º, 48008 Bilbao
Tel. + 344 444 2504

Confederación Española de
Organizaciones Empresariales, CEOE
(Confederation of Spanish Employers)
Diego de León 50, 28006 Madrid
Tel. + 341 563 9641
Fax + 341 262 8023

Confederación Española de Pequeñas y
Medianas Empresas (CEPYME)
Diego de León 50, 28006 Madrid
Tel. + 341 261 6757

Associación Española de Directores de
Personal (AEDIPE)
Moreto 10, Madrid
Tel. + 341 468 2217
AEDIPE is Spain's largest personnel
management association and is a member
of the European Association of Personnel
Management. President: Pedro Blásquez.

Main sources

JORDANA, JACINTA. 'Trade union membership in Spain (1977–1994)', *Labour Studies Working Paper No. 2*. University of Warwick, Centre for Comparative Labour Studies, 1995

MARTINEZ LUCIO, MIGUEL. 'Spain: constructing institutions and actors in a context of change', in Anthony Ferner and Richard Hyman (eds), *Industrial Relations in the New Europe*. Oxford, 1992

RIGBY, MIKE, and LAWLOR, TERESA. 'Spanish trade unions, 1986–1994: life after national agreements', in *Industrial Relations Journal*. Vol. 25, 4, 1994

Ministerio de Trabajo y Seguridad Social, *Boletín de Estadísticas Laborales*, various issues

Ministerio de Trabajo y Seguridad Social, *Guía Laboral*, various issues (annual review of labour legislation)

LEFEBVRE, EDERSA-FRANCIS. *Memento práctico, Social*. Lefebvre, Madrid, 1992

Ministerio de Economía y Hacienda, *La negociación colectiva en las grandes empresas*, various years (annual survey of collective bargaining in large companies)

VIDAL SORIA, J. *Código de las Leyes Laborales*. BOE, Madrid, 1991

Industry collective agreements, published in *Boletín Oficial del Estado* (Official Gazette)

12

Sweden

The development and transformation of the Swedish system of industrial relations has traditionally been the subject of much outside interest, in part because of its exemplary character in the past as offering one of the institutional preconditions of a third way between communism and capitalism, and in part because of the convulsions in the system since the early 1980s.

Swedish industrial relations were traditionally characterised by centralised and co-ordinated collective bargaining, rather than legislation, on pay and labour market conditions, steadily growing trade union influence, an active state labour market policy and – with the exception of historic set-piece confrontations – a relatively low level of industrial disputes in the post-war period. These generally stable conditions provided a solid platform for the growth of such large Swedish companies as Volvo, SKF, Ericsson and Electrolux.

However, this constellation of features, which did not reach full flower until the mid-1950s, began to unravel in the late 1960s. A strong grass-roots trade union movement organising around qualitative issues in the late 1960s and early 1970s contributed to a union push for legislative intervention in fields such as the working environment and industrial democracy. This resulted in many of the collective agreements on employment conditions – with the notable exception of pay – being replaced by a raft of legislation which was passed in the 1970s. The period in particular saw the introduction of two of the most important pieces of labour market legislation – the Co-determination at Work Act, and Security of Employment Act. The employers responded by mounting negotiated and political opposition to the legislation, especially in the fields of co-determination and 'wage-earner funds', which were beginning to place large sections of industry under employee control.

Full employment was also being translated into problems both of containing rising wage costs and difficulties in recruitment of skilled workers: both led the employers to reappraise their commitment to centralised bargaining.

Since the early 1980s pay bargaining has exhibited a steady movement towards decentralisation (from national to industry-level deals), with increasing scope for pay-setting at company level. There was one major departure from this trend with the adoption of a central incomes policy in the early 1990s, in the face of the inability of employers and the main unions to contain a burgeoning wage–price spiral. However, the – probably temporary – return to centralised pay-setting coincided with an enhancement of management prerogatives over pay issues at workplace level.

None the less, negotiation remains a major feature of employment regulation, with collective agreements covering four-fifths of the labour force. And despite the increase in employment legislation, one notable feature of much Swedish labour law is that it is 'semi-dispositive', that is, many legal provisions may be departed from provided it is by collective – but not individual – agreement, affording continuing scope for employment issues to be governed by agreement.

The main players

Trade unions and employer organisations have traditionally been strong and centralised, with the main impetus to consolidation among employers coming from their need to confront a powerful union movement in the early years of this century. Subsequent consensus has been rooted in earlier trials of strength between the two sides, Sweden being one of the few countries in Europe (like Germany) with a tradition of lockouts in response to strikes.

Freedom of association for employees – and employers – is currently guaranteed by the Co-determination at Work Act 1976 (*Medbestämmandelagen*).

Trade unions

Workers began to form trade unions in the mid-nineteenth century, but organised labour as a potential social force only really emerged when the industrial revolution took off in the 1870s and 1880s. The first national trade unions were formed in the 1880s, mostly on craft lines. In 1898 a number of unions joined forces to establish a central organisation, the Landsorganisationen i Sverige (LO), the Swedish Trade Union Confederation, which is still the main central union organisation.

Trade union density, in common with other Nordic countries, is high, and, as with other Nordic countries, high membership is rooted both in the sustained role of collective bargaining in employment regulation and concrete services, such as the administration of unemployment benefit, offered by trade unions. Union density peaked at around 85 per cent in the mid-1980s, and has since declined to just over 80 per cent. Commentators ascribe the fall to a number of parallel processes. First, the erosion of the 'Swedish model' during the 1980s has weakened the influence of traditional pro-union values, such as a commitment to social solidarity and collective resolution of employment and pay issues. Second, the very high levels of employment during the phase of economic overheating up to the onset of recession in 1991, combined with greater scope for individual pay-setting, may have diminished the attraction of union membership to employees most in demand by employers. New management approaches, encouraged by the greater decentralisation of pay from the early 1980s, may also have contributed to some weakening of union ties.

The LO, the largest union confederation, is overwhelmingly blue-collar in nature. It has 21 nationwide member unions, with 900 regional and about 10,000 local branches. Together these have roughly 2.2 million members, or almost 85 per cent of blue-collar workers. Two of the largest unions in the LO have exclusively public-sector membership: the Municipal Workers' Union (Svenska Kommunalarbetareförbundet), with 660,000 members, and the State Employees' Union (Statsanställdas förbund) with 196,000. Of the private-sector unions, by far the largest is the Metalworkers' Union (Svenska Metallindustriarbetareförbundet) with 440,000 members. Other leading unions in the LO are the Commercial Employees' Union (Handelsanställdas förbund) and the Building Workers' Union (Byggnadsarbetareförbundet) with 177,000 and 154,000 members respectively. The LO and its member unions have around Skr 10 billion in strike funds at their disposal.

The main phase of organisation for white-collar workers was in the 1930s, with the expansion and adaption of existing professional organisations independent of the LO. Post-war membership growth was extremely rapid. The present Confederation of Professional Employees (Tjänstemännens Centralorganisation, or TCO) was formed in 1944 as a result of a merger between two white-collar confederations representing private- and public-sector employees.

The TCO, with around 1.3 million members (or 75 per cent of the clerical workforce) in 20 unions, is the main confederation of white-collar employees, with membership more or less evenly divided between the private and public sectors. Its largest constituent trade union is the private-sector Union of Clerical and Technical Employees in Industry (Svenska Industritjänstemannaförbundet, or SIF), with 312,000 members. The two other main member unions are from the public sector: the Teachers' Union (Lärarförbundet), with 202,000 members, and SKTF, the Union of Municipal Employees, with 183,000. The TCO and its member unions have around Skr 4 billion at their disposal in strike funds.

The Swedish Confederation of Professional Associations (Sveriges Akademikers Centralorganisation, or SACO) was formed in 1947, at which time a university degree was a membership requirement – a condition since lifted. SACO has around 385,000 members, compared with some 30,000 just after its foundation, most of whom are employed in the public sector. The largest of its 25 member unions is the 62,000-strong Association of Graduate Engineers (Civilingeniörsförbundet), followed by the National Union of Teachers (Lärarnas Riksförbund), with 56,000 members.

The landscape of union organisation is also characterised by an important phenomenon in the context of collective bargaining – that of negotiating 'cartels' consisting of a number of individual unions which pool resources. The most significant is the white-collar cartel Privattjänstemannakartellen (PTK), established in 1973, which represents some – but not all – TCO and SACO unions. It bargains on behalf of some 580,000 union members – 513,000 from the TCO and 67,000 from SACO – in the private sector. The founding of the PTK marked an important stage in the centralisation and co-ordination of collective bargaining, and created an institution of comparable strength to LO in the blue-collar area with which the central employers (SAF – see below) could negotiate. There is also a corresponding cartel in the public sector.

Trade union workplace rights and functions   As Sweden has no system of separately elected works councils, union workplace organisations, with rights and obligations anchored in the law, are the main form of employee representation. Union organisations in the workplace play a major role in local bargaining, enhanced during the 1980s, in negotiations over workforce reductions, and in exercising rights under co-determination legislation and subsequent accords (see below) as well as handling individual grievances and representing the union organisation itself.

The exact structure of the union workplace organisation varies – large workplaces may have complex structures with many subdivisions, whereas small workplaces may have no formal local union organisation but may be represented in negotiations by an official from the local branch.

The rights of a union representative   The rights of union representatives (*facklig förtroendeman*) are guaranteed by the 1974 Law on Union Representatives (*Förtroendemannalagen*). This applies to any union representatives who can meet three conditions:

- They have been appointed by a trade union with which the company has a collective agreement.
- They are responsible for representing employees on union business.
- The employer has been informed of the appointment and of the representative's specific tasks.

The definition of 'union business' may be fairly broad and may include, among other things: providing employees with information on company matters, undertaking negotiations, involvement in dispute procedures and arrangements under co-determination procedures, and preparations for negotiations, including meetings with individual employees, and exercising rights under the law or collective agreement. In fact almost any union activity with relevance to the workplace can be included, embracing, for example, activities such as participation in courses and at conferences.

'Union representative' may include employee board members, health and safety representatives or members of health and safety committees, shop stewards and study organisers.

However, such activities as courses unrelated to an employee's workplace, political activity and time spent purely on internal union affairs have been deemed not to constitute 'union activity' within the meaning of the act.

Qualification as a union representative under the Act gives an employee certain rights. Union representatives are entitled to reasonable *time off* to perform their duties. The exact extent of this is a matter for local negotiation, and will typically depend on the duties to be performed, the number of employees represented, the type of business activity and the extent to which work may be disrupted.

Representatives have the right to *full pay* whilst carrying out their duties, including overtime payments if an employer decides that negotiations must take place outside normal working hours. They also enjoy wide-ranging protection of employment conditions. Representatives may not be given worse conditions of employment because of their status – indeed, the requirement that employers must let them carry out their functions unhindered means that they may be exempt from certain types of work or transferred to less onerous tasks while receiving the same pay. Representatives are also allowed access to parts of the company other than those in which they work. In the event of redundancies, representatives may be exempt from dismissal if their activities are of 'special importance' to union activity in the company.

If local agreement cannot be reached on any of these matters the union view will customarily prevail until the matter can be finally resolved, although exceptions are made, for example, if the time off would endanger workplace safety or essential public services.

Employers' organisations

The leading employers' organisation is Svenska Arbetsgivareföreningen (SAF). Founded in the wake of a general strike in pursuit of universal suffrage in 1902, it has just over 41,000 private-sector member companies employing almost 1.2 million workers. Although many large concerns are members, over half SAF's membership (57 per cent in 1994) consists of companies employing five or fewer workers. However, large internationally active firms have played a decisive role in moving industrial relations towards a more decentralised model since the early 1980s.

Companies join one of SAF's 36 member federations. Most of these federations have banded together into a number of industry-based groups, which coordinate bargaining in their respective sectors. The largest of these groups is the Manufacturing Industry group, whose member firms employ 265,000 workers. Other large groups are Almega, the general employers' group, with companies employing 260,000 workers, the Commercial Employers' Group, with 192,000, and the Construction Group, with 110,000.

Outside the SAF are a few smaller employer organisations representing banks, publishers and co-operative employers.

Employers in the large public sector are represented by three bodies. The National Agency for Government Employers (Statens Arbetsgivarverk (SAV) represents the national authorities, who have around 312,000 employees. The country's 23 county councils, with 340,000 employees, are represented by the Landstingsförbundet. Lastly the 286 *kommuner* (local authorities), with 725,000 employees, are represented by Svenska Kommunförbundet.

Role in bargaining   Centralised collective bargaining between the SAF and LO constituted the core of employment regulation up to the late 1960s. This was formalised in the 1938 Saltsjöbaden agreement which regulated the conduct of industrial relations and bargaining between the two sides.

Much of the drive towards the centralisation and national co-ordination of bargaining, which emerged in its full form in the mid-1950s, came from the employers as they sought to match union strength and consolidate employer forces, and tie union pay bargaining policies in a phase of full employment into a national framework.

Although the legislation of the 1970s displaced some of these central agreements, some issues continue to be governed by such agreements. Most of the provisions of the Saltsjöbaden agreement were abandoned in 1977 with the introduction of the Co-determination Act. However, the procedural provisions of the agreement concerning the duty to negotiate on disputed issues before any industrial action is taken are still in force. The SAF and PTK still have a central agreement on general conditions of employment and a centrally agreed minimum wage covering white-collar employees represented through the cartel.

There are also central agreements on other issues. One of the most important is the 1982 Development Agreement (*Utvecklingsavtalet* or UVA) concluded between the SAF, LO and PTK. The UVA (discussed in greater detail below) was rooted in the statutory provisions on co-determination introduced in 1976, which required implementation to be via collective agreement. After six years of delay in the private sector, characterised by resistance to the mandatory co-decision-making aspects of the legislation, the UVA registered a number of important concessions to the employers by embracing greater decentralisation in the implementation of the law.

Other examples are SAF–LO–PTK agreements concerning special treatment for workers who have been exposed to asbestos, and on the equal treatment of men and women.

A further important area covered by central bargaining is the plethora of social provisions agreed between the SAF, LO and PTK. These include, for white-collar workers, supplementary pensions, life insurance, industrial injury insurance and medical insurance; for blue-collar workers there is also a fund which finances severance payments. For both blue- and white-collar employees there are collectively agreed and funded bodies which make grants and help with training for those threatened with redundancy. The overall costs of these agreed schemes in 1995 was 6 per cent of gross pay for blue-collar workers and around 7 per cent for white-collar employees.

Consultation at national level

There is no formal tripartite machinery for consultation on economic and legislative matters. However, against a background of permanent Social Democratic government, with close ties to the LO, in the 1950s, 1960s and early 1970s, national-level negotiations between central labour-market confederations such as the LO and SAF were responsible for much of the regulation of the labour market. This picture began to change, firstly with the raft of employment legislation in the 1970s, and secondly with the challenging of the bargaining *status quo* by the employers from the early 1980s.

Until recently unions and employers were also extensively represented on government bodies and commissions, of which the most strategic in the past was the Labour Market Board (Arbetsmarknadstyrelsen). At the height of corporatist involvement these representatives were numbered in thousands. Representation on public bodies was seen by the employers, in particular, as a way of exercising influence over government during the long period of Social Democratic rule. However, in the light of a more friendly political climate – that is, the election of a non-Social Democrat government in 1992 – the SAF withdrew from all such corporatist bodies, with the exception of the Labour Court. Shortly thereafter the LO also announced its intention to withdraw from most government bodies.

The employers are now engaged on a more 'political' strategy of trying to influence government policy by campaigning and participation in informal advisory groups rather than through corporatist arrangements. The success of this strategy may be seen in the decision in 1995 of the newly elected Social Democrat government to appoint an *ad hoc* group of top business leaders to advise them on industrial policy.

Incomes policies

The government began to intervene in pay bargaining in the 1980s in an effort to break emerging wage–price spirals and prevent krona devaluation – intended to kick-start the economy in the early 1980s and transfer resources to the corporate sector – from spilling over into domestic inflation. Incomes policies were usually introduced in conjunction with the central unions and employers, typically offering tax cuts in return for compliance with pay norms. The last direct intervention by the government in collective bargaining was the so-called 'Rehnberg' commission set up by the government in 1990 in an attempt to halt the wage and prices spiral of the late 1980s (see below).

Workplace/enterprise employee representation

As noted above, workplace industrial relations are characterised by the dominance of union representation: there are no separate avenues of representation such as works councils. However, some employee rights are legally guaranteed even where there is no union presence.

Employee representation in the workplace may be divided into three main areas:

- health and safety representatives and committees
- employee board representatives

- the right to information, consultation and, possibly, codetermination under the Co-determination Act and the 'Development Agreement'.

Health and safety representatives and committees

Employees' right to representation in health and safety matters is guaranteed by the 1977 Working Environment Act (*Arbetsmiljölagen*, or AML).

All workplaces with at least five employees must have a *health and safety representative*, who is normally appointed for a three-year period. The law also states that, should circumstances warrant it, workplaces with fewer than five employees may also have a representative. The total number of representatives is decided between the employer and workplace trade unions, taking into account establishment size and working conditions.

Representatives are appointed by workplace trade union organisations. If more than one union is represented in a workplace the relevant unions can decide how to apportion the number of representatives between them. It is usual for a number of reserves to be appointed. Even where the workplace has no trade union, employees are still entitled to appoint representatives. The law states that one of these should be nominated as chief representative, and made responsible for co-ordinating the work of the others.

Irrespective of how representatives are chosen, those responsible for the election have a duty to inform two bodies of the fact; their employer and the Factory Inspectorate, a state body which is part of the National Board of Occupational Safety and Health (Arbetarskyddsstyrelesen) and is responsible for workplace-level policing of the working environment and legislation on working hours. Health and safety representatives have the following tasks:

- representing employees on health and safety issues
- securing a satisfactory working environment
- ensuring that an employer respects the legal requirements
- involvement in the planning of work organisation
- ensuring that employees engaged on dangerous tasks do not work alone.

Employees who regard their work as dangerous have the right to stop work immediately and consult their supervisor or health and safety representative. The representative will then negotiate with the employer; if no action is taken (or if the employer is unavailable) the representative has the right to order the work to be stopped immediately. If negotiations become deadlocked, the representative may inform the Factory Inspectorate.

Health and safety representatives also have the right of access to any documentation which may be relevant to their duties. It may include statistics on accidents, records of industrial injuries reported to the authorities or details of safety checks carried out. Representatives are bound by a duty of confidentiality about such information, but they may consult a member of the executive of the union organisation which elected them, or a health and safety expert from the central union. If either of these is consulted, the official concerned is bound by the same duty of confidentiality as the representative.

Representatives have the right to time off for the performance of their duties without loss of pay or other benefits. It is illegal for representatives to be discriminated against for performing their duties; employers who do so are liable to be fined.

In law, employers and employees have equal responsibility for the training of representatives. Training is usually agreed at company level.

A *health and safety committee* must always be established in workplaces with 50 or more employees. A committee must also be set up in workplaces with fewer than that number should employees request it. Employers may not establish a committee on their own initiative under such circumstances. The committee should meet at least once every three months.

The number of members and the form of the committee are a matter for local negotiation. It is usual for at least one employer representative to be a company manager. Employee representatives who are appointed to cover as many categories of employee as possible do not in theory have to be health and safety representatives, but at least one usually is. The chair and secretary of the committee are appointed by the employer unless it is agreed otherwise.

The duties of health and safety committees are broadly the same as those of representatives. They also cover matters relating to company health care, and education and information on health and safety matters.

If any matter discussed by the committee cannot be resolved satisfactorily, the issue may be passed to the Factory Inspectorate at the request of any committee member.

Board-level representation

The representation of employees on company boards is guaranteed by legislation (*Styreleserepresentationslagen*). The law applies only to private-sector limited companies, commercial associations, banks and insurance companies with at least 25 employees during the previous financial year. If the number should subsequently fall below 25, representatives are allowed to stay on the board for the remainder of their period of office.

When counting employees, all companies within a group are taken into consideration, so that, even if constituent companies each have less than 25 employees, workers will still have the right to nominate representatives to the parent company's board. It also means that if constituent companies within a group have 25 or more employees they are entitled to be represented on the board of their own company as well as on that of the parent.

Apart from this numerical threshold, there are other conditions to be fulfilled – the company must be bound by a collective agreement, and the company union organisation must have expressed a desire to have representatives on the board.

Employees are normally entitled to have two representatives on a board, plus two reserves, even if the board only has two members elected by the annual general meeting; however, if a board has only one AGM-elected member, employees have the right to one representative plus one reserve. Consequently, workers may potentially have as many board members as the shareholders, although the casting vote is held by the chair of the board, who will normally be appointed by the AGM. In companies with 1,000 or more employees workers have the right to appoint three board members plus three reserves.

Employee board members must be employed within the company or group, and are nominated by workplace trade unions. If there is more than one union, there are procedures under the law to establish which union(s) are entitled to representation. For example, if more than 80 per cent of employees are covered by a particular union's collective agreement, that union has the right to appoint all employee board members. However, if another union represents at least 5 per cent of employees, it has the right to nominate one of the reserves. If no union represents more than 80 per cent of the workforce, the two unions with the greatest percentages each appoint one board member and one reserve. If workers have the right to three board members, the largest union appoints two members and reserves and the second largest one member and one reserve. These rules may be changed by local agreement between unions.

The period of office for employee board members and reserves is decided by local unions, but may not exceed four years.

Employee board members are entitled to sufficiently detailed information to take part in the decision-making process. This means that they must receive information in sufficient time, and also that they are entitled to translation facilities if the information is in a foreign language. They are also entitled to time off with pay to attend board meetings. Training for employee board members is usually arranged by trade unions, and may also take place during paid time off.

During board meetings reserve board members have a right to be present and to make contributions – but they have no right to vote under these circumstances. Board members are also entitled to be present and to take part in any discussions in any working parties attached to the board.

Although in other respects employee board members have identical rights to other board members' there is one significant exclusion: they may not be present when the board discusses matters in which the unions' interests may conflict with management's, such as when discussing collective agreements, industrial action and so on. They are also bound to observe secrecy about matters discussed in board meetings.

Employee participation and co-determination

As noted above, Sweden has no system of works councils comparable with those found in a number of other European countries. This was not always the case: under a collective agreement between the SAF and the union confederations TCO and LO works councils did operate between 1946 and 1977, but were never particularly strong. The unions withdrew from the agreement in the late 1970s as part of a strategy designed to get employers to sign co-determination agreements after the passing of the 1976 Co-determination Act (*Medbestämmandelagen*, usually shortened to MBL).

Although many employment issues have traditionally been regulated via collective agreement, employee representation and participation rights in the workplace are secured through the 1976 Co-determination Act, which came into force in 1977, and which reflected the labour movement's desire to push for legislative measures during the 1970s. The act applies to all workplaces where one or more union members are employed. The act's main concern is to ensure employees' influence on company decision-making, although it also governs other issues such as rights of association and rules concerning mediation and conciliation in disputes.

The act gives all unions and employers or employers' organisations a general right to negotiate – but not necessarily to come to agreement – on any question affecting the employment relationship. In particular, employers are obliged to consult local unions before implementing decisions which involve major changes, such as transfers of undertakings or redundancies, which affect either employees in general or an individual employee. For other, less important, matters unions have the right to demand consultation. If agreement cannot be reached at a local level, the matter can be referred to discussion at national level. Employers may be required to pay damages if they fail in their duty of consultation.

The most important effect of this system is that employers are obliged to wait until negotiations have finished before taking any planned action. Although the statute literally refers to 'co-determination at work', in the final analysis employers retain the right to make the final decision, without an employee veto, provided they have carried out their duty of consultation.

The act also obliges employers to provide unions with information. They are expected to provide information on the production and financial situation of the business, together with personnel policy guidelines. Furthermore, unions have the right to examine (and copy) on request any document – for example, accounts and reports – which they need to look after the interests of their members. Employers are also obliged to assist unions in analysing such documents.

In the case of employer–employee disagreements, the law distinguishes between conflicts of right, involving differences in the interpretation of collective agreements, and conflicts of interest, involving matters not governed by collective agreement. In the case of the former, since industrial action is illegal while an agreement is in force (see below), conflicts must be settled by local and/or central negotiations, or ultimately by reference to the Labour Court. The 1976 act regulates whose view should prevail before final resolution of the issue. In the case of disputes over co-determination and an individual's obligation to work, priority is given to the union interpretation: in the case of disputes over pay, priority is given to the employer's point of view.

The provisions of the 1976 act have also been supplemented for the private sector by an important national agreement concluded between the SAF, LO and PTK, the 1982 'Development Agreement' (*Utvecklingsavtalet*, shortened to UVA) or, more fully, the Agreement on Efficiency and Participation. The agreement has been viewed as marking a retreat by the trade unions from the more ambitious co-determination goals of the 1970s and an acceptance of corporate objectives in the conduct of employee participation. It makes a number of provisions, for example, subject to the overriding goals of 'developing and improving the efficiency of the enterprise . . . [and] safeguarding employment'. The UVA is more a set of broad guidelines than specific prescription, and is based on the principle that each company should develop employee participation systems suited to its needs.

At the same time, the conclusion of the UVA enabled the central unions to maintain some influence over developments and initiatives at workplace level during periods of rapid innovation in managerial approaches. The vehicles for participation may be either negotiations or joint bodies set up to implement specific policies or to ensure longer-term partnership at workplace and enterprise level. The following main areas are covered:

Work organisation   The main thrust of the agreement's provisions in this area is that 'an employee should be given the opportunity to contribute to the planning of his own work' and that work should be organised in a 'varied and stimulating' way.

Technical developments   Technical changes 'involving major changes for employees' should be carried out with trade union involvement. Stress is also placed on an employer's duty to inform employees of the rationale for, and consequences of, the introduction of new technology and the need for employee training.

Information on the company's financial situation   The agreement provides for the disclosure to workplace trade unions of information on the company's financial/economic situation, planning and budgeting. This is meant to 'enable unions to participate at an early stage with ideas and proposals'.

Right to hold union meetings in working hours   The UVA gives union members the right to five hours' annually paid time, during working hours, to attend union meetings. However, if meetings held in normal working hours would prove disruptive to production, meetings may be held at other times – but, in that case, overtime rates are payable. Any subject which 'touches upon employer–employee relationships or is otherwise connected with union activity in the company' may be discussed.

Employee consultants   In companies with over 50 employees, in the case of questions 'which have special importance for the company's economic situation or for employment', unions have the right to use the services of an employee consultant, who may be (but does not have to be) an employee of the company. If outside consultants are used, they are usually accountants. Consultants are used to help unions analyse a particular situation, but may not conduct negotiations on their behalf, and are paid for by the employer.

The EU works council directive

At the time of writing, implementation of the Directive on European Works Councils could be seen to have followed a typically Swedish pattern. After meetings between trade unions, employers' organisations and the Ministry of Labour, attempts were to be made to introduce the directive's provisions via collective bargaining. However, the Ministry is prepared to take the legislative route should bargaining fail.

Given the extensive rights to consultation and negotiation already available to unions, Swedish employers are perhaps more amenable to the process than those in some other countries. Indeed, as with the various corporatist approaches of the past, consultation is seen as having a positive role to play in keeping unions in touch with economic and corporate realities.

For a small country, Sweden is the location of the headquarters of a large number of multinational companies, and around 20 companies are expected to be covered by the directive. Companies such as Ericsson, Volvo and Electrolux have moved swiftly to establish arrangements by voluntary agreement. One Swedish multinational – the ball-bearing manufacturer SKF – has for some years had the only known example of a world works council, with representatives from as far afield as Malaysia and Argentina as well as from its European subsidiaries.

Collective bargaining

Coverage by collective agreements is high, reflecting the historic role of negotiation in employment regulation and the organisational strength of the trade unions during the formative phases of industrialisation. Some 85 per cent of the workforce are covered by collective agreements, broadly corresponding to the level of union membership. There are no mechanisms for extending collective agreements to non-signatory companies.

From the 1950s until 1983 the collective bargaining system was highly centralised. There was a remarkable degree of co-ordination in bargaining, with public- and private-sector employees belonging to the same national confederations, and blue- and white-collar organisations joining forces to bargain together on many issues other than pay. Pay was set by the so-called 'three-stage rocket' system, with central, sectoral and local negotiations.

Centralised bargaining was seen by the LO as essential to its solidaristic wage policy, which it has not yet entirely abandoned. The policy consists of two elements: first, the principle of increasing pay for the lowest-paid employees by compressing differentials; and, second, the pursuit of the same level of pay for work of equal value throughout the economy, regardless of the productivity or profitability of any given sector – with the implication that industries which could not afford to match rates would either have to raise productivity or contract down to the most efficient producers (or in some cases, disappear). A further implication was that highly productive industries or firms would have to pay out in increases agreed centrally less than they could afford: this was useful for the exporting sector, and created some scope for wage flexibility, but also generated the possibility of wage drift, which, in turn, was brought under a degree of central negotiated control.

The LO's policy, pursued since the 1950s, has had a great influence on pay determination, with wage agreements geared to levelling out what the confederation has described as 'unfair wage disparities'. The policy was also adopted by the TCO, the main white-collar union confederation, but with the qualification that it should not erode differentials between blue- and white-collar employees: SACO, representing professional employees, has never subscribed to it. By the early 1980s the traditional dominance of the LO over other union confederations gave way to greater pluralism in approaches with the growth of unions representing non-manual and public-sector workers.

It is often forgotten, particularly in view of its recent strenuous attempts to decentralise bargaining, that for many years the SAF was also in favour of this policy; in fact, SAF was the main driving force behind the centralisation of the bargaining system. This was seen as necessary because of the lack of co-ordination between its member organisations.

The system began to show serious strains in the early 1980s, and initially took the form of tension between the union confederations, which the employers – convinced of the need for a more decentralised approach – were able to use. The two main issues were, firstly, the tension between blue- and white-collar unions over the erosion of differentials as a result of solidaristic bargaining and, secondly, the difficulty of urging wage restraint on the more militant unions, often with a skilled membership. This meshed with the employers' concern over labour costs and a desire for more local flexibility, leading to the first crack in the system, in 1983, when the engineering employers' federation VF and the metalworking union Metall broke away to sign an industry agreement. Since then the degree of decentralisation in collective bargaining has fluctuated – sometimes from year to year – and has to some extent reflected differing employer priorities. Whilst the export sector, which has benefited from a number of krona devaluations, has argued for decentralisation, the domestic sector, which now employs the bulk of the labour force, has tended to favour some form of centrally set norm.

The 1980s also saw an increasing tendency to government intervention in wage bargaining, mainly because of the weakening of the LO–SAF consensus and the solidaristic wage policy, which had been an alternative to a government incomes policy. This tendency reached a high point in 1990, when the government set up the 'Rehnberg Commission', with a mediator presiding over employer and union representatives, in an attempt to find a consensual solution to the wage–price spiral. The commission was largely successful in dramatically cutting agreed pay rises during the 1991 bargaining round. This was achieved by restricting pay negotiations to the sectoral level and granting employers a monopoly of wage-setting at local level.

In the two subsequent rounds (1993 and 1995) collective bargaining on pay has been at industry and local level. This is mainly because of SAF's decision, in 1990, to withdraw entirely from central bargaining on pay and conditions, although the federation retains a co-ordinating role during bargaining rounds. SAF's long-term ambition is to have bargaining devolved completely to company level, and ultimately to employee level, but the fulfilment of this wish would seem to be a long way off. This is not least because of the fact that some employers – particularly the large number of small firms among SAF's membership – feel that such arrangements would be too cumbersome.

The LO has been effectively forced to accept industry-level bargaining by the removal of its central negotiating partner. Although it continues to seek to co-ordinate bargaining by member unions, this proved difficult in the 1995 bargaining round. The dual nature of the economic recovery – burgeoning growth in the export sector and relatively stagnant demand in the domestic market – put renewed strains on the 'solidaristic' pay policy, and member unions were unable to agree a unified set of demands before the 1995 round. In particular, the fact that negotiations still taking place for public-sector workers are likely to yield wage rises well below those in private-sector settlements will only serve to increase internal tensions in the LO; its largest member union by some margin is Kommunal, the municipal workers' union.

Types of agreement

The 1976 Co-determination Act defines a collective agreement as 'an agreement in writing between an employer or employers' organisation and a trade union on the terms of employment of employees or otherwise on the relations between employer and employee'. A collective agreement which has been signed by an employers' organisation or trade union becomes binding on all that organisation's members. In addition, the SAF, LO and PTK have agreed that the provisions of industry-level agreements should be extended to all employees in SAF member companies, whether or not they are union members. There is, however, no procedure through which a collective agreement can be declared binding on non-signatory parties.

There are five different types of collective agreement which may be concluded. These are:

Main agreements   The main surviving example of this type of agreement is the 1982 Development Agreement (see above). However, they were common before the widespread programme of labour market legislation undertaken during the 1970s. The most famous such pact was the 1938 Saltsjöbaden agreement between the SAF and LO regulating the procedures of collective bargaining and matters of co-operation. Most agreements of this type have now been abandoned, although some survive, at least in part. For example, the provisions of the Saltsjöbaden agreement setting out negotiating procedures for the settlement of disputes, and measures to avoid disputes in essential public services, are still in force. Similarly, the negotiating rules in the SAF–PTK central agreement are still in force, although the rest of its provisions were abandoned in 1977.

Central (or framework) agreements   These are signed by the national organisations, and deal with both pay and terms and conditions of employment. They lay down the overall scope for increases in pay and labour costs over the period of the agreement, taking into account the country's general economic performance.

The employers' refusal to take part in centralised bargaining has made this type of agreement virtually redundant as far as pay is concerned. However, central agreements on other matters continue in force.

Industry-level agreements   These are agreements signed between a trade union and an employers' federation at industry level. This is currently the highest level at which binding pay agreements are signed.

Local agreements   These are agreements signed by an individual employer and a trade union branch at company or plant level. They may cover pay, co-determination or terms and conditions, although most companies tend to follow industry-level agreements in the latter case.

Since many industry-level pay agreements set only minima, exact rates of pay depend upon local agreements – highlighting the substantial degree of effective devolution of regulation within the system. Many questions regarding working hours – such as shift patterns, working time distribution, and the introduction of flexible working hours – and pay systems – such as result-based pay and bonus systems – may also be dealt with at local level, but only usually within an industry-level framework.

Auxiliary agreements   These are agreements signed by a trade union and a non-organised employer. They bind the employer to follow the terms of relevant industry-level agreements. They are a typical form of regulation for small companies which choose not to belong to an employers' association.

The bargaining cycle

Bargaining begins as old agreements are about to expire. The length of time for which agreements are valid has varied since the move to decentralisation started in the early 1980s, with some lasting as little as six months and others covering two years. Many agreements struck during the 1993 and 1995 bargaining rounds have been for two years; however, two important deals – in retailing and metal-working – last for three, and others are for less than two.

From 1956 until 1983 bargaining was conducted in three consecutive stages, a system which was often described as the 'three-stage rocket'. After 1983 the first stage – that is, central bargaining – was increasingly omitted, notably during the 1984 and 1988 pay rounds. No central pay bargaining has taken place since 1990, when SAF unilaterally withdrew from negotiations at that level.

Traditionally, central bargaining was initiated by the central organisations (the SAF, LO and PTK), and their discussions centred on the scope for wage rises and other labour cost increases. The resulting settlements – central or framework agreements – took the form of recommendations to industry-level unions and employers' federations.

Industry-level negotiations then took place, sector by sector, within this frame-work, with the results being binding on the parties. Although industry agree-ments were formerly concerned with adjusting industry pay rates in accordance with the framework agreement, they currently form the top level of bargaining on pay and other labour costs.

Local bargaining at company and plant level ensures that pay rates are adjusted according to the relevant industry-level agreement. Local negotiations are particularly important where, as often happens, an industry-level agreement provides a *pott*, or kitty, for local bargaining as well as a general pay increase. Unions have traditionally used these to target specific groups of workers who they feel are underpaid; management are more likely to see them as an opportu-nity to use the funds to finance productivity-related measures.

Agreed provisions and objects of bargaining

Pay   There are no statutes governing general pay determination, nor any provi-sions on a minimum wage or pay indexation; these matters are left entirely to bargaining, either individual or, as is the case for around 85 per cent of employ-ees, collective. There is no legal provision for collective agreements to be extended to non-unionised employees, but the LO and SAF have an agreement to that effect.

Small companies who are not members of an employers' organisation often choose to sign an 'auxiliary agreement' (*hängavtal*) which binds them to follow the terms of the relevant industry-level agreement.

Pay agreements for blue-collar workers generally use two systems: fixed hourly rates (*tidlön*) and piece rates (*ackordlön*). Piece rates may either be com-prehensive or may consist of a fixed rate plus a variable element. There are also two types of agreement: agreements on actual pay and agreements on industry minima. The main example of the latter is the manufacturing industry agreement.

It specifies minimum fixed and piece rates for four types of workers, divided by degree of job difficulty, together with minima for young workers under 18. The agreement also has provisions specifying higher minima for workers with two and four years' seniority.

The fact that many agreements set only minima leaves considerable scope for local-level pay bargaining and individual supplements, and real wages are often considerably higher than the rates specified in agreements. For example, the highest minimum hourly wage in the metalworking agreement in the first quarter of 1995 was SKr 67.06 (£6.60); the average wage in the sector in the corresponding period was SKr 88.10 (£8.60). The trend to more local bargaining seems to be spreading. Many agreements signed by Almega, the general employers' federation, in the current bargaining round put much more emphasis than previously on local bargaining. There is a general increase plus whatever local increases the partners can agree on; there is, however, a 'safety net' amount which comes into effect if local agreement cannot be reached.

Pay for agreements with white-collar employees do not usually set anything other than minima, and much more emphasis is put on individual wage-setting, although most guarantee a general percentage pay increase. But again, Almega has had an innovative agreement since 1993 with members of Ledarna, the supervisory staff union, which devolves wage-setting totally to company level, with no recommended percentage increase.

Overtime pay is also set by industry-level collective agreements, as are payments for work in specialised areas and shift work.

Ordinary working time Working hours are subject to statutory regulation under the Hours of Work Act (*Arbetstidslagen*). However, departures from it may be permissible by collective agreement. The law specifies a maximum length of 40 hours for the normal working week. Under some circumstances this figure may be achieved by averaging out over a maximum reference period of four weeks, subject to weekly maxima set by collective agreement.

Ordinarily this legal maximum of 40 hours is the norm in collective agreements. However, where shift and other forms of working are practised, there are usually complementary provisions. For instance, the blue-collar metalworking agreement has a normal weekly maximum of 40, with 38 hours for workers on discontinuous three-shift systems, 36 hours for continuous rotating shifts and 35 hours for continuous shifts, with regular work on public holidays. The white-collar agreement for the same industry has maxima of 40, 38 and 36 hours a week.

It is also common for averaging periods to be varied by collective agreement, and industry-level agreements often specify that these may be further varied by local agreement.

Overtime Overtime regulations for blue-collar workers generally stick closely to those in the working time law, which sets an annual limit of 200 hours. However, there is scope for industry-level unions to grant short-term exceptions to this upon application from employers. Unions have recently been much tougher in granting these exceptions; they find the amount of overtime being worked during the present economic recovery disquieting, and would prefer the slack to be taken up by the creation of extra jobs.

White-collar workers are often covered by an SAF–PTK collective agreement on working hours, which specifies a maximum 'ordinary overtime' of 150 hours a year. An extra 75 hours can be worked by local agreement and a further 75 hours by agreement between an individual employer and the PTK.

Annual leave Although annual leave entitlement is set by law (*Semesterlagen*) at 25 days a year, collective bargaining may improve upon this. This is most common for white-collar employees; for example, the banking agreement gives up to 30 days' leave a year, depending on age and responsibility.

Because of the generous rights to time off granted by law, other types of leave are not usually subject to collective agreement. However, agreements sometimes specify employer payments to top up State benefits when leave is taken. In addition, agreements sometimes specify short (one to two-day) paid periods of absence for various reasons – usually the illness or death of a close relative and visits to a doctor or hospital.

Industrial conflict

Swedish law on industrial conflict and collective agreements distinguishes between a conflict of right (*rättstvist*) – that is, a difference in interpretation of a collective agreement – and a conflict of interest (*intressetvist*) – a conflict involving matters not governed by collective agreement.

In the case of conflicts of interest, the 1976 Co-determination Act permits industrial action to be taken while an agreement is in force in the following cases:

- To regulate matters not covered in a collective agreement.
- Sympathy action in support of lawful primary industrial action.
- To enforce payment of undisputed and due demands for wages or other remuneration for work performed.
- To obtain co-determination agreements.

Permissible forms of industrial action include strikes, boycotts, blockades or 'other comparable offensive action' such as overtime bans, go-slows and working to rule.

Sweden is one of the few European countries in which employers resort to the use of lock-outs in the course of industrial disputes – a weapon which has played a crucial role in a number of historic disputes. Unusually, public-sector employers also have a right to lock out, and actually used the tactic on a few occasions during the 1980s.

In the case of conflicts of interest, the full panoply of these measures is available to both sides. However, written notice of any planned industrial action must be given to the counterparty in the dispute and to the State Conciliator at least seven days before the action is scheduled to start. The Conciliator's Office, regulated under the co-determination law, follows developments in the labour market and, if industrial unrest seems imminent, appoints a mediator. The mediator may not, however, impose a binding settlement, and there is no obligation to restrain industrial action. If mediation fails, the parties may be asked to take the dispute to arbitration and, if it affects the national interest, parliament may legislate to end the dispute. Such measures are extremely rare.

As far as conflicts of right are concerned, it is always illegal to take industrial action, since collective agreements entail a 'peace obligation' (*fredsplikt*) while they are in force. Disputes concerning the interpretation of laws and contracts of employment are also classed as conflicts of right.

Conflicts of right are resolved by a special procedure. This procedure is governed by law, although central and industry-level collective agreements regulate what happens before legal proceedings are taken. Typically, there will be a duty to try to resolve the dispute by local-, or, if these fail, industry-level negotiations.

If negotiations fail, recourse is had to law, although the exact procedure will vary. If union members are involved, and the union is willing to represent them in the case, then it will be heard straight away by the Labour Court (*Arbetsdomstolen*), a statutory body composed of two employer- and two union-nominated members, plus two judges and an independent member. If unorganised workers are involved – or union members whose union is unwilling to represent them – the case is heard by a civil court. However, any appeal against the civil court's decision is taken to the Labour Court. In either case, the Labour Court's decision is final.

Organisations

Swedish Employers' Federation (Svenska Arbetsgivareföreningen, SAF)
Södra Blasieholmshamnen 4A
S-103 30 Stockholm
Tel. + 46 8 762 60 00
Fax + 46 8 762 62 90

Ministry of Labour
(Arbetsmarknadsdepartementet)
Drottninggatan 21
S-103 33 Stockholm
Tel. + 46 8 763 10 00
Fax + 46 8 20 73 69

Swedish Confederation of Trade Unions – blue-collar (Landsorganisation i Sverige, LO)
Barnhusgatan 18
S-105 53 Stockholm
Tel. + 46 8 796 25 00
Fax + 46 8 20 03 58

Central Organisation of Salaried
Employees (Tjänstemännens
Centralorganisation, TCO)
Linnegatan 14
S-114 94 Stockholm
Tel. + 46 8 782 91 00
Fax + 46 8 663 75 20

Confederation of Professional Employees
(Sveriges Akademikers
Centralorganisation, SACO)
Lilla Nygatan 14
S-103 15 Stockholm
Tel. + 46 8 613 48 00
Fax + 46 8 24 77 01

Main sources

HANDELNS OCH TJÄNSTEFÖRETAGENS ARBETSGIVARORGANISATION and HANDEL-SANSTÄLLDASFÖRBUND. *Avtal 1993–94*, Stockholm, 1993.

KJELLBERG, ANDERS. 'Sweden: can the model survive?', in Anthony Ferner and Richard Hyman (eds), *Industrial Relations in the New Europe*. Oxford, Blackwell, 1992.

RUNHAMMAR, URBAN and STARE, PETER. *Handbok i arbetsrätt*. Allmänna Förlaget, Stockholm, 1991

SVENSKA ARBETSGIVAREFÖRENINGEN. *Arbetsgivarens ABC*. Stockholm, 1992

SVENSKA ARBETSGIVAREFÖRENINGEN. *Företagets sociala kostnader 1994*. Stockholm, 1994

SVERIGES VERKSTADSFÖRENING, SVENSKA INDUSTRITJÄNSTEMANNAFÖRBUNDET, SVERIGES ARBETSLEDARFÖRBUND and SVERIGES CIVILINGENJÖRSFÖRBUND. *Tjänstemannaavtal 1993–94*. Stockholm, 1993.

SVERIGES VERKSTADSFÖRENING and SVENSKA METALLINDUSTRIARBETAREFÖRBUNDET. *Verkstadsavtalet 1993–94*. Stockholm, 1993

13

Switzerland

In industrial relations terms Switzerland continues to constitute an enclave of peace and relative stability, compared with most of its European neighbours, a condition rooted in the epoch-making 1937 peace accord between the engineering employers and the engineering workers' union. Collective bargaining, which covers around half the workforce, and individual negotiation tend to outweigh statute law in the shaping of terms and conditions, with a large measure of employer prerogative on many issues.

The conduct of collective negotiations is not only shaped by the almost total relinquishment of industrial action as an instrument in collective disputes, backed up by tried and tested methods of conciliation, but also by the role of 'good faith' and consensus in public, and mostly private, relationships between the two sides. Agreements, which are legally binding, also often allow for a good deal of flexibility in their implementation, enhanced in recent bargaining rounds, and are open to amendment by mutual consent during the period in which they are in force.

This generally high degree of trust in industrial relations has been tested but not overturned by the recession and heightened competitive pressures. Indeed, in some areas there are attempts to develop joint initiatives to retain and enhance Switzerland as a location for business activity. Nevertheless, there are some signs of erosion in the system of collective bargaining, and unions have had to accommodate demands for flexibility on pay and hours from firms and employers' associations.

Against a background of high wage costs, albeit offset in good measure by high productivity and flexibility, the recession of the early 1990s gave rise to increased pressure on employers' associations, and since 1993 in particular to a generally more resolute attitude by companies and employers' associations in collective bargaining. Real pay levels are expected to fall by 0.5 per cent between 1991 and 1996, compared with substantial increases in profitability. Although the system is characterised by consensus, this is often confined to the strictly contractual relations between the social partners. At plant level the system has been under strain, and managements have been eager to retain and extend their prerogatives.

Corporate strategy has seen a return to fundamentals and a curbing and winding down of diversification embarked on in the 1970s and 1980s. This has been combined with a marked spinning off of companies into focused profit centres – one consequence being the nominal increase in the number of firms affiliated to some employers' associations. Hand in hand with this has been severe rationalisation, with job cuts, delayering and selective closures and relocation of businesses. These have given rise to anxieties about the priority given to rationalisation as against innovation – among other things prompting the engineering union SMUV (see below) to embark on a publicly funded study intended to foster innovation.

The increase in registered unemployment has been one of the most dramatic changes in the labour market in recent years, making visible a phenomenon that official statistics previously underrecorded. The rate of unemployment rose from 2.5 per cent in 1992 to 4.7 per cent in 1994 (8.5 per cent for foreign, 3.5 per cent for Swiss, workers), and is expected to moderate only slowly as rationalisation and productivity improvements overtake economic growth. These figures may seem low by comparison with the rest of Europe, but they should be compared with Switzerland's past experience of unemployment rates below 1 per cent until the early 1990s. The higher figures reflect the growing residential population of foreign workers, who make up some 16 per cent of the workforce and who are no longer exported or exportable during downturns. Compared with the 1970s and 1980s, the unemployed are also registering themselves more rapidly and in greater numbers, and being dismissed more readily by companies during downturns. Companies have been moved to abandon traditional job security policies, but have tended to replace them not by a hire-and-fire culture but by enhancing their workforce's employability: Switzerland is reported to have one of the highest incidences of outplacement provision by companies.

One of the most important outcomes of all this has been the rising cost of the generous system of unemployment benefit. Social security – as regards both financing and expenditure – is likely to prove a major area of difference between employers and the trade unions, with the central employers' association, ZSAO (see below), calling for a moratorium on new social policy initiatives.

For this reason, and populist fears about the labour market being overwhelmed by foreigners, the labour market occupies a crucial role in domestic economic and fiscal policy as well as, via negotiations with the EU on various areas of co-operation, interacting with foreign policy.

The regulation of employment is governed by general principles set out in the federal constitution, federal law, cantonal law and case law. Collective agreements, concluded under the provisions of the Code of Obligations (see below) are legally binding. Individual contracts of employment may either improve on collective agreements or may ignore them, provided no binding collective agreement applies. In addition, company handbooks, custom and practice and in the final analysis the employer's right to direct and control also constitute sources of regulation which may be considered by the courts in the event of a dispute over terms and conditions of employment.

In what follows, only German terminology is used. Swiss German is spoken by about 65 per cent of the population. French is spoken by just under 20 per cent, Italian by 10 per cent. Approximately 1 per cent of the population speak Romansch.

Federal law comprises

- the Code of Obligations (*Obligationsrecht*), which sets out the legal foundations of contracts of employment, both collective and individual. There is separate federal legislation on the extension of collective agreements. The provisions of the Code of Obligations are normally binding absolutely, but deviation is possible so long as it is to the benefit of the employee. Contracts may also deviate from the code to the disadvantage of the employee subject to a written individual agreement to that effect.
- the Labour Code (*Arbeitsgesetz*), and its associated regulations, which is public law governing working time and breaks, safeguards for women and young people, provisions on company rulebooks, and special provisions on working time in industry and other specific types of establishment.
- specific legislation covering temporary work, vocational training, employee information rights (see below), sickness and accident insurance, transfer of undertakings, collective dismissal (see below) and sex equality.

Cantonal law in the employment field is concerned primarily with the procedures of labour jurisdiction, conciliation and arbitration, and does not regulate substantive matters.

The main players

There is a general, though not constitutionally established, freedom of association for employees and employers, and also a 'negative' freedom of association – that is, a right not to join an organisation. The closed shop would therefore be unlawful. In addition, collective agreements frequently acknowledge the freedom of association of the two parties and require them to respect it.

Both employer and trade unions have central organisations whose role is primarily lobbying, general policy development, information and loose co-ordination of the industrial affiliates.

The state does not play an active or highly visible role in employment issues. This reflects the consensus-based and voluntarist character of the system of industrial relations, where private law determinations play a greater role than statutory controls. It is also illustrative of the fact that the system of government in practice does not operate in an adversarial way, with marked public clashes, but has tended to incorporate the broad span of mainstream opinion within a series of coalitions which also consult and negotiate with the principal interest groups.

Where the state has taken legislative initiatives in the field of European legislation (see below) the main direction of policy was thwarted by popular opposition in a referendum.

Trade unions

There are number of, essentially competing, union confederations, with a generally socialist and a Christian confederation, and a smaller liberal confederation. Important for the organisational divisions within the trade union movement is the split between trade unions which represent predominantly blue-collar employees and associations of white-collar staff: 90 per cent of organised white-collar workers are in associations not affiliated to the two largest confederations, the SBG and CNG. In a number of sectors, collective agreements apply only to blue-collar employees, and, with the 'tertiarisation' of the economy, this has led to an erosion of the coverage of collective agreements. The larger confederations have separate industry affiliates.

In general the trade unions have not suffered massive membership losses during the 1980s and 1990s, and have not experienced political or social marginalisation. Aggregate union density is estimated at some 27 per cent, with considerable variation between branches of the economy. Whereas 80–90 per cent of public servants are organised, in the engineering industry density is running at some 33 per cent but is as low as 5 per cent in the private-service sector.

The right to trigger a national referendum on legislative proposals provided 50,000 signatures have been obtained (or to suggest legislation on the basis of 100,000 signatures) has been regularly used by the trade unions, although with declining success. Proposals for co-determination and shorter working hours were defeated, and trade union opposition to raising the retirement age for women also lost in a referendum in June 1995.

The largest central union confederation is the Schweizerischer Gewerkschaftsbund (SGB), with some 430,000 members in 1993 compared with a peak of 460,000 in 1980, 85 per cent of them men. Whereas the SGB has lost 40,000 male members since 1980, it has recruited 10,000 women. Membership losses were greater in German-speaking cantons than in the French-speaking ones, and there was a small rise in the Italian-speaking Ticino region. The SGB accounts for around half of all union members, and – reflecting status differences – predominantly organises blue-collar workers. However, it does seek to recruit white-collar employees and is planning to remedy weak organisation in the service sector, currently organised through a white-collar union, with a new initiative to be co-ordinated by the two main individual SGB affiliates, the engineering union SMUV and the chemical and construction union GBI (see below). The SGB is broadly socialist and has ties with the Social Democrat Party (SPS).

The SGB has 15 industry affiliates, the most important of which are

- the engineering and watchmakers' union SMUV (Schweizerischer Metall- und Uhrenarbeitnehmer-Verband), with 106,000 members. Together with the engineering employers' association ASM, the SMUV was responsible for negotiating the 1937 peace accord (see below). It is seen as a moderate union, if only by virtue of its commitment to the peaceful resolution of disputes, and it has been active in fostering initiatives in the area of industrial innovation, which it sees as entailing more employee involvement. In the engineering industry, non-union members pay a so-called 'solidarity contribution' of SFr 60 (£33) a year, deducted from pay. Union members also make the same contribution, with the proceeds from both sources going to a general-purpose fund.

- Gewerkschaft Bau und Industrie, with 125,000 members, is the result of a merger of the chemical, textile and paper union and the construction union. The GBI is regarded as more militant, openly debating the possibility of industrial action on pay.

The Christian union confederation, the CNG, has some 106,000 members, also divided into industrial affiliates, the largest of which is the construction and woodworkers' union, with 43,000 members.

The SGB and the CNG have both been passing through a phase of organisational renewal, and are seen as more combative than formerly.

The Liberal Democrat Party also has a central union confederation, the Landesverband freier Schweizer Arbeitnehmer, with around 20,000 members.

The largest white-collar federation is the VSA (Verband schweizerischer Angestelltenverbände), which has had a co-operation agreement with the SGB since 1944. The VSA had 130,000 members in 1993, divided into 12 affiliates, of which the general association, the SKV, was the largest. Status divisions remain important in many areas, and white-collar organisations refer to themselves as *Verbände* (associations) and not as *Gewerkschaften* (trade unions).

There is an association of public-sector unions, some of which are affiliated to the SGB and others not. There are also a number of smaller unions, based on occupational divisions, professional associations and a growing number of enterprise-based employee organisations. In the private sector one of the most important of these is the bank employees' association, the Schweizerischer Bankpersonalverband, with around 25,000 members.

Employers' organisations

The principal national employers' association is the Central Association of Swiss Employer Organisations (Zentralverband schweizerischer Arbeitgeber-Organisationen, ZSAO). The ZSAO was founded in 1908, principally as a reaction to the strike wave of 1904–7. The ZSAO represents some 30 industry-level employers' associations and a further 30 regional associations. Firms affiliated to member organisations employ around 1 million employees – approximately a third of the labour force.

The ZSAO does not have individual companies as members, although this has become possible under exceptional circumstances through a recent change in its constitution, intended as a response to concern about the diminishing coverage of employers' associations. At the time of writing, for example, negotiations were in train with a number of major companies – notably Nestlé, Swissair and Migros (retailing) – which have never been members of, or have withdrawn from, industry associations.

Whereas the ZSAO represents company interests as employers, the Swiss Trade and Industry Association (Schweizerischer Handels- und Industrie-Verein), customarily known simply as Vorort, represents industrial and trade interests. A specific employers' organisation, the Swiss Handicrafts Association (Schweizerischer Gewerbeverband), represents the interests of small firms and the craft sector. Close co-operation is maintained between all three bodies.

The ZSAO does not engage in collective bargaining and does not seek to steer or co-ordinate the course of industry-level negotiations, although it has done so in the past and still functions as a central source of information. Its main tasks are to generate and represent an overall employer policy on all other matters which do not fall within the ambit of its member organisations, to represent employer concerns to government on appropriate commissions and policy-making bodies, to inform its members, and represent the standpoint of employers in the media and in public debate.

On collective bargaining policy, the ZSAO – like its members – is keen to remove pay from industry-level collective agreements and devolve it fully to company level. As noted below, some movement in this direction can be discerned in recent bargaining rounds. On social policy the ZSAO has been arguing for a moratorium on new initiatives, in particular those which add to employers' non-wage labour costs.

The most important industry-level employers' association, by virtue of membership and economic importance, is the Association of Swiss Engineering Employers (Arbeitgeberverband der schweizer Maschinenindustrie, ASM). The ASM, together with SMUV, also laid the basis of the dominant culture of industrial relations with the 1937 agreement on industrial peace (see below). The ASM has 600 or so member companies, an increase of some 100 over the past 10 years, thanks primarily to corporate subdivision into more targeted units. However, the number of employees working in member companies has declined from a peak of 243,000 in 1980 to 149,000 by the end of 1994 out of a total of 350,000 working in the industry. Excluding small companies, the ASM covers approximately 50 per cent of employment in the industry. Although most prominent Swiss companies are members, multinationals such as IBM, Philips and Bull remain outside. The ASM has also occasionally had a struggle to retain existing members, some of whom have objected to the reductions in weekly and annual working time it has negotiated (though they remain the longest in the industrialised world after Japan) and some of whom, to quote the ASM, have begun to take the industrial peace sustained by the industry agreement for granted.

In response to some of these concerns the ASM succeeded in negotiating a clause in the framework agreement allowing divergence from agreed terms in respect of working time and thirteenth-month salary payments (see below).

Given the individual character of pay determination in the engineering industry, the ASM fulfils the important task of collecting pay figures from member companies, which are then available to other members.

Consultation at national level

There is no formal system of tripartism comparable to the bodies which exist in the Netherlands or Belgium. However, the government is required by law to consult interested parties in the formulation and drafting of legislation. The social partners are also represented and involved in the administration of a number of bodies in the field of social welfare, as well as policy commissions.

Consultation at regional and industry level

There is extensive co-operation at industry level in some sectors, notably the engineering industry. The engineering industry agreement, for example, calls on all contracting parties 'to discuss matters of common interest, create joint organisations, and mount campaigns'. In particular the agreement provides for joint commissions to be established, either on an *ad hoc* basis or permanently, to deal with issues such as training, equal opportunities, health and safety, work organisation and equipment, and the environment. Moreover, in certain fields the parties to the agreement have agreed to establish joint institutions, financed by contributions from either side. Such institutions, which are well financed, play an especially important role in the organisation and provision of vocational training (see *Recruitment, Training and Development* in this series). For example, there is a jointly run association for further training (Arbeitsgemeinschaft für berufliche Weiterbildung) and, together with the federal authorities, both sides of industry maintain a technical school, the Schweizerische Fachschule für Betriebstechnik. Individual employers and employees pay regular contributions to finance further training.

The engineering workers' union SMUV has undertaken research into the promotion of innovation, with support from public funds, and has proposed a number of underlying principles on innovation in the engineering industry which have been agreed with the employers.

Although most employers are committed to continuing such arrangements, there are undercurrents of discontent. Some firms find the obligation to consult irksome and would prefer to exercise unilateral control. Some trade unionists have expressed concern that the structure of joint funds, and their associated institutions, could weaken trade union determination and autonomy.

Workplace/enterprise employee representation

The dominant form of employee representation is the industry-level collective agreement, of which the agreement in the engineering industry offers the most developed example (see below), or company-level provision. Since 1994 statutory provisions have existed, but the legislation has yet to make any practical impact – and one employer has expressed the view that there was no upsurge of interest among employees for the rights. In general, employee rights are largely confined to information and consultation: full joint decision-making, with an employee veto of managerial decisions, is highly restricted. In particular, companies retain and adamantly defend their decision-making prerogative: consultation is overwhelmingly confined to workplace, social – and importantly – training issues. Although sceptical about the legislation, the main employers' organisations have accepted the new *status quo*.

In practice, many medium-sized and small establishments, especially in the small trades and handicraft sector (*Gewerbe*), have no genuinely independent functioning system of employee representation, although individual trade unionists, functioning as shop stewards (*Vertrauensleute*), may serve as an informal focus and, paradoxically, exercise more influence in smaller workplaces.

Statutory provision

Up to 1993 there was no statutory provision for employee representation. Indeed, a trade union initiative to introduce co-determination via statute law was rejected in a referendum and numerous subsequent attempts to legislate for enterprise- and workplace-level participation have also come to nothing.

However, in 1992, as part of a package of laws intended to harmonise Swiss legislation with that of members of the EU and the European Economic Area (EEA), known as Eurolex, the government introduced some statutory provisions in this field, primarily because existing directives (on collective dismissal and the transfer of undertakings) implied some form of employee consultation. Although the Swiss declined to join either the EU or the EEA in a referendum held in December 1992, the package of laws went ahead, renamed Swisslex, and was passed, as one commentator noted, with 'uncommon speed' – reflecting the continuing commitment to economic integration with the EU still retained by large sections of the establishment (including employers and trade unions). None the less, the central employers' organisation, the ZSAO, insisted that its previous acceptance of the package was conditional on entry to the EEA and reaffirmed its fundamental opposition to additional statutory obligations on companies.

The measures on employee representation (the Federal Law on Information and Consultation of Employees in the Workplace, December 1993, effective from 1 May 1994) complement other parts of the Euro/Swisslex package governing collective dismissal and transfers of undertakings (see below).

The law allows employees in establishments (*Betriebe*) with 50 or more workers to set up representative bodies by ballot, provided at least one-fifth of the workforce (or a minimum of 100 in establishments with 500 or more workers) call for it and there is a majority vote in favour. Employee representative bodies must consist of at least two people, with their size above that number to be settled between the employer and elected employee representatives.

Employee representatives must be recognised by the employer. They enjoy two broad rights:

- information, which must be 'comprehensive and conveyed in good time', on all issues knowledge of which is required for them to exercise their tasks. The employer must report at least once a year on the effect of the course of business on the number employed and on those employed at the establishment.
- participation on questions of health and safety, a transfer of the undertaking, and in the event of collective dismissals. (These rights also apply to employees in establishments where there is no elected representative body.)

The statute enjoins both sides to co-operate in good faith (*Treu und Glauben*) and requires the employer to support employee representatives in their duties by providing office space and technical and administrative facilities. Employers must not put elected employee representatives and candidates at a disadvantage during their period of office, or thereafter, for reasons arising from the exercise of their office. Moreover, under article 336/2 of the Code of Obligations, the dismissal of an employee for trade union or representative activity during their tenure of office is *prima facie* 'abusive' (*missbräuchlich*) (see *Contracts and Terms and Conditions of Employment* in this series). Where appropriate, employee representatives may take time off to carry out their duties.

In keeping with the legal tradition of allowing departures from the law not only to the advantage of the employee but also, in certain circumstances, to the disadvantage of the employee, the statute provides for the following.

The law may be deviated from to the advantage of employees on any matter dealt with by the legislation. Certain clauses may not be deviated from to the disadvantage of employees. These include

- the minimum number of employees required to permit representation
- election procedures
- core rights to information and consultation
- the protection of employee representatives
- confidentiality requirements.

In other respects, derogations from the law may take place provided it is by collective agreement.

Experience with the law is, as yet, limited and no overview of its practical effect existed at time of writing. However, both employers' organisations and the Swiss Trade Union Confederation (SGB) report active interest at workplace level, and the SGB regards the law as offering an important opportunity for extending consultation into workplaces not yet covered by agreed mechanisms – most of whose provisions go considerably beyond the statutory ones.

Under the same package of laws there is now statutory provision for consultation with employee representatives in the event of a transfer of the undertaking or collective dismissals. These innovations, introduced via amendments to the Code of Obligations, are as follows.

Legislation regulating collective dismissal was passed in December 1993, amending articles 335 and 336 of the Code of Obligations. Under the new provisions collective dismissal is defined as economic dismissals over a period of 30 days affecting

- at least 10 employees in establishments usually employing more than 20 and fewer than 100
- at least 10 per cent of the workforce in establishments usually employing at least 100 and fewer than 300
- at least 30 employees in establishments with at least 300 employees.

The law requires the employer to consult employee representatives or, if none has been elected, individual employees. The workforce must be given the opportunity to make proposals as to how the dismissals could be avoided, the number reduced and the consequences mitigated. The employer must also give either employee representatives or the workforce itself all pertinent information, and specifically, and in writing,

- the reasons for the dismissals
- the number of employees affected
- the usual number of employees in the workforce
- the period over which dismissals will take place.

A copy must be forwarded to the cantonal labour authorities. In addition the employer must inform the cantonal authorities about the consequences of employee consultation; in turn the authorities are required to look for a solution to any problems created by the dismissals. Employment for those affected ends 30 days after the authorities have been notified, unless a collective agreement or individual employment contract provides for a longer period of notice.

The transfer of undertakings is regulated by article 333 of the Code of Obligations. This provides for employment to continue on transfer, with all rights and responsibilities, provided the employee does not reject the transfer of the employment relationship. The transferee must respect the terms of any applicable collective agreement for a period of one year, unless the agreement expires or is properly terminated. Both the transferor and the transferee are jointly liable for any obligations arising out of the employment relationship prior to the transfer.

The employer is required to inform either employee representatives or, in their absence, the employees directly, of the reason for the transfer and its legal, economic and social consequences for the workforce. Consultation must take place before any measures related to the transfer are initiated.

Agreed provision

Most existing arrangements for formal employee representation, information and consultation are provided through industry-level collective agreements (*Gesamtarbeitsverträge*), implemented through company-level provisions. It has been estimated that around half the workforce in companies with more than 50 employees are covered by such arrangements (broadly corresponding to the incidence of collective bargaining).

The most developed example is that of the agreement in the engineering industry, which has its roots in the 1937 agreement on industrial peace in the industry, which in turn set a new framework for the conduct of industrial relations (see below). As a consequence the provisions on employee representation and participation cannot be divorced from the broader institutional and cultural framework of collective bargaining, consensus-seeking and approaches to the resolution of differences which characterise the Swiss system.

The engineering agreement provides a framework for employee participation at three levels:

- at the level of the individual employee, through the constitution of employee representative bodies, in theory independent of trade unions
- through co-operation at plant level
- through co-operation between the parties to the agreement at industry level.

Detailed arrangements for the election of employee representatives (most typically termed *Betriebskommissionen*), their office facilities and time off, their powers and activities, are left to workplace agreements, subject to the framework in the industry agreement. Under the agreement, if no works commission already exists, a representative body may be established if at least one-fifth of the eligible workforce so requests. The agreement sets out procedures to be followed where employees wish to change the scope of representation. Where no employee representative body exists, trade unions or white-collar associations may directly represent the interests of employees, although the agreement specifies that any such activity or involvement by unions does not constitute formal negotiation. There is a general injunction on all sides to foster co-operation through mutual information on all important matters related to the organisation of work.

Rights and duties of employee representatives Elected representatives are protected against dismissal on grounds arising out of their office, and may generally be dismissed only for serious reasons warranting summary dismissal. Should an employer wish to dismiss an employee representative there is provision for an appeal procedure involving management and employee representatives, if necessary drawing on the national parties to the agreement. Dismissal proceedings may not take longer than one month, and notice of termination may not become effective for at least one month, unless accepted by the employee to be dismissed.

In addition to any workplace arrangements allowing time off for the duties of their office, employee representatives, including those concerned with the management of company pension schemes, are entitled to four days' paid leave each year for training in representative duties. Under the agreement, two jointly financed institutions exist for the organisation and delivery of such training.

The duties of employee representatives are to hear issues or grievances brought to them by employees, and to put them before local management, unless the matter is one which needs to be resolved formally through 'official' channels. Regular works meetings may be held in working time for representatives to report on their activities, and managements have a right to attend such meetings and state their position. Should representatives decide that an issue needs to be put to a vote, management should offer appropriate facilities.

Participation rights   Under the engineering agreement, representatives can exercise four basic participation rights: how the rights are to be applied at workplace level is left to the parties concerned, though the agreement offers guidance.

- Information (*Information*): employee representatives are entitled to regular and adequate information from management on the course of the employer's business and prior to major business decisions, especially those affecting the financial or technical nature of the company.
- Consultation (*Mitsprache*): company affairs must be discussed with employee representatives before a decision is taken, and the management's decision justified if it is at odds with the standpoint of the employee representatives. The agreement suggests that such rights should apply in all areas of working time, job evaluation systems, equal pay and opportunities, health and safety, the working environment, workplace communications, data protection, profit-sharing, ecology, and the broader role of the company.
- Co-determination (*Mitentscheidung*): decisions may be made only with the consent of employee representatives. This provision covers those issues which are subject to the arbitration procedures envisaged in the agreement (see 'Conciliation and arbitration' below), the introduction of flexible working hours (varying between 30 and 45 per week, to average 40 over a reference period of one year), temporary departures from agreed working hours in periods of economic difficulty (see below), and measures intended to avoid large-scale redundancies.
- Self-administration (*Selbstverwaltung*) covers the organisation of the system of employee representation and social activities.

Other industry agreements make similar provision. In the chemical industry, for example, which covers the four main chemical companies (Sandoz, Ciba-Geigy, Hoffmann la Roche, Schweizerhall), separate provision is made for workers' commissions (*Arbeiterkommissionen*) and for time off for trade union representatives. The agreement also defines participation rights in a different way from the engineering agreement, and grants broader rights of co-determination.

Even where co-determination rights are weak, as in the banking sector, there is formal industry provision and detailed company arrangements, specifying precisely which rights (information, consultation, co-determination) apply in each case.

Employee representation at board level

There is no statutory provision for board-level representation.

New industrial relations strategies

The incidence of 'new employee relations' strategies is difficult to gauge. Many medium-sized enterprises are still characterised by paternalistic managements. These may adopt more innovative human resource management approaches when they are run by an entrepreneur with an individual predisposition to change and flexibility; however, traditional approaches are often deeply entrenched in smaller firms – to the exasperation of those eager to spread technical and organisational innovation more systematically beyond large internationalised companies.

A recent survey of Swiss management culture (Bergmann 1995) identified the following elements: a basically strong work ethic, with a desire for fairness, but with work seen as an intrinsic good. The enterprise was generally viewed as a community of interests (not as a family but also not as a site of class struggle) with qualified loyalties on the part of employees. Power is broadly accepted and there is no great call by employees for extensive co-determination rights. However, managers are expected not to intervene excessively and to allow employees considerable freedom of action in doing their job. Interestingly for the culture of teamworking, the Swiss were found to favour decentralisation, clinging to a 'myth of small-scale' organisation but combining it with an aversion to teamworking. Management was marked by a search for consensus, by pragmatism, a lack of legal formality and a degree of conservatism – even generating fears of 'helvetosclerosis' based on complacency about the success of the Swiss approach in the past.

It is generally felt that high-tech companies have adopted the most innovative approaches, with the banks, for example, tending to retain more formal systems. However, change is imminent here and some banks are developing TQM.

Some companies have experienced a culture shock as a result of international mergers and acquisitions. It is reported, for example, that the merger of Asea (Sweden) and Brown-Boveri (Switzerland) to form ABB led to an upheaval in workplace culture where communications, bureaucracy, remuneration, the management of working time and the age of incumbents was concerned. Swedish managers were often 10 years younger than their Swiss counterparts. Many Swiss companies are highly international in terms of trading relations and organisation, and in the case of the chemical industry employ large numbers of highly qualified R&D specialists in Switzerland.

The engineering workers' union SMUV supports initiatives such as teamwork but insists that they should not displace existing forms of employee representation. In a survey the union found that a mere 25 companies had introduced team-working in the general engineering industry.

The EU works council directive

A number of large undertakings will be covered by the directive, including all the major pharmaceutical concerns (Roche, Sandoz, Ciba-Geigy), Nestlé and the engineering and medical systems group Sulzer, together with ABB. Such companies will need to choose an EU country in which to locate their 'agent' for employee representation. At the time of writing there was no clear indication of which would be the preferred option, although linguistic ties may prove decisive in some cases.

Collective bargaining

Collective bargaining covers an estimated 53 per cent of the total labour force. Although most main sectors are included in collective agreements, either directly or indirectly via extension (see below), many agreements exclude white-collar employees and managers, who often account for 40–50 per cent of the workforce.

Collective agreements

Status of collective agreements   Collective agreements (*Gesamtarbeitsverträge*, often shortened to GAV) are regulated by statute, under clauses 356–8 of the Code of Obligations. Under the law a collective agreement may be concluded by a trade union and an individual employer or employers' association. In practice, only industry-level employers' organisations and individual employers, not the central association, ZSAO, conclude and sign agreements. In order to be deemed competent to bargain, an organisation must meet one of the central statutory requirements of such an agreement, the ability to maintain industrial peace (see below).

Agreements are normally signed by a number of trade unions, reflecting the confessional and status divisions within the trade union movement. Often, as in the engineering industry, the various individual white-collar unions may negotiate together at a single table, with the SGB affiliates bargaining separately. However, there is a good deal of informal co-ordination of positions, and the outcome is, in any event, a single collective agreement.

Collective agreements, which must be in writing, are legally enforceable and directly bind the employers and employees with the force of law. Their terms may not be forfeited, unless the agreement itself allows for it. Under certain circumstances, derogation from the Code of Obligations is possible, but only by collective agreement (or the so-called 'standard contract of employment', *Normalarbeitsvertrag*; see *Contracts and Terms and Conditions of Employment* in this series).

The signatory parties are required by law to ensure that the terms are complied with, and to influence (*einwirken*) any members to do so. Under article 357a of the Code of Obligations all parties to a collective agreement are obliged to maintain industrial peace and refrain from taking any form of industrial action in connection with matters which are governed by the agreement. Further provisions on industrial peace may be governed by the agreement itself, including an 'absolute peace obligation' which extends to all issues not just those covered by the agreement, and applies whether or not the agreement is currently in force (see 'Collective agreements and "peace obligations" ' below).

Collective agreements contain two types of provision:

- contractual provisions (*schuldrechtliche Bestimmungen*) binding the signatory parties, and typically regulating procedural matters and contractual penalties
- substantive provisions (*normative Bestimmungen*) setting standards for the commencement, content and termination of employment relations under the agreement.

Procedures for resolving differences play an important role and are usually integrated into industry-level agreements. (These mechanisms are dealt with in greater detail under 'Conciliation and arbitration' below.) Great emphasis is laid on the principle of negotiation in good faith (*Treu und Glauben*).

Should either party wish to change the terms of an agreement while it is still in force, they customarily allow for discussions in good faith. However, if no understanding can be reached the existing provisions remain in force.

A collective agreement terminates

- on the expiry of its agreed term
- following an event which has been agreed by the parties to constitute grounds for termination
- by mutual consent, usually following negotiations
- by due notice.

Under article 356c II any collective agreement of unspecified duration may be terminated at six months' notice provided it has been in force for a year, unless the parties agree otherwise. An agreement may also be terminated if there is a serious breach by one of the parties or if the circumstances under which the agreement was concluded have changed fundamentally.

The legal situation following the expiry of an agreement (or an employer's withdrawal from it) is not definitively established. Because the provisions of collective agreements are directly binding on employees, rather than becoming so by incorporation into individual contracts, in contrast to Germany, some authorities hold that agreements do not continue to regulate employment relations once they have expired (*Nachwirkung*). In theory, therefore, an employer who resigns from a signatory employers' association ceases to be bound, and is subject only to the legal minimum requirements. However, other authorities argue that in this situation the previous terms will have been incorporated *de facto* into individual contracts, leaving the employer free to change them but only by mutual agreement or through termination to amend the contract (*Änderungskündigung*), offering a modicum of protection against arbitrary and immediate changes.

Extension of collective agreements   Statutory procedures exist for extending collective agreements to non-signatory parties under the 1956 federal law on the extension of collective agreements (*Bundesgesetz über die Allgemeinverbindlicherklärung von Gesamtarbeitsverträgen*). This measure allows the authorities, on application from the signatories to a collective agreement, to apply an agreement to a whole industry. Enforcing it then becomes a matter for the original signatory parties. Agreements may be extended at national or cantonal level.

In order to apply for extension, the signatory employers' association must account for more than half the individual employers and the signatory trade union more than half the workforce. The latter condition may be dropped if the sector is characterised by low trade union membership. In addition the procedure must be in the public interest, may not encroach on the legitimate economic interests of specific groups and must not breach statute law or violate the right of free association (see above).

The practice of extension is not especially widespread, and is mainly confined to traditionally low-paying, weakly organised and dispersed industries, such as hotels and catering, construction and small engineering firms. In mid-1994 nine national and nine cantonal agreements had been extended, covering some 360,000 employees out of a national labour force of 3,570,000. The single most important case was that of hotels and catering, which accounted for 222,000 of the total. The central employers' association, the ZSAO, is generally opposed to the practice of extension, especially outside the field of small firms (*Gewerbe*), which continue to see the procedures as establishing an important regulatory safeguard against undercutting.

Levels of bargaining

There are no national multi-industry agreements. Collective agreements are negotiated at industry level for the whole of Switzerland, for particular regions, and at company level, and may be concluded between a trade union and an employers' association or a single employer. Around 88 per cent of those covered by collective agreements fall within the scope of an industry agreement, and 12 per cent within the scope of a company agreement. Most industry agreements are signed at national level, with around a fifth confined to individual cantons.

Whereas the negotiation of industry or company agreements is the legal prerogative of trade unions deemed competent to bargain, most agreements require elaboration and implementation at workplace level. In the case of industry agreements – such as those for the chemical or the confectionery industries – which establish minimum rates, grading and the relationship between the various elements of the wage is left to joint committees at company level. In the engineering industry the establishment of pay levels is left entirely to individual negotiation between employer and employee, with annual reviews negotiated between local managements and works committees.

Employees covered by collective bargaining

The employees covered by the collective agreement are usually specified in the agreement itself. Those excluded vary from industry to industry, and in some cases may comprise middle-ranking white-collar and managerial staff.

Agreements may also contain provision for maintaining coverage. For example, the chemical industry agreement includes a commitment by the individual employers in the association not to restrict the scope of the agreement by putting employees normally subject to it on individual contracts. Employee representatives have a right of consultation on the classification of new posts.

In general the extension of white-collar and service activities within traditional industries has eroded coverage, as such employees are excluded from many agreements. For example, in the chemical industry two-thirds of employees are now white-collar staff, outside the agreement, compared with one-third in the late 1960s. The GBI union is hoping to negotiate an extension of the terms of the framework agreement, excluding pay, to these employees.

The pay round

The pay round for industries covered by collective agreements begins in the autumn. Pay reviews normally take place in two phases, with a general industry settlement subsequently implemented – in various ways – at company level. The first industry to settle is banking. However, there is no leading sector as such – although observers do on occasion point to the benchmark role of the banks. In some industries the increases actually paid out at company level are not known until the industry round is complete.

Industry agreements no longer provide for automatic cost-of-living increases but pay adjustments are still often oriented to the rate of inflation in the year to November.

Switzerland has no committee of economic experts reporting on developments and making pay recommendations. However, the general forecasts prepared by the banks can be influential. Within individual sectors, employers' associations may survey firms as to their salary intentions – especially in engineering, where there is no agreed pay provision – but the findings do not necessarily correspond with the ultimate outcome. Negotiations in most sectors are relatively low-key, although industries such as printing and construction have seen more public controversy. The negotiations over the renewal of the five-year framework agreement in the engineering industry are customarily and famously held in hermetic isolation from the media, with the outcome announced only when the agreement has been formally ratified.

Recent trends

Although the conduct of bargaining has remained generally peaceable – in line with the culture and formal obligations which govern industrial relations – recent years have seen a toughening of the employers' stance in various areas. In 1993, for example, the engineering employers' association ASM, for the first time, entered negotiations with its own platform of demands, centring on the pursuit of greater working time flexibility, after several decades in which the renewal of the agreement had entailed concessions from the employers' side. The pressures on employees' real incomes, which fell in 1993 and were expected to fall by a further 2 per cent in 1995/96, have also begun to foster greater resoluteness on the part of some unions.

It is a long-standing employer objective at national level and in some industry associations to weaken or remove industry-level provisions on pay, and employers have succeeded in eliminating automatic compensation for cost-of-living increases. In the 1994 pay round, which set agreements for 1995, general or cost-of-living-related increases were frequently combined with scope for individual increases, with agreement on a percentage of the total pay bill to be made available to managers for the purpose. For example, in the construction industry the agreed increase in the pay bill for 1995 was 2.3 per cent, one-third of which could be used to pay individual increases. Minimum rates for starters were actually lowered in the 1994 pay round.

Some commentators have expressed the view that the weakening of pay provisions could gradually call into question the role of collective bargaining and the status of trade unions – which accepted the unique situation in the engineering industry as a special case, due to unique circumstances. The unions themselves still feel that such fears are exaggerated, although there is concern about the increase in employer discretion achieved in recent pay rounds.

Pay deals have been at or below inflation for several years running, and real incomes seemed likely to be hit again in 1995/96 through the introduction of VAT. The average settlement at industry level for 1995 was 1.2 per cent (on minimum rates) with actual pay at company level up by around 1.4 per cent, compared with consumer price inflation during 1994/95 of 1.5–2.0 per cent. (Pay increases outside the area covered by collective bargaining are put at 1 per cent.)

Working time flexibility has been a prominent feature of recent pay rounds, against a background of weekly and annual working hours which remain above the OECD average. (In 1994, for example, nominal annual hours in Swiss manufacturing stood at 1,838 compared with 1,752 in Britain and 1,620 in Germany.) Flexibility, as introduced in the engineering, construction and printing industries, is directed mainly at allowing variations (either on a monthly or on an annual basis) without incurring overtime rates: a typical range is 37–45 hours a week. There has also been a general trend towards longer holidays, with five or six weeks now usual in most industries, and an identified preference for cuts in working time to be taken as additional days off rather than in a shorter working week. However, there have been moves in several industries to cut the working week from 42 hours to 40 hours, although unions characterise their own progress towards shorter hours as 'modest'.

In the engineering industry the most recent renewal of the framework agreement in July 1993 saw the negotiation of a 'crisis clause', with renegotiation of this clause in 1995. (The whole agreement runs until 1998.) The clause allows temporary divergence from agreed terms in respect of working time and the thirteenth-month salary to firms in economic difficulty. Any such deviation requires the agreement of workplace employee representatives or, if none exists, of the majority of the workforce. Since 1933 37 companies have been allowed to invoke the clause, 26 of which wanted to introduce longer working hours, nine a cut in the thirteenth-month payment and two a cut in overtime rates.

One recent innovation in bargaining is the introduction of equal opportunities programmes and/or direct action on low and unequal pay for women. However, in one or two sectors, where agreed industry minimum rates have actually been lowered, women may have been more hard hit.

Agreed provisions

There is, in general, no rigid distinction between framework agreements, setting broad terms and conditions and with a prolonged validity, and pay agreements. In many industries, all issues regulated collectively are contained in a single agreement which sets working time, minimum pay rates, agreed bonuses, holidays and time off, and includes provision for consultation, local negotiations and dispute resolution machinery. Agreements may contain provisions both on minimum rates and also on guaranteed increases at the place of work.

The engineering industry is an exception in this respect in that pay – aside from overtime rates and provision for a thirteenth-month salary – is wholly excluded from the agreement. Rather, rates are individually agreed between the employer and the employee, based on the type of work, performance, and degree of responsibility. General changes in pay levels are negotiated annually at plant level between management and employee representatives, the works commissions, although such accords do not enjoy the status of legally binding collective agreements. However, in most developed organisations there are job descriptions and procedures for job evaluation, the latter requiring the agreement of works commissions.

In practice, works commissions know pay rates and the *de facto* grading system which underlies them and can therefore detect major anomalies. Control by employee representatives can also be exercised during company-level pay negotiations, when the works commission asks for a list of individuals' pay, allowing grading problems or excessive differences to be corrected.

Pay flexibility has always been a major feature of pay-setting. One growing trend in recent years has been for pay negotiations to include a general increase, broadly tied to consumer price inflation, and a performance-related element, usually defined as a percentage of the total pay bill, to be determined at company level. The individual performance element has always played a major role in the engineering industry. Systems of job evaluation and performance appraisal will typically be agreed with employee representatives at workplace level in larger and medium-sized companies. As noted elsewhere, there has also been more general flexibility since 1991, with real pay declining.

The individual pay package for a manual or routine white-collar occupation typically consists of basic pay (*Grundlohn*) with a service-related element, plus a payment-by-results component which is often re-evaluated every six months. In some companies it may account for as much as 50 per cent of total remuneration, although trade unions are eager to restrict it to no more than 30 per cent. Companies also pay premium wages, especially where there is no easily calculated form of payment by results, with pay-outs usually tied to meeting delivery deadlines and quality goals.

During pay negotiations, basic pay, seniority allowance and the PBR element are subject to general increases, but not premium pay.

Industrial conflict

Switzerland has one of the lowest strike incidences in the industrialised world. The culture of industrial relations and the legal and agreed framework have both been shaped to minimise industrial action in the course of bargaining. In some years no strikes at all have been officially recorded, and the incidence was especially low in the 1980s and early 1990s. Between 1983 and 1992, for example, the Federal Labour Ministry recorded a total of 23 strikes in all, which on average affected 4.5 employers and involved 244 workers. The only major strike in recent years has been in the printing industry.

The basis of industrial peace was laid in 1937 by the accord between the engineering employers' confederation ASM and the metalworkers' union SMUV, together with the two Christian trade unions and one other union. As explained below, the unusual feature of the agreement was its absolute character: that is, it ruled out all forms of industrial action, even over matters not covered by the substantive terms of the agreement, and provided for a dispute resolution procedure beginning in the workplace and extending to arbitration (see below). Uniquely, the engineering agreement does not make any provision on pay, which is determined individually between employers and employees, and reviewed in annual negotiations with employee representatives. The 1937 agreement was renewed in 1939, and since then has been renewed and renegotiated on the basis of a commitment to industrial peace every five years: the current agreement expires in 1998.

Although arrangements in other industries differ – notably by a less stringent peace obligation and by the fact that they typically include pay – the 1937 agreement still forms the basis of the culture and practice of industrial relations, and is seen by both sides as a major locational advantage, even if it is occasionally called into question and possibly vulnerable to broader social changes.

The background to the accord was an attempt by the SMUV to gain recognition from the employers and negotiate a collective agreement from a position of some weakness, a demand consistently rejected by the ASM since its foundation in 1905 on the grounds that the union had revolutionary political aims. After a transitional period from 1929 in which there was a provisional peace accord, during which time the union abandoned its overt political objectives, final agreement was reached, crucially, in 1937, after a threat by the state to impose compulsory arbitration in wage disputes where the two sides could not come to an agreement. A decisive role was played by the leading personalities of the two organisations, in terms of their perception of the benefits of forsaking industrial conflict and their ability to convince their memberships. The external threat from the surrounding dictatorships also pushed the parties together.

The peace accord reinforces a basic principle of conduct in relations between employers and trade unions which still characterises public debate and negotiation: the principle of 'good faith' (*Treu und Glauben*), according to which neither side will seek to weaken or discredit the other, and each party will demand of the other only what is within their capacity to deliver. With few exceptions, the process of bargaining remains cordial, principled and generally conducted with relatively little publicity. Nevertheless the ASM and SMUV both maintain funds to support members in the event of industrial action (Schmid, 1989).

There is sporadic, and increasing, controversy about the maintenance of industrial peace. The employers argue that they have paid too high a price for it, in terms of pay levels, and have taken to the offensive in recent negotiations. On the trade union side, officials note that real pay has fallen in three of the last six years, and on balance – according to official figures – is expected to fall by 0.5 per cent between 1991 and 1996, compared with substantial increases in company profits. They see it as industrial peace 'for free', and are looking for stabilisation and an increase in real purchasing power. There have always been voices within the trade union movement critical of the commitment to industrial peace – and they have often been used by union officials to extract concessions from the employers, whose public commitment to industrial peace remains solid.

The right to take industrial action

Both strikes and lockouts are implicitly allowed in law for most employees, as a consequence of the constitutional guarantee of freedom of association, but there is no express statutory provision. Public servants may not engage in industrial action because they are subject to public law, not collective agreement. Senior managers are also generally assumed not to be entitled to withdraw their labour without breaching their contract of employment.

Whether any given instrument in industrial action is lawful – does not breach a collective agreement or individual contract of employment – is essentially a matter for the courts, applying general legal principles (see below).

To be lawful, a strike (or lockout) must have been called by an organisation which is competent to bargain and therefore to conclude industrial action by accepting a new collective agreement. Unofficial strikes (*wilde Streiks*), unless made official by a union, are therefore unlawful, and imply a breach of the employment contract. The strike must be directed at an objective which can be embodied in a collective agreement, hence a strike at plant level over a matter beyond the scope of a collective agreement, or a political strike, would be unlawful. Sympathy strikes (in the UK 'secondary industrial action') are also unlawful in so far as the employer subject to the action cannot meet the union's demands within the framework of a collective agreement. Strikes to assert a legal right would also be unlawful in most circumstances, as the appropriate route would be through the courts. (One exception allowed by statute is a stoppage of work in circumstances where the employer is in breach of statutory safety regulations.) Finally, the industrial action taken must be in proportion (*verhältnismäßig*) to the ends – that is, it must be reasonable, must not involve illegal tactics (such as violent picketing, factory occupations, etc.), must not prevent essential maintenance and safety work, and may not impede essential services (gas, electricity, water, hospitals).

Industrial action must be initiated via the due procedures of signatory organisations. In the case of trade unions, this will involve a qualified majority vote by secret ballot and a decision of the main administrative body of the union.

Crucially, industrial action in breach of a 'peace obligation' (see below) or with no attempt at an amicable resolution would constitute breach of contract.

The effect of industrial action on the contract of employment have been dealt with in only a small number of court cases. Lawful industrial action is held to suspend the contract of employment, and does not constitute grounds for termination. Unlawful action, if persistent and unreasonable, might constitute a serious breach of contract, so allowing an employer to proceed to summary dismissal.

Collective agreements and 'peace obligations'

The Code of Obligations imposes a 'qualified peace obligation' (*relative Friedenspflicht*) on the parties, requiring them to abstain from any form of industrial action during the life of the agreement in connection with any issues governed by the agreement. This duty was added to the Code in 1956, partly as a result of the peace accord negotiated in the engineering industry in 1937. By agreement of the parties, it can be converted into an 'absolute peace obligation' (*absolute Friedenspflicht*) under which the parties agree to abstain from industrial action during the life of the agreement, whatever the issue, and commit themselves to resolve all differences via an agreed procedure.

In some industries a mixture of the two may be found. The chemical industry agreement, for example, requires both sides to preserve industrial peace during its lifetime, but states that, if annual pay negotiations remain unconcluded by 31 December, industrial action may be taken over pay.

Around two-thirds of agreements contain an absolute peace obligation, binding not only on the parties but also on individual employees and employers. Such agreements are estimated to cover around 45 per cent of all employees, including public employees.

In general, since peace obligations are included in framework agreements which remain in force for years, an absolute peace obligation will effectively rule out industrial action during annual pay talks – unless an express exclusion clause is agreed. Any breach of a peace obligation would be deemed a fundamental breach of contract, in theory allowing claims for damages and entitle the injured party to resort to defensive industrial action.

All forms of industrial action which breach the basic peace obligation set out in the Code of Obligations will be deemed to be unlawful. Beyond that, the provisions of industry agreements will be decisive. As noted above, in the majority of cases these provisions rule out industrial action, regardless of the cause, during the lifetime of the agreement. However, some exemptions – as in the chemical industry example – may be granted.

Although the engineering industry, for example, is bound by an absolute peace obligation, and other industries by relative peace obligations, there are still diverse ways in which employees may manifest discontent and bring it to bear during negotiations. It is entirely lawful under most agreements to hold works meetings and work to rule. In some industries, short stoppages and brief demonstrations have occasionally characterised recent pay rounds, although support is often confined to activists.

Conciliation and arbitration

The 1937 peace accord in the engineering industry was prompted primarily by the threat of compulsory official arbitration. In most instances the parties to collective agreements prefer to establish their own mechanisms and procedures for conflict resolution on a private basis.

Official conciliation and arbitration There is statutory provision for official conciliation in and arbitration of, collective disputes at federal and cantonal level. The service is free of charge. Industrial action either during conciliation or during arbitration would, in general, be unlawful, although specific regulations and qualifications exist at cantonal level. Should conciliation fail, the matter can be taken to voluntary binding arbitration with the consent of both parties.

Conciliation and arbitration in collective agreements   The most important and frequently used means of resolving collective disputes are the procedures available under collective agreements. In many cases the mere involvement of parties outside the immediate workplace can serve to resolve problems rapidly.

In the chemical industry, there is a three-stage procedure:

- resolution of the problem at company level between management and employee representatives
- reference to the employers' association and the union for clarification and conciliation
- if that fails, reference to a court of arbitration for a final resolution.

The court of arbitration is constituted by the parties under the chairmanship of the court of appeal in Basle: the employers' association and union each have three representatives. The court's decision is final, with no appeal.

In the engineering industry the parties commit themselves via the absolute peace obligation to resolve all differences through agreed procedures. A similar staged procedure exists, though with an important proviso which puts pressure on a negotiated settlement. If internal discussions between management and employee representatives fail to resolve the problem, they may call on the employers' association and the union to clarify the matter in associated negotiations if the dispute is connected with general adjustments of wages, deviations from normal working hours, changes in methods of wage calculation or the general interpretation of the industry agreement.

If negotiations fail, *either* party may submit the issue to a court of arbitration. The court may put forward a conciliation proposal but if the proposal fails to gain acceptance can proceed immediately to announce a binding decision. The court of arbitration consists of one representative of each side, plus a president appointed jointly. The agreement enjoins the parties to 'avoid public confrontation before a decision is handed down'.

Organisations

Federal Ministry of Industry and Labour
(Bundesamt für Industrie, Gewerbe und
Arbeit, BIGA)
Gurtengasse 3
3003 Berne
Tel. + 41 31 322 2948
Fax + 41 31 322 7831

Central Confederation of Swiss Employers
(Zentralverband schweizerischer
Arbeitgeber-Organisationen, ZSAO)
8034 Zurich
Florastraße 44
Tel. + 41 1 383 0758
Fax + 41 1 383 3980

Association of Swiss Engineering
Employers (Arbeitgeberverband der
schweizer Maschinenindustrie, ASM)
Kirchenweg 4
8032 Zurich
Tel. + 41 1 384 4111
Fax + 41 1 384 4242

Confederation of Swiss Trade Unions
(Schweizer Gewerkschaftsbund, SGB)
Monbijoustraße 61
3007 Berne
Tel. + 41 31 45 56 66
Fax + 41 31 371 0837

Institute for the Study of Employment and
Labour Law (Forschungsinstitut für Arbeit
und Arbeitsrecht)
Guisanstraße 92
9010 St. Gallen
Tel. + 41 71 302800
Fax + 41 71 302807

Main sources

BERGMANN, ALEXANDER. 'Le "Swiss way of management"'. *Employeur Suisse.*
No. 6, 16 March 1995

FEDERAL CHANCELLERY, *Arbeitsvertragsrecht* (extracts of collective and individual contracts of employment from the Code of Obligations). Berne, 1992

FLUDER, ROBERT, et al. *Gewerkschaften und Angestelltenverbände in der schweizerischen Privatwirtschaft.* Zurich, 1991

FRITZ, MAX. *Das Mitwirkungsgesetz.* Zurich, ZSAO, 1994

HOTZ-HART, BEAT. 'Switzerland: still as smooth as clockwork?', in Antony Ferner and Richard Hyman (eds), *Industrial Relations in the New Europe.* Oxford, Blackwell, 1992

OECD. *Employment Outlook.* July 1994

REHBINDER, MANFRED. *Schweizerisches Arbeitsrecht.* Berne, Stämpfli, 1995

SCHMID, HANS. *Friedensabkommen und Sozialpartnerschaft in der Schweiz.* St. Gallen, 1989. (Reprint series of the *Forschungsinstitut für Arbeit und Arbeitsrecht*)

SCHWEIZERISCHER GEWERKSCHAFTSBUND. *Vertragsverhandlungen 1994.* Berne, 1995

La Vie économique/Die Volkswirtschaft, various issues

Collective agreements for engineering, the chemical industry, the confectionery industry, banking, hotels and catering, and the metalworking trades.

The United Kingdom

Industrial relations and collective bargaining in the United Kingdom differ fundamentally from the rest of Europe in three key respects. First, the arrangements are almost entirely voluntary, the only exception being the regulation of health and safety at work. Collective representation depends entirely on the employer's decision whether or not to recognise a trade union, although, once recognised, representatives do enjoy some statutory rights. Second, and as a consequence of this lack of regulation, there is far greater diversity in employee representation and collective agreements than in any other country in Europe. And, third, the duality of representative structures seen in most other EU countries is largely absent. Most employee representatives are trade union members, except where employers have unilaterally established their own arrangements for consultation.

Any realistic account of employee relations has to reflect this diversity, but is bound to be both selective and incomplete. A wide range of different practices has grown up for historical reasons in different industries. At company level there is even greater diversity, sometimes within a single firm. Moreover a large proportion of the workforce is not covered by collective arrangements at all. This proportion has grown in recent years because of the contraction of manufacturing employment, the continuing decline of national pay agreements, and the abolition of legislation which provided a guaranteed minimum rate in certain industries.

Whereas there is some debate about how many employees are now outside the scope of collective bargaining, it is generally agreed to be over 50 per cent. There is no statutory provision covering collective representation for such employees. However, the UK is now obliged to introduce certain legislative changes, following decisions by the European Court of Justice (ECJ), which will entitle those employees without a recognised union to consultation in the event of redundancies or a transfer of the business. Under government proposals responding to the ECJ ruling in October 1995 employers would have to consult workforce representatives only when 20 or more redundancies were expected. Representatives would not have to be from a recognised union. Nevertheless, it is possible that in future the UK may move some way towards a system where the right to collective representation on a wide range of issues would exist for all employees, particularly now that the Trades Union Congress has adopted the principle. Thus employee relations may be at a significant turning point.

The main players

Trade unions

Freedom of association   There is no positive right to trade union membership or activity. The law in effect gives employees the right to join – or not to join – a trade union of their choice and a further right to take part in the activities of a union at an appropriate time. Employers are prohibited from discrimination in recruitment – either in favour of or against trade union members. Dismissal on grounds related to membership (or non-membership) of an independent trade union or to union activity is automatically unfair. Further, employees are protected against action short of dismissal aimed at preventing or deterring membership of an independent union or taking part in its activities. The employee is also protected against action imposing membership of any union (whether independent or not). There is therefore no longer any legal basis for a closed shop.

In all cases the employee is required to present his or her case at an industrial tribunal. The only significant exceptions are employees who ordinarily work outside the country, members of the police service, and those excluded on grounds of national security.

However, these rights do not afford all union activities complete protection. Employers are free to refuse an applicant a job because of union activities in previous employment: it is for a tribunal to decide whether this is in fact discrimination on grounds of union membership. Protection within current employment applies only when what an employee does, or proposes to do, falls within the definition of 'activities of an independent trade union' and is 'at an appropriate time'. Tribunals have taken different views of what is appropriate: in general they have drawn a distinction between the activities of union officials – especially workplace union representatives – and rank-and-file union members.

While action by an employer to deter union membership is unlawful, this protection does not prevent an employer discriminating against employees who refuse to accept individual contracts. Following two court cases in 1993, the government introduced legislation which allows an employer to pay extra money to individuals who accept 'personal' contracts while withholding payments from those who refuse to sign such contracts on the grounds that they wish their terms and conditions of employment to be negotiated by a trade union.

In practice, therefore, while the individual's right to trade union membership is protected under the law, the right to exercise that membership, either as an individual or collectively, is significantly constrained.

Evolution   Trade unions developed earlier than in any other country and, when initial attempts to establish general trade unions in the 1840s failed in the face of opposition from employers, established themselves mainly on craft lines, often at local level. Collective bargaining, usually organised along strict craft lines, became well established for skilled workers from the mid-nineteenth century on. In some industries, notably coal mining, workers came to be organised on industrial lines, but it was only at the end of the 1880s that general unions catering for the mass of semi-skilled and unskilled workers were formed. The first unions for white-collar workers were founded before and after the First World War, and took a variety of different forms.

This long period of evolution largely explains the great variety and complexity of trade union organisation which persists today despite mergers and rationalisation, which have seen the number of unions affiliated to the Trades Union Congress fall to around 70, compared with 110 in 1975.

Structure and organisation   Unlike in many other European countries the trade union movement is not divided on political lines, but many individual unions are affiliated to the Labour Party, which was established as an instrument of political representation by the unions in 1906. Some 30 unions are affiliated to the Labour Party and over 50 unions operate a political fund which may be used for campaigning purposes. Individual unions continue to play a major role in Labour Party policy-making through formal constitutional as well as less formal ties. Affiliated unions exercise 50 per cent of votes at the Labour Party's policy-making conference. However, their constitutional powers have been considerably weakened in recent years, and there is continuing debate – and conflict – about the future relationship between the party and the union movement, with strong pressure from the Labour Party leadership, echoed by the majority of union leaders, for a more distanced and less organic relationship.

The Trades Union Congress   Despite some sharp political divisions in the 1980s – notably over the issue of single-union agreements for workplaces on greenfield sites – the trade union movement remains under the single umbrella of the Trades Union Congress (TUC). The TUC was founded in 1868, primarily to lobby Parliament with the aim, in particular, of lifting the threat of criminal prosecution from workers taking industrial action. However, it was not until the 1920s that it acquired its own administrative apparatus independent of its affiliated unions.

The TUC has no power to bargain direct with employers, nor is there any national tripartite structure through which binding accords could be concluded. The TUC's role is much reduced compared with previous eras when its General Council (elected by delegates to the annual conference) negotiated the terms of incomes policies with the government, especially during the period 1974–9. In the past the TUC has played a major campaigning role – for example, against trade union legislation or cuts in public expenditure – but it has now adopted a much lower profile, streamlining its organisation and focusing its interventions. Its main functions are in representing the trade union movement as a whole, in trade union education and in enforcing its rules over disputed areas of recruitment (the so-called Bridlington principles). How far this disciplinary role can be enforced at present is in doubt because under the 1993 Trade Union Reform and Employment Rights Act employees have the statutory right to join any trade union they wish.

The main unions   There have traditionally been two main forms of trade union: craft or occupational unions and general unions embracing workers in a wide range of industries and occupations. Industrial unions, organising all employees in an industry, have always been a rarity, although certain occupational unions such as the Fire Brigades Union function as such. The huge changes in the structure of industry and employment over the past two decades have had a major impact. Unions which used to be predominantly craft or occupationally based, such as the Amalgamated Engineering Union, have increasingly developed a wider role – in this case by merging with the electricians' and plumbers' union (the EETPU) to form the AEEU in 1992. Other craft unions, such as the Boilermakers, have merged with general unions or, in the case of the Sheet-metal Workers, with white-collar unions. The general unions have also taken over smaller industry-based groupings such as textile workers. Meanwhile privatisation and competitive tendering mean that a number of former public-sector unions now represent workers in private-sector organisations.

The largest union affiliated to the TUC is Unison, formed from a merger of three unions in 1992, with around 1.4 million members, largely in the public sector. The other major unions are the Transport & General Workers' Union (TGWU), with more than 900,000 members across a wide range of industries and services; the General Municipal Boilermakers and Allied Trades Union (GMB), another general union, with nearly 850,000 members; the Amalgamated Engineering and Electrical Union (AEEU), with over 800,000 members, mainly skilled industrial workers; and Manufacturing, Science and Finance (MSF), a general union mainly made up of white-collar workers, with around 500,000 members. These figures almost entirely reflect 'active' members. Unlike in countries such as Belgium and Italy there are relatively few retired union members.

There are a number of large unions which are not affiliated to the TUC, notably in the public sector: the Royal College of Nursing, the Police Federation and two of the four teachers' unions. In the private sector there are several important non-TUC unions and staff associations representing staff in banks and building societies, most of which are loosely grouped together in the Financial Services Staff Federation. Such organisations have traditionally adopted a more 'conciliatory' approach to relations with management than their TUC counterparts, but this has changed significantly in the past few years.

The basic unit of all unions is the branch, which may represent a single workplace or cover a number of different establishments. Branches usually have a major role in union policy-making and elect delegates to annual (in some cases two-yearly) conferences. Branches are usually run by elected lay officers, who may or may not be workplace representatives.

Workplace rights One key characteristic, distinguishing UK unions from the rest of Europe, is that they are strongly rooted in workplace organisation. Trade union dues are generally quite low and incapable of sustaining a large apparatus. Strike funds too are usually small – compared with German unions', for example. A great deal depends on the activity of shop stewards and other workplace representatives who are largely responsible for maintaining and increasing union membership, for representing individuals and groups and in many cases for collective bargaining as well. These representatives are almost always elected on an annual basis, although such elections may be informal and candidates are often unopposed. The number of employees represented by each shop steward varies enormously according to the union, the type of workplace, the nature of the work and 'custom and practice'. It can be as few as 10 or 12 and as many as 100 or more. In larger workplaces there are often agreements defining the number of shop stewards and their role.

Workplace representatives are entitled to reasonable time off work, paid by the employer, to carry out their functions. The arrangement is often informal and mostly involves only a few hours a week. However, in larger workplaces there may be full-time union representatives, sometimes known as senior shop stewards or convenors, with office facilities provided by the employer.

One effect of the successive waves of restrictive trade union legislation since 1980 (see below) has been to increase the authority of the full-time trade union official *vis-à-vis* the workplace representative. At the same time, however, the decentralisation of bargaining and the breakdown of national agreements in the private sector and, increasingly, in the public sector enhanced the negotiating and representative role of shop stewards. The formal and informal 'balance of power' within different unions varies a great deal and there are no generally hard and fast rules defining the relative authority of officials (who are mostly appointed), the national executive members, who are elected by secret ballot, and stewards elected by ballot or a show of hands. Shop stewards are not usually bound by the decisions of their 'superiors' and they can, and frequently do, adopt a position against the advice of officials. Where union representatives make decisions collectively, for example in joint shop stewards' committees representing members of several different unions, their decisions are normally binding, even if they run counter to the policy of a minority union. Some unions, however, do have considerable authority to discipline shop stewards.

The shape and pattern of representation of unions has thus changed profoundly in recent years, and continues to do so. One by-product is the virtual disappearance of the traditional inter-union demarcation disputes which used to be commonplace in some industries. Another consequence is the gradual rationalisation of union representation at company level. Inward investors now invariably negotiate recognition of a single union at any new site, and existing companies are following the pattern where they can. Elsewhere companies and unions have agreed 'single table' bargaining, where different unions agree to negotiate together while retaining their separate identities in representing individuals or groups of members. However, there are still a large number of firms which negotiate separately with different unions, particularly where distinct arrangements remain for blue- and white-collar workers.

Trade union law   The 1993 Trade Union and Employment Rights Act (TURERA) is the most recent example of a series of legislative changes which have significantly altered the relationship between trade unions and their members since 1980. The major changes relate to the law on strikes and industrial conflict (see below). One major effect has been to force unions to exert control over the collective action of their members to a much greater extent. At the same time, however, other changes have reduced the ability of unions to discipline individual members, and opened up areas of union administration to greater electoral accountability.

The legal status of trade unions is best described as hybrid. At common law they are unincorporated associations: groups of individuals banded together under a collective name, which have no legal identity distinct from those members. However, legislation gives unions a legal personality and certain powers and attributes of corporate bodies although it expressly stops short of bestowing corporate status on them. Many of the rights accorded in law to unions and union members depend upon the union being 'independent', as defined in the law. Basically this means that the union is (1) not under the domination or control of an employer, and (2) not liable to interference by an employer (arising out of the provision of financial or material support or by any other means). Unions can obtain a certificate of independence from the certification officer provided they satisfy the statutory definition of independence.

Like companies, unions have to comply with certain administrative requirements. The most important are

- the duty to keep a register of members
- the duty to keep accounts and make annual returns
- requirements concerning the operation of union pension funds.

The 1988 Employment Act introduced the right of union members to inspect accounts and records and also made it unlawful for unions to use union property to indemnify an individual for a criminal offence or for contempt of court.

A specific statutory procedure sets out the rules covering union mergers, whether by amalgamation – where both unions cease to exist – or by transfer of engagements, where one union becomes part of another. Ballots of members are necessary for both amalgamation and transfer, although in the latter case it is only members of the dissolving union who are entitled to vote.

Unions may set up funds for political purposes (after a ballot), but since the 1984 Trade Unions Act they are required to hold 'review' ballots at least once every ten years. The act also sets out a detailed list of activities which are considered to be 'political' in the eyes of the law, which means that unions are able in certain circumstances to pay for non-party political activities out of their general funds. The balloting procedure, intended to test membership support for political funds, proved in many respects a watershed for the unions in the mid-1980s: very large majorities were won in most cases, and many unions developed sophisticated communication strategies, often for the first time, to highlight the case for the maintenance of funds to their own members.

An important change introduced in the 1993 Trade Union Reform and Employee Rights Act concerns the system by which employees agree to pay their union dues via the employer, by automatic deductions from pay. Known as the 'check-off' system, this arrangement became widely established in the 1970s and 1980s, particularly in the public sector and large firms, because of its advantages for both employers and unions. The 1993 act requires that employees must give their individual consent to the arrangement every three years. The change was generally seen as imposing an unnecessary barrier to union membership and was opposed by employers as well as unions. In the event the unions responded with successful campaigns to retain and recruit union members during 1994.

The other major change was introduced in 1984, the requirement for the election every five years by postal ballot of general secretaries, presidents and members of national executives. Many unions already held elections for these positions, but not by postal ballot. As an inducement to accept the change the government provided funds to cover the cost of balloting. These were, however, withdrawn in 1993, along with a government subsidy for trade union education.

Membership and density   The trade unions have a history of high levels of membership. In the early 1920s membership reached 8 million, a figure not achieved again until 1945. Subsequently membership rose steadily – and strongly during the 1970s – to reach an all-time peak of more than 13 million in 1980. (All these figures include non-TUC unions.) The following years, above all the deep recessions of the early 1980s and 1990s, have seen a consistent reduction in the total to below 9 million in 1993. The whole brunt of this decline has been borne by unions affiliated to the TUC, with non-TUC trade unions experiencing modest growth.

This is the longest sustained decline since records began, although it still leaves the UK with a relatively high rate of union membership. Membership as a proportion of employees in employment is still around 35 per cent. Not surprisingly there is great variation in union density between different sectors. Industries that were formerly in public ownership, such as the utilities, have a union density of 80–90 per cent for manual workers and 50–60 per cent for white-collar staff. Union membership in hotels and catering or the retail sector is 10–20 per cent. It is typically much higher among full-time workers, at 39 per cent, than among part-timers (21 per cent). Among occupational groups it is highest in professional and technical occupations and lowest for salespeople.

The reasons for the decline in union membership have been the subject of much debate. It has been argued that the political climate was hostile to the trade union militancy of the 1970s and that government policies, such as anti-strike legislation and the abolition of the closed shop, made it harder for trade unions to function effectively. Persistent high unemployment obviously inhibited trade union activity. It is also argued that fundamental changes in the structure of employment mean that collective bargaining and trade unions are in inexorable decline.

Certainly, major structural factors are involved. The huge decline in manufacturing employment, particularly in heavy industry, where unions were strong, coupled with the growth of a fragmented private service sector, has inevitably led to a decline in membership. The continued increase in white-collar employment is also a factor (although, as we noted above, a large number of trade union members are white-collar workers). Meanwhile the estimated number of people in self-employment rose by nearly 70 per cent during the 1980s, to more than 3 million. More than a quarter of those in employment are now part-time.

In political terms perhaps the most important reason for the decline is that trade unions have been on the defensive for most of the period. While trade union organisation showed remarkable resilience in the face of a hostile government and, sometimes, hostile employers, it did not seem to offer much to those outside its ranks. However, there is no sign that people in general are now hostile to trade unions. On the contrary, opinion polls consistently show that a large majority consider they do an important job in the workplace. Despite profound structural changes continued decline is by no means inevitable.

Employers' organisations

Employers' organisations have a consistently lower profile than in most other EU countries. During the 1980s such bodies seemed increasingly irrelevant as the focus of collective bargaining shifted more and more to company and establishment level (see below). Many of the largest employers, such as ICI and Ford, always operated independently. During the last 15 years other big companies have gone their own way, either leaving employers' associations, as in the case of GEC and British Aerospace, or dissolving them altogether, as in the case of the major banks and the supermarket chains. However, in some industries employers' federations have been developing new roles and are more important than they may appear.

National and industry structures   The main representative body of employers is the Confederation of British Industry (CBI), with a membership of some 250,000 firms. Most industry-based employers' associations are also CBI members. The CBI has a strong regional profile and its council is made up of regional representatives as well as representatives of small firms, and so on. Its annual conferences (which began in 1977) were initially promoted as policy-making forums for business and to counteract the public impact of TUC conferences, but their role has been substantially downgraded.

At industry level the most important employers' associations include the Engineering Employers' Federation, the Building Employers' Confederation and the Chemical Industries' Association. Again these associations have a strong regional presence, particularly in the engineering industry.

Their role in bargaining   The role of employers' associations in collective bargaining varies greatly. At national level the CBI has no direct role in industrial relations. Periodically it has urged pay restraint upon its members and even suggested pay bargaining targets at its annual pay presentations which take place at regional level during the middle of the year. It continues to provide members with regular briefings on pay and bargaining trends (as well as regular surveys of business prospects).

At industry level certain employers' associations are directly involved in national pay bargaining. This is the case in the building industry (and the various specialised sectors of construction), in chemicals, printing, motor vehicle retail and repair, footwear, clothing and textiles. The importance of these arrangements varies a lot (see below), but in general the role of the employers' association is greatest in sectors with a large number of small and medium enterprises.

Where industry-wide bargaining no longer exists it does not necessarily mean there is no longer a role for the employers' association. The clearest example is the engineering industry, where regional associations render important services to member companies at local level, providing information on pay, advice on industrial relations, and representation at industrial tribunals. A large number of smaller companies rely extensively on this support.

Consultation at national level

The tradition of tripartite consultation between government, employers and trade unions is much weaker than elsewhere in Europe. That said, there have been periods when this type of arrangement has been extremely important, notably under the Labour government in the second half of the 1970s, when trade unions and – more reluctantly – employers were involved in policing the terms of government incomes policies. The Social Contract, as it was known, collapsed in 1978, first because the main employers' organisation – the Confederation of British Industry (CBI) – was unwilling to continue this policing role and subsequently because the trade unions were unable any longer to contain their members' wage demands.

The consequent strike wave, the so-called Winter of Discontent, was a major factor in the election of the Thatcher government in 1979, which set out from the beginning to eradicate what it described as 'corporatism'. The Trades Union Congress has since that time been rigorously excluded from any role in policy-making, and its status as a consultative body has been systematically reduced. During the 1980s the government, the CBI and the TUC continued to meet under the auspices of the National Economic Development Council (NEDC), the tripartite body set up in 1962 to promote policies aimed at faster economic growth, but the NEDC was gradually stripped of most of its functions and was finally wound up in 1992.

Traditionally, training was a field where unions and employers were represented equally, and this principle persisted through the 1980s with the tripartite Manpower Services Commission and its 1985 successor, the Training Commission – despite the abolition of most of the sectoral Industrial Training Boards. But tripartism ceased in 1990 with the move to central government control over training policy backed by local Training and Enterprise Councils, two-thirds of whose members have to be managers from private industry.

There are, however, two important statutory bodies at national level which continue to involve equal representation of unions and employers. These are the Health and Safety Commission (HSC) and the Advisory, Conciliation and Arbitration Service (ACAS).

Since the 1974 Health and Safety at Work Act trade unions have enjoyed significant statutory rights in the workplace, and the whole field of health and safety (including the protection of the public from risks associated with work-related activities) has been overseen at national level by the HSC. The HSC has the duty of promoting the general purposes of health and safety legislation and of preparing specific regulations and codes of practice. It also oversees the work of the Health and Safety Executive, in effect the operational arm of the HSC.

ACAS

ACAS was established in 1974 as an independent body which essentially took on the roles of conciliation, arbitration and advice which had previously been the responsibility of the Department of Employment. Its main functions are

- providing facilities for conciliation, mediation, arbitration and enquiry where the parties involved request them
- providing a free advisory service on employee relations and personnel practice
- publishing codes of practice. These codes cover such as issues as disciplinary procedures and the right to time off work for trade union representatives. They do not have the force of law, but can be quoted as an authority in courts and at industrial tribunals
- providing individual conciliation – for example, where an employee claims unfair dismissal – before cases are heard by industrial tribunals.

When ACAS became a statutory body (in 1975) its independence was made explicit in the legislation: 'The service shall not be subject to directions of any kind from any Minister of the Crown as to the manner in which it is to exercise any of the functions under any enactment.' This independence was and has remained a key element of ACAS's success, and the service has on occasion taken a distinctly different line on industrial relations from the government. At the outset the ACAS remit was the improvement of industrial relations and the encouragement of the extension of collective bargaining. The latter objective was removed by the 1993 Trade Union and Employment Rights Act, but the change appears to have had little practical impact.

By far the largest part of ACAS's work is individual conciliation – over 79,000 cases were received in 1994, of which some 58 per cent were claims about unfair dismissal. But there were still over 1,100 cases of collective conciliation completed in the same year, around half involving disputes about pay and terms and conditions of employment. Arbitration forms a relatively small part of ACAS's work, particularly as there are no powers to arbitrate without both sides agreeing. Originally the Central Arbitration Committee (CAC), set up at the same time as ACAS, had a wide range of powers, including the right to impose improvements in terms and conditions of employment in cases where an employer unreasonably refused to recognise a union. Most of the CAC's functions were abolished in the 1980s. The CAC's role is now limited to rare cases of voluntary arbitration and the issue of disclosure of information to recognised trade unions for bargaining purposes.

CBI–TUC consultation

In general the amount of joint consultation, let alone policy co-ordination, between employers and unions at national level is minimal. But the last few years have seen occasional attempts to set up a bilateral dialogue at national level between the CBI and the TUC, symbolised by invitations for the CBI to address the TUC's annual conference, and vice versa. In future there may be closer relations between the two organisations. However, both bodies have always been relatively weak, and now have less power than in the 1970s.

Government's role

Despite appearances the government continues to keep a close watch on employee relations, with regular reporting to Ministers on the progress of pay rounds, particularly in the public sector. A future government could well reintroduce some national forum for discussions on economic and social issues – including employee relations – but it would be unlikely to have the authority to draw up policies, let alone enforce them.

In the past there has been much discussion of the need for reform of collective bargaining, particularly when rapid inflation has led to escalating pay demands, but also as part of a broader sweep of institutional change urged by some unions, with co-ordinated bargaining and a council of independent economic experts. With the combination of lengthy recession and low inflation reform has either slipped down the political agenda or run aground on entrenched structures. A further factor is that collective bargaining has become so fragmented that a co-ordinated approach would be extremely hard to achieve on a voluntary basis, and the central institutions capable of supporting such a policy have now lost many of their functions and powers.

In July 1995, following a Cabinet reshuffle, the government announced the abolition of the Department of Employment and divided its roles between a

newly constituted Department for Education and Employment and the
Department for Trade and Industry.

Consultation at regional and industry level

Consultation between the social partners at regional level is virtually unknown.
The major exception is Northern Ireland, where the special circumstances of the
last 25 years have periodically led to joint meetings and declarations.

At industry level there has been a long-term decline in the importance of
national agreements on pay and conditions which has inevitably led to a down-
grading of consultative arrangements as well. There is no obligation on private-
sector employers to consult the unions at industry level, although some
public-sector employees enjoy a statutory right to consultation. In certain industries there is a continuing process of low-profile consultation, usually through the
machinery of Joint Industrial Councils – bodies established particularly in the
1920s and 1930s to set minimum pay rates at industry level. Industries which
retain this type of machinery include chemicals, textiles, clothing and construction. Some segments of the construction industry, such as civil engineering and
electrical contracting, have highly developed formal machinery for bargaining
and consultative purposes.

Workplace and company employee representation

There is no statutory form of employee representation, nor is there any obligation
on employers to recognise trade unions or any other employee representatives for
collective bargaining purposes, or for representing individual employees, even
where a trade union is shown to represent the majority of employees. Any of the
legal obligations which an employer has to an independent, recognised union –
for example, allowing its representatives time off work for union activities –
depend entirely on the decision of the employer to recognise the union.

Employers may also derecognise unions if they choose to, either completely
or partially. Usually this involves an employer giving the union notice that
recognition will be withdrawn on a certain date, although this notice period is
not a legal obligation. In a number of cases employers have offered employees
inducements – extra pay or particular benefits – in order to secure a favourable
result in a ballot. The ability to offer inducements to individuals to leave the
scope of a collective agreement and accept a personal contract, effectively discriminating against those who choose not to accept the offer, successfully challenged in the courts in the past, is now guaranteed to employers in law.
Derecognition has been seen as a growing trend over the past few years,
although in reality it has been confined largely to one or two industries (notably
printing and publishing) and individual companies, such as BP. Successful

union claims for recognition continue to exceed the number of cases where recognition is withdrawn.

Union recognition can thus take different forms. Recognition usually implies full collective bargaining on behalf of some or all employees. But certain employers recognise a union only for the purpose of representing individuals. In some cases there is a combination of the two, for example where collective bargaining has been removed for managers but the union retains the right to represent individuals.

Health and safety representation

Unions may also have recognition rights for health and safety purposes – a collective issue – where collective bargaining for other purposes does not exist. This is important, because health and safety is one area where employers have significant statutory responsibilities towards employee representatives. As part of the general health and safety framework, regulations were issued in 1977 on the training and the functioning of safety representatives. An independent, recognised trade union can appoint a safety representative from among the employees anywhere it has membership. These safety representatives are entitled to receive from the employer sufficient information to enable them to carry out their tasks. They have the right to carry out inspections and a right to consultation. Where there is more than one safety representative the employer has a duty to set up a safety committee if requested. Representatives have a right to as much paid time off as is necessary for the performance of their functions, which are laid down in some detail in the regulations. A separate code of practice covers training, which stipulates that safety representatives should be allowed to attend a basic training course approved by the TUC or the safety representative's own union. However, in-house courses also qualify under the regulations, provided they cover the issue of union policies and practice on health and safety matters.

Statutory rights of representatives

Despite the fact that there is no legal right to recognition, statute law confers a number of rights on independent trade unions which have in fact been recognised. In addition to rights on health and safety, these are

- the right of union members and officials to time off work for trade union reasons
- the right to disclosure of information for the purposes of collective bargaining
- rights to consultation on redundancies (collective dismissals)
- a right to consultation and other rights in connection with the transfer of undertakings
- the right to information and consultation on occupational pensions
- the right to hold a workplace ballot on the employer's premises.

A union does not acquire these rights simply by virtue of holding the right to representation and consultation. However, once an employer has agreed to negotiate – for example, on matters of discipline, or working conditions – the union is entitled to them. Exactly what is involved – for example, the sensitive issue of when union representatives are entitled to be paid for their union duties – is spelled out in codes of practice published by ACAS. In general the test is what is 'reasonable' and hence will vary according to circumstances.

The rules on consultation in the event of redundancies or a transfer of undertakings were successfully challenged by the European Commission in 1994 on the grounds that they did not meet conditions laid down in European directives. In October 1995 the government introduced regulations on workforce consultation in the event of redundancies and transfers of undertaking to take effect from 1 March 1996. Under the provisions, employers must consult with workforce representatives where 20 or more redundancies are expected over a period of 90 days. To remedy the ECJ's criticism that previous UK law envisaged consultation only where there was a recognised trade union, the new regulations allow the employer to consult with elected representatives without these having to be from a recognised trade union. Provided the workforce elects representatives, the employer may choose to consult with these even where a trade union is recognised. There is no provision for a permanent form of employee representation, and in theory they could be elected on an *ad hoc* basis.

Employee involvement

Reflecting the absence of statutory arrangements for consultation, there is a strong tradition of voluntary employee involvement, ranging from team briefing and quality circles to the formal consultative committees which exist in some firms. However, analysis of these arrangements has often revealed that they have a short life span and that consultation goes in cycles. Unions have a long history of attempts to increase workers' participation, but their main focus has been on collective bargaining – albeit complemented now by greater interest in works councils as a possible vehicle for employee representation.

The formalisation of collective bargaining in the 1960s and 1970s, particularly by large employers, led to the growth of formal consultative arrangements. Subsequently the influx of Japanese-owned firms and the trend towards single-union bargaining (or single-table bargaining – several unions negotiating as one) all led to renewed interest in the idea of company councils in the 1980s in a context of new emphases in personnel management (HRM, total quality, etc.). Union derecognition was also a factor. However there is no sign that such councils have displaced trade union bargaining. Indeed, many of them coexist with trade unions and directly involve union representation.

According to the periodic official surveys of industrial relations, around a third of workplaces have joint consultative committees. The most recent Workplace

Industrial Relations Survey (WIRS) – conducted in 1990 – showed a decline in formal consultative arrangements, compared with 1984, but the WIRS authors noted that this change reflected a decline in the number of large establishments and in trade union recognition. (See Table 7.)

As for other methods of consultation and communication, WIRS figures suggest that systematic use of the 'management chain' for communication remains by far the most common approach, although the use of surveys, employee ballots and team briefings has grown significantly.

Trade union attitudes towards initiatives such as quality management, direct communication through team briefings and functional flexibility changed markedly during the 1980s, especially in the private sector, primarily because of competitive pressures. In some instances trade unions have been identified as more active promoters of change than middle-management employees, many of whom have felt threatened by – and have been hard hit by – the slimming down in management hierarchies and demands for the acquisition of new skills. However, there is no single unambiguous trade union view of employee involvement strategies: opinions range from regarding employee involvement as an opportunity to discuss a wider range of issues, such as training, to suspicion that it is simply a tool to displace existing representative arrangements.

Table 7　*Methods of communication and consultation, 1990*

	% of private-sector establishments	
	Manufacturing	*Services*
Work-group meetings	23	33
Meetings with junior managers ('team briefing')	31	47
Meetings with senior managers (at least once a year)	38	40
Management chain	57	58
Suggestion schemes	14	31
Regular newsletters	22	44
Surveys or ballots	7	17
Other methods	11	13
None of these	14	11
Workplace consultative committee or higher-level committee with local representatives	25	25

Source WIRS

Employee participation at board level

Company law requires only a single board, in contrast to many mainland European countries, where two-tier boards (supervisory and administrative) in large enterprises offer scope for the inclusion of employee representatives at a level divorced from day-to-day management.

With a few notable exceptions, UK employers have consistently mounted strong opposition to the idea of employee representation at board level. Union opinion has been divided between partisans of a voice for employees in decision-making and those who believe that employee representatives would be isolated and irrelevant. The issue has not been on the agenda since the end of the 1970s, when the Labour government proposed that under certain circumstances there should be employee directors. The only examples were in the steel industry (then in public ownership) and the Post Office.

The only requirement on companies at board level is that annual reports to shareholders have to state what the employer's policy is on employee involvement, a formal obligation introduced in the 1980 Employment Act.

The EU works council directive

The government's refusal to sign the social protocol attached to the Maastricht treaty has allowed the UK to opt out of the EU works council directive. The rules therefore do not generally apply. Employees do not count in the calculation as to whether companies are obliged to set up works councils, and they are not entitled to any representation.

While the government has continued to denounce the legislation as a costly irrelevance, employers' organisations have been more pragmatic, recognising that their counterparts in other EU countries have accepted the directive and that foreign companies operating in the UK will tend to include UK employees in works council arrangements.

As for UK-owned international companies, they are of course obliged to follow the directive, if applicable, so far as employees of any of their overseas subsidiaries are concerned. Just over 100 companies fall into this category. Once legislation is implemented in September 1996, UK companies – unless they have a voluntary arrangement – will also have to select one of their subsidiaries as an 'agent' for their European works council.

Early signs, from such companies as the food manufacturer United Biscuits and the textile firm Coats Viyella, are that companies will include their UK employees in voluntary works council arrangements. However, the process is not inevitable – a number of the firms affected are conglomerates or holding companies which have hitherto kept the management of their different subsidiaries strictly separate.

The unions have been enthusiastic about European works councils, partly because of the government's opposition and partly because of the complete absence of any statutory right to consultation outside the fields of health and safety, redundancies and transfers.

Collective bargaining

According to the most recent Workplace Industrial Relations Survey, covering 1990, collective bargaining embraces 54 per cent of employees in workplaces with more than 25 employees, compared with 71 per cent in 1984. Allowing for the fact that the incidence of collective bargaining is likely to be less in smaller establishments, WIRS suggests that the overall incidence of collective bargaining could be below 40 per cent for the workforce as a whole. Since 1990 the incidence may have fallen further because of employment losses in manufacturing during the 1991–3 recession. On the other side, there is some debate as to how the million or more public-sector employees whose pay increases are set by pay review bodies, not collective bargaining, should be dealt with. Whereas WIRS excluded them from the scope of bargaining, other commentators have pointed to the fact such employees remain highly unionised, with active negotiations, encouraged by government policy, at local level, and union involvement in discussions on a broad range of issues.

The status of collective agreements

Collective agreements are not legally binding or enforceable between the signatories unless they expressly state that such is the case. Substantive, but not procedural, terms of collective agreements are 'incorporated' into employees' individual contracts, and thus become enforceable in civil law and subject to procedures for variation and termination. Thus all collective agreements are binding in honour only unless otherwise stated. Legally binding agreements are extremely rare. An outstanding exception is the agreement covering electrical contracting employees, which is almost unique in setting standard rates across an industry. (The only other example is in engineering construction.)

Levels of bargaining

The structure of pay bargaining has been progressively decentralised over the past 40 years. Recently the government has pushed the public sector in the same direction, with the introduction of compulsory competitive tendering for contracts and the decentralisation of management. However, there is considerable resistance on the part of public sector trade unions.

Consistent figures are not available, but the pattern which emerges from successive surveys shows a widespread shift in the private sector away from reliance on pay rates and conditions determined at industry level. In the mid-1950s industry-wide arrangements affected some 80 per cent of private sector employees. There were no more than a few hundred distinct formal bargaining units in the country, although in practice there was a lot of informal bargaining within individual workplaces, in particular on piece rates, especially in such industries as engineering, coal mining and textiles.

By 1980 the number of separate bargaining units in the private sector covering 25 or more employees had risen to well over 30,000, according to the estimates in the first Workplace Industrial Relations Survey (WIRS). The second WIRS found that by 1984 multi-employer bargaining was the principal means of fixing pay for only about one-fifth of private-sector employees. In 1986 a CBI study noted that two-tier bargaining – industry-wide agreements modified or supplemented by local negotiations – was in rapid decline. In the next four years 16 major national bargaining arrangements covering over a million private-sector workers either collapsed or were dissolved, including, most importantly, the agreements covering engineering, the clearing banks, food retailing and independent television.

Pay determination has always been more decentralised than elsewhere in Europe. It has now become fragmented. A major force behind this shift to bargaining at company or establishment level is the need to respond to local labour market pressures and to tailor pay arrangements to business needs. But these are not the only factors. In the engineering industry the strength of trade union organisation at workplace level made national bargaining increasingly irrelevant over many years. And it was the unions' successful selective strikes for shorter hours in large companies which led to the collapse of the national agreement on pay in 1989.

Nor has national bargaining entirely disappeared. In the chemical industry it continues to set a benchmark level for 'conforming' companies to apply to their local pay rates. In printing, the national agreement sets basic pay in some companies and provides the basis of local negotiations in others. And, as noted earlier, national bargaining continues in construction, taking a variety of forms in the different branches of the industry.

In addition, certain industries retain national agreements on non-pay elements – for example, annual holiday entitlement or premium payments for shift working – which companies continue to follow. Procedural arrangements to resolve disciplinary matters or disputes may also follow terms laid down at industry level.

Many large firms negotiate (or set pay) company-wide, particularly in the service sector – for example the banks and retail chains. Although there has been some devolution of bargaining to divisional level in the finance sector, most employers have preferred to retain central controls. This is less true in manufacturing industry. Some prominent manufacturing firms – such as Ford and ICI – continue with centralised company bargaining over pay and conditions, as do some of the privatised utilities, notably British Telecommunications (BT) and British Gas. But elsewhere plant- or site-level negotiations are widespread. Prominent examples of this very decentralised approach include major companies such as Unilever, BTR and GEC. In many of these decentralised companies pay awards are, of course, coordinated by management at divisional level, and enforced by centralised financial reporting systems.

Employees covered by collective bargaining

In those firms where unions are recognised collective bargaining generally covers all employees up to professional/technical grades and junior management. Above those levels the situation varies a great deal. There has been a definite shift away from collective bargaining for management grades and some professionals, such as scientists, with the widespread adoption of pay systems based wholly or partly on individual performance. Where pay increases are entirely dependent on individual performance unions are rarely involved.

The position is different in the public sector, and to some extent in privatised (denationalised) firms. Here white-collar unions have represented management and professional groups for many years and collective bargaining is much more entrenched. Privatised firms have sometimes 'bought out' collective bargaining, for example by awarding company cars to managers at BT.

The pay round and negotiating procedures

Annual negotiations are the norm but there is no formal pay round. In the period of incomes policy the pay round began in August each year and the tradition lingered for some years afterwards, at least in people's minds. However, the key months for pay negotiations are now clearly January and April, followed by July. Companies without collective bargaining also tend to follow the pattern.

In the past there were a number of leading settlements and sectors. Pay negotiations in the car firms (especially at Ford) and at national level in the engineering industry tended to set the pattern for much of the private sector. In the public sector, coal mining was for a time seen as a barometer for other negotiations. The pattern is somewhat different today. The car firms have moved to a pattern of two-year agreements; the engineering agreement no longer exists; the mining industry is a fraction of its former size. As a result other bargaining groups have assumed more significance, although the concept of leading settlements is less prevalent than in the past. Key companies in the private sector include ICI and BT, while Ford's negotiations remain prominent in the media. In the public sector, negotiations for local government staff have become more important, despite moves to decentralisation and to contracting services out. The independent pay review bodies, which decide annual awards for various groups of public employees, notably nurses and teachers, are also important because they have the authority of government backing, even though the government is not obliged to accept the recommendations.

The most powerful influence on pay is without doubt the retail price index (RPI). Despite the promotion of alternative statistics, and years of exhortation from both government and the CBI, negotiators continue to look to the index as a benchmark. The period of prolonged recession in the early 1990s marked a partial break from the habit, with large numbers of firms postponing pay reviews or freezing pay completely. However, the subsequent recovery has seen the index re-emerge as the key influence. RPI forecasts are provided by a number of institutions, such as banks and stockbrokers, as well as independent economic forecasters. These provide negotiators with useful short-term indicators. Although the Treasury has equipped itself with a small group of independent economic experts, their independent forecast at the time of the budget in November has not acquired the status enjoyed by similar bodies abroad and tends to exhibit marked variations around the consensus forecast, depending on the theoretical standpoint of the expert in question.

The CBI's databank reports give monthly information on pay trends. A more detailed account is supplied to participants in the survey (a cross-section of businesses). The CBI publishes a report every other month with articles, policy statements and statistics on employment and collective bargaining; it also provides members with an annual review of trends.

The UK tends to be much more open about pay and collective bargaining developments at company level than other countries in Europe. This is largely because the very fragmentation of the system entails a greater need for independent information on a regular basis. Analysis of pay and bargaining trends is provided in the fortnightly *IDS Report*. Incomes Data Services also publishes fortnightly *Studies*, comparing personnel policy and practice in different organisations, as well as a monthly *Management Pay Review*, which analyses trends in pay and employment practice at more senior levels. Other organisations providing information include Industrial Relations Services and the trade union-backed Labour Research Department. The CBI and the Engineering Employers' Federation also compile pay databases and assess trends amongst member companies.

Recent trends

Recent bargaining has tended to focus almost exclusively on pay, with economic recovery and the slow rise in inflation feeding through to a gradual increase in pay settlements. Settlements in manufacturing industry were mainly between 3 and 4 per cent in the first half of 1995. Increases in the service sector were a little lower, reflecting the patchy recovery in domestic demand and the government's efforts to hold public-sector pay down. Earnings growth over 12 months was significantly higher in manufacturing than in services, at around 5 per cent, compared with 3 per cent. These figures are for basic pay rises only: they do not reflect the growing complexity of pay settlements. The spread of profit-related pay (see *Contracts and Terms and Conditions of Employment* in this series, pp. 404–5), additional awards for performance, lump sum bonuses and all-merit reviews have made it increasingly difficult to assess how much overall settlements are actually worth.

Although there is no formal limit on public-sector pay increases, during 1994/95 the government in practice was seeking to hold public-sector rises at around the inflation rate. The official policy was that any rises had to be funded from within existing budgets, and this freeze in pay costs was intended to last into 1996. Overall in the public sector pay rises are thus meant to be funded by increased efficiency, which almost inevitably means a reduction in employment. The policy led to increasing signs of unrest in the first part of 1995.

Working time reductions have largely been off the agenda since the 1989–91 campaign by unions in the engineering industry reduced the basic working week for manual workers in many companies to 37 hours. However, economic recovery has prompted the engineering union AEEU to raise the issue again, and some moves may be likely in companies where workers still have a basic 39 hour week, for example in the motor industry. Elsewhere, employers have been looking to revise working patterns and thus extend the working day, particularly in retailing, the banks and customer service departments of the major utilities. Seven-day opening is now common across the retail sector and there are likely to be extensions to evening and night working.

Pointing to some issues in managing recovery after a long recession, the 1994 ACAS report commented that employers had in many cases been compelled to deal with immediate pressures rather than manage change in a positive way, and warned of tensions beneath the surface which might break out into disputes as the recovery gathered pace. Pressure points noted by ACAS included flexible working patterns, management restructuring, contracting out and performance-related pay.

Agreed provisions and the objects of bargaining

The evolution of employment regulation has been predicated on the Victorian *laissez-faire* principle that adult male workers did not need the protection of the law and could determine their conditions of employment through individual or collective negotiation. The almost complete lack of statutory regulation of terms and conditions of employment, and the absence of a superstructure of binding collective agreements at industry level, means that virtually all aspects of pay and conditions are determined essentially at company level, either by agreement or unilaterally. The implementation of the EU directive on working time, the first such regulation in the UK for the bulk of employees, may change this voluntarist approach and philosophy in some respects. Where unions are recognised there are no restrictions on the issues which may be the subject of collective bargaining. Equally, there is no obligation on an employer to bargain on any issue. Employers can change terms and conditions without union agreement. However, because the terms of agreements are incorporated into individual contracts such unilateral action can only be carried out lawfully only by giving due notice of changes and securing the consent of individual employees (see *Contracts and Terms and Conditions of Employment* in this series, p. 386).

The traditional pattern of pay bargaining, with separate arrangements for blue-collar and white-collar employees, still persists in many sectors. However, integrated pay structures have become more common and there has been steady progress towards harmonised conditions of employment such as sick pay and holidays.

There is no system of statutory job classification, and industry-level agreements – where they still exist – usually set out only rudimentary pay structures. Job grading is almost entirely fixed at company or establishment level. More and more employees are paid on a monthly basis by credit transfer, but there are still companies with weekly paid staff where payment is made in cash.

Most agreements set out pay structures, usually based on formal job evaluation – although recently there have been some moves towards classifications based on skills or competences (see *Contracts and Terms and Conditions of Employment* in this series, p. 400). Pay structures and grading are usually subject to collective bargaining, sometimes through formal joint job evaluation panels.

White-collar pay structures usually consist of a set of pay scales. Pay progression is increasingly based on individual performance, although in some cases progression is automatic or semi-automatic up to a specified level. For manual workers, most pay structures continue to set out a rate for the job, although some firms have adopted progression based on the acquisition of skill 'modules', where increases are paid on the basis of the employee passing tests or showing competence at particular skills.

Basic pay is normally reviewed once a year. Although certain firms have agreed two- or three-year pay deals, these almost always include annual rises, either set in advance or based on a formula linked to the retail price index.

Bonuses and supplements   In the past the earnings of many manual workers were often made up of basic pay plus supplements, principally bonuses (individual or group) linked with production or productivity and overtime and shift payments. In addition there could be a variety of additional payments such as bonuses for good attendance, call-out payments, supplements for working in arduous or unpleasant conditions, and so on.

These additional payments were defined in different ways. Overtime and shift premium payments were often laid down in industry-wide agreements. Other supplements were agreed at company or establishment level. The disappearance of most industry-wide agreements has changed the pattern, although some manufacturing companies continue with the old arrangements.

There has been a gradual movement away from such systems, however, with companies consolidating most supplementary payments into basic pay or, increasingly, an annual salary. This partly reflects moves towards annual hours systems, above all in continuous process industries, where payment for overtime is either abolished or applicable only where an agreed number of banked hours has been exceeded. In such cases Saturday or Sunday working, for example, is paid as if it were a normal weekday. In return for this flexibility employees receive additional days off. Another factor in the move towards consolidated salaries is the employers' desire to control wage costs more effectively. The traditional arrangements sometimes allowed a great deal of scope for drift, and inevitably meant that wage costs were unpredictable.

Supplementary payments linked with productivity became widespread in the

1970s as employers sought to replace piecework payment systems with more controllable bonuses – and because they were a way of avoiding the rigours of incomes policies. Although the 1980s witnessed a backlash against such deals – and against the idea of negotiating about productivity at all – there are nevertheless many examples of bonuses linked with output targets. In such cases the bonuses (and sometimes the targets) are subject to collective bargaining. Individual piecework also continues to be an important payment system in parts of manufacturing.

As far as individualised merit pay is concerned this usually applies only to white-collar employees. Firms operate a variety of policies, with some reviews based entirely on individual performance and others incorporating a general increase. Annual pay reviews at a fixed date are usual, although some firms operate rolling reviews, with individuals receiving pay awards at different times of the year. Increases based on performance are usually consolidated into salary, although some firms award performance bonuses.

The general view is that increases based solely on merit have been rapidly gaining ground compared with other forms of award. IDS figures on managerial pay reviews show that out of 450 such reviews in 1990 64 per cent were to some extent based on merit. Of these 44 per cent were based entirely on individual performance.

Financial participation   Payments linked to the performance of an organisation are well established in the UK and there are a variety of methods which firms can adopt (for details see *Contracts and Terms and Conditions of Employment* in this series, pp. 402 ff). For the most part such systems have generally been introduced by employers outside the terms of collective agreements as an incentive for employees to stay with the firm and identify with its success. Thus most profit-sharing has been introduced unilaterally by employers, with the rules and pay-out varying periodically according to decisions at board level.

However, the rapid growth of profit-related pay (PRP) arrangements, covering some 2.4 million employees at the start of 1995, has changed this slightly. The intention behind PRP was that it should become a variable element of normal pay which would be free of tax. The rules do not require employees' consent to the introduction of such schemes. However, if PRP is intended to replace an element of basic pay, it is in reality necessary for the employer to gain consent. Such consent must be not only to the principle of converting a proportion of pay to variable PRP, but also to the amount of guaranteed pay to be converted. Where there is a recognised union this inevitably means that some sort of collective bargaining will be involved. In practice, however, most PRP schemes do not substitute for basic pay increases. They are tax-efficient bonuses which ride on top of normal pay.

Working time   Pending implementation of the EU Working Time Directive (see *Contracts and Terms and Conditions of Employment* in this series, pp.

392–3) working time remains almost entirely unregulated by statute law and therefore generally the subject of collective bargaining. Unions and employers are free to choose any working time arrangements they wish, including provisions on overtime, shift patterns, flexibility, breaks and so on. Part-time work is widespread, with most part-time workers on contracts for 16–20 hours a week. But other patterns are widespread, including so-called zero-hours contracts in some retail establishments, where working time is not laid down in the contract and employees are told when they will be needed.

For full-time employees the basic working week for manual workers is usually 39 hours, with a substantial number on 37 hours. Annual hours agreements, time-banking arrangements and flexible rosters have all become more widespread in recent years. For office workers a basic 35 hour week is normal, although 37 hours are also common.

In manufacturing, agreements on working time are now usually concluded at company or workplace level. Actual working time may vary, as management and unions in different establishments have agreed many different working arrangements. Negotiations over shift breaks and flexible working have been common for many years in industry, with unions agreeing periodically to give up or reduce breaks in return for extra pay. Agreements or understandings on overtime working and allocation were also widespread. Although such practices have become less common in recent years, with the assertion of 'management's right to manage', such bargaining still takes place.

Shift working, according to the periodic Workplace Industrial Relations Surveys, exists in a little over one-third of establishments, being concentrated in manufacturing and the public sector (over 40 per cent). In some industries there are agreements on shift patterns and premium payments concluded at national level which companies continue to follow. Premiums typically range from 20 per cent for conventional shifts up to 100 per cent for weekend and night working.

Holidays   There is no statutory holiday entitlement, whether to annual leave or to public holidays (usually termed 'bank holidays'). In practice the most common basic holiday entitlement for full-time workers is 25 days a year (plus public holidays), with around half of employers rewarding long service with additional leave. (Amounts vary widely.) Holiday arrangements in many organisations are still based on entitlements agreed at sectoral level during the 1970s and 1980s. The national agreement in the engineering industry was particularly influential in establishing 25 days as a norm.

Restrictions on when employees can take their main holiday and the number of days which can be taken at a time are common in manufacturing industry and in parts of the service sector. Some companies shut down completely for a week or two every summer. There are traditional breaks in certain parts of the country which tend to influence the dates when these shutdowns occur. Such arrangements in some cases form part of the collective agreements.

Time off   Employees are legally entitled to time off work for trade union duties and activities, public duties and jury service. Time off for trade union purposes – sometimes known as 'facility time' – is the subject of periodic negotiation, formal and informal. Certain agreements lay down formally both the number of employee representatives, their constituencies and representational rights, and the amount of time allocated for their duties.

Other time off work, for personal and domestic needs, has increasingly become a subject of negotiation over the past few years. Such arrangements are almost always agreed at company or establishment level and typically cover family occasions, illness, bereavement, medical and dental appointments.

Other types of agreed provision   There are no limits on the issues which may be covered by collective bargaining, and companies sometimes have a range of different agreements and notes of understandings with trade unions drawn up over the years. There is considerable variation in the subjects considered appropriate for collective bargaining.

Training was an issue traditionally subject to considerable joint regulation at industry level, and unions with a large proportion of skilled workers usually regard training as a matter for collective bargaining. Other unions have begun to take training more seriously, as it has become more important to their members, particularly where employers have linked pay with acquired skills. Detailed agreements on training have been a key element in the introduction of new working practices in manufacturing industry, and they have often involved joint regulation of training on a continuing basis. Such agreements may cover the type of training, how it is to be delivered, payments to those involved, and joint administration. Other agreed provisions which relate to training may include career breaks as well as provision for employee development such as sabbatical and study leave, assistance with fees, etc.

Job security is often mentioned in agreements, with measures to avoid job losses listed alongside agreed procedures in the event of redundancies, levels of compensation, etc. Job security agreements are usually short-term commitments from employers, often agreed in exchange for union restraint over pay. Over the years, unions have sought to regulate redundancy by procedures specifying that the first criterion for redundancy should be length of service. These 'last in, first out' (LIFO) agreements were designed to prevent arbitrary selection of employees. Latterly many employers have in effect withdrawn from such agreements; in some cases unions have agreed new procedures which allow for selection according to different criteria such as the employer's need for a balanced workforce or the work record of individual employees.

Agreements on redundancy usually specify compensation levels well in excess of the legal minimum entitlement. They may also specify measures to assist redundant employees, such as time off to look for work and the use of outplacement services.

Maternity leave and allowances for child care are other areas where unions have sought to improve on the statutory minimum entitlement. Most commonly this involves enhanced maternity payments and bonuses on return as well as time off work before the birth. In the absence of statutory provisions on paternity leave, unions have sought to negotiate leave entitlement for fathers. It has become far more widespread than it used to be, although entitlement is usually limited to a few days.

Sick pay and absence are often the subject of agreed procedures for notification and control, especially where bonuses are tied to good attendance. Other areas of bargaining include sick pay entitlement related to length of service. Other agreed provisions may include a range of employee benefits such as cheap loans, subsidised transport or employee discounts on company products.

Industrial conflict

The legal context and incidence of industrial action have changed profoundly since the early 1980s, and by the mid-1990s the number of days lost through industrial action had fallen to historically low levels.

Collective agreements, ballots and procedures

The fact that collective agreements are not legally binding, and do not customarily establish contractual relations between the signatory parties, means that there is no enforceable 'peace clause' comparable to those in many continental countries. In general, however, it is extremely rare for an official dispute on a substantive (economic interest) issue to occur during the lifetime of an agreement. Collective agreements frequently include procedures for handling collective disputes.

Normally agreements specify the steps to be followed in the event of a dispute, with time limits on the various stages. The stages may be both internal and external, using the offices of an employers' association. Many agreements include provision for conciliation through ACAS where both parties agree. Some agreements specify that the *status quo* will prevail until otherwise agreed, although this is less common than in the past. Agreements often commit both sides to avoiding disputes and sometimes to arbitration. There are also instances of agreements which specify that binding arbitration will take place as the final procedure, and forbid industrial action. Such so-called 'no strike' agreements are, however, unenforceable unless the agreement is specifically stated to be legally binding.

Recent legislation has had considerable impact on the way in which unions conduct their affairs, particularly ballots on strikes or other forms of action (see below). In some cases the requirement to ballot has been incorporated into procedure agreements.

The right to strike – and to lock out

There is no positive 'right to strike'. For many years trade unions were guaranteed immunity under the law from prosecution for acts which would otherwise be illegal – most obviously action to induce employees to breach of contract. Thus in effect unions enjoyed considerable freedom under the law. Since 1980 that freedom has been steadily curtailed in a series of Acts of Parliament. Most of this legislation does not automatically render certain trade union actions illegal. Rather it removes immunity from prosecution unless certain rules are followed. This enables employers – and others – to obtain injunctions preventing industrial action, or to sue unions which do not comply. The main impact of the changes in the law has been, first, to limit severely the scope of industrial action and, second, to oblige unions to undertake stringent and complex balloting procedures to make any action lawful.

Formal lockouts are unusual, although the suspension of employees for refusing to work normally (itself a form of industrial action) is quite commonly the prelude to a stoppage. There are no legal restrictions on lockouts as such, although employers may find themselves open to claims for unfair dismissal in some circumstances.

As far as the individual employee is concerned the legal position differs markedly from that in many other European countries in that taking industrial action entails a breach of contract: there is no provision for a suspension of contract. However, the employer may lawfully dismiss strikers for breach of contract in the event of an official dispute only if all the strikers are dismissed. Selective re-engagement is possible after three months. (Dismissal for union activities alone, as noted above, is automatically unfair.)

Permitted and unlawful industrial action

Broadly speaking, strikes and other forms of industrial action are the same in the eyes of the law. To retain immunity under the law a dispute must be between workers and their own employer. Sympathy or 'secondary' action is unlawful. Action to enforce union membership has no immunity. There is no statutory definition of industrial action, but the courts have in practice tended to apply the test of whether an action is concerted and designed to put pressure on the employer. Disruptive action, particularly a ban on overtime working, has become more widespread than strike action in the past few years.

For industrial action to be lawful a ballot is required. The balloting regulations are elaborate and confer a number of rights on employers as well as imposing duties on trade unions. An official code of practice on ballots, published by ACAS, gives details of the full requirements, among which are the following:

- Ballots must be secret and conducted by post.
- Ballots must be held not more than four weeks before action.

- Where more than one site is involved the general rule is that each site likely to be affected must vote in favour.
- The employer must be given at least seven days' notice of the ballot, together with details of those involved.
- The employer must be given a sample copy of the ballot paper.
- Once the result is known the employer must be given full details of the outcome and, in the event of any action, at least seven days' notice together with details of those involved.

Unofficial action – action called without the authority of a union – has no legal protection. Unions can be sued for damages unless they go through an explicit and defined process of repudiation of the action. Employees involved in such action have no right to claim unfair dismissal and can be dismissed selectively.

Picketing

There is limited statutory protection for picketing in the course of disputes to 'obtain or communicate' information or 'peacefully persuade' any person to work or not to work. Broadly speaking, this protection is limited to employees of the organisation concerned who are picketing their own place of work. There is, however, no tort or crime of 'unlawful picketing' as such. Picketing which does not have statutory protection is therefore not in itself unlawful.

The incidence of strikes and lockouts

The number of recorded work stoppages (strikes and lockouts are not differentiated) has fallen drastically in recent years, from well over 1,000 a year in the early 1980s to a little over 200 a decade later. The number of days lost per thousand workers dropped from an average 400 in the period 1984–88 to 70 in the period 1989–93. In 1993 30 days per thousand workers were lost in labour disputes. Disputes about pay have continued to be the main cause of strikes. Strikes have been concentrated mainly in the public sector and there have been more one-day or 'protest' stoppages than in the past. (A number of these are not recorded in the figures because they are not 'trade disputes'.)

The figures largely reflect official strikes. They do not include most unofficial disputes – usually of short duration – nor do they include other forms of industrial action, such as overtime bans, which have become more widespread.

Conciliation and arbitration

As described earlier, ACAS is the main body involved in conciliation and arbitration, continuing to be involved in over 1,000 disputes a year. Almost all this work is conciliation, either before or during disputes. Outside arbitration remains rare. Disputes can be referred to ACAS by either side, or by both – and ACAS may offer its services without being formally requested to do so. There is no obligation on unions or employers to accept conciliation, to follow set procedures or to suspend any action that may be taking place.

Organisations

Department of Education and Employment
Sanctuary Buildings
Great Smith Street
London SW1P 3BT
Tel. + 44 171 273 3000

Advisory, Conciliation and Arbitration
Service (ACAS)
27 Wilton Street
London SW1X 7AZ
Tel. + 44 171 210 3000
Fax + 44 171 210 3708

Confederation of British Industry (CBI)
Centre Point
103 New Oxford Street
London WC1A 1DU
Tel. + 44 171 379 7400
Fax + 44 171 240 1578

The Institute of Personnel and
Development (IPD)
IPD House
Camp Road
Wimbledon
London SW19 4UX
Tel. + 44 181 971 9000
Fax + 44 181 263 3333

Trades Union Congress (TUC)
23–8 Great Russell Street
London WC1B 3LS
Tel. + 44 171 636 4030
Fax + 44 171 636 0632

Main sources

EUROPEAN FOUNDATION FOR THE IMPROVEMENT OF LIVING AND WORKING CONDITIONS. *Management-initiated direct participation: United Kingdom*, Working Paper WP/95/03/EN. Dublin, 1995

GALL, GREGOR, and MCKAY, SONIA. 'Trade union derecognition in Britain, 1988–1994', *British Journal of Industrial Relations*, September, 1994, 433–48

INCOMES DATA SERVICES. *Employment Law Handbook*, various issues

INCOMES DATA SERVICES. *Report*, various issues

INCOMES DATA SERVICES. *Studies*, various issues

KESSLER, SID, and BAYLISS, FRED, *Contemporary British Industrial Relations*, 2nd edition, London, Macmillan, 1995

MARSH, DAVID. *The New Politics of British Trade Unionism*. London, Macmillan, 1992

MILLWARD, NEIL. *The New Industrial Relations?*. London, PSI Publishing, 1994

MILLWARD, NEIL, *et. al. Workplace Industrial Relations in Transition*. Aldershot, Dartmouth Publishing, 1992